Shoot Like a
Gentleman!

A Memoir

Major General
Freddie Plaskett

For Dean and Carol Bristol.
Friends from a river trip in Europe.
With warm regards and best wishes
Freddie· Plaskett

February 2006

© F.J.Plaskett 2005
Shoot Like a Gentleman!
ISBN 0-9547805-0-7

Published by:
Maximilian Publishing
P.O. Box 1998
Salisbury
SP5 4YD

The right of F.J.Plaskett to be identified as the
author of this work has been asserted by him in
accordance with the Copyright, Design and
Patent Act 1988.

Design and production co-ordinated by:
The Better Book Company Ltd
Havant
Hampshire
PO9 2XH

Printed in England

The Author. Painted by William Dring R.A. and exhibited at the Royal Academy Summer Exhibition of 1982. Reproduced by permission of The Trustees of the Institution of The Royal Corps of Transport.

Foreword

General Plaskett has produced a most striking memoir – light in touch, elegantly phrased, entertaining and exceptionally interesting. It will convey to future generations, as well as to contemporaries, the realities of soldiering in the British Army in a position of responsibility, as well as the considerable variety which such a life has contained.

GENERAL SIR DAVID FRASER, GCB OBE DL

Introduction

This started as a brief history of my service career at the urging of my four married daughters and was originally intended to give my twelve grandchildren some idea of what their maternal grandparents got up to in 'the olden days'. My youngest daughter, now following in her mother's footsteps as a journalist, having read snatches of the manuscript, suggested that I should write it for publication.

"You've had quite a colourful career," she said. "It's covered much of what has been described as 'the dissolution of Empire' and you were in on it in several places, notably India before and during the Partition. Apart from showing us those ghastly photographs once, I can't recall you saying much about it. It is, after all, a slice of modern history and there must be lots of people out there who would be interested to read about it."

So here is my salute to 'the olden days' – although they are still well within living memory. My thanks are due to those who have helped me to bring this memoir to the light of day. Son-in-law, Fergus, who read the first draft and made helpful suggestions, and Pat, my wife, who recalled old proof-reading skills from more than twenty years ago when we first met. Thanks are due also to General Sir David Fraser, now a noted military historian and novelist, for his supportive comments along the way and for his generous Foreword, and to Colonel Geoffrey Powell who has permitted me to quote from his *History of The Green Howards*. Finally, to my dear daughters, simply for 'being there' and for encouraging me to get on with it.

FREDDIE PLASKETT
AUTUMN 2004

1
Cast Off

Whoop! Whoop! A destroyer? Yes. It had to be.

Notebook in hand on that late spring morning in 1939, I gazed entranced as the slim and sinister grey beauty crossed the bar and slid effortlessly upriver through the Mersey shipping. A white ensign fluttered fitfully at her stern in the light breeze. She moved along the line of docks to fetch up at her Pier Head berth on the Liverpool side of the river.

I was twelve years old and a seat at the big bay window of the drawing room at my paternal grandmother's house was my favourite perch at weekends and on any other free afternoons. The house stood on a bluff overlooking the Mersey on the Wirral side at a place called Seacombe, near to the landing stage for the ferries carrying commuters across the river to Wallasey, long the dormitory for those engaged in commerce in Liverpool.

Years later as I walked with my father to the railway station of the little country town where we had settled 'for the duration' as we used to say during the war years, I thought of 'my' destroyer; the thrill of that pre-war moment had made me decide that come what may I was going to choose a life at sea. It was now June 1944. The D-Day landings in Normandy were only weeks behind us. The years of war had not deadened my ambition, but time and proximity to a fighter station had provided the Royal Navy with a rival. The RAF had been generous to the local Air Training Corps and as a member I had learned to fly a glider and had flown on training flights in the old Avro Anson that the station held as a 'dogsbody' aircraft. I had caught the flying bug.

Like most young men at the time, I was keen to get into the war, but I was hard-pressed to choose between the navy and the RAF. The army was out of the question for I had no ambition to be a soldier. Then I learned by chance that the Fleet Air Arm had introduced a scheme known as the 'Y' Entry that accepted suitable young men for aircrew training at the age of seventeen and a half. This seemed to be the ideal solution to my problem of satisfying a passion for flying combined with a love of the sea and I decided to volunteer on reaching seventeen – the earliest age for applications.

I had reckoned without my father, however, a taciturn but determined man of Victorian values. He had suffered a rough First World War in the trenches and refused point blank to countersign my application, parental consent being necessary at seventeen. At eighteen I would be called up anyway and probably into the army, but with a chance of being sent down a coal mine as a Bevin Boy, the fate of ten per cent of the national call up. With the arrogance of youth I was annoyed that he was not prepared to support my plan.

Years later I came to realise that beneath his dour northern exterior lurked a soul more sensitive than I had ever given him credit for. It dawned on me that the shattered and wasted landscapes of Flanders would appear before his eyes for the rest of his life whenever war was mentioned or discussed. So he would not willingly donate his offspring to the armed services. Fortunately my mother was more pliable and could be worn down. She was eventually persuaded to sign and on my seventeenth birthday I was able to volunteer.

Shortly afterwards I was summoned to a fairly rigorous medical examination followed by three days at the requisitioned Grand Hotel in Torquay undergoing 'suitability tests' for aircrew training. These hurdles cleared, I appeared before a selection board that turned out to consist of two academics and several genial air and nautical heroes. It was a comprehensive grilling that seemed to go on forever although when it was over I realised that it couldn't have lasted more than forty-five minutes. I was not told whether or not I had been found suitable for training as a pilot: they said "we will let you know."

I had enjoyed a contented but not particularly memorable childhood. My father had been demobilised from the army at the end of the First World War and had then trained as a constructional engineer. He married and I was born in the late autumn of 1926 when he was involved in the installation of structures for an oil company on Merseyside. He was doing well. We lived in Wallasey and he became a Mersey commuter involved in the design and construction of oil installations. I am hazy about the details of what went wrong but I know he had a bad accident during a site visit in the depression years of the late nineteen twenties. While his bones were mending he lost his contract with Socony Vacuum, his main employer at the time. This, in effect, meant the loss of his livelihood and could have spelled disaster. When I was growing up in the depression years and afterwards in the thirties, the social safety nets that we know today didn't exist. Those who fell on hard times had to fend for themselves.

Fortunately, for my father, his family was well-to-do. His mother was the daughter of a prosperous Liverpool businessman and had inherited property from her father; the house we lived in had been a wedding gift to my parents. Her family came to the rescue and my father joined their business in Liverpool in some sort of administrative capacity. My early memories are of him leaving the house each morning to catch the Mersey ferry complete with bowler hat, briefcase and umbrella. A more unlikely Mr Pooter could not be imagined. It must have seared his soul, although he was no doubt grateful for the opportunity to do a salaried job while attempting to get back to his chosen walk of life. But my mother's dreams of private education for her only son had gone out of the window and I attended a local state school until the age of ten when I took and passed what was known as 'the scholarship exam' that entitled me to a higher education to the age of sixteen.

This was a stroke of luck, not realised at the time, but looking around today, I'm pretty sure that the much maligned 'elitist system' dismantled in the nineteen seventies with the dissolution of the selective state schools did a great deal more for my generation's youth than the 'one size fits all' comprehensives do for today's young. I couldn't have had a better grounding for the future. My headmaster, a classicist, took selected senior pupils and gently led us towards an appreciation of literature and poetry that will undoubtedly last a lifetime – a priceless gift.

So my early years were spent near to the sea. My frequent visits to my grandmother's house at Seacombe gave rise to a love of the sea and ships that has never left me. I was much in awe of the old dear; she could not be described as a warm personality but in retrospect she treated me with a gruff 'children should be seen and not heard' sort of kindness. I visited her as often as I could, however, because from my favourite window perch I could see all the activity of the river.

I would spend my free time with a notebook recording the comings and goings of the Canadian Pacific Line ships, *Empress of Britain*, *Empress of Canada*; the Lamport and Holt liners, the West Africa ships, *Apapa, Appam, Abosso*; the pink coloured Union Castle liners and of course the mighty Cunarders before they moved en bloc to Southampton. There were many others of lesser pedigree. A special treat was a Saturday morning trip on the Liverpool overhead railway along the line of docks to the Gladstone Dock at the seaward end.

My mother was half Irish; her English father had been lost at sea in the First World War and her mother spoiled her many grandchildren disgracefully. My cousins and I loved our Irish granny. When we misbehaved her favourite comment on her daughters' scoldings was,

'Ah, who'd be worrying?'

She had a good voice and taught us many of the sad, lilting songs of Old Ireland. Years later, in Korea, I surprised our Irish quartermaster officer with my knowledge of his native ballads – as well as the rebel ditties.

Came the Hitler war and my father thankfully reverted to engineering, taking a post in the Midlands. When I left school my mother and I joined him and while waiting anxiously for news from the Royal Navy I took a clerical job in the local headquarters of the Air Ministry Works Directorate. I did my best to settle in to the gentle rhythms of rural life based on the church and the local grammar school that most of my new found friends had attended.

Time crawled by until one day out of the blue and shortly after I had reached seventeen and a half –the minimum age for enlistment – I received instructions from 'My Lords Commissioners' at the Admiralty to report to HMS *St Vincent* in Gosport to be embodied as a Naval Airman 2nd Class (CW) to undergo pilot training. The navy, different as ever from the other two armed services, reserved the description 'cadet' for its gilded youth training at Dartmouth's Royal Naval College. Others undergoing officer training were CW (or Commission Worthy) ratings firmly anchored to the lower deck until all the obstacles obstructing the path towards the coveted gold braid had been overcome.

Hence my walk to the railway station on that memorable evening in the summer of 1944. My father, who had by now accepted my ambition to fly and anyway had decided that the naval air arm was a better bet than the army, cleared his throat.

"I suppose," he said, "I ought to give you a few words of advice."

We walked on and reached the station where the train had just pulled in and was waiting, steaming gently. I loaded my suitcase aboard and leaned out of the window

"Just remember these two things and you won't go far wrong," he continued, as though there had been no pause in our one-sided conversation.

"Keep your bowels open and stay well clear of loose women." He shook hands briefly and departed.

At that time I was too excited at the prospect of what was to come to take much notice of what he had said. I had attended a single sex school and I had no sisters. My experience of girls had been confined to friendship and teenage horseplay with the chaste maidens of the tennis club. But those words of wisdom from my home grown Polonius had stuck in my mind and I have pondered them many times since. Sixty years of subsequent life have convinced me that it was indeed wise advice but I have often wondered at his choice of priorities. Why bowels before birds? Sadly, I failed to ask him and it's too late now. He was run over in his mid-eighties crossing the road to his favourite pub and he died in hospital before I could get to him. My wife, Pat, however, is sure she has the answer. "There's no mystery," she says. "All Englishmen are fixated with their bowels. It's to do with the teachings of nannies or grannies in youth and lasts a lifetime."

The Y Entry Selection Board had given me an outline of the Fleet Air Arm pilot training pattern. After a short introduction to the Royal Navy that was to take place at HMS *St Vincent*, some trainees would attend a long course at Chelsea Polytechnic to study subjects with a bearing on maritime aviation. Friends had told me that there were weeks, if not months of desk work before you were allowed to set foot anywhere near an aeroplane and that this penance was normally endured in a Nissen hut on some draughty airfield in the deepest countryside. To be offered instead a chance of some months in Central London at the taxpayers' expense was a considerable bonus.

HMS *St Vincent*, on the Gosport shore of Portsmouth Harbour, was a well-known naval shore establishment converted to the basic training of would be Fleet Air Arm aircrew from its peacetime role of training boy seamen. For some time after D-Day and while the fighting was raging along the northern coast of France, it was also used as an occasional clearing house for the overspill of light battle casualties – usually walking wounded. My arrival there along with the remainder of a lorryload of Y Entry recruits coincided with the appearance of a heavily bandaged busload of casualties. Our magpie chatter was stilled and gave place to a thoughtful silence as we came face-to-face with some inkling of what was actually happening a mere sixty miles away on the other side of the Channel.

Being in a 'shore ship' was a complete change of lifestyle. So far as we, the trainees, were concerned, we were in a ship, and you learn very early on as a seamen recruit that you are 'in' – never 'on' a ship. Our ship was to all intents and purposes afloat. We went ashore when the liberty boat came alongside – actually we paraded at the main gate in our 'fore and aft rig' of bell bottomed trousers and tunic to be inspected by the officer of the watch before the appointed time. Caps were checked to ensure that the CW white bands were clean and that they were worn square to the head and neither tilted Admiral Beatty style nor worn 'flat a back' as depicted in most of the photographs of naval ratings that the public saw. Our blue collars had to be clean and carefully pressed and the three stripes round the border generally, but incorrectly, held to commemorate Nelson's three famous victories of The Nile, Copenhagen and Trafalgar had to be shining white. The dovetailed black ribbons on our tunics had to be regulation length and those trousers that had been painstakingly ironed to display the seven horizontal creases popularly supposed to represent the seven seas that we had yet to see, were carefully checked. Returning was a similar exercise. Those who 'missed the boat' had to wait outside for the next one. Missing the last boat of the evening meant being hauled inside and charged with an offence.

Our beds were hammocks; the barrack rooms were messdecks. Windows were scuttles – the navy's word for portholes – ceilings became deckheads, the floor was the 'sole' and we 'darkened ship' at lights out. We did our own dhobi (washing) and carried out running repairs to clothing at the weekly 'make and mend'. Whereas soldiers and airmen performed guard duties, we 'stood watches'. The middle watch from midnight to four in the morning on Vincent Creek, the tidal inlet that flows in from Portsmouth Harbour, had a true graveyard feel. We strained our eyes in the gloom for the enemy raiding parties that never appeared – how could they, for they were fighting for their lives in France. But the imagination of a seventeen year old standing guard with an ancient and unloaded rifle in the middle of the night is pretty fertile.

We were thoroughly and deliberately immersed in the arcane and unique language of the seagoing Royal Navy until we spoke it as naturally and fluently as though we had been born to it. Our introduction to the navy was great fun and by no means intellectually challenging at that stage but there was a serious purpose to it. We had to be taught that although we were all aspiring airmen and thus most of our training would necessarily be under the stewardship of the RAF, and using that service's assets and training staff, we were first and foremost members of the senior service and that much of our life after training would be spent at sea.

The outdoor part of the General Naval Subjects (GNS) course was a mixture of sadism and unalloyed pleasure. We were instructed by genuine old salts in the mysteries of 'bends and hitches' – knots to you – and blocks and tackles (pronounced tayckles). We rehearsed man overboard drills. Over half a century later, with short term memory often an absentee, I am still able to recall without difficulty the sequence of commands to 'call away' a seaboat's crew. We were taught to sail 32 foot cutters and 27 foot whalers in Portsmouth Harbour with a petty officer sitting in the sternsheets applying correction where necessary with a handy rope's end. Despite this politically incorrect method of imparting knowledge, a passion for small boat sailing has remained with me ever since.

In all this there was a distinct whiff of Nelson's navy.

The trainees were a varied bunch. Mixed in with the young civilian element from Britain, there were many members of what we now call The Old Commonwealth – Australians, New Zealanders, Canadians and a few South Africans, as well as a sprinkling of volunteers already serving as naval ratings and somewhat older than the rest of us. Drill and weapon training, universally regarded as the sadistic element of the course, was generally disliked and none of us could really understand why it made up such a large part of the syllabus. It may have been that the majority of our petty officer instructors had been gunnery specialists. That meant that they had spent a good deal of their service at HMS *Excellent*, the Whale Island gunnery school on Portsmouth Harbour where all outside activities during working hours are carried out at the double, wearing knee length khaki gaiters. All our drill instructors wore these – the Mark of the Beast!

Most days included a period of drill with or without weapons. At that time the navy's personal weapon was the old Lee Enfield bolt action rifle, supplemented by the semi-automatic Lanchester, which can best be described as a maritime version of the Sten, well known throughout the other two services. Naturally, we made many mistakes to start with. These were dealt with quickly and ruthlessly in two ways. In the centre of the vast parade ground at *St Vincent* stood a very tall mast rigged as the mainmast of a square rigger, a relic of boy seaman training. I guess the height to have been about forty or perhaps even fifty feet. Near to the top was a single platform, a crow's nest, accessible only by climbing the rigging, which ended just below the platform. An opening had been cut into the platform just above the rigging, making entrance quite easy. This opening was known as the lubbers' hole.

A separate set of rigging had been led from the mast below the crow's nest to the platform's edge about six feet out. This rigging was known as the futtock shrouds. A minor misdemeanour on the parade ground meant a trip to the top of the mast; no particular problem for a fit teenager with a normal head for heights. If, however, the order was accompanied by a terse command to achieve the crow's nest by the futtock shrouds it became more tricky – you were climbing the last six feet leaning outwards not far short of the horizontal. The vast safety net eight feet from the bottom of the mast looked a long way down from there and certainly none of us wanted to test its strength. It was permissible to claim no head for heights and opt for the other penance which was to hop round the edge of the parade ground in a knees bent position with your rifle held horizontally across the back of your neck with one hand grasping the barrel and the other hand the butt. Few chose this option for fear of being marked out as wimps.

It was about this time that we were introduced to 'annual classification'. This, I think is common to all three services; it consists of being taken to a weapons range to be invited to fire live rounds at a target some two or three hundred yards away. In our case it was done at the fearsome Browndown Ranges at the edge of the Solent so that even if the targets and the earthworks behind them are missed altogether, the 'wide' rounds will fall harmlessly into the sea. Our Whale Island trained instructors loved it but we didn't share their enthusiasm, mainly because as luck would have it we classified in the depths of winter. I have since conducted annual classifications all over the world but I still remember vividly trying to get my teeth into a cold and hard Pusser's (navy issue) 'tiddy oggie', laughingly described officially as a Cornish Pasty, while crouched behind a wooden shelter at Browndown in the biting onshore wind and rain. Good character building stuff.

If our drill instructors served as ogres, the chief ogre and memorably so, was one Chief Petty Officer Wilmot who could have held his own with any regimental sergeant major I have met since. At the time, the name of Wilmot was well known throughout the Fleet Air Arm aircrew component of pilots, navigators and telegraphist air gunners or TAGs – many of whom were remustered pilot candidates who for one reason or another had failed to achieve a pilots' badge. I mention him specifically because wherever we foregathered either singly or in groups after *Vincent*, someone came up with a Wilmot story. And this situation ran down through the years. In the late nineteen seventies, when I was serving in London as a 'Whitehall Warrior' I met a member of the Department of Trade's Sea Transport Branch who mentioned in conversation that he had been a naval pilot in the war. Inevitably *St Vincent* came up but all he could remember about it was the name of the CPO gunnery instructor – Wilmot, who had sent him up the mast twice during drill training.

In fact I have reason to know that CPO Wilmot was not only an excellent instructor, he was also something of a closet softie. On one occasion I was volunteered, on the lines of 'three volunteers, you, you and you' to be a waiter in the Petty Officers' Mess for a formal function. The senior member was the Chief Ogre himself and serving drinks nearby I heard him singing the praises of 'my boys' to a group of visiting civilians. I heard years later that after retirement he became a postman in Southsea and that he had died at a ripe old age. His honourable epitaph could be that he played a major part in bringing many young men to disciplined adulthood.

It was not all work. Portsmouth was only a short ferry ride across the Harbour from Gosport. The city was as much the wartime home of the Royal Navy as any other port and more so than most. Sailors were its favoured citizens, and although the white bands around our caps marked us out as CWs – or 'seagoing wrens' – the mocking description of officer candidates by the other members of the lower deck – to the civilian population we were simply sailors and we had our collars touched for luck by Portsmouth's young ladies along with the genuine crews of visiting naval vessels. We committed few misdemeaours however; it was sensible and seemly to keep clear of the crushers – the navy's regulating police – always on the lookout for conduct unbecoming, and the sheer ignominy of being ploughed from the course always loomed.

Came the day when some of us 'embarked' on the train for London and our course at Chelsea Polytechnic. In those days the School Certificate, taken at sixteen, could be followed by the Higher School Certificate taken a year or two later. Those who had not taken 'Higher' due to having left school too early – or not having bothered – were required to undergo an intensive course of higher education with particular reference to disciplines that would be useful in further training such as mathematics, physical geography, astro navigation and similar technical subjects. There were about thirty of us in this situation including several colonials – not an acceptable description these days but no offence intended and in any case their nicknames for the Brits were sometimes unrepeatable. We were quartered in a large requisitioned house in Thurloe Square, South Kensington, almost opposite the Victoria and Albert Museum, and we took our meals in an attic that was rigged out as a canteen above the Polytechnic building in Manresa Road just off the King's Road in Chelsea.

If we had expected to participate in the pleasures of wartime London, we were disappointed. My leanings had always been more literary than technical and I found the course hard going. The pace was fast, the standard high and we experienced the real meaning of the word 'intensive'. Others may not have found it so, but I can't recall any stories told about evening drinking bouts and no one appeared to spend nights elsewhere than in the allotted dormitories.

But there was one outing that comes vividly to mind. Glen Miller, a name to conjure with even as I write, was the legendary leader of the US Air Force Band. In late 1944 the band was touring US airfields in England and word had reached us that it was due to perform at the Queensbury Club in Shaftesbury Avenue, open to allied servicemen and women only. I recall that it was early December and the band was due to travel to France next day to entertain the troops. Miller's popularity in my teenage years can be compared to the emotions aroused by the Beatles for a later generation and some of us were determined not to miss a sight of the great man in the flesh. We all arrived early and managed to get in. Predictably the place was packed and the wide stage, set up for dancing, allowed a close view of the band and the maestro himself. During a pause and for a bet, I approached him nervously and asked if he would mind if I asked the blonde girl singer to dance. He gazed on me benignly through those large spectacles.

"Go ahead son. She's free for the next number but it's her call." She was a nice young lady, a few years older than me and I seemed to have started a fashion, for during the orchestral numbers she had lots of dancing partners. It was a splendid break from our daily grind and the news that Miller had been lost in the Channel without trace while flying in a light aircraft to France was received with great sadness by a whole generation of British and American youth.

Through all this, the life of Chelsea Polytechnic went on around us. We were a part of the student body and most of us were of a similar age to the civilian majority. But there was a social life in which we did not, could not, take part. There simply wasn't time. To be sure, there were pretty girls in abundance but amorous dalliance was on hold for us, at least until the critical end of course examinations. I suppose our 'module' could be described as a crammer tucked into a higher educational establishment. Our teachers were good, the best, and anyone with two clues to rub together could not fail to absorb much of the instruction.

Although London in 1944 had not seen much of the Luftwaffe for a couple of years, Hitler and his scientists hadn't finished with us yet. It was flying bomb time. The V1, that strange, sinister, pilotless flying machine known to Londoners as the Doodlebug, puttered in the skies above us. When its engine stopped, it went down in a steep glide to the ground and exploded. The received wisdom was that if the engine stopped directly above you, the angle of the glide path to earth would ensure that it would explode well away from those directly below, and this theory seemed to work. On several occasions I recall seeing one of these things above – it flew quite low – and watching it glide before hearing the bang. The Royal Air Force became adept at shooting V1s out of the sky before they reached London, but many got through.

There were rumours of an even more deadly weapon on the way. Trailed in speeches by Hitler as the ultimate secret weapon, this was to take the form of a rocket ascending from its launch pad in Germany into the stratosphere and programmed to descend on London with its cargo of high explosive. Despite the desperate efforts of our troops to get to the launch pads of these weapons, known to be in Northern Germany, a number of rockets reached their target. They were indiscriminate, undetectable, there was no warning and no defence. We were having breakfast at the Poly one morning when there was a massive explosion that seemed to be quite near to us. Heads and eyebrows were raised and comments such as 'that was a near one' and 'I didn't hear the engine' were interrupted by someone racing in and shouting,

"That one landed on the pensioners' barracks."

The Royal Hospital, Chelsea, to use its correct title, is home to the army pensioners famous for their familiar uniform of red coat and black shako type hat. The hospital is a short walk and an even shorter run from Manresa Road, and some of us piled out of the Poly and ran to the hospital to see if we could help.

We were met by a scene of carnage with masses of helpers milling about full of good intentions but not really knowing what to do. Fortunately, the police, fire brigade and rescue services were on the scene very quickly; the area was cordoned off and we were thanked and bidden to return to our studies. I was pleased and honoured years later, after my retirement from the services, to be appointed a Commissioner of the Royal Hospital, and when attending Board meetings, which entailed passing the brass plate that commemorates the bombing, it always brought back memories of that eventful day. It later transpired that the Chelsea Hospital explosion of 1945 was caused not by a Doodlebug, but by a rocket, one of the first V2s as they came to be known. It had hit and destroyed the same block that had previously been bombed by a German airship in 1918 and then rebuilt in 1922.

Final examinations in all subjects eventually took place and it became evident that the Polytechnic course had been no sinecure. We lost a number of students who failed to reach the minimum pass mark. For my part I knew that while happy about most subjects I must have scraped through higher maths by the narrowest margin. But ahead of us lay a return to *St Vincent* to join the 77th Pilots' Course, a short burst of instruction on aviation preparation then ho! for flying training, initially with the RAF.

Moreover, somewhere about this time we were all promoted. From the lowly rank of Naval Airman 2nd Class, below which it was impossible to sink, we skipped one grade (1st Class) and became Leading Naval Airmen. This entailed sewing a shiny gold anchor, or 'killick' on to our best going ashore uniform and a very few bob a week more at pay parade. Flying pay, however, was in the offing and that was a substantial bounty.

2

Tigers and a Ship

Over the war years a standard pattern for pilot training had emerged within the Fleet Air Arm. It ran through Induction, which I had now completed, Elementary Flying Training (EFTS), courtesy of the RAF; Service Flying Training (SFTS), courtesy of either the United States Navy or the Royal Canadian Air Force which took place in the US or in Canada, and finally conversion to deck landing and take-off after qualifying as a pilot.

EFTS for the 77th Pilots' Course took place at Clyffe Pypard, a prewar Marshalls Flying School in Wiltshire, converted to RAF use and furnished with De Havilland 82A training biplanes – better known as Tiger Moths. There was no messing about. On the day after our arrival, having drawn basic flying kit consisting of helmet, parachute, Gosport tubes for verbal communication with the pilot instructor plus a flying jacket for warmth, we were marched out to our aircraft, introduced to our new teachers and we were each plonked into the second cockpit of a two seater trainer to be taught cockpit drill, culminating in the 'vital actions check' before take-off.

We were in seventh heaven. This was what we had volunteered for and no instructors could have had more keen and attentive pupils. It was now early spring 1945 and the ritual of being marched to the aircraft parking area – the 'apron' – each morning was eagerly anticipated. The dewy dawns were full of the promise of spring and the smell of the 'Tigers', an amalgam of aircraft dope, fuel oil and an element that we attributed to be unique to Tiger Moths, gave exquisite pleasure. To paraphrase Wordsworth 'Bliss was it on those morns to be alive.'

It couldn't last, of course. Bliss tends to fade before the application of hard graft and this was represented by the shallow learning curve of 'circuits and bumps'. Before you can fly an aeroplane, it is obviously necessary to learn the techniques of take-off and landing and in the forties this was done by repetition until the pupil had grasped the knack of doing both successfully irrespective of weather and wind conditions.

This took time and some never succeeded for no other reason than that nature had failed to endow them with an adequate ability to coordinate hands, feet and eye. We lost several hopefuls from our course because of this. I imagine that these days an advanced link trainer would root out those with poor coordination long before they progress to actual flying training, thus saving on sorely bruised egos and considerable expense.

When the instructors were satisfied that we could get the aircraft into the air and then land it safely we went on to aerobatics, and how to get out of a spin. This was when we appreciated the true value of all those dreary lessons on theory of flight covering lift, weight, thrust and drag, angles of attack (of an aerofoil to wind) and the elements of a stall. Our instructors had all been operational pilots but they told us that they relished flying trainers because it was 'back to basics' flying with very few instruments, the wind in your hair and a true 'feel' for the aircraft. It probably explains why so many pilots of commercial jets these days fly vintage biplanes for fun when off duty.

So we looped and rolled our way across the Wiltshire Downs as spring led into summer; we learned how to recover from stalls and spins, those most dangerous of situations. Until that wonderful day when returning to the field before lunch after, in my case, nine hours dual instruction, the instructor got out of the front cockpit and said, and I shall always remember the words:

"Do me a good one," turned his back and walked away, waving his hand in a forward motion.

Going solo for the first time is one of those pinnacle moments in one's life. The knee trembling stage – taxiing down to the take-off point – is followed by the hollow stomach feeling while you are trying frantically to remember the mnemonic for the sequence of the vital actions check that you knew so well this morning. The vital initials suddenly appear in the mind's eye – TTM FF; throttle nut tight for take-off, trim tab lever half to two thirds forward, mixture control at rich, fuel gauge indicating full, flaps and rudder mechanism free. Then elation kicks in as you thrust the throttle forward, the aircraft tells you it wants to go when you reach airspeed, and you are away for the thrill of a lifetime, in control of your own personal third dimension. We didn't 'soar' away, the Tiger Moth and I. They don't do that; they are kindly aircraft, gently resisting attempts by the inexperienced to do daft things and so there were very few accidents during our EFTS phase.

The first solo is a simple take-off and landing, just one circuit and bump. Not many are perfect so I wasn't too unhappy when I did a short, skittish bounce before setting both wheels and tailskid firmly on the ground. The instructor's verdict was "OK, but make damned sure the next one is a good three pointer with no bounces." By implication his comment gave me licence to become a free spirit, to wander solo at will within a thirty mile radius practising the techniques and manoeuvres which we had been taught during dual instruction. I recall that the weather was near perfect for low altitude flying. Except for spin recovery where spare altitude is a necessity, we seldom flew above three thousand feet. So sometimes alone and sometimes in company with a friend, I made the most of over twenty hours solo flying across the lovely Wiltshire countryside, always being careful to avoid the circuit of RAF Lyneham, an operational airfield close by.

There was also a general lightening of spirit, a new euphoria. Social life was still limited; Clyffe Pypard is on an escarpment of the Wiltshire Downs, miles from anywhere that could offer anything approaching a wild evening out and anyway we were still treading carefully for fear of putting a foot wrong. So evenings were spent in the Naafi canteen, chatting about the day's flying and perhaps joining the group singing obscene songs. I recall celebrating the ecstatic condition of the lady who was coming round the mountain, rejoicing in the testicular disadvantages of Messrs Hitler, Goering, Himmler and Goebbels as well as Mr Samuel Hall, the trials of O'Reilly and his daughter and an unprintable version of the battle between Abdul the Bulbul Emir and Ivan Stavinsky Skavar. There were many others that escape the memory.

Wrapped up in our own little world, we were only vaguely conscious of the great events outside, but it had become obvious that the war in Europe was drawing to a close. One of the side effects that had become noticeable to the RAF was the sudden surplus of aircrew, and stories began to appear in the papers of expensively trained pilots driving shunting engines on the railways and even helping farmers to harvest crops. At this time, having successfully completed EFTS, we were all awaiting our postings to SFTS in North America. Wonderful tales of flying training at Pensacola in Florida had reached us and that was the prime ambition of most. Mobile, elsewhere in North America's southern states, and Canada, being slightly less favoured.

As the days passed with no news of postings, we became restive and petitioned the RAF administrators of the station for information. The frank answer was, "It's unlikely that you'll be going to the States or Canada and as yet the Navy hasn't decided what to do with you." This was a bitter blow and gloom descended. Eventually the UK element of the course was packed off to Portsmouth and the Commonwealth trainees were sent to a holding unit while their future was discussed with their respective high commissioners.

While 'they' were deciding what to do with us, we were sent back to *St Vincent* for a few weeks, during which VE Day, the end of the war in Europe, occurred. We joined in the manic nationwide celebrations and incidentally, I blotted my copybook in a big way. *St Vincent* boasted a large concrete outdoor swimming pool, well fenced and closed during the winter months. It was filled in May of each year and opened in June. Three of us joined three young ladies of *St Vincent*'s small administrative Wren contingent in an illicit swim in late May before the pool was opened but as luck would have it we were caught by the Regulating Police, the infamous 'crushers', and we were all placed on Commanders' Report, the naval equivalent of Regimental Orders.

It was obviously no heinous offence and Lieutenant Commander Williams, our Divisional commander, and reputedly the brother of Emlyn Williams, the actor, looked rather bored until the crusher giving evidence intoned, "They was all unclothed." Whereupon he looked distinctly interested.

"You mean they were naked? Girls as well?" The crusher, obviously a man of some sensitivity beneath his forbidding exterior, shifted uncomfortably.

"Yes sir, all of them. Not a stitch on." It must be remembered that we are discussing events in 1945, when morals, even during a world war, were meant to be tighter than today. It was our good fortune that Williams had a sense of humour and the lecture he gave us plus the seven days Number Elevens, translated from naval jargon into English as stoppage of leave and pay, was belied by the twinkle in his eye. The girls, tried and judged by their own 'Queen Bee', the Wren officer, also got a lecture and a minor punishment after gallantly admitting complicity in the skinny dip.

Soon after this we were packed off to HMS *Daedelus* III located near

Havant on the south coast and near to Portsmouth. With apologies to the good citizens of Havant, a pleasant little town, in 1945 HMS *Daedalus* III was an unlovely place; it was a collection of superannuated Nissen huts inhabited by all manner of transitees and it was clear that the ship's administration had problems with finding employment for them. *Daedalus* remains in my memory solely by virtue of the curious affair of Stoker Preston. From time to time the Tannoy would pipe 'Stoker Preston to the Captain's cabin'. This occurred four or five times a day and speculation ran rife. It reached fever pitch when it was discovered that Stoker Preston was a Wren – and a Leading Wren at that. Fertile imaginations created stories of the methods by which this lady achieved her elevated status. But in the end the Captain, credited with being something of a navy blue swordsman, proved to be of lesser clay, just like the rest of us. Leading Stoker Preston was apparently a dab hand at ministering to the coke stove that graced the Captain's cabin, and who more entitled to have first call on her services than the captain of the ship.

In due course their Lordships at the Admiralty decided to do what came naturally to them and they sent us to sea while they were still considering our future. Thus after a mercifully short time at Havant, we were embarked in HMS *Pretoria Castle*, a prewar Union Castle liner that had been converted to an aircraft carrier. Her task at the time was to run up and down the Channel testing the deck landing hooks on Seafires, the naval version of the Spitfire. What the lower deck thought of fifty or so 'seagoing wrens' masquerading as leading seamen and embarked as supercargo became painfully obvious very quickly. We were viewed with amused and cheerful contempt that dissolved quickly as the good humour and good nature of the ordinary matelot came to the fore and many of us, stifling our disappointment at the turn of events, soon began to enjoy the experience.

The GNS training that we had been given at *St Vincent* was immensely helpful. For a start, and to the surprise of the crew, we spoke the language, albeit lacking any experience of the working of a 'grey funnel line' ship at sea. But it was no surprise to us that the sea was the 'oggin' (hogwash) or that the Royal Navy was to the lower deck, the Andrew – I never found out why. We had stood watches and were familiar with the watch divisions of the twenty four hour clock. We were aware that a broadcast announcement aboard ship was a 'pipe'. We knew that the First Lieutenant was 'Jimmy' and that the Master at Arms was the 'Jaunty', and incidentally the only man on the lower deck permitted to wear a sword.

There were nevertheless many things that were new to us. We had not lived on real messdecks before, where each day two members of the complement of each table were designated 'cooks' and on the pipe 'cooks to the galley', each had to take a large pan known as a Dixie to the galley to be served the meal for the whole table and then had to return and share it out. We were issued with lifejackets and with hammocks. These were lashed to a traditional formula each morning and then stowed in a hammock rack until collected in the evening. Properly lashed, each hammock would support a man in the water we were told, and someone was detailed to throw lashed hammocks overboard if it became necessary to abandon ship. There were hammock hooks all over the ship, some in the messdecks over the tables and some on the weatherdecks for use in fine weather when one could sleep under the stars. You simply had to find two that were the right distance apart and climb in for the night. Much too early each morning a petty officer chosen, we thought, for his insidiously penetrating voice, would wander round the decks reciting a mantra which went something like – "Wakey, Wakey, rise and shine, You've 'ad yer time and I've 'ad mine. Evo, Evo, lash up and stow. Come on me lucky lads, the sun's burning yer eyes out." And then, after a pause "On oilskins."

Of course we were subject to the tricks that have always been played on greenhorns. A friendly rating would volunteer to assist with your hammock and would helpfully tie one end. A minute or two after settling in comfortably you would become aware that it was a 'granny', cunningly designed to let you down painfully but not dangerously. Or, if the knot was good, you find that you are sleeping with your feet slightly higher than your head. This, when one sleeps on a moderately full bladder, causes even the young adult male to get up for relief several times during the night, a joke which takes time to mature, as the victim will have no idea that he has been targeted for several nights until a good Samaritan puts him wise to a little known medical fact. This was all in good part and in no way malicious. Standard naval rituals and practices were taken in our stride. Morning Colours and evening Sunset when bugles blew and flags were raised and lowered were old hat to us, as were parts of ship. When the ship's Tannoy piped 'Libertymen to muster at the Brow', we knew where to go. When on parade the order 'turn forr'ard, dismiss' was given, we knew which way to turn from the start. Settling in to ship's routine was no problem.

Our main job at sea was to shadow various members of the ship's company in tasks related to flying. We became assistant 'batmen' when deck landings were taking place. This involved standing in a small gully at one edge of the flight deck holding a baton shaped like a table tennis bat in either hand with arms outstretched. The task was to help the pilots to guide their aircraft on to the restraining wires stretched across the deck to bring them to a halt before they reached the crash barrier at the end of the flight deck. In a calm sea it was not a difficult operation and we became quite good at it, although watched carefully by the real batmen. When the sea was even slightly rough it was considered better for the morale of the pilots for the permanent ship's company batmen to take over.

When there was no night training for aircrew we would usually spend time alongside at Portsmouth Dockyard, casting off next morning and moving down the ancient harbour leaving Kings Stairs to port, familiar to Nelson's captains as their embarkation point all those years ago; past the hulk of *Foudroyant* to starboard, a ship of the line from the Napoleonic wars, pensioned off and used during our war and afterwards for sea cadet training. Gliding on at three or four knots past Gunwharf to port, owned by the Army and crammed with tank landing craft, and then the traditional salute to Fort Blockhouse which flew the flag of the Commander in Chief to starboard at the seaward end of the Harbour. Out into the Sound past Southsea Castle where Henry VIII watched as Mary Rose foundered near Gilkicker Point and on along the swept channel through the passage between the twin forts guarding the entrance to the Solent.

We did this many times and I have done it since times without number in small boats. It is as much liquid history as the Thames is said to be and it has never failed to bring to me the lump in the throat and that feeling of pride in one's country and history that elements of the chattering classes have attempted to make so unfashionable today. This journey is still done on the ferries from Portsmouth en route to France and Spain, although *Foudroyant* can no longer be seen and Gunwharf has been developed into something else. But Nelson's flagship still looms over the naval dockyard and there is a fine memento of more recent history in the refurbished HMS *Warrior*, the Royal Navy's first ironclad warship, located in a dockyard berth.

Then there were those nights at sea, with the gentle roll of the ship and sometimes cloudless skies with the stars shining seemingly much more brightly than on land. In this area, the CW element, so eager to absorb seagoing knowledge from the ship's company, became the teachers. During our astro-navigation instruction we had been required to learn the names and positions of the constellations in the night sky. This was a revelation to Pretoria Castle's ratings who enjoyed being able to find Polaris, the North Star, through the twin pointers of Ursa Major, to recognise Orion with his sword and belt and to identify constellations such as the Plaeides. A useful spin off, as a Welsh rating told me, was its impact on girl friends, "Very romantic, see!"

But throughout this otherwise agreeable seagoing interlude, there was an undercurrent of unease. We were all concerned about what was to happen to us.

Then occurred an event that increased our options for the future. One fine day when there was a lull in flying and we were idling along off St Catherine's Point on the southern tip of the Isle of Wight, a strange machine settled down on the flight deck. It was one of the new autogiros, out of which stepped a soldierly looking gentleman. He turned out to be Brigadier Ponting late of the Indian Army and from the War Office. He had specifically come to see and speak to the redundant pilot trainees and he addressed us in the aircraft hanger. His exact words are long gone but I recall that having commiserated with our situation, he reminded us that there was still a war going on in the Far East and that the Indian Army, short of officers because of the long Burma campaign, would be happy to consider us for officer training. Furthermore, he said, those who would care to volunteer, although required to undergo a War Office Selection Board, or WOSB, would find that this would not be rigorous as we had already been selected for officer training by the Royal Navy. Successful candidates would attend a pre OCTU course in England and then be sent to India for further training before being commissioned into a British Indian Army regiment of their choice.

This required some thought. I had been firm in my lack of ambition to be a soldier. The alternatives, however, were not encouraging. The

Navy had still not made up its mind what was to be done with us. It seemed likely, given the pressure to reduce the Home Fleet and the subsequent surplus of manpower, that we would be out of the Service in short order and looking for jobs in a swollen labour market. Also the prospect of India and service abroad was mightily attractive to a generation that had been brought up to be familiar with stories of the North West Frontier and the poems and tales of Kipling.

I volunteered along with the majority of the rump of the 77th Pilots' Course. Not long after this, two atomic bombs were dropped at Hiroshima and Nagasaki on the main Japanese island of Honshu and the Japanese decided to call it a day. This gave rise to mixed feelings. While we had to be pleased that the killing had stopped, there was also a feeling of disappointment that we had missed the war after all. Dreams of travel to India, we thought, were unlikely to be realised. But full marks to our guardian angels at the War Office; they appreciated our probable disquiet and we were reassured. The Indian Army would still need officers in the immediate aftermath of the war.

1936. The Matriarch. My paternal grandmother. *Elle etais formidable!*

The 75th Pilots' Course. HMS *St Vincent* 1944. Author top right.

Accommodation Block (Cabins). HMS *St Vincent* - showing mast.

At sea. Preparing for a deck landing.

Clearing the deck for the next one.

3

Going for a Soldier

Transfer to the Army was a shock to the system. It is not widely known that naval ratings are not sworn men. They operate under the direction and authority of King's (now Queen's) Regulations and Admiralty Instructions and take no oath of allegiance to the Crown. Not so the other two services. After our visit to the War Office for the WOSB, which amounted to little more than a formal interview by three senior officers who had our educational details and service records in front of them, we were issued with railway warrants to Maidstone where we were required to report to Invicta Lines, the depot of the Royal West Kent Regiment. As we arrived, in civilian clothes by direction of the War Office, we immediately took the oath of allegiance to His Majesty and we were kitted out as private soldiers of The Queen's Royal Regiment. The concession to our status as officer cadets was a white circle of celluloid behind the cap badge and narrow strips of white tape on each battledress epaulette. The shock to the system came with the sleeping arrangements. The Navy had provided metal beds with springs and mattresses and sheets when ashore and comfortable hammocks with good blankets when at sea. The RAF's arrangements were even more 'ritzy' with soft hospital type blankets and sheets. Invicta Lines, where we spent two nights, provided beds made out of 4 x 2 wood criss-crossed with strong string. Three hessian 'biscuits' filled with straw served as a mattress. The Army did not offer sheets and the blankets that were issued would have been rejected by a well brought up horse. We began to wonder if we had chosen wisely. Rupert Brooke's 'rough male kiss of blankets' became an itchy reality and one that we were destined to get used to.

We were then sent on leave with instruction to report two weeks later to Wrotham Camp in Kent. None of us had the faintest idea of what we were about to face. I recall that my father, not having seen me for about eighteen months, but aware of course that I had transferred to the Army, greeted me with the words:

"Good God, they've put him in the Mutton Lancers."

This was soldiers' talk, a reference to the Queen's Royal Regiment cap badge which depicted a paschal lamb carrying the banner of Catherine of Braganza. This featured somewhere in the regimental history. I realised that it would have been a mistake to make any reference to a poor first impression of my new Service; my father, never one to refrain from I told you so's, would have had a field day. He was, however, nobody's fool. Just before I returned to duty he clapped me on the shoulder and said with his wolfish grin.

"Not the same is it? You'll get used to it. All part of life's rich tapestry!"

Wrotham Camp in Kent was a pre-OCTU, that is to say that potential officers were sent there to be toughened up before being despatched elsewhere to formal officer training. We were placed in the India Wing and we were formally referred to as Indian Army Cadets. Our course was expanded by a large number of 'schoolboy cadets' also destined for the Indian Army. These young men were about eighteen months younger than us and at seventeen and a half, they were also under age volunteers. Many had family connections to the Indian Army or to the Indian Civil Service (ICS), with parents still living in India. It was a happy mixture and we made lasting friendships.

The pre-OCTU course was, in present day jargon, something else. Our instructors were in the mould of the traditionally brutal corporal with a mission to 'show up' these sailors in particular. It wasn't difficult for them. We had to unlearn naval drill, which differs considerably from army drill, and then learn an entirely new set of commands. Even saluting was different. The navy's 'shortest way up, shortest way down' was replaced by a more vigorous 'longest way up, shortest way down' and the navy's actual salute with the angled hand touching the brow as though peering out to the horizon, was replaced by a head high vertical palm placed against the forehead. The army sloped arms. You can't easily slope arms in a ship; the navy shouldered arms, and so on. Our corporals had a great time. Wrotham Camp sat below a steep escarpment. Punishment for infringements usually consisted of a timed trip up the escarpment and back laden with rifle and a backpack full of house bricks with a certainty of having to do it again right away if the allotted time was exceeded. But all this had been anticipated and was accepted. We were introduced to the army's answer to the tank at infantry platoon level. This was a truly fearsome weapon for its operator called a Projector Infantry Anti Tank, or PIAT. It had a padded butt to fit into the shoulder and a trigger that when pressed projected a bomb type missile by means of a spring. It had the kick of an angry mule. I fired it twice and then because of shortage of ammunition I was thankfully denied further acquaintance.

One skill I took away from Wrotham was how to ride a motor bike. We travelled the lanes of Kent in 'packets' of five or six, each led by an instructor. Among the Army issue bikes at that time were the 500 cc Triumph and the Matchless 350 cc G3L model. Wrotham offered either and it fell to my lot to be trained on a Matchless. There was a good deal of motor bike instruction with some useful periods on maintenance but there was very little chance of 'going solo' because of the number of accidents and ensuing damage to commercial premises. I recall that Woolworth's window in Maidstone situated opposite a sharp ninety degree bend was a regular casualty. Nevertheless, the ability to handle a motor bike was a useful skill for the future.

Our main gripe was the food. It was an outdoor life and we were taking much more physical exercise than we had been accustomed to when we were in the navy or when we were with the RAF. Food was still restricted, indeed rationed, in Britain and we were constantly hungry. Brown Windsor soup featured heavily on the menu, followed by stew. It was gobbled down but any thought of emulating Oliver Twist was met with a hollow laugh. The weekly treat was a breakfast meal on Sundays consisting of a fried egg, sausages made of soya and a slice of bacon. If you were at the back of the queue the egg could have doubled as a new sole for an army boot and the sausages, or soya links as they were officially known, had long ceased to bear any resemblance to the genuine article.

There was no privacy. In the communal latrine hut eight or nine holes had been cut side by side into a very big earthenware pipe and partly lined with wood. The holes were of a size to accommodate the average backside. Here we sat to perform our natural functions. Every now and then the long pipe was flushed with water and after one or two nasty incidents we became keenly aware of the need for caution. It was not unknown for drunks from other courses returning to camp at night to creep into the hut and slip a lighted newspaper into the end hole just as the flushing started, causing the paper to float past the other holes and shrieks and general mayhem further down. I can't recall anyone being seriously hurt and the student code of Omerta ensured that the camp authorities didn't know that this was going on. Sleeping arrangements mirrored those of Invicta Lines except that at Wrotham the weather also took a hand.

By now it was early November and it was both cold and wet. We slept in Nissen huts that had been badly sited and this caused them to flood in wet weather. If you happened to be on a bottom bunk, as I was, it was not unknown for the water level to reach the sagging string below the straw palliasse and then by capillary action reach the unconscious sleeper around dawn. The floodwater would usually put out the coke stove that kept the hut reasonably warm. Waking up at dawn with a wet backside in a freezing cold hut probably did wonders for our characters; it certainly increased the scope and fluency of the profanity of those on the bottom bunks.

4

Passage to India

All things, even pre-OCTU at Wrotham, come to an end, however, and details emerged of our passage to India. Most were to go by troopship but some were to travel by air as part of a trial of a new air trooping service being strongly marketed by the RAF. As yet there were no long range aircraft in service that were specifically designed to carry passengers. The DC3 Dakota would have been ideal but its range was too short. The RAF had surmounted this little local difficulty by sewing up the bomb bays of surplus long range bombers and offering them up as troop transports. I was told that I was to be one of those who would be in the party to test the new air trooping system. You, they said, will be one of the lucky ones.

We were packed into the belly of a converted Liberator bomber at RAF Bourne in Cambridgeshire in the early spring of 1946 and took off for an airfield in North Africa. It was extremely exciting. Few of us had been abroad before and it was possible by standing on tiptoe to peer though the tiny portholes which had been set into the side of the aircraft. Down across France and over the Med we flew until we landed in Tripoli at RAF Castel Benito during the late afternoon at what had been, less than a year previously, a wartime operational airfield. The evidence for this was clearly visible from the mounds of crashed and broken aircraft bulldozed to the side of the runway and craters not yet filled in where they did not interfere with air traffic.

We staged there for one night sleeping under canvas and as newcomers to desert living, we were gathered together to receive a short talk on the location of the facilities together with a few local lifestyle tips. We had already noticed that the black ants that infested the place were about eight times the size of the ones at home and we were advised to clear them out of our tents without touching them for they could offer a nasty nip to the unwary. We were also warned about the presence of snakes and scorpions, with particular emphasis on the tendency of scorpions to seek out the warmest place to sleep during the cold desert nights, often ending up someone's warm and recently discarded shoe. It was therefore accepted practice to rap each shoe smartly on the ground before putting it on next morning.

We were also told to keep clear of the desert outside the camp perimeter because nobody could yet be sure that the surrounding mine strip had been completely cleared. Such minor but important details as learning to strike locally made matches away from you to avoid the flaming head landing on your clothes, and the advisability of knocking the issue 'hard tack' biscuits on the table before eating them in order to evacuate the weevils, we had to learn by experience. It was nevertheless thoughtful of the camp authorities to put their transitees wise to the potential dangers of a seemingly bland and innocuous place, despite it looking like a military aviation scrapyard.

We took off across the Western Desert for Cairo next morning. It was a memorable and moving journey. As we flew over the desert, not at any great speed or height, and long before the scrap merchants had cleared away the saleable debris of war, we could see below us clear evidence of desperate battles. Sometimes there would be signs of a major encounter with wrecked and abandoned tanks, guns and vehicles littering a wide area; at other places there might be a ring or line of shell craters around a small wired and fortified feature that told a story of a strongly defended position eventually overrun. At one place where the sea was visible in the distance on one side of the aircraft, there was a crashed fighter plane that must have been a good thirty miles inland. We speculated. Did the pilot survive? If so, did he realise that he was reasonably close to the sea? Was he rescued or did he die of thirst and exposure? This journey passed in a flash and we landed at Cairo West airfield with our rations untouched.

Then the aircraft broke down. Or more accurately, one of the engines developed a fault and we had to wait in Cairo until a replacement could be flown out and fitted. We were quartered at Mena Transit Camp, no great distance from the Pyramids and the Sphinx. They could be viewed from Mena camp's main claim to fame and were well worth seeing by moonlight. The transit camp was famed throughout the British Army as having the deepest deep trench latrines in any theatre of operations. Flash to bang time, so to speak, was several seconds and the hideous possibility of one of the decrepit thunder boxes collapsing haunted the thoughts of most of us.

We were allowed out into Cairo while we were waiting for our aircraft to get back into service. The city was a byword for sin and soldierly delights but our problem was acute lack of cash. Cadets were paid as private soldiers so private soldier type entertainments had to be the norm. We had been told that walking alone around Cairo at night was not a good idea so we visited one or two nightspots in groups. I have to say that neither before nor since have I seen more athletic contortions done by young ladies with a variety of animals or objects than in those short trips into Cairo's nightlife. It was an education, of sorts. Hamburg's Reeperbahn was a girl guide's tea party in comparison. Cash was so short that we had to rely on locally produced cigarettes. These were called CTC – the correct title was Cape to Cairo. The resident British troops, however, had other names for them, Camel to Consumer and Consumption to Coffin being the most repeatable.

Cairo was, in parts, a gracious city with a strong continental flavour. Crammed with soldiers waiting to go home while we were there, although some were in transit to Palestine where there was still a good deal of unrest. But the Nile was serene and beautiful, lined with houseboats in the smart areas and the weather was pleasant compared to the March winds at home. I would like to have stayed longer there and I still regret that I have never returned to the city.

We waited about ten days for the aircraft to be repaired and then we flew on to RAF Habbaniyah in central Iraq. A leg stretch was decreed by the captain of the aircraft and we got out on to a blisteringly hot tarmac swept by a strong, dust laden wind, thankful that it was merely a refuelling stop. To our eyes, a godforsaken place in the middle of nowhere. Then on down the Gulf and across the southern tip of Persia to Mauripur airfield, Karachi, where we were to wait a day or two for a DC3 Dakota to complete our air journey. We had arrived in India.

Impressions of Karachi were coloured by the fact that the local vendors of trinkets and the shoeshine boys realised right away that we were new to the country and therefore easy marks. It was hard to get rid of them and the standard response of the shoe shiners in particular when they realised that they were getting nowhere, was to say 'OK sahib,' and move off only to run past a few seconds later and smear black polish over brown shoes or vice versa. Annoying when you have been looking forward so much to arriving in a fabled place but thankfully not experienced again as we moved south.

The final and mercifully short leg of the air trooping experiment was by DC3 Dakota from Karachi to Poona, famed as the spiritual home of Colonel Blimp, that proud army officer stereotype well known to all at home. It was in fact an easily forgettable little town snoozing quietly in the Indian sunshine. It was also the place where the Wrotham contingent split up for the onward journey to their various officer training establishments in India. We, the Indian Army infantry element, were destined for the Officer Training School at Bangalore and we were pared down to a small party of about ten. On the small railway station platform where we boarded the train for our two day rail journey to our destination, I saw no sign of the leading player in one of the many tales of Poona. It relates to a colonel in full fig of khaki drill uniform and red banded hat striding backwards and forwards on the platform while waiting for his train when he was approached by a stout Indian gentleman who embarked upon a lengthy diatribe about the lack of station facilities and demanded to know what was to be done about them. The exasperated colonel cut him short.

"How the devil should I know?"

The Indian said, "Are you not stationmaster?"

"Of course not," replied the colonel.

"Then," said the Indian, equally exasperated. "If you are not stationmaster, why is it that you are walking so proudly?"

Travelling on trains in India during those last years of the Raj, was an agreeable way of spending time. The system, operated by a devoted and long serving Indian workforce and managed by equally devoted Anglo Indians with a smattering of Europeans, was very efficient. The Hindu religion was, and probably still is, hierarchical in the extreme with a rigid caste system only slowly being eroded by the march of progress. The lower castes tended also to be the poorer element of the population, travelling third class. Journeys often took days rather than hours and they were often accompanied by children and small domestic animals; they would usually take their food and prepare it either at convenient stops along the way or on the train if they could get away with it. There was a middle class in more comfortable seats operating under a similar system, but Europeans and richer, usually higher caste Indians, travelled in style in cabins with separate sleeping, sitting out and washing facilities. Fit young locals without funds or not prepared to subscribe to the wellbeing of Indian Railways, just waited until the train was moving and jumped on to any protruding part which would take their weight and keep their feet off the ground. There they hung on and either clambered unseen to the roof or ran away as the train slowed for the next station. Travelling on the roof was no problem in a country where there were very few bridges and little wind.

Although we had been issued with the unpopular dehydrated 'K' ration for our two day journey we noticed that the few other Europeans on the train, all civilians, took their meals at one of the many branches of Simpsons, a chain of small restaurants that operated at a station of any size on the journey. Turbanned waiters in spotless white ministered to the patrons and we decided to take breakfast there on the second day of the journey. It was a great success and we lingered over the meal until some time after the other Europeans had departed. Then someone noticed that there was a grimy looking character hanging round outside the café and occasionally peering timidly through the doorway. We called over a waiter and asked him about this.

"Oh," he said. "That is the fireman. The driver has sent him to see when the sahibs have finished their breakfast so that he may carry on with the journey!"

This was when we realised that the Raj was still alive and kicking. Wrotham was suddenly worlds away.

As the train trundled southwards across the undulating countryside, stopping briefly at small towns with exotic names like Sholapur, Gulbarga, Raipur and passing uncounted small hamlets with an occasional black water buffalo placidly chewing and gazing at nothing in particular, I looked out on the unchanging scene of villagers toiling in the sun and reflected on the impact of those first few days in India. I was going to like the place, of that there was no doubt. The sights, sounds, smells, the friendliness of most of the people I had so far encountered and the sheer timelessness of it all combined with the pleasant spring climate to make it captivating. Also my teenage reading of Kipling and other writers who had fallen under the spell of India made it all seem strangely familiar.

5
Bangalore

Arrival at the Officers' Training School (OTS) Bangalore late at night saw us quartered in pleasant 'bashas', two to a room with solid metal charpoys (beds), and, praise be, spotless sheets. The first morning was a revelation. There was no bugle for reveille; there was a discreet knock at the door, which opened to a beaming Indian face surmounting an impeccable white dhoti and carrying a tray with a teapot, two cups and saucers, milk, sugar and two plates; each held a banana and two biscuits.

"Good morning sahibs. Salaam. I am Okri, your bearer and this is your chota hazri". No one had given us any idea that on arrival at OTS we would be given a personal servant, but it was a situation which we felt we could accept without stress. We thought at the time that, assuming chota hazri meant breakfast, a banana and a biscuit was a bit thin for growing lads, but we very soon learned that while hazri did mean breakfast, chota meant small and that it was the custom at OTS for a snack to be offered before First Parade and breakfast to be taken later.

As part of the new intake of cadets we were spared parade on the first day and simply instructed to make our way to the cadet mess for breakfast. A further revelation. Our mess was a cool, airy colonial type building with silent servants ministering to every need. After the lifestyle we had so far encountered in the Army, all this took some getting used to. In fact, eating a hearty breakfast we felt like 'the condemned man etc...'

All was well however. After a greeting and introductory pep talk by our course commander, Major Charnock, the rest of the day was spent familiarising ourselves with our surroundings, meeting the rest of the new intake and being kitted out with most of what we would need for our six month course of training. We were issued with two sets of one piece overalls, khaki berets and bicycles, cycling being the normal mode of transport at the OTS, situated just outside the city of Bangalore on Agram Plain and including a vast training area. We had arrived wearing the comfortable but ill fitting soldiers' tropical rig of flannel shirt and drill trousers; this was well below the standard required by the OTS for walking out and for formal parades, so we had to be measured by the tailor for two suits of khaki shirt and shorts and two suits of khaki bush jacket and trousers together with a side cap.

My room-mate was Alan Colley from Birmingham, a good friend I had known since those seemingly far off days at *St Vincent*. We agreed that we were both contented with the turn of events and we resolved to enjoy whatever was now to be thrown at us.

Morale had certainly ascended since our arrival at Bangalore. We met and made friends with our Sikh neighbours in the next room, Harbans and Gurbax Singh, who went out of their way to help us with the more difficult passages of Urdu, which all Indian Army officers had to speak to a passable standard. Our munshi, or language teacher, was a Muslim, by name Abdul Gafoor, a gentle soul who did his best for us. I have often wondered if he survived the bloodbath that scarred the face of India before and during the Partition process in 1947. During those halcyon days at OTS, Muslims and Hindus lived integrated working lives with no hint of the horrors that I was to see later, although in retrospect there must have been an undercurrent that was not evident to us.

The officer training course covered a multitude of subjects; it also differed from anything we had been exposed to previously. Our training with the navy, after immersion in the customs and language of the senior service, and our brief experience with the RAF, was all aimed at control of a flying machine, ultimately to make us proficient at landing that machine on a heaving flight deck at sea. The army's *raison d'être* is to gain and hold ground in war and certainly in India at that time, to be trained and prepared to act in aid of the civilian authority when called upon to do so. So the wide syllabus at the OTS covered platoon and company level tactics in all the phases of war – advance to contact with the enemy, attack, defence, withdrawal and concomitant subjects such as patrolling, weapon handling and radio procedure, which was different in the army to the other two services. Administration and man management was also covered, now known in more upmarket jargon as behavioural science or human resources. We took part in exercises in both jungle and desert country – all found within striking distance of Bangalore. The OTS staff even managed to find some bare rocky terrain similar to conditions encountered on the North West Frontier of India and we tried hard to emulate a demonstration company of Gurkhas who made light work of running up steep hills and securing the summits. On these occasions we wore coloured flashes on our backs to distinguish us from (notional) hostile tribesmen and so ensure that we were recognised as 'friendly forces' by the column moving along the valley.

These exercises stretched us rather more than they would have done in a temperate climate but the compensation arrived when hot and sweaty and bitten by numerous unidentified insects, we emerged from, say, a jungle 'bash' to be greeted by our beaming mess staff with the mess set up under canvas and a full meal available. We had never had this at home, but it was standard at OTS in India. Exercises usually ended in the morning and on these occasions it was customary to carry one's meal away from the mess tent to eat, gossiping in Kipling's 'morning cool'. Invariably the kitehawks, common sights in the Indian sky, having located food, divebombed us while both hands were engaged with mug and plate, whipping away sausages, bacon, eggs and anything else edible. Some sadistic mind devised a revenge ploy which was to conceal a lighted cigarette butt in a piece of bread and carry it out of the tent on a plate. The swoop of the bird was followed by a shrill scream and a rapid departure into the distance. This cruel practice was not popular and it was eventually outlawed by general consent.

It was sometimes necessary to spend an extra night in the field under canvas after an exercise while waiting for stragglers to report in and for transport to be marshalled for the return to camp. On these occasions we were always so tired that sleeping was no problem at all. The threat of 'Henry' however, was usually sufficient to bring the most comatose student to morning parade on time. Henry was an excessively flatulent mule who had been trained to perform on command – not that he ever needed much urging, in fact he practised for a good deal of his waking life. The 'special wake up procedure' was to back Henry up to the space occupied by the erring sleeper, get him to lower his backside to the most effective level and order him to open his gas tap. I never saw Henry in action but his handler described the results with relish. According to him, the gasping spluttering and cursing victims never re-offended.

Internal security, or IS training was taken very seriously, perhaps with a portent of the horrors to come. The British establishment in India was still conscious of the tragic mistake made years earlier in the nineteen twenties by Brigadier Dyer at Amritsar and we covered that situation from every angle. Briefly, the Brigadier, faced by what he decided was a hostile mob in the town square, called upon the crowd to disperse; when they failed to do so, he ordered his troops to open fire. Many civilians were killed or wounded and the subsequent enquiry found that the crowd had been unable to disperse quickly because the exits from the square were too narrow to cope with the press of people. The lessons learned from this incident were hammered into us.

In 1946 the army in India was still teaching methods of controlling and dispersing hostile crowds that would have been familiar to Brigadier Dyer as they were based on a bugle, a banner, a roll of barbed wire and a piece of chalk! The drill was to march to the incident normally at section strength with loaded weapons at safety and confront the crowd. A chalk mark was drawn across the road with a line of wire some yards behind it. The troops were lined up behind the wire standing at ease. A single blast from a bugle followed to claim the attention of the crowd; they were then told that they were an illegal assembly and that they must remain behind the chalk mark and disperse in an orderly manner. Should the crowd fail to disperse, bayonets would be fixed and a second bugle blast would be followed by another message ordering the crowd to split up and leave the area. At this stage a banner would be raised behind the line of soldiers bearing the message 'disperse or we fire'. It was accepted that probably at this stage stones and other missiles would be thrown at the troops although in those days there were no riot shields, rubber bullets or tear gas. The problem of how to get the message over in the local language was meant to be solved by the civil authority providing a local magistrate to accompany the troops. His job was to draw the crowd's attention to the law relating to unlawful assembly.

Of course we listened carefully to all this – we had to – but with a considerable degree of scepticism; it seemed so old fashioned and we doubted if it would work in practice. In fact, when faced with the problem of hostile crowds several times later on in Calcutta, I cannot recall using the 'school solution' at all. Now and then we had time to draw a chalk line or lay a strip of white tape and loud hailers had taken the place of bugles but lack of time ruled out wire and banners. Magistrates reluctantly appeared from time to time but they invariably vanished when the situation began to look uncomfortable. Who could blame them; they would very quickly have been marked men had they stayed with us. I did, however, come across a bugle blast and barbed wire solution used in West Africa years later, but more of that in due course.

It was the custom at OTS for monthly mess meetings to take place when a student committee met with the Indian catering staff to air complaints and make suggestions about the food. The meals were generally excellent and the European element of the course was well satisfied but the several Indian cadet members of the committee had a point to make. Our course was the first with a much increased Indian cadet element and they thought that the practice of serving all European style meals on most days was a bit unfair. After some discussion a Solomon type solution was arrived at. In future we would be offered exclusively Indian food at lunchtime and a European evening meal. Curry had not previously featured much in our diet and the insipid dishes masquerading as curry at home bore little relation to the genuine article that we encountered in India, so at first we were not too happy about this arrangement. We had to eat it, however; we were perennially short of cash and anyway there was neither time nor opportunity to eat at lunchtime elsewhere than in the cadet mess.

Real Indian curry is an acquired taste and it took us about six days to acquire it, after which we looked forward every day to the midday meal, wondering which of India's multitudinous curries had been selected for us to try that day. The caterers had risen nobly to the challenge of educating our palates and although now a lifelong addict, I cannot recall finer curries than those served at OTS.

Bangalore was in Mysore Province, and the Maharajah of Mysore had very kindly offered to place his riding school at the disposal of a few cadets from each OTS course. After suitable instruction, which took place one evening a week, those chosen for this privilege would be allowed to hack around the countryside on his well behaved mounts. Lots were drawn and my number came up. It was immensely enjoyable. We started from scratch sitting astride wooden horses being taught the correct seat and the use of the reins by the fiercely moustached Rajput riding master of the Maharajah's Cavalry Regiment. From there we progressed to the walk, the trot, the canter and finally the gallop. Along the way we were introduced to the grid; this was a series of timber poles lying horizontally about four feet apart and eighteen inches high. These produced lots of spills, being just high enough and wide enough to create a most awkward motion that would easily dislodge the inexperienced rider, but in the bloom of our youth we almost bounced so it was all good clean fun. The final session, about four months later, involved elementary tent pegging. It soon became evident that you need more than a few months' riding instruction to have any chance of success at that popular Indian activity. I don't suppose that his Highness the Maharajah of Mysore thought of his kindly act in PR terms but it certainly pushed much goodwill in his direction.

Early in the course we had been required to choose three Indian regiments in order of priority for our eventual commissioning. We had also to choose two British regiments to act as 'parents' for administrative purposes. My first choice was The Frontier Force Rifles, followed by the Rajputana Rifles and the Mahrattas, all northern regiments with which I felt I could feel at home. My British Army choices were my father's regiment, The Cheshires, and The Green Howards, a Yorkshire regiment that I had encountered along the way and admired.

Bangalore was a pleasant country town and for the first time in our service we had some evenings to spare for social jaunts. The main activity, which took place on pay day, was a trip to the local Chinese restaurant by rickshaw where we would gather for beer and a massive Chinese meal. The evening would invariably end with a rickshaw race with the grinning rickshaw wallahs seated in their vehicles and four or five rickshaws being raced along the road to the camp at Agram Plain with cadets between the shafts. Someone had acquired a genuine hunting horn and the air was filled with view halloohs and sundry other pagan cries.

The big event for every course was passing out parade and we prepared for it for about four weeks, practising our drill movements until the regimental sergeant major professed himself satisfied: as in most officer training establishments throughout what was still known as The Empire, he was a guardsman, but I have long forgotten which regiment bore him. My course photograph tells me that we were 'D' Company, Cadet Course 94 and I recall that my platoon commander was Captain Allah Dad followed by Captain 'Tug' Wilson of the 5th Royal Gurkha Rifles. Both were regular officers and both in after dinner conversation were gloomy about the short term prospects for peace in India, predicting wide unrest as the negotiations for a transfer to Indian independence progressed.

For most of the European cadets on our course, a by-blow from these negotiations fell just before we were due to be commissioned. It was decided that there were to be no more European officers commissioned into Indian regiments, which were to be 'Indianised' as soon as possible. This meant that we were to be commissioned into one or other of our British Army choices. Some of these regiments, including my first choice, the Cheshires, had no battalions in India, which would mean a sad departure from a country for which I had developed a great affection. As luck would have it, however, the Cheshires were up to establishment in subalterns and I learned that I was to be commissioned into The Green Howards which did have a battalion in India – the 2nd Battalion – stationed at Barrackpore about eighteen miles to the north of Calcutta and part of the 19th (Yorkshire and Lancashire) Brigade quartered in and around the city. Those cadets who had opted for Gurkha regiments were not affected by Indianisation and happily went off to join those superb soldiers wherever they were stationed.

Not long before our passing out parade, a curious emergency faced us. Two West African regiments had been withdrawn from Burma and quartered at Avadi Camp near Madras, not a great distance from Bangalore. The senior course at OTS, which was ours, was placed on standby to draw rifles and ammunition and be prepared to embus for Madras to be employed as 'security troops'. No more was said and in the event we were not needed, but I learned later what had happened. Apparently the West Africans had been geared up to leave India by troopship on a certain date and this had been put back for reasons which they didn't consider either fair or appropriate. So they refused to parade and threatened outright disobedience. Apparently all available British battalions were rushed to the area to surround the Camp but the situation was saved by negotiation and a potentially nasty incident was avoided.

We were duly commissioned amid scenes of great delight and I spent ten days' leave with friends in the pleasant seaside city of Madras at an establishment known as Madame Andre's. Despite a name that always attracts sharp glances when I reminisce about it, Madame Andre's was an eminently respectable establishment and recommended by the OTS as a suitable place for newly commissioned officers to spend a leave period. Madame herself, a motherly lady of uncertain pedigree although I surmised either colonial French or Anglo Indian, was kindness itself. We were introduced to agreeable young women from the European and Anglo Indian element of Madras at parties sponsored by Madame but we were left in no doubt that hanky panky was not on the agenda, certainly not within the bounds of her establishment.

Then there was the enjoyable task of spending the commissioning grant, designed to cover items of uniform that officers have to provide for themselves, our needs up to now having been provided free of charge by the army quartermaster organisation. A new forage cap, Sam Browne belt, two suits of KD and sundry small items took care of the allowance and one of the glories of India was that one could be measured one day, have a fitting the next day and receive the perfectly tailored clothing the following day. Also it was good quality material. The jodhpurs which were made for me for the riding instruction at Bangalore in 1946 were taken in at the waist and worn by Kate, my third daughter, when she was learning to ride at Tidworth in the late nineteen sixties.

My orders were to entrain – the army traditionally uses this manner of shorthand, entrain, embus, embark etc on its movement orders to save time – for Howrah Station, Calcutta where I would be met by my regiment and would report to the Adjutant at Barrackpore. Although I had travelled in style by train as a cadet during the memorable journey from Poona to Bangalore, I hadn't done so as a commissioned officer. It was therefore a surprise to be given a voucher for a sum of money equivalent to three first class fares from Madras to Calcutta. It was explained to me that both British and Indian army officers in prewar India had travelled on postings with their complete households which may have included horses and syces (grooms), servants and domestic goods. It was considered administratively easier to provide a set sum represented by three first class rail fares than to have to meet claims for varying amounts and the practice had continued. I mentally saluted the genius who had thought this one up – and had probably saved money for the civil administration into the bargain.

6

Calcutta and Barrackpore

Shoot Like a Gentleman!

"Some of the work was old fashioned peacekeeping, a task that fell to 2nd Green Howards during 1946 in Calcutta during the time of the communal massacres that marked the bloody run-up to Indian independence in which a million may have died. On one occasion for five successive days in the clammy monsoon heat, young Green Howards did what they could in the stench and smoke to keep the murderous mobs from their screaming victims. With a handful of other units they eventually restored some semblance of peace to the streets of that enormous city, littered by then with 4,000 rotting corpses."

THE ABOVE IS EXTRACTED FROM 'THE HISTORY OF THE GREEN HOWARDS' BY GEOFFREY POWELL AND IS REPRODUCED BY PERMISSION OF THE AUTHOR'.

The two day journey north to Calcutta emphasised once again the vast size of the subcontinent as the train chugged northwards along the coastal plain through the princely state of Hyderabad with its Maharajah famous for his riches and his fleet of Rolls Royce motor cars. On through Orissa towards Calcutta, known then as the second city of the British Empire. In 1946 when I joined my battalion it was a city still reeling from the impact of communal rioting. Followers of the Muslim and Hindu faiths were at odds over the shape of India after the promised independence from Britain had been achieved. The battalion had been temporarily withdrawn from riot control duties in the city only a few days before my arrival so I reported to 2nd Battalion the Green Howards as a newly commissioned 2nd Lieutenant at the battalion base at Barrackpore. The harassed adjutant looked at my shining Sam Browne belt and carefully pressed khaki drill uniform and said, "Those will have to go. Didn't they tell you we wear green? I"ll get you properly kitted out."

There was only one possible reply.

"Sir," I said, concealing my annoyance and despair. Annoyance because no one at OTS had bothered to point out something I could not have been expected to know – that battalions recently withdrawn from fighting in Burma still wore jungle green uniform – and despair because every last rupee of my uniform grant on commissioning had been spent on the now useless and redundant khaki drill. It turned out that I needn't have worried. The regimental darsi (tailor) didn't expect to be paid right away. Regimental funds, controlled by the adjutant, covered the cost of my new green uniforms – produced in the customary couple of days – and I paid for them over a period out of my meagre pay. This had two advantages for the Regiment; the darsi was kept happy and loyal, which was important when you had a good one, and junior subalterns were denied the normal excesses of the young by being kept short of funds.

I met and was welcomed by the Commanding Officer Lieutenant Colonel MacDonnell DSO, who was very senior. Born at the turn of the century in October 1899 and commissioned in 1919, he was within a few years of retirement and was known throughout the Regiment as the Dean, a bachelor of the old school. I realised years later that he was typical of the many bachelors scattered throughout the Army at that time. It was not that they were uninterested in female company; it was simply that the Service and particularly the Regiment always took first place in their lives; they had become comfortably settled in a bachelor existence and they had neither the opportunity nor any inclination to marry and raise a family. The Dean was well respected as a good CO.

I had barely time to settle in and meet the battalion's personalities before we were ordered to deploy into Calcutta once again For me it was the first time and so of besetting interest. I was thrown in at the deep end as a rifle platoon commander, the battalion being perennially short of subalterns. I was given command of thirty-three Yorkshire soldiers; they were all at least three or four years older than me and had spent two or more years fighting the Japanese in the Burmese jungles. What these battle hardened young men thought of a still fresh faced nineteen year old being placed in command of them during a difficult internal security operation is best left to the imagination but they responded magnificently and generously to my inexperience. Perhaps being a fellow Northerner although not born and bred in God's county, helped. My first platoon sergeant, to whom I am deeply indebted but whose name, to my shame, escapes me, had farmed in North Yorkshire before volunteering for the Army. He was a tower of strength. From him I had much wise guidance in those first few weeks and what could have been tricky situations were resolved without the disasters which could have come down on my head had I been relying on my own inexperience. For IS (internal security) operations are as unlike war as they could possibly be. There are no start lines, no set objectives, no supporting barrages; the commander on the spot, be he corporal or colonel, has to deal with each situation as it arises, and every situation is unique. Many thousands of people were slaughtered on the streets of Calcutta in 1946 and 1947 in what are now known collectively as the Partition Riots. Some of the killing had taken place in the weeks before my arrival but it had not by any means stopped. Frequently on patrol we came round a corner to find bodies of victims lying in the road with the goondas (terrorists) nowhere to be seen.

It is no part of my plan in these scattered recollections to go deeply into the political background of the situation in India generally and Calcutta in particular during the years before partition but you would have to be pretty dense not to have absorbed something of the background. A summary will suffice.

The post-war Labour government in Britain had decided to give India its independence and the Viceroy, Lord Louis Mountbatten, a distinguished naval officer and a reputedly Labour supporting aristocrat, was charged with bringing this about. The Indian Congress Party, mainly Hindu and led by Pandit Nehru and the Muslim League, led by Mr Jinnah were the main opposing political parties. The negotiations, which took place in Delhi, were at fever pitch in 1946 and much of 1947 and unrest spread into the major cities of India, particularly into Calcutta, by far the most populous.

In Calcutta the situation was made worse by the return to India from Malaya of the remnants of the Indian National Army, the INA – known also as the Hindu Mahasabah and led by the firebrand Subhas Chandra Bose – the Flying Tiger to his biographer. These people, with independence their aim, had sided with the Japanese during the Second World War and they had been returned to India after the Japanese surrender. It had been hoped that with independence on its way they would be satisfied with the situation, but it was no part of their plan to allow the Muslims a say in the administration of an independent India, so they carried on doing what they did best – fomenting trouble.

The Indian Army, to its everlasting credit, stayed loyal, and Gurkha and Indian regiments did a good job in the dock areas of the city. Keeping the peace in the remainder of Calcutta was placed in the hands of the Yorkshire and Lancashire Brigade, comprising the East Lancashire Regiment, the York and Lancaster Regiment and the Green Howards. The Brigade included a yeomanry regiment, the 25th Dragoons, who were equipped with Stuart tanks mounting a two pounder gun; they operated mainly dismounted. The Brigade Commander was a dour Cameronian brigadier named Eric Sixsmith.

The Calcutta Police, British and Indian officered with Indian other ranks and armed only with lathis – long wooden staves – carried on their normal policing duties so far as they were able but the situation had escalated out of their control long before the Governor of Calcutta had been persuaded to call in the Army, and police morale had suffered. They did, however, have something of inestimable value to us – their local knowledge, and at all levels, but particularly at ground (or platoon) level, it paid us to liaise closely with the police in our respective sectors of control.

The section of the city allotted to my platoon featured a tramline running along a main road in its centre. The power was on but there were no trams operating, the drivers having decided that in this situation self-preservation was more urgent than getting on with the job. So we provided an armed escort for the drivers and used the trams for communication between the observation posts that we set up throughout our sector. I recall taking four soldiers to establish an observation post (OP) at what had been a police post. They replaced about eighteen policemen, unarmed save for their long wooden staves and huddled together for mutual protection. I visited the post next day to find the soldiers seated on comfortable chairs in the sun with their rifles on their laps and surrounded by admiring small boys keen and willing to fetch and carry.

Just as I was getting into the swing of things and enjoying a real job after those years of training I was told that it had been decreed from on high that I was to attend a short course at the School of Infantry at Mhow in the Central Provinces. I tried to get out of it in order to stay with my platoon but without success, so most of November was taken up with re-learning the material we had covered at Bangalore. I was keen to get back to the battalion while we remained on active operations and in fact when I returned to Calcutta it was as though I had never left.

We were still on the streets, with communal mayhem erupting regularly

What I think of as 'the Grant Taylor put down' came out of the Infantry Subalterns' Course at Mhow. While there we were instructed in pistol shooting by one Colonel Grant Taylor. One of those eccentrics who always surface in times of war, he was demonstrably a crack shot with a pistol and claimed to have learned his craft during the prohibition wars in the United States. He told us that he had been a close friend of Legs Diamond, a legendary pre-war gangster. The Grant Taylor theory was that the British Army was much too formal in its approach to pistol shooting; the accepted practice was to stand sideways on to the target in the classic duelling stance with arm outstretched and one eye closed. Much better results are obtained, said Grant Taylor, by adopting the cowboy crouch and shooting with both eyes open. Months later, all battalion officers were gathered for annual pistol shooting classification on the thirty yard range at Barrackpore. Came my turn and true to Grant Taylor's instruction I adopted the cowboy crouch. The voice of the Dean interrupted the proceedings.

"Who the devil does that young officer think he is? Tom Mix? Tell him to shoot like a gentleman!"

Through the remainder of 1946 and much of 1947 we remained on IS duties in Calcutta. I got to know the city very well. The poorer quarters were a nest of bazaars, Shambazar, Bowbazar, Barabazar and the endless game of creating trouble continued. Cattle are sacred to Hindus and wander at will. A dead cow, cruelly slaughtered in an unorthodox manner would appear one morning outside the house of a prominent Hindu. Result, a nasty riot, probably two or three killed and several cut about by knives. A herd of pigs, anathema to Muslims, would be driven down a narrow alleyway into a populous Muslim area. Result – confrontation. Several deaths.

Occasionally there was a major confrontation with no 'lead in' that we could know about, but these were usually foreshadowed by police intelligence which meant we could get between the factions and hopefully reduce the bloodshed. Something I had not learned at OTS during IS training, was the moral ascendancy always achieved over an unsophisticated and disparate mob, sometimes of hundreds or even a thousand or so, by a single line of seasoned soldiers clearly competent in the use of their weapons and prepared to use them on command. Lined up across a road they would stand impassively, wearing the neutral expression that soldiers in this situation invariably display to possible casualties. Their unshakeable confidence and total impartiality always communicated itself to the mob and I know of no occasion when it was seriously challenged.

For most of 1946 and 1947 there was a permanent curfew in Calcutta. From 9 pm until dawn, civilians found on the streets had to justify their presence outdoors. It was not easy to enforce because a goodly proportion of the citizens of Calcutta slept on the streets in normal times, so we all, officers, NCOs and soldiers, had to use our discretion. On one occasion while visiting my detachments I came across a whole family sitting on the steps of their terrace house in a prosperous area of the city a good hour or so after curfew time. The rest of the street was deserted. I approached the patriarch, a stoutish elderly gentleman and advised him that he was breaking the law.

"I know," he replied, "but I am a magistrate and I tell the people living here what to do. I have to stay up late to see that they do not break the law." I had to think quickly.

"I'm glad," I said, "that you are such a public spirited citizen. As it happens we are in need of a magistrate because we have been told of trouble in Dharamtolla Street not far away (untrue). If you would accompany us in our vehicle we can get there quickly and you can act as interpreter for me."

Without further ado he ushered his family inside and slammed the door in my face.

We also did sweeps of one or other of the bazaars at the request of the police, the aim being to flush out terrorist leaders. These were rarely successful because on our arrival usually at platoon strength, the terrorists, either politically motivated or just in it for the aggro and the loot, made themselves scarce. But it did keep them on the move. On one of these occasions, while discussing the operation with the European police inspector and his Indian sub-inspector, a small boy appeared and handed round three chapattis – pancakes – wrapped round what appeared to be sausages.

I was bidden to eat and did so. A pleasant taste but obviously no sausage. "What is it?" I said.

"It's a bull calf's pizzle," the sub inspector replied.

"Pizzle?"

He grinned at me. "His penis!"

Concern overcame revulsion. "But they're sacred. Won't we cause a riot?"

"Not round here," said the inspector. "They're mostly Muslim. Just don't go around asking for pork chops."

At that stage the Muslims and Hindus clearly hated each other and we, the British troops, were the thorn in the middle, so to speak, but there was one issue on which they spoke together; they wanted us out of India. When we appeared on the scene to restore the rule of law the cry of 'Jai Hind' meaning 'get out of India,' was raised by both sides.

Although we were not usually offered any violence there was a phase, allegedly fostered by Hindu Mahasabah members, when white faces were targeted. Leaving aside instances of lone European civilians or soldiers wandering into dangerous areas where they would be vulnerable at any time, irrespective of civilian unrest, there were several incidents involving acid being thrown at troops travelling in lorries – very nasty, as it could result in blindness. The method adopted was to drill a small hole in the end of a light bulb then fill it with acid and seal the end with wax before throwing it into a passing army lorry carrying soldiers. It didn't last long. The troops were alerted; several acid throwers were caught in the act and dealt with summarily, and in due course the open lorries were wrapped in chicken wire as a precaution.

Down by the Hooghly River that runs through the city of Calcutta on its way to the sea, the burning ghats worked night and day disposing of the piles of bodies ferried in by lorries. Many of these victims, with no known kin, were tipped into the water only partially burned, to float down the river with the ever present vultures using them as rafts while stripping flesh from the bones. It was not nice to see; nor was it nice to smell. The stench of burning human flesh remains permanently recognisable to those who have experienced it.

It was eventually announced that India was to achieve independence at midnight on 14th August 1947. This gave rise to a mass migration of people, with Muslims travelling to the newly created states of Pakistan to the north west and to the smaller territory of East Pakistan adjacent to Bengal, while Hindus travelled southwards into India. Horror stories to equate with and even to surpass the goings-on in Calcutta began to emerge. The migration took place by rail and whole trainloads of people, men, women and children were slaughtered on the journey to their new homes.

For us, the formal announcement of partition together with a date to hang it on, represented a respite. Unrest died down considerably and we were withdrawn to barracks. Even better, it became my company's turn to be sent to the battalion detachment at Darjeeling, set among the tea estates six thousand feet above the plains in the foothills of the Himalayas. It was a welcome change from the heat, dirt and humidity of Calcutta's streets. We travelled by rail and to get there we took a normal sized train northwards to Siliguri Junction where we changed to a tiny train on a narrow gauge track to make the ascent to Darjeeling. This had a small but powerful loco and very small open carriages much like those now used for zoos and theme parks in England. Upwards, ever upwards we went, criss-crossing the mountain road with on one side dizzying depths and on the other the solid mountainside. The train moved at a brisk walking pace and astride each of the two buffers on the puffing loco sat a railway employee throwing handfuls of sand onto the metals from a large box secured between them. An American Jesuit priest in our compartment, who told us he was returning to his living in the hills, said:

"I used to wonder why they don't use gravity for that job until I realised that labour is cheaper than gravity in this country."

We stopped halfway up the mountain at a hillside village called Kurseong for bacon and eggs for us and wood and water for the loco. There was a blessed coolness, something we had almost forgotten. Then the track got steeper as we moved higher. The last stop before Darjeeling was the Gurkha Depot, Ghum, at 7,904 feet reputed to be the highest permanent military garrison in the British Empire.

Our company camp at Lebong was about 200 feet below the town of Darjeeling and overlooked a racecourse that wasn't much bigger than a circular running track. It featured two races each week when the small, sturdy hill ponies raced against each other to the cheers and abuse of the stocky, Mongolian featured hillmen who were native to the area. We sat at the tables in front of our mess during race meetings watching the jollity below us and conscious all the while of the magnificent spectacle of the snow covered Eastern Himalayas facing us – dominated by Kanchenjunga, at 28,200 feet, the world's third highest mountain. Everest could not be seen from our camp; it was just out of sight to the west, but Tiger Hill, near Darjeeling, provided a good view on a clear day.

Most of us suffered mountain sickness for those first few days at Lebong and it was necessary to become acclimatised before taking vigorous exercise. Walking on the flat presented no problems but climbing steps or tramping up hills caused the breath to become short accompanied by an unpleasant feeling of nausea. It passed off eventually as we became acclimatised.

Once the few delights of Darjeeling had been sampled, there wasn't a great deal to do, so a fellow subaltern and I organised a trek into the hills. We planned to take some of our soldiers and get as near to Everest as we could without formal climbing equipment Travelling or trekking in Northern India had long been based on a series of government sponsored structures known as Dak bungalows, each placed a good day's trek apart. They were pretty basic. A place to roll into your sleeping bag, a stove and a supply of wood – but most of all a shelter from the biting cold and wind and a chance to get rid of the day's leeches. These unpleasant creatures infested the trekking slopes; they started as little bigger than full stops, able to worm their way under the cloth puttees and long trousers we were advised to wear. At the next night stop they appeared on the legs and sometimes as high as the thighs, as slugs, engorged with our blood and swollen to the size of short, black, thick pencils. We got rid of those on the lower legs with lighted cigarettes and on the more sensitive higher reaches with salt – which took longer to take effect.

It wasn't a simple climb upwards. We climbed one hill to be confronted by a steep valley before we could reach the ascent to the next, higher hill. Often in the valleys and close to the mountain streams there were small villages, the population eking out a subsistence living on the poor pastures available to them. We were invariably received with courtesy but sometimes the headman was an ex British Army Gurkha pensioner and on these occasions we were offered such hospitality as he was able to afford. There was very little in the way of consumer goods to be seen but we noticed that every village had its treadle-operated Singer sewing machine, obviously regarded as community property and very carefully looked after.

The trek was quite successful. We reached Sandakphu, at 11909 feet the last Dak bungalow before real climbing begins. I wrote a short article on the trip for the regimental magazine, The Green Howards Gazette; re-reading it over fifty years later I was astonished that I was able to refer so casually to a 22 mile 'yomp' in one day in that hilly country. We must have been fit!

Leaving Darjeeling to its colonial atmosphere and incomparable views we went back down the khud (hill) to Barrackpore for some formal infantry soldiering. By now I was with Support Company and commanding the three inch mortar platoon. There was a field firing range not far from our barracks and we were able to do some live firing there. I wasn't well acquainted with the three inch mortar which is a battalion support weapon. Platoon support was provided by the two inch mortar and this I knew well. Fortunately, my new platoon sergeant was an expert and gave me some quick instruction before the visit of the Brigade Commander accompanied by the CO. It was what I imagine a first night is like for an actor. I gave the appropriate commands, a mortar barrage happened and the brigadier seemed appropriately impressed. The Dean, not given to fulsome praise, nodded his head – quite an accolade. Had there been a misfire I could have been in trouble. My sergeant hadn't had time to go through misfire procedure. It was all down to my soldiers; they were well aware that I was inexperienced and backed me up splendidly.

Those soldiers were a mixture of regulars, 'hostilities only' conscripts and volunteers. Most of the regulars, mainly NCOs, were 22 year men and happy to be wherever the Army placed them. The others, however, only wanted to get home to their wives and families. We had been given our release, or 'demob' groups and as a hostilities only volunteer, I learned that I was in Group 62, due for demob in March 1948. 'Roll on the boat' became a constant refrain from the non-regulars.

Malaria, contracted by a bite from the female Anapholes mosquito, was endemic to India and on the plains we had to sleep under nets and also take a daily anti-malaria Mepacrine tablet. This was a small yellow pill that after a while gave a very obvious yellow tinge to the skin. Platoon officers were responsible for parading their soldiers each day and personally supervising consumption of this tablet. Somehow, and who knows how these rumours start, word had got round that extended exposure to Mepacrine produced impotence. This disturbed everyone, but particularly those who were returning to wives and families. In vain did the medics plead that the rumour was baseless. As a result the daily Mepacrine parade became something of a pantomime with the soldiers doing their best to outwit the platoon commander by devising methods of pretending to take the pill without either swallowing it or even putting it in the mouth. But Nemesis was waiting in the wings. If, after a week or two there was no yellow tinge to the skin, it became obvious that something was wrong – a matter for the platoon sergeant to deal with.

Barrackpore features in history as the site of the start of the great Indian mutiny of 1857 and it sometimes seemed that matters had not moved on much since. Soldiers slept under their nets in straw or rattan roofed barrack blocks kept bearable in the muggy heat by a system of rattan punkahs swinging overhead and worked by a usually aged 'punkah wallah' who sat at the end of the hut with the cord working the punkahs looped either through a finger or more often through a big toe. Punkah wallahs were supposed to sleep during the day and work at nights but in the nature of things they often fell asleep while working, depriving the barrack block of cooling air. It was therefore customary at night for each man to drop one army boot near the man in the end bed so that when the punkah wallah fell down on the job he could be awakened by a well aimed missile. I have often thought since that if the cooling system had to be labour intensive, it would be hard to devise a simpler or more effective method of keeping it up to scratch.

Personal servants were cheap and in ample supply when in barracks. They gave every indication of enjoying their jobs and many had served with the British Army man and boy, for generations. It was by no means unusual when interviewing a prospective employee, to be presented with a sheaf of 'chits'– testimonials, now and then going back into the nineteenth century, yellowing and dog eared. Sometimes the writer, anxious not to hurt the feelings of a bearer who had perhaps been keen but ineffective, had done his best to alert a future employer to shortcomings without upsetting the servant who was leaving his employ. I recall at least one chit with the comment, 'Ali has performed his duties energetically and to his complete satisfaction'

All the barrack blocks had two or more small boy 'chicos' to fetch and carry for the soldiers and my batman managed to employ one even from the small sum extra to his pay that I was able to give him. At the cry of 'char wallah' the licensed tea vendor would appear prepared to offer tea, egg banjos (a fried egg between two pieces of bread), curry puffs etc. Most of it was on tick and the char wallah kept an IOU book for settlement on pay day. Very occasionally, smart alecs with other plans for their pay, contrived to steal the char wallah's book. It never worked out for them. In order to survive, the char wallah not only had to know every soldier in the unit, he also had to develop a prodigious memory and be able to produce for the regimental sergeant major, details of every transaction with times, dates and names, since last pay day. He usually had a good idea of the identity of the culprit who was denied credit by all vendors from then on and frowned on by the decent majority who considered bilking the char wallah to be 'offside'.

Barrackpore was not far from Dum Dum airfield, now a large international airfield but in those days a concrete strip used at the end of the war by the American War Graves Commission with an American army camp close by. It was customary for the Americans operating in the Far East to fly the remains of their servicemen killed on active service back to the States whenever they could be identified and recovered. In mid 1947, the job completed, they left. We heard stories of loose ammunition lying around and I was sent with a party of soldiers to investigate. The Americans had left all right, but leaving much of their kit behind. There were no weapons but a good deal of small arms ammunition had been abandoned and the area was a mass of small fires on to which the Indian peasants were throwing live ammunition, the idea being to salvage the brass cartridge cases to make trinkets. Stray rounds were whizzing around all over the place and after we'd shooed away the locals we had to wait a while for the situation to settle down. Further investigation revealed other useful stuff; recordings of the latest popular music, office equipment, something that was later identified as an ice cream making machine and canned food still in good condition. We cleared up, taking back the remaining ammunition for controlled destruction and the other booty vanished within the Battalion.

Indian Independence Day duly dawned in mid-August 1947 and all troops were confined to barracks for 24 hours. As it happened, however, Peter Wilde, another subaltern, and I had to visit Fort William in the centre of the city on that day. Our driver with an armed escort travelled in the front of the one ton truck that took us and we sat in the back looking out on wild scenes of jubilation. Calcutta was en fête and communal strife was forgotten for the day. The English language newspaper, *The Statesman*, reported in the following day's edition that there had been no incidents of illegal behaviour reported in Calcutta on Independence Day 1947.

SHOOT LIKE A GENTLEMAN!

The Battalion had been withdrawn from internal security duties in Calcutta soon after the plan for partition of India had been announced and we remained at Barrackpore until just before Christmas. Orders were then received to proceed by train to Bombay, onward by troopship to Port Sudan and then to Khartoum. Release groups 60 onwards would not disembark at Port Sudan but would go on to England and join the 1st Battalion at Newark in Nottinghamshire. British troops were being evacuated from India as sea transport became available.

We travelled as a battalion by train from Calcutta's Howrah Station across India to Bombay. It was a well disciplined three day journey with the exclusive use of a train. We stopped at sidings along the way for meal breaks; at each stop the doctor got out and solemnly checked the station well to see if the water was safe for European stomachs. At Bombay, the UK-bound element, those who were going home for demobilisation, was split from the battalion and and placed in Kalyan Transit Camp, a polyglot place and memorable to me only because walking with my towel to the shower block one afternoon I rounded a corner and came face to face, if that is the right expression, with a very large cobra. He, or she, was lying coiled up in the middle of the narrow footpath that wound through the shrub and tall grasses. I stopped. The cobra raised its head, expanded its hood and looked at me. I turned round, walked slowly back to the corner and once round it, took to my heels. I reported it to the camp staff, who said:

"He's no bother. He lives here. There's plenty of small rodents for him to eat and provided you don't upset him, he's fine."

In due course I embarked in MV Georgic along with many others and we left India from Ballard's Pier, Bombay for the long journey home. Air trooping was still in its infancy and practically all troop movement was still mainly by sea. I had enjoyed my time in India; despite the pre-Partition troubles I had liked both the place and the people and I resolved to return someday. Meanwhile, I would make the most of the journey home.

MV *Georgic*, a prewar ocean liner, had been sunk at Suez during the war. She was then raised and refitted for service as a troopship. I was reunited with a number of old friends from Fleet Air Arm and OTS days who were also Release Group 62, so the time passed pleasantly enough. I watched my battalion disembark at Port Sudan with mixed feelings. I would miss the comradeship of the regimental family, but at just over twenty-one years of age, the future was all there to play for.

We sailed through the Suez Canal at night – always worth waiting up for. As the great ship ghosted along, the decks packed with silent troops, we passed a British Army installation just beyond Ismaliah with a lone sentry standing guard under a light and watching the ship go through. Suddenly a cockney voice rang out from the ship.

"Ain't you lucky mate. All that bleedin' sand to play with!" A great crash of laughter. The sentry raised two fingers, turned from the light and was lost in the darkness.

At Port Said, more old friends from Bangalore embarked. 'Poacher' Harris, from Lincolnshire of course, had been with 6th Airborne in Palestine. He told harrowing stories of units guarding the beaches being swamped by hordes of illegal Jewish refugees, men, women and children leaping out of ancient rust buckets usually from Cyprus and kissing the shore of their Promised Land. He said that no one knew what to do.

"We couldn't send them back, there was nowhere to put them and we certainly couldn't fire on them so we just let them vanish inland."

We disembarked at Liverpool, presumably to typical January weather. I had fourteen days disembarkation leave, a week of which I spent with my parents and a prearranged week in London with friends. Davis, Colley and I hatched a plot to use our service gratuity of about £200 (riches!) to fund a walk through France to the Pyrenees after demob. We planned to do some rock climbing.

I reported to 1st Battalion Green Howards at Newark as instructed but it was patently obvious that they had no idea what to do with me. My new company commander, Captain Wally Burnett, solved the problem by giving me a motor bike and telling me to carry out a reconnaissance for suitable training areas during the few weeks I had left before demobilisation. This was clearly a euphemism for 'make yourself scarce' and I honed up my motor cycling skills against the day when I might need them. Wally, a couple of years older than me, did his best to look after the new arrival. He was engaged to a pretty nurse at the local hospital and took me along to one or two of the functions they attended. Years later Billie Burnett said she remembered well the gangling subaltern in a borrowed suit too short in the sleeves and at the ankles tripping over her feet on the dance floor.

India 1946. Calcutta Street Scenes.

The narrow gauge railway to Darjeeling.

The view of the Himalayas from The Mall. Darjeeling.

Calcutta. A rare treat. A platoon swim. Yorkshire soldiers. None better.

On the way home 1948. By troopship through the Suez Canal.

7

A Civilian Again

Travels with a Rucksack

On the due date in March 1948 I reported to the Demob Depot in York to receive a suit, a gratuity cheque and a rail warrant to London. Having enlisted in June 1944 I had completed just short of four years in the services. Advice on resettlement was plentiful but that would have to wait a while.

I met up with friends Colley and Davis in London as planned. We stayed at the Nuffield Club for Officers which we were entitled to use until our demob leave finished, and we spent a few days buying sleeping bags, haversacks and anything else we might need for our journey through France. We then took the ferry from Newhaven to Dieppe.

It was a voyage of exploration untrammelled by orders from above. It took a little time to appreciate that we could now do as we liked within the law. Although we were seasoned travellers in the Far East, none of us had been to the near continent before. Holidays when we were growing up in the nineteen thirties were traditionally taken at home either by the seaside or in my case in the Welsh mountains. My father's only continental experience had caused him to share forever afterwards with Nancy Mitford's Farve, a conviction that 'abroad is bloody', but he did enjoy touring in his Morris Cowley, his fondness for North Wales only modified by his distaste of their habit of closing the pubs on Sundays.

Dieppe was a revelation. Less than three years after the war, the town was in a mess. Buildings along the harbour frontage had been flattened and evidence of the battle for the town was everywhere. We passed through quickly and moved inland, destination Paris.

Hitchhiking was a normal and successful mode of travel round France at that time, helped considerably by a wartime shortage of fuel. This had forced the innovative French to use alternative means of generating energy to power their vehicles. There were few cars on the roads but goods were being moved from place to place in small and medium sized lorries which carried wood burning boilers serving huge gasbags on top of their cabs. I never grasped the principle but this system certainly provided locomotion and the drivers were willing to pick up those travellers who were happy to travel in the back and keep the boiler topped up with wood. So we went from one forest clearing to the next, swapping lifts whenever necessary when other lorries pulled in to collect fresh boiler fuel. Communication using school French aided by mime was quite adequate and food in the countryside, although basic, was cheap and available.

We stayed some time in Paris where the British and Americans were still very popular. Our French improved with the coaching of the young ladies of the Place Pigalle and its environs who were more than happy to teach us, but we had eventually to tear ourselves away from that city which holds a special quality for those who visit her for the first time when young.

We pressed on down Route Nationale 20 through countryside which showed few signs of war, using the gasbag lorries for some of the time although there was also a good deal of walking. We made good use of our sleeping bags and bivouac tents to economise – Paris had hammered our funds somewhat. We were among the earliest of the postwar backpackers I suppose, and as we moved southwards through small villages we met many kindnesses from the villagers. We became known as 'Les Anglais' along our route and addressed as such. It was no unusual occurrence to walk into a village not long after dawn, drawn by the smell of baking bread, and be invited by the baker to share the family breakfast, offers of payment being waved away.

Word of our journey had obviously gone before us – we met no other backpackers travelling north or south – for on arrival at the small town of Chateauroux we were approached by a matronly lady and on confirming that we were indeed 'Les Anglais' we were invited to a wedding. It was, I recall, a Friday and seemed to involve most of the townspeople. It lasted the whole weekend, long after the bride and groom had departed for their honeymoon. When we awoke and extricated ourselves from this lavish hospitality, the hangover lasted another day. I have driven through Chateauroux, now a sizeable town, many times since and often wondered if the bride still lives there with her family.

On through the pottery and porcelain town of Limoges and then a long flog towards Toulouse. There was no need for any detailed map reading; it was R.N.20 all the way to the Andorran border. South of Limoges we had a lucky break with a lift to Foix, which meant that we saw Toulouse only from the back of a gasbag lorry. Beyond Foix, where we said goodbye to our benefactor, we were in the foothills of the Pyrenees. It was heavily wooded country and we gathered sticks for a fire before pitching our bivouacs. Sitting by the fire to a supper of baguette, beans and butter, we were suddenly surrounded by armed and irate gendarmes who gave us to understand that we were in big trouble. Apparently there had been a spate of severe forest fires in the area and there was a total ban on both camping and camp fires. We escaped the wrath of the local magistrates by pleading ignorance, which was true, and promising to walk through the night until we could take shelter in a village. We had no idea who could have blown the whistle on us, but the forest obviously had unseen eyes.

Toiling upwards and almost out on our feet by next day, we were given a lift to the border town of Bourg Madame. Andorra at last. But the place proved to be a disappointment. Its description had made it sound interesting – romantic even. Ruled by a committee of senior clerics, French and Spanish, it turned out to be a primitive and drab place where the main occupation seemed to be smuggling. Living was cheap, however, and there were plenty of rocks to climb, giving excellent views.

But we didn't stay there long. Back down the mountain to strike out for the fabled Riviera, which had not yet by any means recovered its former glory. The beach obstacles had been cleared away and it was possible to bathe in the clear, warm water. But a few yards out, the concrete 'dragon's teeth' of the tank traps could be clearly seen not far below the surface, visible reminders of the short German occupation towards the end of the Second World War. It was pleasant though, to see places like St Tropez and Tourettes sur Loup when they were real villages instead of the fashionable water holes and expensive boutiques that they have since become. We returned through Provence and up the Route Napoleon, the road that the great man travelled in March 1815, having broken out from his exile on Elba and marching north in a bid to recover his throne, only to be defeated at Waterloo three months later. It was a tortuous road with little traffic and unpaved in places. I doubt if we covered as much ground each day as Napoleon's soldiers had done over a hundred and thirty years earlier. Eventually we reached Grenoble, then on to Lyon and eventually the Channel and home.

Savings were almost exhausted and it was time to get a job. In the autumn of 1948 the country was still full of young men who had interrupted their training for careers in order to volunteer for the services, and the government of the day had recognised their need for jobs by not only expanding the network of traditional labour exchanges but also supplementing them with more upmarket agencies known as appointments offices. These were designed to put to civilian use the specialist training which had been given to all sorts of people during the war years, and ex-officers were among those invited to apply to be placed by them. Having turned down offers from the ordinary labour exchange of jobs in banks at one extreme and heavy labouring at the other, I wrote to the nearest appointments office quoting qualifications and experience. I was pleasantly surprised to be called quite quickly for an assessment interview and after intelligence and literacy tests similar to those for pilot training, which was probably their origin, I was told that I fitted the profile for a career in journalism or 'outdoor management', whatever that might be. I was offered three interviews, none of which related to journalism, which was oversubscribed.

One of these was with a paint and printing inks manufacturing firm based in Wolverhampton that was looking for trainee managers. It looked interesting, mainly because it was a countrywide organisation, perhaps offering a chance to travel. It was also a close knit family firm still chaired by a descendant of the 18th Century founder, Benjamin Mander. I applied for an interview with Mander Brothers, was accepted and with five other recently demobbed army officers, embarked on a course of training that involved weeks in the classroom followed by more weeks in each department involved in the production and marketing of paints, wallpapers and printing inks.

At this time I was committed to the Army Reserve of Officers and I had been told that I was liable to recall in the event of an emergency. No one thought that this would mean anything. After the recent war, the prospect of another looked so remote as to be out of sight.

So I learned about the history of paint – from earth colours, ochres, umbers, encaustic painting and so on, right up to the modern mixtures of the late nineteen forties, that consisted, I was told, of powdered pigment, an oil medium, a drying agent, usually cobalt, and a thinner. Fascinating! I then 'did time' in the technical laboratory, the research laboratory, the accounts department equipped with the latest information retrieval machines based on punched cards, and the warehouse. Finally, we each had to serve in a shop and accompany a representative on the road. All for the subsistence salary of £250 a year; starvation wages of course, but we were commercially unproductive during this process and we all appreciated the opportunity we had been given in a commercial market swamped by returning servicemen. Furthermore, we were used to being broke.

By now it was well into 1949 and I had decided that selling paint was not likely to be my chosen long term path in life, although I was grateful to Manders for giving me an opening to the commercial world. I was simply restless and I knew it. As luck would have it I had been sent to Salisbury to do my shop serving and my 'on the road' travelling had been done in the same area with an ex-army officer who had worked for Manders before the war and had gone back to them as their regional west country representative.

Colley and Davis had gone back to Birmingham and had kept in touch. They too were restless and we cooked up schemes that featured the Southern Rhodesian Police and eventually emigration to Australia on the 'Ten Pound Pom' scheme. The Australian Government still had a White Australia policy at that time and had brought in a scheme, aimed mainly at the youth of Britain, to take in suitable immigrants as citizens, paying their sea passages from England for a contribution of just £10 per head. We applied, were interviewed, medically examined and eventually accepted.

Then everything changed. I fell in love. Heather was a journalist on the Salisbury Times. I met her at a Saturday night Rugby Club function that she was attending as a reporter for her paper. We found we had many shared interests, riding, the theatre, racing – we went to point-to-points together – and I often accompanied her to the offerings at the Salisbury Arts Theatre, now renamed The Playhouse, even being allowed now and then to write the critique for the paper, but published under her byline. She was tall, slim, and had the unconscious ability to look elegant in anything she wore – an attribute that lasted through all our subsequent years together. The second of three daughters of a Salisbury businessman, she had had been a pupil at the Salisbury

Roman Catholic convent school that accepted Anglicans as day girls but not as boarders.

I had a rival to whom she was almost engaged, they had known each other since childhood and there was certainly an understanding strongly promoted by her family. He was a dashing young RAF officer – a fighter pilot and potentially heir to a large farm near Warminster. He was based at an airfield in the north east and at his urging, Heather had taken a job on the Grimsby News, but had returned home because she found that she didn't like the place. As time went by it became evident that there was a chemistry between us that could not be denied. I was besotted. I don't have the lyric power nor is this the place to describe the intensity of my feelings, but to borrow some words from elsewhere – for me 'She did teach the torches to burn bright...'

I made my pitch, leaving the poor girl in a quandary; she confessed that she would like to say yes, but she was living at home and family pressure was intense. A potentially penniless suitor was not the family's favoured solution and I could sense my unpopularity. Bob, the pilot, solved the problem sadly, but neatly, by crashing his fighter plane into the Irish Sea end of the Bristol Channel from which neither he nor it, so far as I know, were ever recovered. I volunteered to stay in Salisbury as the Mander Brothers regional representative for Hampshire, Wiltshire, Dorset and the Channel Islands when my course was completed. They accepted this, bought me a car and gave me a decent salary. Colley and Davis duly emigrated to Australia and after a desultory series of letters, we lost touch.

Heather and I became engaged on my 23rd birthday in October 1949; it just happened to be a convenient date. We had to plan on a long engagement in order to put enough together to rent a flat or possibly service a mortgage on a small house. In those days respectable people didn't live together outside wedlock. It simply wasn't done, but I bought a veteran ex-Army motor bike, a Matchless G3L 350 CC, representing one of the few happy memories of my time at Wrotham, and on it we had a long continental holiday together, getting as far south as Capri. This caused much indrawn breath and presumably a good deal of nugatory counting on fingers by mothers and maiden aunts as the months went by after we returned.

Now international storm clouds were gathering. The situation in Korea, a far off land, was looking troublesome and by early 1950 it seemed probable that Britain might find itself committed to a substantial contribution to the UN military intervention there. I was tipped off that there was likely to be a reservist call-up later in the year. As a reserve officer I would almost certainly be recalled to the Army and this would effectively put me back once again on the labour market when I returned. I was still missing the travel and comradeship of the Service and I suggested to Heather that I should pre-empt the call-up by applying for a regular commission. She, having grown up in a military orientated town on the edge of Salisbury Plain, a major training area, quite liked the idea of being an army wife.

I wrote to the War Office and, wonder of wonders, I had a letter from Brigadier Sixsmith, now a senior staff officer in the personnel department dealing with the Regular Commissions Board. He said he remembered me from Calcutta, particularly my expertise (!) with the three inch mortar on the field firing range. He also said that he had made a phone call to the present CO of 2nd Battalion The Green Howards, Lieutenant Colonel D'Arcy Mander, who had been second in command of the Battalion during my service with it in India. He had said he would have me back if I were accepted for a regular commission. I would therefore be allotted a place forthwith, said the brigadier, on the three day Regular Commissions Assessment Board at Westbury in Wiltshire. Amazing. For the first time I realised that there was some point to the old saying 'It's not what you know, it's who you know'.

8

Back to the Army

I attended the Regular Commissions board in mid 1950, did all the interviews and initiative tests, including the famous one where you had to cross a wide river with two short bits of wood, a barrel and a rope. I was told on the third day that I had passed and would be gazetted almost immediately as a regular officer.

I had been looking forward to marriage and to being re-absorbed into the Regiment when the Government decided that there was no longer any need for infantry regiments to have two regular battalions and that second battalions would be 'ghosted' or in the official jargon 'placed in suspended animation forthwith'. This left an army swamped with infantry officers looking for jobs and I had been lucky to obtain a regular commission before the blow fell. I was contacted by the War Office and asked what I wanted to do. I could apply for a transfer – there were vacancies in the Royal Military Police, the Royal Army Ordnance Corps and the Royal Army Service Corps. Alternatively, I could resign, notwithstanding the fact that I had only recently been accepted. This was out of the question; I had already given notice to my employers. I swallowed hard. The choice was pretty restricted. To be honest, I hadn't much idea of what they all did except that I knew the RASC dealt with transport because I had come across the Royal Indian Army Service Corps and they had seemed a decent bunch, always ready to help with spares or breakdowns. So I took a deep breath and asked to be considered for a regular commission with the RASC.

There was some documentation to be done at Westbury before the formal application for transfer could be completed and the staff officer involved greeted me cheerfully with the words:

"So you're going to join the Jam Stealers?" Puzzled, I asked him to explain.

"It's one of those things dating from the 1914/18 war," he said. "The rumour in the trenches was that the drivers used to pinch the jam from the ration packs before they got to the infantry. Probably apocryphal, but it stuck and it's become a term of affection really, like Pontius

Pilate's Bodyguard" – he mentioned a famous and prestigious northern regiment that boasted its direct descent from the British mercenaries on our northern borders in Roman times.

"Or," I said innocently, noticing that his battledress sported Queen's Regiment shoulder flashes, "The Mutton Lancers?" He glanced at me sharply without replying and the paperwork was completed rapidly.

But it wasn't at all straightforward. The RASC, older than I had realised, with a history dating back to the seconded cavalry officers and soldiers of the Royal Waggoners of the eighteenth century, proved to be on pretty good terms with themselves. They had no intention of being a soft touch. Officers applying to transfer to them would be interviewed and if considered to have potential, would be placed on six months probation to include an induction course. Those completing the course successfully would be gazetted as regular officers of the Royal Army Service Corps.

I was interviewed by a grizzled brigadier at Saighton Camp, Chester. His name was Farquarson Roberts, shortened when he was out of earshot to Farky Bob. His appearance did not belie his interests. He was an ex-amateur boxer and he seemed more interested in the fact that I had done some boxing training in my youth than anything else I had to tell him.

"Right," he said. "You can come on attachment to one of my transport companies and then we'll see if you have the makings of a transport specialist."

Shortly afterwards and still wearing Green Howards flashes on my battledress I found myself reporting to 24 Transport Company RASC at Copthorne Barracks, Shrewsbury, the regimental home of the Kings Shropshire Light Infantry. The second in command of my new company, Major Denys Baker, welcomed me with delight.

"You're the answer to a prayer," he said, "I've been trying to persuade the KSLI to lend me an officer to help with my fieldcraft and weapon training course but they say they're too busy. Now I've got an infantryman of my own so we can get on with it."

My protests that I'd been sent to learn something about the operation of transport were waved aside.

"Plenty of time for that later." So my attachment turned out to be a refresher in weapon training, fieldcraft and infantry section tactics except that this time I was doing the teaching.

I then found myself on a course at Buller Barracks in Aldershot, the home of the RASC, and quartered in its Headquarters Mess that was staffed by civilian mess servants grown grey in the service of the Corps. My fellow students were refugees from infantry and cavalry regiments across the British Army, all caught by the 'ghosting' policy that had deprived them of their hoped for careers.

We all wondered what we were in for, but we need not have worried. The RASC Regular Officers Course was uniformly excellent and a credit to its organisers. We learned that there was a great deal more to modern logistics than any of us had realised. We had all been trained to keep looking ahead and not to worry about how our ammunition had got to us. The methods used to get the stuff to the front line troops in various theatres of war were a revelation. Air supply supplemented by mules in Burma – the RASC had several air despatch regiments in the UK and elsewhere and a mule company in Hong Kong. Supply by sea along the North African coast – the RASC owned and operated many seagoing ships and craft from military port detachments established around the world, but notably in Singapore and Cyprus. The Water Transport Headquarters and nerve centre was at Freshwater on the Isle of Wight.

The mainstay of operations was wheeled transport, the general purpose workhorse of the military world being the ubiquitous three tonner, well known throughout the Army. In addition there were depots holding the three basic necessities for the fighting troops – ammunition, fuel and food. In 1950, when I began to learn about my new Corps in some detail, it was still vast and widely spread; hence its ability to absorb so much new blood.

Heather and I married in September 1950 during my fortnight's end of course leave. My best man was Douglas Petrie, a lowland Scot and also a transfer from infantry. We wore uniform as was the custom. The girls said it was more colourful; Douglas in his trews was particularly admired, but as one of our guests from the course remarked, it was also one of the few perks of the Service because it saved the expense of hiring morning dress! We spent a blissful honeymoon in Polperro, then a sleepy Cornish village, in marked contrast to its situation today.

Marriage under the age of twenty-five for officers was deeply frowned on in those days. There was an old maxim that went 'subalterns can't, captains may, majors should and colonels must.' The

Army gave its feelings on this matter added emphasis by denying the full marriage allowance to those under twenty-five who made this supposedly unwise decision and went ahead. The full allowance was eighteen shillings a day, reduced to eight shillings a day until reaching the permitted age for those who had had the temerity to defy the system. Heather and I were both twenty-three which meant that she would have to go on working because the allowance of twelve pounds a month plus my pay as a lieutenant was insufficient to sustain us both.

I was gazetted to the RASC after the course and posted back to Shrewsbury. We rented a flat in nearby Whitchurch and she freelanced with some success on the local papers while I was picked up by a company 'milk run' vehicle and taken to and from barracks each day. For a few months it was the life of Riley – like nothing I had seen in the Service before. 24 Company was a virtually independent command. Its wide geographical area of responsibility stretching down to South Wales meant that its few officers were given much licence to act independently and provided that their decisions and actions were sensible they suffered few frustrations.

All this changed when my posting as a reinforcement for the British Commonwealth Force in Korea came to hand. I had been operating as a detachment commander at the Z Reservist camp at Castle Martin in Pembrokeshire when I received the fateful phone call from Shrewsbury. It was now early 1951 and we had just learned that Heather was carrying our first child. Her mother had heard the news and was keen that she should return home to Salisbury to have the baby while I was away. This was a sensible solution to our dilemma and we spent my embarkation leave in Salisbury.

9

The Land of the Morning Calm

A Savage Little War

In March 1951 I embarked on the troopship *Empire Pride* for the journey to the Far East along with Geoffrey Pearce and John Riggall, also RASC. We had received posting orders to three different units as individual reinforcements. The ship was one of the smaller troopers and rolled and pitched more than most. I didn't find her particularly uncomfortable, having won my sea legs in my late teens, but the general verdict was that she was a cow. If so, she was short of company because the only female aboard was the ship's cat. It was a long and tedious journey, calling in at Suez, Aden, Colombo, Singapore, and Hong Kong before fetching up at Pusan, the southernmost port of South Korea. We arrived there early one morning to be awakened by a jazzy rendering of Saint Louis Blues from the quayside. This was the 26th US Army Band, its mission to welcome every troopship into the port with a selection of popular tunes with the object of at least starting us off with raised morale. I thought it was a great idea although I wasn't really a beneficiary as I had to go on in the ship to Japan to spend a short time with the UK detachment on the main Japanese island of Honshu.

Kure, on the Inland Sea about ten miles south of Hiroshima, had been the Australian Army Base after the Japanese surrender and there were still quite a few Aussies left. It had shed its identity as British Commonwealth Occupation Forces, or BCOF and had become the headquarters of British Commonwealth Forces Korea, or BCFK. Having been a Commonwealth organisation when in Australian hands, it possessed an infrastructure easily modified to provide a firm base for the growing UK and Commonwealth operations in Korea, just across the Yellow Sea. I reported to the small detachment of my Company located at Kure, and was surprised to find that it was commanded by none other than Wally Burnett, late of the Green Howards and my company commander at Newark for the few weeks before my demob in '48. Wally had also been a victim of the sudden reduction of infantry battalions although in his case he had been surplus to the requirement for captains and he too, had volunteered to transfer to RASC.

Having made my number with the moguls at BCFK, I was keen to get over to Korea, but there was time for a quick trip to Hiroshima to see how the Japanese had coped with the devastation caused by the atom bomb dropped less than five years previously. There had been some rebuilding but to a great extent it was still a ghost city. I saw the famous bridge with the imprint of leaves burned into the stone by the intense heat and there were still open spaces where the mainly wood and paper houses had gone up in puffs of smoke. I also managed to visit Miyajima, the island where the kamikaze pilots had paid their last respects to their Shinto gods before their suicide attacks on US aircraft carriers in the Pacific.

The night before I was due to fly to Korea from the air base at Iwakuni I joined a friend to see a Kabuki Play in Kure. We arrived at the small theatre quite early enough to get a seat in the back row, confident that since we would be unable to understand a word of the dialogue, the further back the better. We watched with growing surprise as the place filled up with British sailors, obviously from the visiting aircraft carrier in the harbour. Jack ashore was clearly expecting to enjoy himself – but at a Kabuki Play? Had we come to the right theatre? The place was full when the play started and as the demure maidens fluttered their fans and the villain flourished his sword with the samisen music twanging in the background, it was Jack's turn to be surprised. As the catcalls grew in volume the body language of the actors began to reflect severe nervousness until a burly sailor displaying the propellor badge of a stoker on his sleeve leaped on to the stage and in thick Liverpudlian accents shouted:

"All right lads, if they won't give yer a show, I'll do yer one meself." He proceeded to disrobe to shouts of "Gerrem off".

Amid the uproar my friend, fresh out of Sandhurst, began to be restive.

"Here I say, we've got to do something about this." Clearly he had forgotten, if he had ever been taught, the golden rule that commissioned officers in uniform must avoid becoming involved with drunken other ranks – not to protect the officer, but to spare the soldier or as in this case, sailor, the mandatory court martial and subsequent severe punishment meted out to those found guilty of 'offering violence' to an officer.

"Keep quiet and be thankful we're in the back row," I hissed. "The crushers will be here any minute."

Sure enough, after a few minutes four large sailors in uniform, wearing white canvas belts and gaiters and sporting white armbands marched down the aisle, leaped on to the stage and removed the offending exhibitionist, by now naked to the cheering audience. We discovered later that the theatre played Kabuki five times a week with a strip show on the sixth evening. Either by accident or by malign design, the crew of the carrier had been given the impression that they were attending on a strip show night. I've often wondered since what the Japanese actors thought of it all. Certainly the sailors would have had a shock had they made overtures to the 'actresses' for in Kabuki, like our mediaeval theatre, the actresses are men!

My short visit to Japan had taken place in Cherry Blossom time and had I been deprived of my sense of smell I would have found it an enchanting place. Cherry trees in full bloom lined all the roads; it was a picture postcard. The downside, however, was that it was also an agricultural area and the Japanese fertilised their fields with any manure they could find, human manure being the main and strongest smelling ingredient. The result was that the whole area stank to high heaven at the time that I was there, although I was told that later in the year the smell was hardly noticeable.

I flew to across the Yellow Sea to Korea and the war, landing at Kimpo, the main US air base and an operational station for bombers, fighters, fighter ground attack and transport aircraft. It seemed to be ordered chaos – pulsing with life. I was picked up by a Company Jeep and driven north through Seoul, the capital of South Korea. The city had only a short time before been liberated from the grip of the invading Chinese and had been badly knocked about.

Much of it was still in ruins although some of the older brick buildings had survived, but they were all badly scarred and holed by shellfire. I arrived at 78 Company's field location somewhere north of the small town of Uijongbu that lay astride Korea's ancient invasion route for armies travelling south. The war was moving along at its own pace to the sound of orchestrated artillery fire. This was to become the normal backdrop for the next two years, so much so that when the guns fell silent, although never for long, it was something to be noted and remarked upon.

78 Company RASC had started life as a motor ambulance company, its purpose to support the field medical units of the Commonwealth element of the UN force. The ancient ambulances with which it had originally been provided, however, were no match for Korea's roads – or the lack of them, so the unit had been re-equipped with a menagerie of four wheel drive vehicles capable of surviving Korea's washboard laterite highways and tracks. I was allotted a platoon equipped partly with British built Bedford three tonners and partly with Chevrolet trucks manned by soldiers of the Royal New Zealand Army Service Corps. Our tasks were wide ranging and therefore more interesting than the standard logistic support tasks of a brigade transport company. We moved infantry units from the front line to the rear and the rear to the line; we re-supplied the field artillery with ammunition, often directly to the guns while they were in action, a stirring sight at night, gun flashes illuminating the piles of empty shell cases and the sweating gunners stripped to the waist. The New Zealand drivers of my platoon were delighted when we had a job in support of the 16th New Zealand Field Regiment. Gossip reigned supreme on those occasions. We also got involved with the American units on our flanks for the provision of unusual commodities such as flame throwing fuel.

The 'Kiwis' are well known to make excellent soldiers and they mixed extremely well with the mainly reservist Brits. Harmony ruled except that the New Zealanders had not received some special stores from their homeland – spare parts for their vehicles and other specialist items. No information could be culled from the US stores organisation and a New Zealand sergeant was despatched to the main US supply depot in Pusan to find out if they had arrived and if so where they had got to. He returned with the stores, suitably outraged. We managed to keep a straight face – just – when we heard his story.

He had arrived at the American supply depot, which was located on the coast and was a hive of activity; at that time the depot was still being stocked using DUKWS, amphibious road vehicles left over from the Second World War. They were acting as lighters, ferrying the stores from freighters anchored offshore. The result was that while the US supply chain was operating quickly and efficiently, anything even slightly out of the ordinary was placed firmly on the back burner. The

British were unaffected as we had our own line of communication based on Hong Kong through Kure in Japan.

The Kiwi sergeant's report went something like –

"This Yank officer scratched his head and said he didn't know anything about specialist stores for New Zealand troops."

'Ain't you looked after by the Brits?' he said.

"I explained that while we were generally operating on British rations, fuel and ammunition, there were certain specialist things such as vehicle spares that had been sent through the US line of communication and that they were long overdue. He called over his sergeant and told him to have a look into the store where they kept items for other UN troops. The sergeant went off and came back shaking his head. 'No suh. Nuthin. All ah could find was some boxes marked Kay One Dubbya One with a picture of a big fat assed chicken!'"

By now the 'yo yo' phase as the Americans called it, that had characterised much of 1950 and the early part of 1951, had been checked and the front line was in the process of being stabilised by a series of short, bitter battles to seize and secure tactically advantageous high ground that followed a roughly east/west path slightly to the north of the Imjin River. This came to be known as Line Kansas.

We were kept busy and time passed quickly from late spring to summer and then to autumn. I had arrived in reasonable weather but stories of the intense cold and associated horrors of the previous winter were in constant circulation. By all accounts it had been something of a 'dog's breakfast', order, counter order and disorder being the norm. For those who would like to know the full story of this savage little war of over half a century ago, the book *The Korean War* by Michael Hickey published in 1999 captures the agony and chaos of the early stages and is well worth reading.

The villages in our sector were all quite substantially damaged but we saw few civilians. Those who had not trekked southwards as refugees had been moved below our divisional boundary by the Americans who had established a 'no civilian line' behind us but slightly to the north of Seoul. This had the dual aim of guarding against sabotage and removing civilians from under our feet while we were getting on with the war. It also served to avoid the inevitable civilian casualties that would have occurred had the peasants been allowed to work their land, for the hills and fields were widely sown with mines for which there were no known maps.

We lived partly in holes in the ground and partly under canvas. When I arrived at the Company's location I found conditions to be less primitive than I had imagined. There was an officers' mess consisting of a deep marquee sized hole in the ground, a marquee sized flysheet acting as a roof, and earth steps hacked out of one side to reach ground level. The Company had recently moved and officers slept under hastily erected canvas. Individual holes in the ground were not necessary in the mild months, but according to the old hands they would certainly be needed when winter arrived. Wherever you happen to be, they said, excavate your sleeping hole with explosive before the ground freezes to the consistency of granite. Air supremacy provided by the massive American combat air element removed the need for camouflage and this situation existed for the two years that I was there. Now and then there would be an echo of the Second World War's Tokyo Rose when an enemy aircraft hovered over us on dark nights to tell us by loud hailer what a good time our civilian countrymen were having with our women at home. There was also some leaflet dropping; these were highly prized by collectors.

Inoculations and vaccinations are a normal part of service life but in Korea we were inoculated against a variety of diseases hitherto unknown to most of us. There was Japanese B Encephalitis, Weill's Disease – caught apparently by exposure to the urine of rats, plentiful in the Korean summers and Bilharzia, familiar to those who had served in Egypt.

The hills were teeming with game; pheasant, partridge, small deer and ground game. A six shot repeating shotgun could be had from American sources for a couple of bottles of whisky. But getting at the game was another matter. It was sheer folly to venture off the roads anywhere that had not been swept for mines. In time the sappers taped off the suspect areas. These became, in effect, game reserves where the local fauna seemed to know that they would be safe.

Although the war was given respectability by virtue of UN sponsorship, by far the largest contribution was provided by the United States with the rest, including the Commonwealth force, as junior partners under overall US command. The Commonwealth made the second biggest contribution. When I arrived in spring 1951 our force was still growing, having started out as two infantry battalions with meagre support and reinforced the previous winter by a full infantry brigade.

We all had to get used to working and living in an American dominated environment. Our radio entertainment was based on AFN, the American Forces Network, which used its civilian advertising expertise to broadcast precautionary messages to the troops. VD is a menace to efficiency in any operational theatre and at that time it was rife in both Korea and Japan, so an AFN broadcast featuring those popular singers Kirk Mathews and 'Liltin Martha Tilton' would be interrupted by a 'commercial break' perhaps a soldier on R and R in Japan, talking to his friend and obviously looking at a Japanese lady of the night. "Gee Hank, she's beautiful." Voiceover: "Sure, she's beautiful. But she's *diseased*! Remember, soldier. Five minutes with Venus could mean twenty years with Mercury!"

And those wonderful Burma Shave signs that the American higher command used as cautionary PR and so brightened up the main supply routes (MSRs). In the early stages we bathed in the rivers to get clean – before the arrival of the mobile bath units in late 1951. The rivers were fast flowing and subject to flash floods; there were several drownings. The US 1st Marine Division was our left flanking formation and on their MSR leading to a bathable river was the following Burmah Shave type tale spaced about 400 yards apart. 'Sergeant Jones went for a swim' – a two minute drive – 'full of vigour, verve and vim' – a two minute drive – 'He didn't look before he dived' – a full five minute drive – 'Vacancies, pay grade five!' We kept a weather eye out, however, for the Australians and New Zealanders when bathing. A supposedly friendly rivalry existed between these neighbours. This gave rise to some pretty 'heavy' practical jokes. In the winter, snowballs filled with gravel were exchanged. When bathing in summer a primed grenade was sometimes tossed in the deepest part of the river giving the perpetrators a few seconds to get out. A grenade burst will stun fish for a considerable distance. The effect on naked bathers approximates to a swift kick in the most sensitive part of the male anatomy and since the curve of the river where we bathed looked like some outlandish naturist colony with only the dressy or ultra modest wearing any form of clothing in that exclusively male community, it paid not to be there if the Aussies and Kiwis were in the water together.

Our official currency was British Armed Forces Vouchers, or BAFVs, shortened in conversation to 'Baffs'. The US Army used Dollar 'Scrip' but when dealing with the Americans at soldier level the currency was gin, whisky or any other potent spirit issued through the NAAFI. When on active service US forces were denied any form of hard liquor, and our NAAFI ration being very generous, a thriving black market existed. I was innocent of this when I arrived and while I was sitting in our below ground Mess one day as duty officer while all others were absent on various tasks, there was a polite cough and an American officer wearing a captain's bars of rank peered down at me.

"Say, I'm looking for Sergeant Atkinson."

I replied. "He's out I'm afraid but do come down and have a drink."

Accompanied by a companion he came down the earth steps into the Mess and I asked him what he wanted. He said, "I've come for some Redeye." I looked mystified. He added "You call it gin. Sergeant Atkinson is our contact and we only just found out where you'd moved to."

In the interests of promoting good relations with our allies I indicated a box in the corner and said, "How much do you want?"

"How much is it going for?" they countered.

"I think we pay about four shillings a bottle. Let's call it a dollar a bottle. We can probably spare you five bottles."

They looked at each other, eyes wide. Then one of them said, "Say, is this the Club? Are you an officer?"

When I said yes and introduced myself, he said, "Goddam racketeers. We've been paying twenty bucks a bottle for this stuff."

Before they went off with their booty they were at pains to get me to promise that they could come again.

They turned out to be the officers of a small reclamation unit behind the Divisional rear boundary. Their job was to salvage and bring back to serviceable condition all manner of equipment and clothing. My OC, Major Frankie Potter, one of the Corps' great characters, was quite relaxed about my small initiative but later on we all derived great benefit from the association with our new found friends who insisted on repairing typewriters, radios and anything else within their capabilities for as long as they could buy booze from us at the rate that we paid for it. It also added to our hoard of Dollar Scrip, useful for R and R in Japan. Sergeant Atkinson was told to discontinue his racketeering but since the black market in spirits had contributed so much to the wellbeing of the Commonwealth contingent in that first wickedly cold winter, it had become a fact of life and it's doubtful if he took much notice.

In September of 1951 I learned by signal from UK that I had become the father of a baby girl, an excuse for a 'thrash', not that much excuse was ever needed then. But it could have resulted in trouble. Our Officer Commanding (OC) was in Japan, leaving his monkey in the care of his batman. The monkey was a beast of uncertain temper and sharp teeth. The OC had acquired it from a New Zealand naval ship during the Inchon landings and he doted on the little monster – who was named Kiwi for obvious reasons. I don't like or get on with monkeys, dating from an episode in India when I was chased from an abandoned temple by a troupe of guardian baboons, escaping by the skin of my teeth and the speed of my bicycle. Kiwi sensed my dislike, and having lulled me into a false sense of security he waited until I was within the scope of his chain and bit me on the leg.

"Of course he didn't mean it," said the OC. "He likes us all really"

Apparently, for I had little recollection of the incident next day, I emerged from the Mess tent on the night of the 'wetting the baby's head' celebration to find the monkey sitting on his perch a few feet away, and glaring balefully at me. I then, according to my friends, drew my pistol and shouting:

"Dance, you little bastard," got off three rounds before the subalterns who had been celebrating with me rushed out from the Mess, threw me to the ground and put me to bed. My loyal friends made sure that the OC didn't hear of the incident and I am not proud of it. I tried to make amends but Kiwi wasn't having any and made sure he had his revenge by biting me again before the OC left and the monkey was passed on to someone else.

In the late autumn of 1951 the disparate Commonwealth field units and formations were gathered together and the 1st British Commonwealth Division was formed under the command of Major General Jim Cassels; it was to operate as an element of 1st (US) Corps of the US 8th Army. We now fielded a full divisional headquarters with an integrated Commonwealth staff, one wholly British brigade of three infantry battalions plus armour, supporting troops and logistic backing, one Canadian brigade group organised on similar lines and one

Commonwealth brigade with British and Australian infantry, New Zealand gunners, Indian medics and other Commonwealth elements. There was now an exclusively Commonwealth line of communication stretching back to Japan. It had built up to a substantial force, although still dwarfed by the US contribution.

Korea is known as 'The Peninsular of Morning Calm' in the local language and this does sum up the exquisite dawns in spring and autumn, the summer being hot and very humid. In late autumn, however, there occurs what I believe is known to meteorology as a 'diurnal wind change' when the warm winds from the Yellow Sea are replaced by strong icy winds from Siberia.

This happened almost overnight; the temperature dropped suddenly, the wind increased and it became colder than I have ever known it before or since, even during trips to Northern Norway, well inside the Arctic Circle. We had listened to the old hands with tolerant amusement when they recounted the horrors of the previous winter. It couldn't possibly be as bad as that, but as they had had such a rough time we were prepared to let them 'swing the lamp'.

The first few days of winter proved that they had not exaggerated. No matter what precautions you took to keep out the numbing cold, it was always there, waiting to strike the unwary. Metal tools stuck to the flesh of mechanics who had shed their gloves to unscrew an awkward nut. Fountain pens had to be in a pocket next to the skin, otherwise the ink froze. One of our party tricks for visitors was to throw an uncooked egg in its shell full tilt against a stone; the egg bounced off unbroken and still frozen solid. Our vehicle radiators were filled with an anti-freeze mixture supposedly sufficient to withstand the winter, but we could take no chances. Night sentries had to start each vehicle every hour and run the engine for five minutes to eliminate any failure to start in the event of an emergency evacuation of the location or, more likely, a sudden middle of the night troop carrying job. We ate like bears just out of hibernation, probably doubling our daily calorie count without putting on much weight.

The long awaited winter clothing had arrived just at the onset of the extreme cold. This put us in a better position than those who had arrived in the middle of the last winter and had been forced to scrounge warm clothing from the well equipped Americans in exchange for booze or, unusually, our tinned composite (compo) rations. This needs some explanation. American tinned combat, or 'C' rations were highly desirable to our troops from a land still suffering post-war food rationing. American rations contained such luxuries as chicken, turkey, ham and lima beans and were supplemented by a PX pack with sweets, Hershey bars, chewing gum and both rolling and chewing tobacco. Sometimes on long journeys we were able to draw C ration compo from US ration points and this was always a popular move for us. Our compo rations eschewed such fripperies, but to American eyes they were much valued for their bulk. Steak and kidney pudding, oatcakes, stewed steak and other stodge, went down well with those suffering a diet of ham and chicken in the bitter cold of a Korean winter. When eventually fresh rations became available, the British Army's expertise with curry became known and in quiet periods we were never short of American guests when there was a curry on the go.

Also operating during that second winter after the Division had formed, were the three separate brigade mobile laundry and bath units (MLBUs), providing a welcome opportunity to get clean, albeit for a short time. Attendance was rationed of course, but here you could be deloused if necessary, take advantage of a shower in really hot water and at the end of it all change your grimy uniform for clean and dry outer clothing, courtesy of the operators, the Royal Army Ordnance Corps. Most of us tried at least once to visit the Canadian MLBU where the battledress issued was of darker cloth and better quality than the UK issue. The fact that the clean effect was destroyed on the way back from the MLBU by the clouds of yellow laterite dust from the Korean roads didn't lower our spirits at all. Those MLBUs were great morale builders.

With the formation of the Commonwealth Division, efforts were made to relieve those who had suffered that first winter and 78 Company was relocated to Pusan on the south coast of Korea for Line of Communication duties. I watched them go away; as a spring reinforcement I could not join them and neither did I wish to. If I had to be there, I preferred to serve with the field formation which held more interest for me because the variegated tasks given to us made the time pass more quickly. I was transferred to 57 Company supporting 29 British Brigade and part of the Commonwealth Division.

Operating all the time on the roads as we did, mention must be made of the American engineers, the Construction Battalions – I was told that they were the descendents of the famous SeaBees of the South Pacific war. They worked wonders on roads that had been little more than tracks used to carrying carts and light vehicles and now lumbered with armour and very heavy wheeled traffic. Although during off road trips our drivers became expert in getting our three tonners to places a mountain goat might think twice about, once back on the MSR they could knock up a fair speed, only restricted by the clouds of laterite dust which caused a permanent fog for following traffic.

Our sector's MSR was policed by a platoon of the 35th USMP Co, commanded by our friend Lootenant Jimmy McGovern, a Scotch fancier and a frequent visitor to our Mess. I recall that Jimmy was visiting us on one occasion when we were entertaining our Colonel from Divisional HQ, an agreeable but extremely proper officer with strong views on most things and of course we treated him with kid gloves. He was telling us about his recent R and R trip to Japan.

"I think that those little Japanese girls are most attractive," he said "especially when they wear national dress. Don't you think so lieutenant?"

Jimmy swilled his Scotch round slowly, wearing a judicious expression. "Waal I'm not sure about that colonel. Ah can't say ah agree with you. Ya see, I'm a tit man maself!"

It was one of those occasions when no one knew quite what to say next. Jimmy, however, was good value. He had served in Australia during the Pacific war and he was sometimes very funny on the subject of two cultures separated by a common language. "Ah wondered what the hell ah was at when ah got off the boat and saw a sign saying 'keep your pecker up'. Ah thought, what the hell do these guys do all day?"

But there was one mystery that Jimmy and his policemen never solved. There was a speed limit on the main supply route dictated mainly by the clouds of dust created by speeding vehicles; unless it could be proved that the journey was one of real emergency the penalties, usually financial, were quite severe. All our drivers knew this but their enthusiasm sometimes got the better of them, occasionally resulting in the attentions of a US military traffic cop. The usual reaction of our drivers was stout denial of any intention to break the speed limit.

"In fact," they said, "you can't do it because these three tonners won't do over thirty mph. If you don't believe me, you try."

This usually resulted in a warning but once or twice the policemen did try and to their great surprise they found that thirty was about the maximum that the truck would do, even at full revs. What they didn't know was that unlike their US workhorse trucks, the British three tonners had a low ratio all wheel drive facility that was engaged by operating a lever out of the direct line of sight of the driver. This was quickly and surreptitiously engaged before the driver gave up his cab to the policeman. A good deal of head shaking went on and although Jimmy knew that there was something fishy about this he didn't get to the bottom of it before he was 'rotated' to the States.

In early spring 1952, it fell to my lot to set up a joint British/Canadian transport element in Seoul. We occupied a ruined school not far from the centre of the city. The British element was equipped with the ubiquitous three tonner while the Canadians, led by Lieutenant Bud Atkin of the RCASC, had US built 2.5 tonners, the equally ubiquitous 'dooce and a half'. It was easy to settle in; there was unaccustomed shelter and plenty of parking space in what had obviously been a well appointed and high grade educational establishment now shattered by shellfire and abandoned. We were initially troubled by the reek of rotting flesh that hung over the place. A thorough search revealed the science laboratory that had been well stocked with anatomical specimens bottled in formaldehyde; the bottles had been shattered in the fighting for the city and the decaying specimens had made the air foul. Once they had been cleared and disposed of, the atmosphere reverted to Korea's normal summer miasma that we were used to.

The job was general transport, looking after the needs of the burgeoning Seoul Garrison. It was a dull, uneventful task, enlivened only by marathon poker sessions with visiting Americans. One evening in the middle of one of these convivial gatherings, Bud Atkin noticed a flame shoot out of the door of a small wooden hut used by a local Korean civilian, a barber, who visited us from time to time. It was well away from the building and normally locked and unoccupied, but it was furnished with a small diesel stove for the comfort of the barber and his clients when he visited. He had been there that day but had left earlier and assuming that the diesel had not been switched off and had somehow ignited we all raced across to the fire. By the time we got there the intensity of flames made it impossible to get near enough to the hut to see inside, but we were both confident that there had been no one in it, and organising a bucket chain we did our best to damp down the flames. The large wheeled fire extinguisher that had recently been delivered to the location was useless. It had arrived without the cylinders of powder necessary to its operation and constant bids to the Seoul garrison headquarters for them had gone unanswered.

The fire went out when the hut had burned to the ground and moving closer I recognised an unforgettable smell – burning human flesh. My platoon sergeant, who was there, was immediately told to check the whereabouts of all our soldiers and I told Bud that he should do the same. Also the garrison medical officer was called to check for human remains. At this stage we both agreed that it was perfectly possible that a local civilian intruder might have evaded our gate guard and broken into the hut seeking a warm billet for the night. All my men were quickly accounted for but the Canadians were short of one man. Vehicles were checked but a thorough search failed to produce the missing man. One of the Canadian soldiers said he knew that the man had returned to our location and that he had been pretty drunk because he had that day received a letter from his wife to say that she was leaving him for someone else.

The MO confirmed a residue of human remains and we were left with the sad conclusion that the distressed soldier, not wishing to sleep in a crowded barrack room, had forced the flimsy lock, lit the stove and sunk into a drunken sleep. The diesel stoves were notoriously dangerous and unreliable and should not be left unwatched at night. There was, shamefully, an attempt by the garrison headquarters staff to turn this incident into a witch hunt and find a scapegoat – preferably an officer, to blame for the accident. But this rapidly fell flat when we were able to produce orders forbidding use of the hut at night as well as telephone logs and written requests for fire equipment for our location on which action had clearly not been taken by that same HQ.

I was once again under the command of 78 Company, now based in Pusan and led by a different OC. Frankie Potter, Wally Burnett and the others I had served with during those live wire days of the previous year had gone home, having been required to serve only a year in Korea. Because my company headquarters was now in the far south, I spent a good deal of time driving the length of the peninsular from Seoul to Pusan, a distance of about 300 miles. The rear areas, below

Inchon, had become much more settled with the establishment of a more or less static line of battle north of Seoul. Apart from a good deal of military traffic around Taegu, the headquarters of US 8th Army well to the south of Seoul and our higher commanding formation, the war seemed further away as one travelled down the peninsular. Moving in convoy as a platoon when it was sometimes necessary to stage overnight, we tended to find a suitable open space, park the vehicles facing outwards to the road – standing operating procedure in a war zone – and with a guard mounted, we would settle down for the night. The drivers slept in their trucks and the platoon HQ, officer, sergeant and jeep driver, bivouacked under canvas. In the mild weather months it was pleasant enough, if unexciting.

Now and then I had to travel south in my jeep accompanied only by my driver/batman. It was much more interesting without the shepherding involved in convoy travel. There was sometimes a country inn still operating. Even though there was no food to spare and we had to feed on compo rations, a hot bath was possible – luxury indeed. You sat up to the neck in a bath shaped like a cannibal cooking pot while a young woman continually replaced the hot water, the offer to wash and dry the weary traveller having been politely declined on grounds of prudery. Then a good night's sleep on Tatami matting, Japanese style.

Once when we were passing through a hamlet on the way south, the air was filled with the shrieks of an animal in pain. My driver, a tough reservist road haulier from the Midlands, said, "It's over there."

We pulled up outside a door in an earth wall and on bursting through it we saw a plump but pathetic looking dog having the life beaten out of it by a Korean man, presumably its owner. Outraged, my driver laid out the man with one blow, while I tended to the dog which, still shrieking and clearly beyond help, had to be despatched. There was nothing more we could do, so we left. We didn't know why that Korean peasant was beating his dog to death, although we had our suspicions; other countries, other customs however, and it's pointless criticising those hallowed by time. But that man must have wondered for the rest of his life why two armed foreign soldiers should burst in on him, knock him out and shoot his dog before vanishing completely.

I had been lobbying strongly to get back up to the Division where the pressure of events made the time pass much more quickly than doing mundane jobs on the Line of Communication. But first I had to do a short stint in Pusan, a sea of mud in the rainy autumn, leavened only by the fact that my wife's sister's husband, a merchant navy officer, was second engineer on one of the liners requisitioned as troopships for the Korean war. He called in to see me in Pusan twice while I was there with first hand news of what was happening at home. Despite the fact that Heather and I wrote every day, it was not possible to put everything down on a couple of sheets of airmail paper and to speak to a family member who could fill in the gaps was a great bonus.

More signs. American units in the field, certainly in Korea, seemed to vie with each other to decorate the supply routes with directions to command posts (CPs) at all levels. Also they tended to invent macho code names for them. As a result the roads were littered with stakes bearing wooden signs pointing to 'Skullcap CP' or 'Bayonet CP' and similar legends. One sign was particularly memorable. A professional soldier has no right to bleat about his postings and we maintained the traditional stiff upper lip. But our reservists and the national servicemen of both the Commonwealth and the US did make their views of the country and their armies in general widely known. The US operated a policy of six monthly 'rotation' to Japan or to the States for those who wanted to go. British troops did one year if they were there during the winter of 1950 and eighteen months if they arrived after that. Korea was not a popular posting and on the road north there stood an enormous sign which read 'Drive carefully soldier. You may KILL your replacement!' I reckon that sign did a good deal for road safety.

Eventually, still with some months to go before 'rotation', my wish to get back to a Divisional unit was granted. I rejoined 57 Company within the Commonwealth Division and now well qualified for Rest and Recreation (R and R) I was able to take leave in Tokyo for five days. I teamed up with a friend from the Company who was also due for leave. Although unspoken, this was really for mutual support. We were both newly married and within a few months of returning home. The pleasures and pitfalls of Tokyo's Ginza and its offshoots were notorious and we had no intention of falling foul of them. In fact, we struck lucky. We stayed at the officers' leave hotel near the Ginza, the Hotel Maronouchi.

At that time Tokyo had a growing British business community based on the great Far East trading empires of the pre-war years. In the early nineteen fifties these commercial enterprises were re-establishing themselves in their traditional markets. A card on the notice board at the Maronouchi invited British officers who would like to see traditional Japan to ring a Mrs Smith-Wright at her Tokyo number. This we did and were rewarded with an invitation to visit this lady and her businessman husband at their Tokyo address. They were kindness itself. They placed their country bungalow at our disposal and explained that because of the pressures of business they could not be with us there but that they would have us taken there and returned to Tokyo when our leave expired.

Picture postcard time again, but this time without the smell because it was autumn and the harvest was imminent. We were driven through traditional Japanese countryside in the Smith-Wrights' old Rover car to their bungalow in an exquisite setting on the shores of Lake Fuji. The outlook was stunning. Across the lake, calm and shimmering in the sunshine, the great mountain loomed, the permanently snow covered upper slopes making more pronounced the concave vent that marked it as an extinct volcano. We were lucky when we arrived because Japan, like England, suffers an autumn of mists and fog and we didn't see much of Mount Fuji after that first day. But the welcome was sincere and friendly. The house staff comprised two or three young girls kept in order and chaperoned by a Mama San who brooked no nonsense from either them or us, while at the same time seeing that all our domestic needs were properly attended to. She was clearly a wise old girl who had seen as much of life as anyone would want to see and responded to a wry smile with a toothless grin from time to time. We got by with mime supplemented by the few words of English she had learned from her employers.

The car was left with us for the two or three days that we were there so that we could see something of the surrounding countryside, but just following the traditional pattern of life in a Japanese bungalow was an experience of itself. We were not allowed to wear shoes in the house, which was carpeted throughout in traditional Tatami matting. Shoes were removed at the door and slippers were provided. We ate Japanese food. I suspect it was Europeanised for our benefit but it was plentiful and palatable. The time sped by, so much so that we returned late to Tokyo and missed the leave Globemaster aircraft to Korea, but we managed to hitch a lift on a DC3 (Dakota) mailplane that landed at Kimpo later than the Globemaster.

There was no Company vehicle to meet us. We put this down to the fact that we had missed our assigned aircraft but we didn't worry about it because there was always traffic from Kimpo to the forward Divisions and we were sure we could hitch a lift.

It was obvious that some great emergency in progress at Kimpo; we were told that an aircraft had crashed and caught fire and that there were many casualties but we were too busy crafting our excuses for missing our flight and arriving late to enquire deeply.

We eventually arrived at the Company's field location via a series of lifts and almost a day late to be met by an ashen faced Guy Newberry-Cobbett, our OC. "My God, where have you come from and are you all right? I've just posted you both as missing!"

It turned out that the aircraft that had crashed at Kimpo was the Globemaster we should have caught at Tokyo. We were on the aircraft manifest as passengers but had not been identified after the crash so it had been assumed that we were among the casualties. The signals posting us as missing on active service had got as far as Japan, but thankfully they were cancelled before being transmitted to the War Office, saving our young wives and our families a deal of heartache. Guy Cobbett, a tough and strict disciplinarian but an excellent officer, knew when to ease the pressure and no more was said about our lapse.

From time to time I met John Riggall and Geoffrey Pearce, with whom I had travelled to Korea and we were all looking forward to the troopship home, hopefully before the next Korean winter had properly got into its stride and arriving before Christmas 1952. But it was not to be. All the reservists had gone home and the national servicemen who had replaced them had to return in time to be discharged from the Army no later than the expiry of their statutory eighteen months military service. Troopship capacity was limited and this meant that regular officers and soldiers had to go to the back of the queue until space became available irrespective of their entitlement to repatriation. We had to recognise that there was no other decision to be made although that was small consolation to those of us on the wrong end of it. But to quote Mr Truman at the time on another issue "If you can't take the heat, get out of the kitchen!" So we soldiered on through a second Korean winter.

By early 1953 the peace talks that had begun at Panmunjom in No Man's Land between the opposing armies in 1952 and had dragged on sporadically, punctuated by battles of varying intensity, began to look as though they might bear fruit. I had been promoted to Captain and was commanding the Composite Platoon of my company. We looked after and delivered the petrol and ammunition for 29 Brigade. I had left the company location and had established my platoon headquarters at the forward petrol point on the reverse slope of a hill overlooking the Imjin River with my ammunition point across the river close to our infantry 'customers'.

The pontoon bridges that the CBs had established over the river had suffered from the attempts of floating debris to sweep them away and the tanks of the Canadian Lord Strathcona's Horse had been detailed to break up the debris with direct fire from their main armament. The shells regularly ricocheted over the hill, landing in the valley below us where the Royal Engineers had located their divisional field park, carrying their heavy plant and equipment. It was uncomfortable for the sappers who were in danger of casualties from 'friendly fire' and when the tanks were operating they tended to cross the valley to watch from our location, but had a short round landed on our petrol point there would have been spectacular fireworks. This prompted me to reflect that as we were within range of Chinese artillery, an enemy sympathiser in our area with a radio set could wipe out my location with a few rounds of observed fire, so we ringed the area with trip wires attached to flares which would at least have given us warning of an infiltrator.

It didn't happen though and we were probably being overcautious. One thing that did happen was the loss of my invaluable staff sergeant and second in command. He had gone on a routine visit to our forward ammunition point located across the river in the mountainous infantry echelon areas. He had been driving himself and his vehicle was found in a ravine. I was later told that he had been evacuated to an American MASH with critical injuries. I tried without success to locate him visiting the MASH units on either side of our Division.

On one of these visits, looking into the tented wards accompanied by one of the doctors I noticed a Korean patient tied down to his bed. He was clearly agitated and looking fearfully and frantically from side to side. "What's wrong with him?" I said. The doctor frowned. "Not much of an advertisement for us," he replied, "but he's a North Korean soldier and he's been brainwashed into believing that we do away with all our prisoners. There's no way he'll let us treat him without restraint. Fortunately he's not critical and we can wait till he's calmed down. At present the interpreter can't do anything with him."

My invaluable staff sergeant didn't return to me. He had obviously been evacuated down the American medical evacuation system. I wrote to his wife explaining what had happened and hoping that she would soon have some news. He was a long serving professional soldier but our paths did not cross subsequently until fifteen years later when I was a guest at a regimental dinner at Aldershot. I found myself seated next to a Captain Hallowes. We were both in Mess Dress and although my memory was stirred, the penny didn't drop until I noticed the Korea and United Nations medals on his mess jacket. Before I could speak he said, "Yes. I wondered when you'd catch on. Bert Hallowes, your late staff sergeant from Korea." In the interim he had been commissioned and he told me that he was now the personal staff officer to the head of the Corps. He then said he had a bone to pick with me. "Whenever my wife and I have words, she gets out that letter you wrote to her and says 'Whatever happened to that paragon your officer wrote to me about in this?' I'll never live it down."

The job of a composite platoon commander requires frequent liaison with his customers, and my staff sergeant and I spent a good deal of time separately visiting the forward units on Line Kansas. Apart from minor skirmishing and the ever present rumble of artillery somewhere along the front, things had become less frantic by early 1953 with the interminable peace talks taking place at Panmunjom. It became possible in daylight for light traffic to use short stretches of the roads and tracks that were under enemy observation from across the valleys. The trick was to drive to the 'shellfire notice', lower the jeep windscreen, then ensure that the journey could be completed in dashes short enough to deny the enemy a chance to range his light artillery.

I did this in my jeep accompanied by my driver while visiting forward units several times without incident until one day there was a whine and a crash just behind us as we rounded a bend into cover. It was clearly an opportunity shot, both short and wide of us. I wouldn't have thought that there had been anything like time enough to have seen us and ranged on us before we had slid out of danger until it was pointed out with some asperity by the infantry company commander I had come to see, that my driver had failed to lower the jeep windscreen, giving an alert Chinese forward artillery observation officer a glimpse of light on glass and that vital few seconds to range and shoot. Of course I was just as much at fault for not having noticed, thus drawing unwelcome fire down on a forward position. I kicked myself and apologised profusely, only too well aware that while we would return to our location on the unobserved reverse slopes across the river, it was the fate of the infantry on both sides to live on the forward slopes, each under the eyes of his enemy. Fortunately for me there were no repercussions; the company commander didn't make an issue of it and it was in my interests not to broadcast my culpability.

There were 'movement light' units on some of the higher hills, allowing the front at critical points to be flooded with searchlight in the event of a night attack alert. These locations provided an excellent and unencumbered view of large sectors of our divisional front and in quiet periods they were much visited. I recall on one occasion watching a napalm attack on a suspected enemy observation post. The aircraft approached as though on a demonstration, quite slowly and seemingly with no opposition, certainly none that I could see. A banana shaped object dropped from it and fell to the ground as the aircraft zoomed away. As the object hit the ground a sheet of flame leaped high into the air then swept forward unrolling a carpet of intense fire. I couldn't see how any living being could have survived, although the evidence is that they did, simply by diving deep into the tunnels they had mined into the hills until the heat had dispersed.

As the Army's transport corps, we found that we had many friends among the motor transport officers (MTOs') of other units. All units have organic transport – some much more than others. Infantry, sapper and signals units have large quantities of wheeled transport, sometimes not very well maintained; after all, moving people and things is not their primary purpose but simply a means to an end. They were always pleased to find a sympathetic ear in the matter of 'borrowing' spares or tools and in the interests of goodwill we generally did our best to accommodate them. We were particularly friendly with the Royal Northumberland Fusiliers; their MTO, Jumbo Watson, was a jovial character, great value at a party and an all round good egg. He kept his battalion transport in good nick and was generally held to have a good career ahead. His battalion was rotated before we left and we were sad to see them go.

In due course, the backlog of national servicemen being cleared, in the spring of 1953, months beyond our planned rotation date, I embarked with my two companions, Riggall and Pearce, in the troopship *Empire Pride*, the same ship that had taken us to Korea. Most of us had a souvenir or two. I had a 9mm Luger pistol that I had acquired along the way. I had no ammunition for it but since I wasn't proposing to shoot with it that didn't matter. The authorities, however, thought otherwise. We had a message from the Ship's Commandant to the effect that anyone with any sort of weapon had better get rid of it before landing at Liverpool because Her Majesty's Customs would be conducting a rigorous search. This was followed by a list of the penalties for illegal possession and importation of arms into the United Kingdom. As a result of this my Luger rests at the bottom of the Indian Ocean, together with a vast armoury of weapons thrown overboard from a stream of troopships returning from Korea. There was no rigorous customs search at Liverpool. It was a sensible ploy, adopted, I imagine, by all ships' commandants on the Korean run.

These are meant to be reminiscences of a fitful drift along life's river and as such, emotive ramblings have no place in them. But Korea, to my mind, should not be as comprehensively forgotten as it is generally by the British public. It was not an internal security action, nor was it a guerrilla campaign. It was a vicious three year conventional war, albeit small by world war standards of measurement. More than that, it was an infantry soldiers' war, supported by those other elements of the 'classic triumvirate' – armour and artillery. Those of us behind the immediate line of battle who were not infantrymen suffered hardships due to extreme weather and primitive living conditions it is true, but we were not required to face with outdated bolt action rifles and a few automatic weapons, unprecedented 'human sea' attacks by a fanatical enemy contemptuous of the lives of his soldiers. That our reservists and mainly teenage national service infantry soldiers not only faced them but either beat them or fought them to a standstill, was a noble thing.

Korea. Where it all started. The 38th Parallel.

Korea. The 'shellfire notice'.

Korea. New Zealand gunners in action during Operation Commando.

Korea. A tricky recovery problem.

But this one is kaput! A British bren carrier. Knocked out by enemy action.

But this is 'one of theirs'. Russian built Chinese tank knocked out above Seoul and bulldozed aside.

10

Interlude at Home

We arrived back from Korea in Liverpool in the spring of 1953. Heather met me at the ship and we stayed a couple of nights at the Adelphi Hotel before embarkation leave in Salisbury and an introduction to my eighteen month old daughter, Helen, auburn haired and bonny. The RASC personnel branch told me I was to be posted as adjutant to a field unit in Germany – 'good for your career'- but I asked to stay in England if possible as it would be unlikely that I would get a married quarter in Germany for a year or two and I hadn't seen much of my young wife yet. The point was taken but I was told that there was no 'good career' post available. All they could offer was a 'fringe' job as adjutant to a 'potty little petrol depot' in Dorset.

"Done," I said and in due course I became the Adjutant at the Petrol Depot at West Moors.

It was the start of an idyllic two years. Early on in my stint at West Moors the newly formed Army Air Corps advertised in Army Council Instructions for officers who would like to train as light aircraft pilots. The bug was still there and I volunteered; I was interviewed at Middle Wallop, told that aptitude and previous aircrew training made me a suitable candidate and that I would be called forward in due course. At about this time my unit fell due for its annual administrative inspection, an ordeal all army units have to undergo. To my great surprise and pleasure the inspecting officer was to be Major General Eric Sixsmith, my brigade commander in Calcutta, my patron for my return to the Army and now the General Officer Commanding the South West District – our administrative headquarters. He questioned me closely on my career ambitions and openly derided my bid to become an Army Air Corps pilot.

"That won't amount to anything," he said. "You can take it from me that anything worthwhile that flies will be collared by the RAF and the AAC will become a military air taxi service. What you must do is go on a colonial secondment and study for the Staff College examination."

As it happened, my highly eccentric CO, Lieutenant Colonel Ronnie

MacDonald, had been an Army Lysander pilot in the Second World War. After the General had left he called me into his office and gave me some 'Dutch Uncle' advice.

"I've kept quiet until now," he said. "Because you are obviously keen to go back to flying, but the GOC is right. Before the war I did what you're now doing and eventually I became an Army pilot. I spent my time with Lysanders, flying clandestine missions and as you know I was caught and put in the bag."

He had been captured and spent most of the war in a German prison camp.

"When I came back to the Corps my contemporaries had moved onwards and upwards and I was a virtual stranger. You've got a choice between having your fun and satisfying your ambitions for a good career."

I talked it over with my wife, now pregnant for the second time. She was not keen for me to go flying but loyally left the decision to me. I decided to let the chips lie where they fell and left my application in.

It was pleasant serving in that attractive corner of Dorset. I ran a branch of the Army Sailing Association in Christchurch Harbour, fished on the Hampshire Avon near Ringwood and thoroughly enjoyed the antics of my CO. Serving with Ronnie was never dull. He was a superb raconteur and probably the funniest man I met in the Army. One of his senior majors once said at a weekly conference when the laughter had subsided.

"One of these days, Colonel, I'm going to write down some of the things you say, put them in a book and make a fortune."

Being rail served, the Depot employed a number of MOD railwayman to look after the metals and the wagons and do the shunting up to the junction with the British Rail network. Most of these people were long serving employees, both loyal and hardworking and gave no trouble. But there were one or two young men who made it their business to prove at every opportunity that they were not subject to military discipline and that 'these soldiers' would not be allowed to order them around. They were, in a word, 'stroppy' and offered confrontation at every opportunity. I had not come face to face with this sort of thing before. Unions and industrial unrest had played no part in my short experience of commerce and that would have remained the situation had we not had a problem one weekend.

A consignment of special oils for the tanks and specialist equipment in Korea had been called for urgently and it was necessary to work on a Saturday to get the supplies away to meet a critical shipping date. Two MOD railwaymen had been called in and had worked a short shift but had refused to put in the extra time needed – a matter of an hour or so – to complete the procedures to get the consignment away. The young officer in command of the pioneer soldier workforce had done his bit and the oils were loaded but he was unable to cope with the intransigence of the railwaymen and his company commander being away, he rang me in desperation. I went down to the loading bay and spoke to them, explaining the urgency, confirming that they would be paid for the extra time and asking them in effect to help support the war effort. They refused point blank to respond, quoting what these days are known as 'unsocial hours' and claiming that they weren't being paid enough anyway for Saturday morning working. One of these men had only recently completed his National Service and was clearly enjoying his confrontation with two officers.

"You must realise," I said, "that I have no power to authorise any more money than your union has already negotiated for you. This stuff is badly needed by your own people fighting a war on the other side of the world. If you won't do what is necessary to complete the procedures for securing the load, I'll get the soldiers to do it and you can get out and not come back."

As I was told later, I had played into their hands. My chief tormentor drew himself up to his full height and said portentously, "Are you discharging us?"

"Call it sacked if you like," I replied. "Now beat it and we'll get the job done ourselves."

I told the CO on the phone when we had despatched the consignment – that did in fact just meet the deadline for the ship. Ronnie said, "Of course I'll back you up Freddie; I'd have done the same thing myself, but there'll be all Hell to pay – mark my words."

Three days later an elderly gentleman – to me then, but in retrospect he must have been something short of sixty – turned up at the Depot and asked to see the CO. He was wearing a dark suit and tie and carried a briefcase. He looked and seemed to be a gentle and benign soul. I asked his business and he said he had an industrial relations case to discuss with the Commanding Officer. He handed me his card; he was the regional representative for the National Union of Railwaymen.

I said, "I think I'm involved in this. I'd better come in with you." He inclined his head.

According to the report put in by the local Union man, those two young railwaymen had encountered Attilla the Hun brought back to life. They had said, in effect, that the only reason they were not flogged at the stake was that there were no whips or stakes handy. I put my case, stressing the urgency of despatch to a war zone. The CO added.

"My adjutant has only recently returned from two years in Korea and naturally realised more than most the urgency for the consignment."

The union man said, "One of my sons did his National Service there and I've heard all the horror stories about the place, but there was no call to sack two of my members on the spot. Can I be assured that they will be reinstated and that this won't count against them?"

He got his assurance and I received from him a finger wagging lecture on the folly of clashing with organised labour. In fact, as I learned later, I had no authority whatsoever to sack them; that privilege was reserved for 'higher authority' after a painful enquiry and negotiating process had been gone through.

One day we were visited by two rather grim looking citizens who came into my office and asked to see the CO. They showed Foreign Office identification. I led them through and kept an ear cocked to the drone of conversation in case the CO wanted any documents. Suddenly there was a roar of laughter and Ronnie appeared at the door leading to my office, beaming.

"Let's have a cup of tea." In due course the two Foreign Office wallahs came out grinning widely. Ronnie saw them out and then perched himself on the edge of my desk.

"You know what those two wanted?" I shook my head.

"Before the war I had a little sports car and went up to Town a good deal. But even then it was hell's difficult to find a place to park it. Then someone told me that if you registered with the Moseley Movement you could use their car park on the Embankment. So I became a bogus Blackshirt and had easy parking until I had to sell the car and of course when the war started I jacked in my membership. Those boys found my name in the old records and I had to be investigated for possible Fascist leanings!" He laughed. "When I told them that my debriefing notes from prisoner of war camp would prove that I spent a good deal of time in detention for making fun of the Master Race, they seemed to think it was OK."

As the Adjutant and personal staff officer to the CO, I didn't have much to do with the technical side of the Depot. The company commanders were graduates of the Long Petroleum Course and obviously knew what they were doing. After retirement some of them reached high positions in the oil industry. Ronnie knew as little as I did about the technicalities of POL – the Army's acronym for petroleum, oils and lubricants. We looked after discipline and administration and this, for a very good reason, was a full-time job. The reason had to do with the fact that before the days of mechanical handling, stocks of POL were held in jerrycans, filled from immense tanks at the Depot. It was a rail served depot and the jerrycans were manhandled on to the rail wagons, labour being provided by Royal Pioneer Corps national servicemen.

Many of these tough and hardy young men were illiterate and when bored, prone to throw 'good order and military discipline' to the four winds. I stress that they were not bad lads and they were certainly hard workers. They couldn't find solace in reading, although comics were popular, and so we strained every nerve to keep them interested and occupied in their off duty hours. The Royal Army Education Corps provided an officer and two young graduate sergeants to run an education programme but with the best will in the world it could not claim to be successful. I used to walk round the camp at least once every day and purposely included a visit to the hutted classrooms in my tour.

Walking up the concrete path towards each hut, the noise of an unruly schoolroom could clearly be heard. As soon as the door opened you could have heard a pin drop. The whole class was giving the obviously nervous teacher its full attention. As soon as the door closed behind me and I walked down the concrete path, bedlam was restored. The CO, the Regimental Sergeant Major and others in authority reported similar experiences. The mass of minor offences we had to deal with on Monday mornings made me familiar with large sections of the Manual of Military Law, which is one of the qualifying papers for the Staff College Examination and it is thanks largely to the Royal Pioneer Corps and its soldiers that I achieved a high pass mark in that subject when I eventually took the examination.

As time went by and I heard nothing from the Army Air Corps, I made enquiries, only to be told that they had a surplus of candidates and I would have to wait my turn. So as a backstop I applied to take the Staff College Examination. My CO readily endorsed my application and it was duly sent to the General's headquarters in Yeovil.

It should be explained that to an Army officer, attendance at the Staff College, which is dependent on selection after qualifying at a competitive examination, could be a seminal thing, something that could and usually did, colour the whole of his subsequent career. Competition for a place was therefore very keen indeed. In the nineteen fifties there were seven papers to take at the annual examination; this normally lasted three days. There were three tactics papers covering respectively, organisations, what was then known as imperial policing and finally limited and general war. Then military history, military law, current affairs (geo politics) and administration. A minimum of 50% in each paper was needed for a pass in each subject and an aggregate of 60% was needed to pass the examination. You were allowed a window of three tries and I knew of several who actually tried three times to improve on their pass marks obtained in the two previous years. It was generally recognised that candidates should study for about a year before taking the examination.

During this time it was advisable to take every course that had a bearing on the examination papers and most commanding officers looked tolerantly on potential examinees who were usually allowed time off for courses and study. The Metropolitan College of Woking ran a correspondence course specifically aimed at the Staff College Exam and it made sense to buy it, as most of us did. We became familiar with, among others, the bandit Rodrigo who was busily laying waste on paper to large areas of the Isle of Man. I've never actually been there but from midnight oil map exercises I reckon I could find my way around it to this day.

I was on a military law course in London when Heather phoned me and said, "You've been posted!"

Surprised, because my three year stint at West Moors had a year to run, but thinking that perhaps the Army Air Corps had claimed me at last, I asked where to.

"Well, so far as I can gather, you are to be seconded to the Royal West African Frontier Force in Nigeria. We're going to Lagos, the capital, and you are to be the Staff Captain to the South Nigeria

Brigade. I haven't seen the actual posting order but Ronnie gave me the details over the phone. He also said with some satisfaction that the General had been as good as his word, but I don't know what he meant by that. Anyway, there's plenty of time. We don't go until after Christmas by which time Wendy will be toddling and it will be easier to travel."

She was referring to our second daughter who had arrived in November 1954. Wendy Elizabeth, also auburn haired and equally bonny.

So 'the General had been as good as his word'? I had a feeling that I had been the victim of a plot – no doubt justified as for my own good. I suspected that there had been collusion between my CO and General Sixsmith. The General had certainly not offered me 'his word'. He had merely expressed a view that I was moving in the wrong direction careerwise. Ronnie Macdonald had agreed with him for the reasons he gave me. I taxed him with this; he responded with stout denial, but then he always did. Actually I was quite taken with the idea of a secondment to a colonial force so I didn't press the issue and as it turned out, they were right.

It was traditional while the Empire still existed for young officers to be seconded to what were still known as 'colonial forces' to gain experience. There was quite keen competition for secondments while you were still young enough to enjoy colonial soldiering in the years before your parent regiment demanded undivided attention. This ensured that such exotic sounding formations as The Aden Protectorate Levies, The King's African Rifles, The Malayan Military Forces, The Royal West African Frontier Force and others were never short of keen new blood for their officer corps. Authority encouraged this. With the Empire dissolving during the decades after the Second World War, the value of young and 'middle piece' British officers making friends and contacts with the future officer corps and potential rulers of these emerging colonial countries was not lost on our politicians and on members of the Army Council. In fact it was sometimes said at the time that government of ex-British colonies swung between Sandhurst and the London School of Economics.

11

Beware, Beware, The Bight of Benin!

But no Knickers on Saturday Nights

Had it not been for the long tongue of flame streaming from one of the engines on the port side, I could have dozed off easily as the old Albemarle, an ex-RAF charter aircraft, droned southwards over the Sahara Desert on that January evening of 1956. I was on my way to my new posting in Nigeria. Air trooping had developed strongly in the post-war years and although a few troopships still crossed the oceans, mainly to move formed units with their portable kit, individual reinforcements and replacements usually moved by air, either in RAF transport aircraft or more often in aircraft chartered by the Army Movements organisation.

The flames had been hardly noticeable in full daylight but as the evening advanced and the sunlit desert below changed to old gold and then to deepening shades of violet, it became possible to read a newspaper without benefit of the cabin lighting. The air charter company cabin staff seemed totally unconcerned and when I and several others drew their attention to the phenomenon the air stewardess smiled brightly and said, "Pretty isn't it. But don't worry. With this aircraft it's quite normal and not at all dangerous. You get used to it after a while." But it's a safe bet that all her passengers were mightily pleased and relieved to arrive without incident at Ikeja, the airport for Lagos – Nigeria's capital city on the Bight of Benin.

The South Nigeria Brigade of the Royal West African Frontier Force was a new formation – soon renamed Southern Sub District to embrace the mass of military depots and static installations in and around Lagos. To all intents and purposes, however, it was a brigade command of three infantry battalions. There was a sister formation, Northern Sub District. This was based in Hausa and Fulani country with its headquarters in the northern town of Kaduna. The controlling Headquarters for both was HQ Nigeria Military Forces co-located with our Sub District at Apapa Camp in Lagos.

Ours was a small headquarters commanded by a Brigadier known to all and sundry as Mad Max – one of the Army's many Mad Maxs and Mad Mikes serving at that time. His staff comprised two General Staff officers – a major G2 supported by a captain G3 and two Logistic Staff officers – a major A/Q and a staff captain. Our Brigadier, a bachelor, was both volatile and unpredictable. Within six months of our arrival at this new formation headquarters, both his senior staff officers had fallen short of his exacting standards and had departed, leaving the headquarters staff pared down to a G3, Captain Peter Windeler of the Border Regiment, and a staff captain, me. We probably survived because allowances were made for the fact that we were not 'staff trained' – we were not graduates of the Staff College.

One of the characteristics of our multi-faceted Brigadier was that he never even attempted to dissemble; if he didn't like someone or something it immediately became apparent, and he didn't much care for the General Officer Commanding (GOC) Nigerian Military Forces, a Major General, who was himself a peppery straight talking character plagued by attacks of gout that made him extremely bad tempered. It could have made our lives difficult because we shared a camp with the GOC and his staff, but fortunately we found the HQ NMF staff sympathetic to our situation and relations at our level were perfectly cordial.

There were few married quarters available in Lagos when I arrived although more were being built. Although I would qualify for one of the new quarters being built in the military hospital compound, initially I had to wait until a suitable private house or flat could be hired before I could arrange for my family to come out. One of the requirements was security; there were certain parts of Lagos that were not considered suitable as quarters for European officers or soldiers and this made my search more difficult. Consequently, Heather and the two children had to wait four months before they could join me. The flat I eventually found met the Army's standards and was quickly rented for me. It was part of a small detached two storey house divided into two flats by a piece of fibre board tacked across the staircase landing, the upper level accessed by a fire escape of outside steps. We lived on the top floor. The ground floor, or downstairs flat, was occupied by Captain Nigel Spellar and Margaret, his wife. Nigel, or Nibs as he was known to his contemporaries, much to his wife's annoyance, was seconded from the RASC to the West African Army Service Corps (WASC) and was also studying hard for the Staff College Exam. The house was located behind a police station and just outside a military depot. It was owned by an African politician and businessman who must have weighed about twenty-five stones – a mighty man. He was a cultured and agreeable conversationalist and he enjoyed visiting us to chat and drink our whisky. He was realistic on the subject of Nigerian independence.

"We will have a long period of adjustment," he said. "You, our colonial masters, have imposed upon us laws which took you many years, even centuries, to fashion. When we are free of your influence, our tribal laws and customs that you have suppressed will surface, and tribal rivalries will create conflict just as they did in your history. We will have to get over this without your help and this we will do, but it will take time."

Events subsequently proved his prescience and I hope he survived, for many of Nigeria's educated and far sighted citizens were slaughtered in the conflicts which erupted after we left. A particular friend, Captain Sam Ademulagen of our HQ Signal Squadron, who I was later to serve with as a student at the Staff College, was promoted to Brigadier on his return to Nigeria and was killed with all his family during a night assault on his house in the Northern city of Kaduna. The origins of the assault were alleged to be tribal; Sam was a Yoruba from the Lagos area commanding a formation in Hausa and Fulani country. There were many other well documented casualties of Nigeria's turbulent recent history which included the Biafran War, fought as a result of the Eastern Region attempting to collar for itself its newly exploited oil riches by seceding from the parent country. This resulted in much bloodshed before the attempt failed.

Nigeria, particularly the humid southern part of the country, was not an ideal place for white people in the nineteen fifties. The climate was enervating; diseases such as malaria, TB, blackwater fever and rabies were endemic. The unpleasant effects of the climate were recognised by the Army by a grant of three months 'recuperative leave' at home in Britain in the middle of a three year tour of duty, a unique concession by a government not normally celebrated for its generosity to its servicemen and women. We were living in what had been known to previous generations as 'the white man's grave' epitomised by the old rhyme 'Beware, beware, the Bight of Benin, where few come out though many go in.' Lagos lies on the Bight of Benin and Benin City, the region's ancient capital, stood about 150 miles to the east of us.

The country was pretty stable, however, during the last few years of its colonial existence and despite the humid heat and the poverty of most of its citizens, Lagos was a colourful and cheerful place. The vendors in the teeming market places all wore multi-coloured clothing and the 'mammies' as the more matronly ladies were generally known, were noisily friendly. All Africans love children; they can do no wrong, and our two red haired little girls were much admired. We had struck lucky with servants, essential in that enervating climate. Umaru was a Hausa man from the north, a Muslim, whereas most of the inhabitants of Lagos were of the Yoruba people and either Christians or pagans of one sort or another. He had a nice young wife and a 'piccan' – the local pidgin for a baby. Wendy, our youngest, was still a piccan to the locals and Heather, who became an accomplished pidgin speaker, always spoke of 'my piccan' when discussing children with Umaru's wife. Pidgin, which I never really mastered, had its own logic. As in standard English, superlatives were often based on comparisons. In West Africa these were invariably local. For instance, kerosene was an expensive and highly desirable replacement for wood as a source of domestic fuel. So a reply to the question "Was it good?" might be "Yes. Fine fine pas(t) kerosene." Or, because the new port under construction at Takoradi on the nearby Gold Coast was a potential life enhancing event for all, "Fine fine pas Takoradi," eventually shortened to just "Pas Takoradi."

The administrative and commercial centre of Lagos is on an island, accessible in the nineteen fifties by one modern road bridge – Carter Bridge. The remainder of the city, which we shall call Greater Lagos, although each district had its own identity, sprawled out into the mainland for a distance of about eight miles, a mixture of shanty type dwellings and quite modern houses brightly colourwashed and with wide verandahs and window openings. There was very little air conditioning. The more upmarket houses boasted ceiling fans and there was usually a brief respite from the humid heat around January when the cool Harmattan wind blew briefly from the Sahara, but most of us just sweated out our time there and it wasn't too bad when you became acclimatised.

The military headquarters were located at Apapa Camp on the mainland although the General and the Brigadier both had houses at Ikoyi on Lagos Island in the smart area close to Government House. Military installations were spread around Greater Lagos on the mainland in random fashion – workshops, an ordnance depot, a large military hospital – and they were responsible for their own security. There was, however, an infantry detachment of two companies of the 2nd Battalion Nigeria Regiment also based near to Government House on Lagos Island. They were for internal security duties in the City if and when called upon for assistance by the civil authorities. The officer corps of both the army and the police, hitherto white officers and native other ranks, were rapidly being Africanised in preparation for Nigeria's independence. Civil unrest was not expected but the population was quite excitable, easily stirred up, and minor security incidents were fairly common.

For civilian administrative purposes Nigeria, a huge country, was divided into three regions, each dominated by a tribal people and each with its own language and customs. The Northern region, with its military sub district, was the home of the Hausas and Fulanis while the Western Region was mainly inhabited by the Yoruba people and the Eastern Region by the Ibo people. Our brigade covered the Western and Eastern regions and our three infantry battalions were all stationed up country. One was at Abeokuta, sixty miles north of Lagos, another at Ibadan, the university town about 120 miles to the north and the third at Enugu, across the Niger River in the Eastern region, about 300 miles away. Communications were not particularly good and commanding officers had considerable autonomy. Our brigadier also commanded the mass of depots in and around Lagos.

There are pros and cons to every Army posting and while it wasn't hard to see the cons in Nigeria, one of the pros was the hours of work. In traditional colonial style we worked in the cool of the morning from 7 am to the start of the hottest part of the day at 1 pm. A siesta after lunch was followed by 'exercise hours' supposed to last from about 3 pm to 6 pm. Situated as we were, about 300 miles north of the Equator, there was no gloaming. The sun rose quickly and set equally quickly at around 7 pm all year round. My chosen exercise was sailing. Heather and I quickly became members of the Lagos Yacht Club and although funds wouldn't run to exclusive use of a boat, we were able to buy a half share in a Hornet dinghy with the OC of the signals squadron, Malcolm Stears and his wife, Ellen. The Hornet was a racing dinghy with a sliding plank amidships on which the crew member perched four feet out from the side of the boat to counterbalance the pressure on the sails and keep her upright and stable when the wind was strong. Our wives became experts on the plank and we raced and planed all over the vast harbour of Lagos, capsizing regularly into the warm, tropical water without a thought for the monsters that might lurk beneath our keel. Salt water crocodiles, the most aggressive kind, abounded in the tidal mangrove swamps surrounding the harbour and attacks on attacks on humans were regularly reported in the local paper, but I can't recall any accounts of attacks actually within the harbour.

There was a garrison recreation area on the Atlantic shore accessible only by sea around a rocky groyne at the harbour entrance. It was known as Tarquah Bay and was owned and maintained by the military. It had safe bathing on a white, sandy beach, showers, changing rooms for both sexes and a few primitive but clean bedrooms for those who wished to spend a weekend there. It also boasted a contracted out 'canteen' where you could get drinks, ice creams and snacks. It was run by Sergeant Ogun of the Nigeria Regiment, a 'dead ringer' for Idi Amin – in appearance only for he was a gentle soul although not over endowed with either speed of reaction or depth of thought. But he ran the small detachment of civilian staff well because in the local vernacular he had 'plenty power' being big and strong and an ex-regimental boxing champion.

Sergeant Ogun was responsible to me for this haven of cool breezes and white sand and one of my more pleasant duties was to sail out to Tarquah Bay for a fortnightly inspection of the facilities and to pay the detachment. HQ NMF had been provided with a RASC vessel for duties such as this. She was a harbour launch; a seaworthy craft with a crew of six soldiers but since she had long been virtually commandeered as the General's launch and was under the control of his ADC, the vessel was rarely available although she was allowed to operate a ferry service for families at weekends. So I usually sailed our boat to the Bay, a distance of about four miles from the Yacht Club. This resulted in one of those incidents that are laughable only in retrospect.

Our families had gone to Tarquah Bay on the launch one Saturday and Malcolm and I sailed over in the Hornet, with the detachment's pay secured in a waterproof cover inside the boat's buoyancy chamber. On the way out with a falling tide and a stiff headwind, Malcolm, out on the plank, missed his footing when we had to tack and we capsized just in sight of the harbour groyne. Normally it was easy to right the boat by standing on the centre board and this he did but the wind was so strong that as soon as we got her upright she went over again. In this situation the drill is to get the mainsail down but the tide was racing out and by the time we had done that we would have been way out in the Atlantic and so we persevered. Three times she went over and we realised that our strength was failing. Mercifully on the fourth attempt we were sufficiently in the lee of the groyne to keep the boat upright and instead of negotiating the groyne at the ocean end, we crept round to where there was a small foetid creek leading to Tarquah Bay by the back door, so to speak.

We splashed up the creek, towing the boat by its painter and came up behind the groyne lined with people looking and pointing out to sea. Something had obviously happened. We asked one of the European ladies who was not known to us what all the fuss was about and she told us that two people in a small boat had capsized and had been swept out to sea. The launch had been sent to search 'for the bodies!' At that moment we were spotted by Melissa, Malcolm's six year old, who ran to our wives and the mix-up was swiftly unravelled.

It transpired that Sergeant Ogun, on finding that his detachment's pay was not on the launch, had placed a lookout on the groyne to alert him when our boat appeared. Seeing the first capsize, the lookout had run to find his sergeant and by the time Ogun had got to the vantage point, we were nowhere in sight, having by that time righted the boat and sailed behind the groyne. Ogun assumed we had been swept out to sea. The news spread like wildfire and everyone had rushed to the spot where the boat was seen to have gone over. Someone had despatched the launch, which returned hours later reporting failure. Many small boats stood off Tarquah Bay at weekends and we later published a piece in garrison orders warning of the dangers of being swept out to sea on a swift falling tide.

An echo of colonial lifestyle was the requirement for officers to 'drop cards' on the Governor. This was modified for junior officers to signing the book at Government House. Eventually this resulted in an invitation to a Government House Garden Party – attendance de rigeur, for us anyway. Dress: plain clothes. Standing sipping orange juice in company with the flower of Lagos, black white and brown, on a warm, sunny late afternoon, I noticed a broad back and stance that seemed familiar. It took me back to Korea and Captain Jumbo Watson, the Motor Transport Officer of the 5th (Northumberland) Fusiliers and a good friend to our unit.

I assumed that he had been seconded like me, but to a Nigerian infantry battalion.

"Jumbo, you old soak?" I said interrogatively. He turned.

"Good God," I said.

"Not quite," said Jumbo, his white dog collar a stark contrast to his dark suit. "But with His guidance I'm seeking the path."

He told me that he had retired to take the cloth and had become a missionary. He said he had always felt the call.

"Well, Jumbo," I said, "I reckon it wasn't all that loud in Korea." He grinned.

"I trust that we'll remain friends and that you will spread no tales of our youthful excesses."

How could I? The European community resembled a village with gossip its lifeblood. Jumbo's reputation remained unsullied and we did remain friends.

There was an active social life. The British abroad tend to concentrate in cantonments, unlike the French and Spanish who were also West African colonists but more willing to integrate and intermarry. I suppose our reluctance to do this stemmed from being insular islanders. The Army, of course, had always been a rigid hierarchical society and never more so than when in a colony. It was Kipling's Plain Tales from the Hills all over again with several Mrs Hauksbees within our garrison. Rules that would now be considered laughably old-fashioned held sway. Dress, for instance. For the men it was simple and a matter of decree. Either uniform, black tie or plain clothes. The ladies, however, were badly affected. There were times to wear hats and times to wear gloves, times to wear neither and times to wear both. A great deal of telephone time was taken up discussing the niceties and gradations of dress for functions.

Our Brigadier had a bachelor's disdain for all this; he would not have felt out of place tieless and in a sports coat and flannels at a Royal Garden Party. I thought he was going to have a seizure one morning at a weekly conference for COs of local units. We had got to 'any other business' on the conference agenda when the CO of the military hospital, a thoroughly unmilitary man as most hospital COs aspire to be, piped up and asked if ladies were to wear hats and gloves at some function or other. Max's eyes widened and his colour rose. His thumb, arched at the top of his clenched fist, went to his mouth, a sure sign of impending rage. He turned his head to look at me, sitting on his right taking the minutes of the meeting.

"I'll find out," I said quickly, frowning at the doctor, who got the message. The Brigadier rose without a word and stalked out. The aftermath was a ten minute rant in his office which brought him off the boil.

He didn't much like social functions, but he would occasionally dine with his immediate staff. As he was a bachelor we normally arranged for a senior couple to be present when we asked him to dinner; this wasn't difficult to arrange with the big headquarters in the same location. On one occasion when we had moved into a newly built married quarter in the military hospital grounds we had a housewarming dinner party with about eight guests including the Brigadier. Everything went swimmingly. The houseboys, Umaru plus one borrowed for the evening, were both in spotless white with scarlet cummerbunds and white turbans; they knew it was an important occasion and backed us up with an efficient performance. At the end of the dinner Umaru padded in during coffee time and clearly had an important message. He leaned towards Heather at the head of the table. Conversation stilled.

What was it? A riot? World War Three? "Madam," said Umaru portentously. "De baby shit!"

There was dead silence for a couple of seconds. Broken by the senior wife, who laid her head back and screamed with laughter, bless her. Even Mad Max, no lover of children, managed a grin. He then led the men into the garden, as was the custom, for a pee, while the ladies giggled and gossiped behind us.

Lagos boasted a lively nightlife. One nightclub was famous for a sign outside bearing the raunchy message 'No Knickers on Saturday Nights'. It was much photographed by the European element, but potential voyeurs were disappointed; despite appearances there were no weekly orgies. The notice was conveying an innocent and perfectly reasonable message. Knickers in the local patois were shorts and the management, while willing to accept them on weekdays, insisted that male guests wore trousers on Saturday nights.

As the Staff Captain at our small HQ and in the continued absence of a Major, still awaited from the Staff College course, it became part of my job to brief the Brigadier on disciplinary cases. Captain George Beach of the Army Special Investigation Branch – the SIB – reported to me. George, christened irreverently 'Beach of the Branch', gave me details of a case shortly after my arrival that illustrated the thinness of the veneer overlying tribal Africa. Two of the African soldiers in the garrison workshop admired a singer in a local nightclub and visited their native doctor, – to obtain a potion to improve their singing prowess. The potion proved to be useless and when they went back to complain, the native doctor said, "You'd need his vocal chords to sing like him."

He later said at the trial that he had simply made a jocular remark to that effect. The two soldiers took him literally. They waited for the singer to leave the club one evening, cut his throat and extracted what they thought were his vocal chords. They took them to their native doctor. He, appalled, called the police. They were imprisoned for life.

It was impossible to live in Lagos for any length of time and not be aware of the native doctors, or, in the local patois, Ju Ju men. It was sensible to call them in to fend off the rain if a major function was planned, not for their actual value but to appease the staff, who were much happier if the age old custom was observed.

The power of the Ju Ju men was demonstrated when we were caretaking a house for someone away in England on recuperative leave while we were waiting for our married quarter to become available. Umaru came to me one day and said:

"You are going to need another servant when you get your new house. My brother from the north would like to come to Lagos and if you will take him on, I will train him."

We leaped at the offer; finding an honest and reliable servant was a big problem and Umaru's younger brother – he swore it was 'same mother, same father, same bed', the usual way of describing blood kin – would be ideal when trained.

The young man arrived. Mo, shortened from Mohammed, was totally lacking in sophistication having been brought up in a remote peasant village in the dry northern desert area, but he was a nice lad and very keen to learn. Quite unwittingly I scored ten out of ten with him at the start. Someone had given him a torch and this had become his most precious possession. He couldn't wait for darkness to fall so that he could have an excuse to use it. Inevitably the battery expired quite quickly; then he dropped the torch and the bulb gave out. He understood that the torch needed power and that he needed a new battery, but he was defeated by the bulb failure. He came to me doe-eyed and offered the torch. I told Umaru to tell him that I would 'go make him better' and I produced it next day with a new battery and bulb. From then on I was a great wizard – one who thankfully was never called on to prove his prowess again.

As time went by Mo developed a nasty cough. Jean Windeler, Peter's wife and a close friend to us, was a nursing sister and employed at the Shell Oil Company dispensary in Lagos. She came to tea one day and hearing Mo cough, was immediately suspicious. "I'll have him checked," she said and arranged for him to be examined at the civilian Creek Hospital. To our considerable alarm, the diagnosis was advanced and aggressive TB, known to an earlier generation of laymen as galloping consumption. We were told that Mo was not long for this world. I broke the news to Umaru who refused point blank to let his brother be treated in Lagos. He clearly didn't believe the diagnosis and asked if he could take his brother back to his village up country, where he would be treated by his native doctor who would make him better. So much for the white man's medicine. Africa had won again. Umaru left with Mo for the north by 'Mammy Wagon' – Nigeria's all purpose bus system, carrying people, small animals and portable goods around the country.

I asked the doctor how long Mo would have. He said, "When he gets back to the dry desert air, he'll feel better for a short time and no doubt his native doctor will take the credit. But it can only be a matter of time, a year at most. Had he stayed down here in this steaming heat, you could halve that."

We now had to think of our own family. Our children and the friends they regularly mixed with were tested for TB as were Heather and me. We were given BCG vaccinations, which had only recently ceased to be a standard precaution, and we were kept under observation with periodic checks for a further two years. Before we left Lagos, Umaru, with his family also under observation, told me that poor Mo had died.

Shortly after the Mo incident our elder daughter, Helen, contracted recurrent malaria and developed a high fever. We were beside ourselves with worry but she recovered from the initial attack quite quickly. It has recurred over the years with decreasing frequency and potency and now, in her early fifties, it seems at last to have left her.

Amid all this the Staff College Examination was held at Giffard Camp, Accra, the capital of the Gold Coast about 300 miles to the west of us. I travelled there by Nigerian Airways Bristol Freighter, jocularly known as a Bristol Frightener and piloted by a mixture of British, South African and Australian pilots.

Ghana, as the Gold coast was renamed after independence, has a climate more friendly to Europeans than Lagos; it is mainly Savannah country, low scrub, gravel and sand. The temperature is similar but the heat is drier, less enervating and tempered with cool breezes from the Atlantic. The mangrove swamps surrounding Lagos make the place sweaty and humid even when you are acclimatised. Weather conditions on the Gold Coast were therefore reasonable for the examination.

There were about twelve candidates from all over West Africa, all seconded British officers. African officer students at the Staff College were nominated and not subject to examination. Our invigilator was a genial and oldish African major of the Gold Coast Regiment, by name Arthur Ankrah. He knew the rules and saw that they were observed. Years later when I was a teacher at the Staff College I had a Ghanaian student in my syndicate and asked if he had known Arthur Ankrah who I assumed had retired. My student, a major, looked surprised.

"You must mean General Sir Arthur Ankrah, our President and Commander in Chief." I should have known of course, but keeping track of the politico/military shenanigans of former West African colonies at that stage required more time than most of us could spare.

We had a few hours to look round Accra. Christiansbourg Castle, infamous for its connections with the slave trade, stood perched imposingly on a clifftop overlooking the beaches where the boats from the ships moored offshore braved the heavy surf to make a landfall on the beach. Accra's port, at Takoradi, a short way along the coast, was not yet completed and surfboats were still the most economic means of supplying Accra with imported goods. It was fascinating to watch the heavily laden double ended wooden boats being teased through the Atlantic rollers to crash on to the beach. We were told that there was an occasional capsize but we didn't see any while we were there.

Back to Lagos with a four month wait for the exam results. A couple of days after I returned, and with the Brigadier away visiting a battalion up country, Peter Windeler strolled into my office. We kept each other up to date with developments on a casual basis – the formal business being conducted at a weekly conference chaired by the Brigadier with all local COs present. Peter, as the General Staff, dealt with all operational matters while I dealt with transport, discipline and general administration – logistics, in present day jargon.

"Heard about our riot?"

I looked up. "No. Where?"

"On Carter Bridge," Peter replied.

"The Lagos Council have decided to clear those slummy tin shacks at either end before the Queen's visit. The slum landlords are furious at the potential loss of income. They've given free palm wine to the tenants and persuaded them that their homes are going to be bulldozed. Apparently they're all fighting drunk, scragging travellers and throwing bricks around. The police have asked for help and I've called out the 2NR detachment from Ikoyi."

Alarm bells sounded in my head. "It's a shopping bus day."

I rushed to the wall where the timetable for the families' bus was pinned on a board. The main European shopping area was in Ikoyi on Lagos Island, the nearest thing to a supermarket being the Kingsway Stores, owned and run by the British West Africa Corporation, a Lever subsidiary. Twice a week we ran a three tonner, with seats in the back and encased in protective chicken wire, around the garrison quarters for the wives to use as a shopping bus. It was driven by an African WASC driver accompanied by an unarmed British sergeant as an escort. It ran to a strict timetable, ending its journey at the Kingsway Store. A quick check on the timetable showed me that the bus would be crossing Carter Bridge in about fifteen minutes.

"Have the infantry arrived?"

"No," said Peter. "I've only just told them. It'll be about twenty minutes before they get there. The police said it was looking pretty dicey but they thought they could contain it until the troops arrive."

We had to do something quickly. We had two Land Rovers available and our small HQ was located next to the brick built Force Pay Office that was staffed exclusively by British soldiers of the Royal Army Pay Corps. It had no African soldiers for reasons that need not be entered into. It did have a secure armoury. We explained the situation to their CO who readily agreed to let us have eight of his soldiers. We armed ourselves with weapons and ammunition and belted towards Carter Bridge, about five miles away. There was a personal interest. While Jean, Peter's wife, would be working at the Shell Dispensary on the Island and therefore safe, my wife had told me that morning that she was catching the Army bus to go shopping.

We arrived at the Bridge to find it littered with stones and other debris; the infantry were coiling up their Dannert wire barrier. A few locals were lying dead drunk at the side of the road, but no sign of rioters.

"Did you see the Garrison bus?" I asked the detachment commander.

"I didn't see any bus," he said. He waved his arm around. "This lot were all as drunk as coots, but a bugle blast and a couple of shots in the air saw them off. No casualties." His puzzled reply to my next question was, "No magistrate and no time for a chalk line."

We assumed that the bus had broken down or had been otherwise delayed, but having dismissed our small force, Peter and I decided to check at the Kingsway Store. The bus was indeed parked there, the driver asleep with his feet on the steering wheel. The sergeant escort had no doubt found somewhere cooler. I located Heather inside the store and asked her what had happened at the bridge.

"Well there was a lot of shouting and some of the Africans were throwing bricks at the Police. We came up behind the crowd and the sergeant banged on the door of the cab to get their attention." She paused. "He was very rude to them. They saw us sitting in the back and they waved and shouted to the people in front who stopped throwing stones, moved aside and let the bus through. They were all laughing, waving and whistling at us. We saw from where we were sitting that once we were through the police line, they started throwing stones again."

Thanking our stars that there had been no professional rabble rousers among the mob, we returned to the Headquarters. It could have turned out differently. Previous experience had taught me that such situations, seemingly benign, could turn nasty in a flash. We discussed arming the bus escort, but realising that this would be of little practical use and could inflame a given situation we decided against it.

The Queen, accompanied by Prince Philip, visited Nigeria shortly after the Carter Bridge incident. In Lagos she stayed at Government House, to be met by a guard of honour. My job was to stand at the entrance of the long drive to Government House and phone through to the Guard Commander the news that the Royal Party were on the way. I had a perfect view of the young couple as they drove past me a yard away and my salute was met with a smile from both and a personal royal wave. About eighteen months later when the Queen came to the Staff College for its Centenary Year celebration, she made a point of chatting with all the groups of students. She told me that she had enjoyed her visit to Nigeria and even professed to remember the lone greeter at the entrance to the drive of Government House.

Heather and I were among the guests when the Queen presented new colours to the 5th Battalion Nigeria Regiment at the university town of Ibadan in 1956. She also announced that the Regiment would henceforth bear the title of Queens Own Nigeria Regiment (QONR). The ceremony took place on the Battalion's parade ground shortly after dawn at the coolest time of day. Dress uniform for Nigerian infantry soldiers consisted of black boots, short cloth puttees, hosetops (a footless stocking stretching from the ankle to just under the knee), black shorts, red Zouave jackets – similar to a British infantry mess jacket, all surmounted by a fez. The drill, accompanied by a regimental band with a British Director of Music, was impeccable. African soldiers enjoy drill. They are natural dancers with an inborn sense of rhythm and timing and they relish the concerted movements and foot stamping. The calm and smiling dawn, the lines of African soldiers moving in perfect unison to traditional military airs, their shining black faces making a pleasing contrast to their red jackets, created a memorable spectacle that would have attracted the admiration of the late Mr Ziegfield of New York or of a top London impresario.

There were aspects unique to Lagos that remain in the memory. It was quite common to see a naked man walking along the road followed by a policeman on a bicycle carrying his clothes. This was because clothes being a valuable item, captured suspects were often ordered to strip and their clothes confiscated until they reached the police station.

This ensured that they didn't run away.

There were certain times of year when climatic conditions threw up a superabundance of living creatures. Two of these are unforgettable as 'flying ant time' and 'eel dying time'. Flying ant time occurred at dusk several times each year when the air would be thick with these creatures swarming round any light source available. Roasted or fried flying ants were a local delicacy and a good source of protein; at these times every available street lamp in Lagos had a local housewife acting as custodian and gathering the ants into a bowl as they lost their wings and fell to the ground.

Eel dying time happened once a year. The eels were in fact lampreys. They died in their millions and covered the whole surface of Lagos Harbour with a sheet of upturned white bellies. After three or four days the harbour and its surroundings stank to high heaven for about two weeks until the natural predators and carrion seekers did away with them.

Travelling with the Brigadier in the back of his staff car, we often passed a man who lived on a piece of waste ground – his only covering from the often pelting rain an upturned wheelbarrow. Max always waved to him from his staff car sporting its silver star and with his flag on the bonnet and the man waved back, making no attempt to beg. "There," said the Brigadier, "is the most contented man in Lagos."

Enugu, our furthest battalion location, was the capital of the Eastern Region across the mighty Niger River. After a nasty experience on a Bristol Frightener when one of the passengers was sick at his feet, the Brigadier decided that next time we visited the Battalion we would go by road. We used a Land Rover equipped with comfortable seats in the back because a four wheel drive vehicle was essential for some of the unpaved roads we had to use. One of the ladies from a European charity asked if she could hitch a lift. It was quite a normal request and we liked to help out whenever possible.

Mad Max agreed. "But tell her not to chatter."

I couldn't do that of course but I did tell her that he was a very reserved and rather shy bachelor. It was therefore all my fault that she regarded him as a challenge and tried to 'draw him out.' She was a spinster of uncertain age but unlikely to see forty again. She became a pain in the neck to both of us with her incessant chatter to which Max in the front seat beside the driver, responded with grunts and the occasional arched thumb in mouth. Sitting in the back with this lady I tried to take refuge in a book but it was hopeless. It was a day's journey and we started early. We travelled through Benin City, the ancient capital of the coastal region and a notorious slaving centre that I had wanted to see, but the Brigadier, normally tolerant of my interest in what to him were irrelevancies, refused to stop.

Eventually we got to the Niger and we were ferried over by motorised raft to Onitsha on the opposite bank. We drove on to Enugu arriving at about five pm. We both knew the city quite well and to my surprise the Brigadier ordered the driver to make a detour that would take us past the mines – Enugu had a large mining community. At five pm the miners were changing shift and we drove along a road crowded with African miners carrying tin lunch boxes and wearing helmets with headlamps, but otherwise completely and unselfconsciously naked. I saw the lady's jaw drop. They were well set up lads and their manhood swung from side to side in some cases as they walked. For the first time in the journey she was completely silent and wouldn't meet my eye. After she had departed I said, "That was a bit unkind," although I couldn't resist a smile.

"Kept her quiet for the last bit, though," said Max. Then, "She'll dream about that for years and what's the betting that she'll find a way to go back that way at five o'clock one day?"

Dressing after a shower in the well appointed bedroom of our new married quarter one evening, and just about to put my socks on, I noticed that a big toe was moving without any prompting from me. Suddenly, the skin broke and out popped a white maggot which crawled across the carpet. It didn't hurt at all and although it was a distasteful experience, both Heather and I knew what had happened. There was a local insect called the Tumbra Fly which laid its eggs on any fabric it could find. It was the custom in Lagos to dry washed clothes by laying them on the ground. They dried very quickly in the midday sun but should the Tumbra Fly happen to be around it would lay its eggs on, say, a vest or a pair of socks which, when worn by their owner, caused the eggs to hatch and the maggots to crawl to the nearest source of food and heat – a human body would do nicely. The maggot would feed on the body tissue until it matured and then would break out to live an independent life. Our servants had strict instructions to hang washed clothes on a line so that the flies would be put off by the clothes moving in the wind. One of my socks must have blown off. It was unpleasant but it was only harmful in the case of multiple strikes as for instance numbers of eggs on a vest or a pair of underpants when medical treatment was needed.

It was said that West Africa tended to accentuate leanings towards bizarre behaviour. Obsessions took on a new lease of life. Birdwatchers became almost fanatical about their pastime; Despite the tsetse fly, which plagued the ponies, polo players seemed to think of little else and I suppose we became ultra keen on sailing and dinghy racing. Enthusiastic drinkers needed to exercise caution lest their hobby take over. Our Brigadier, who by all accounts had always had a short fuse, seemed minded to let his emotions rip whenever anything displeased him. Neither Peter nor I could complain; he was good to us and overlooked our many deficiencies in staff work due to our inexperience. We didn't mind having the occasional book thrown at us – his aim was never very good anyway. But he did cause us problems in other ways. The Force Financial Adviser, a civil service financial watchdog charged with seeing that we didn't spend too much, was often difficult to placate when my creative accounting was suspect after the Brigadier had been on the rampage and had broken something. Fortunately the FFA was an enthusiastic small boat sailor, a fellow yacht club member and a friend.

The Brigadier was a keen horseman and kept several ponies at Lagos Racecourse. He would ride morning and evening and after breakfast would climb into his staff car to drive to the HQ in the mainland district of Apapa. One morning I was sitting in my office going through the signals, letters and other messages of the day when an apparition appeared – a one ton military water truck complete with trailer and sporting a flag on the bonnet and a silver star on a red background on the front bumper, the insignia of our Commander. In the front passenger seat with the driver grinning hugely sat the Brigadier chewing the end of his swagger cane with a crimson face and angry eyes. I quickly got through on the phone to the OC of the transport company and told him to make himself scarce.

The Brigadier stormed in, poked his head through my door and said through gritted teeth, "Get that – expletive deleted – here. Now!"

I didn't have to ask who he meant. I gave it five minutes and went into Mad Max's office.

"Major Kenworth is out visiting detachments today, sir." The arched thumb went into the mouth but the sullen glare remained. I waited for a moment then turned my back to go out, only to be struck forcibly on the back of the neck by a heavy book, the Manual of Military Law, as it happened. This was too much; it had hurt. I turned back, equally furious and was about to throw it back at him when he raised his hands, roared with laughter and shouted 'Pax'. I think the fact that for once he'd scored a hit had defused the situation.

I learned later from the OC of the transport company, what had happened. The Brigadier's staff car had broken down on the way to his house. When it didn't arrive he phoned the transport company. The duty sergeant answered and said it had left. What he actually said was,

"I go lookum sah. I go seeum. He no dere."

"Then send me something else, man."

The sergeant, a man of logical mind, sent the first set of four wheels that came to hand – the water truck. The Brigadier sent it back to have the star and flag fitted, meaning to exact retribution from the OC for failing to have a suitable spare vehicle available. Mad Max's tempers were like the old sailing adage about strong winds 'Long foretold, long last. Short warning, soon past.'

From time to time our headquarters organised and conducted recruiting marches into the jungle (or bush) up country for the units and installations under our command. The Brigadier enjoyed them and always took a staff officer to take notes. Peter Windeler usually went on these expeditions but once or twice I went instead. They were quite lavish affairs organised by one or other of our battalions and were designed to impress village headmen or chiefs of small tribes. We would take small four wheel drive vehicles either to a government bungalow in the bush or to a prearranged location along a jungle track and set up camp. An invitation would go out to the local headmen and chiefs to meet the Queen's representative on the following morning to discuss recruiting for her Army.

Next morning the chiefs and headmen would arrive with their retinues to find the Brigadier seated on a dais if it was a tented camp or on a verandah if it was a government bungalow. Behind him would be the piled drums of the nominated battalion guarded by a file of African soldiers in full ceremonial dress of red Zouave jackets and fez with shouldered rifles. A bugler would blow a call to obtain silence and the interpreter, a fluent speaker of tribal languages, would say, in effect,

'The Great Queen across the water sends you greetings. She desires more of your fine young men to become soldiers to serve her and help her to protect your lands and your country.'

After this, gifts would be exchanged. The chiefs would receive perhaps a bottle of whisky and the Brigadier would be offered live chickens walked to the meeting place on a string like dogs on a lead, fruit or small artefacts. It was all done with simple dignity and goodwill. The 'fine young men' on offer would be examined by the doctor who always accompanied these expeditions. Those who passed this cursory medical inspection were given half of a Nigerian pound note stamped with the District stamp and told to get themselves to the nearest military unit where they would be given the other half. They were then turned round and the recruiting officer's assessment, arrived at in liaison with the doctor would be written in red wax pencil on their backs. It might be 'Inf', 'Sigs', 'Asc'.

All units knew that a young man arriving at their guardroom clutching a torn in half pound note properly stamped was to be given a whole note and then despatched to the Recruitment and Training Centre where he would be thoroughly examined and re-assessed before undergoing training, often, but not necessarily always in line with what was written on his back. It was an economical and red tape free recruiting system typical of a colonial force unencumbered by a mass of civil servants. It was also pure 'Sanders of the River' brought to life and I often speculated on which of the chiefs would have most resembled Edgar Wallace's African hero, Bosambo.

Now and again if there was an urgent signal or something important in the morning mail, I would jump into our general purpose Land Rover and go to the Brigadier's house on Lagos Island, have a coffee while he was having breakfast and discuss with him action on urgent or important items. On these occasions I would pick up his *Times* from the Kingsway Stores on the way. In Nigeria we had the overseas editions of the London papers anything up to two days late. In those days the results of the Army Staff College Examination were published in *The Times* long before an official notification was received by candidates. One morning I had received a signal from a friend at the War Office to advise me to look in *The Times* for that day. Next day I invented a pretext to visit the Brigadier at breakfast time and I picked up his paper on the way. I got to his house and handed him the morning's mail followed by his newspaper.

"Anything in the paper?"

With as much unconcern as I could muster I replied. "Nothing much. Just the Staff Collage Exam results"

He looked up, pointed a finger and raised his eyebrows.

"Yes. I passed."

He gave his wolfish grin, "I know. Well done," leaving me wondering how he could know. A long time later he told me that he too had contacts at the War Office but obviously at a higher level than mine for he had known the results a few days before they were ratified and issued to the Press.

In late 1956 we had a visit from the Royal Navy. HMS *Belfast* out of Simonstown Naval Base in South Africa called in to Lagos on her way home. It fell to us to arrange a shoregoing programme for the visiting sailors and the job landed in my lap. We knew that this had to be handled with some care because with South Africa under the heel of apartheid, excesses by Jack ashore were obviously dealt with more leniently there than they would be in Lagos where no racial distinctions were drawn. We needed a programme that would keep the lower deck sober and as far as possible out of trouble.

I was discussing the visit with friends at the yacht club and bemoaning my fate at having to organise the programme when Marcus, the Scandanavian manger of the Star Brewery in Lagos, asked if he could help. Would the sailors like to visit the Brewery?

"Marcus," I said. "We're talking about British sailors. I'm trying to think of ways to keep them sober and interested and you're suggesting a visit to a brewery. Thanks, but no thanks."

"Freddie," he replied. "I can organise a two hour tour of my brewery for them ending up with a drink in my cold store and I will guarantee that they will not drink more than four small bottles of beer each – less than two pints."

Marcus was a nice fellow and a fair competitor when we were racing so I passed his offer to the Brigadier who was delighted. I had a feeling he knew it would upset the General when he heard about it but Max said get on with it. With some misgivings, I accepted Marcus's offer.

The interest was intense. Practically the whole ship's company volunteered for the brewery visit. A ships' officer went with each party

– no doubt the Captain had misgivings too. I went with one of the early parties. I had not been round the brewery before and I found it interesting. More to the point I was very keen to check that Marcus could make good his promise. After touring the various floors and being shown the complete process of beer being brewed and bottled, we descended into the cold room. Marcus, who hosted every party, then gave us a twenty minute lecture accompanied by coloured slides. The attention of the sailors tended to wander; entranced, they gazed around them at more filled beer bottles than they had ever seen in one place in their lives before. Racks and racks up to ten feet high. It was very chilly and our thin blood made us feel cold.

"And now boys," said Marcus. "You will find bottle openers on that table. The rack you can use is over there," pointing "and you can drink as much as you like on one condition – that you do not leave this room." Several hefty employees stood by the only door.

"What the hell is he playing at," I said to the ashen faced naval lieutenant who was near to me. "This is a recipe for mayhem."

But not so. Having fallen on the beer and gulped down two small bottles almost without drawing breath, the third went down noticeably more slowly and when it came to the fourth, most of the sailors were holding their stomachs and desperately trying to finish it. So far as I could see, no one could get beyond four small bottles of the ice cold lager type beer.

Marcus explained it to me when we met as guests at a drinks party thrown by the ship's officers aboard *Belfast* before she sailed. Apparently when you go from wet, heavy heat, as in Lagos, to crisp, dry cold, as in a brewery cold room, it takes about twenty minutes for the body to undergo a chemical change which renders it unable to absorb more than about two pints of cold liquid at one go. Hence Marcus's twenty minute talk.

That was the simple secret behind a successful and trouble free visit by HMS *Belfast* to Lagos in the mid 1950s. I have not been aboard her since although I see her from time to time lying in the Pool of London.

In January 1957 our small Headquarters was reinforced by two newly promoted majors from the Staff College Course of the previous year. My immediate boss was an infantry officer of the Black Watch, a man of humour and competence, who got on well with the Brigadier. Peter Windeler's new superior, a Sapper officer, who I did not get to know well, was also a competent professional, so we could to some extent take a back seat as our superiors now reported directly to the Brigadier.

A few months later the General sacked his ADC – his personal staff officer. It must have been a difficult decision because they were both members of the same regiment and the ADC was related to the General's wife. The ADC, an agreeable young man, had obviously decided that his National Service was going to be fun come what may, and several times tried the General's patience, which was soon exhausted. The ADC was sent home. I had been present on several occasions as our District representative when the General was inspecting our units and I had got to know him reasonably well. He decided that I would be a stand in ADC until his regiment could provide a replacement from England. I was appalled. I knew that I lacked both the charm and the necessary social graces to be any sort of ADC, let alone a good one. Predictably, my Brigadier objected, but the General insisted and pointed out to him that now his staff had been increased to the correct level, he could well spare me. With the worst possible grace, the Brigadier gave in.

Fortunately, I avoided having to keep the General's social diary; one of his Headquarters staff officers did that. But I did have to accompany him on visits, attend parties at Flagstaff House and see that life went smoothly for Mrs General, a gentle, delightful and completely vague lady who needed to be steered towards decisions on the numerous committees that she had to attend, usually as chairman.

The General suffered badly from gout and as he was not a sweet natured person at the best of times, he was best avoided when he was subjected to attacks of that painful complaint. It was difficult for me and I began to suspect that the departed ADC may have 'worked his ticket'.

My downfall came one day when we were due to visit the Garrison workshop where as usual there was to be a quarter guard for the General to inspect. I had long known that it was a cardinal rule for an ADC to make sure that his General never ever arrived even a few seconds before the appointed time, for in so doing he could embarrass the CO who, with his RSM, would be doing his own final inspection of his guard. I usually made a practice of instructing the driver to park the staff car a couple of minutes away from the unit to be inspected so that I could give the General a last minute briefing.

"What side of the car will the guard be on?" he said suddenly. He had never bothered about that before and I realised that this, added to a more than usual tetchiness, indicated an attack of gout. He wouldn't seek medical advice for it because he was on his last appointment before retirement and the doctors would have had him home out of the unsuitable West African climate in a flash had he complained about it.

"The right hand side," I said. "We need to change over." Whereupon, instead of getting out of the car on my side and running round to get in the other door as I realised too late that I should have done, I clambered over him, treading on his gouty foot as I did so. He, with a sharp yelp, moved to my side, glaring savagely. There was no time for recrimination. I apologised and we moved on.

These affairs invariably included lunch so that the General could meet the officers in a social setting and after lunch we moved out to the car. Having said his farewells the General turned to me, "You may make an adequate staff officer after further training but you will never be an ADC. Find you own way back to your unit." He got into his car and drove off. So ended my brief, inglorious career as an ADC.

I reported to my Brigadier next morning. He asked me why I'd been sacked. I told him the unvarnished truth.

"That's rich," he roared. He laughed till the tears came to his eyes and even though it was barely mid–morning, he dug out a bottle and insisted we had a celebratory drink.

Shortly afterwards the major sharing the nearby office with Peter Windeler, was given a puppy by a friend and well-wisher. It was a cute little thing and would wander round the offices most mornings. Suddenly it died of no outwardly discernible cause and as rabies was quite widespread in Nigeria, it was examined at the hospital. To our general alarm it had been incubating the rabies virus and both its owner and Peter Windeler had to undergo the course of twenty-one injections in the abdomen which at that time was the fate of known rabies contacts. Both the major with whom I shared an office and I were quizzed about our contacts with the dog but because we had had little to do with it and as we had no broken skin on our hands the medics decided we didn't need the jabs.

The unfortunate spin-off from this was that Peter's system reacted badly to the injections and he was whisked off to the military hospital with a raging fever. Our house was in the hospital compound and Peter's RAMC doctor, by name Kevin Coakley and a friend, came to us one evening shortly after we had heard that Peter had taken a turn for the worse. Kevin suggested I visit Peter as he had had a relapse and in the doctor's words, "We may lose him." I went to visit Peter at once. I found him awake but rambling unintelligibly and being tended to by Jean, his wife. She told me that the doctors had said that his only hope was a new drug, Cortisone, and that the only source in the country was her dispensary at the Shell installation. They were rushing it to the military hospital as we spoke. Jean and the Shell Oil Company saved Peter's life that evening. The drug arrived and he made a rapid recovery.

Max had told me that I would have to 'sweat it out' in Lagos for two years but that I would have a good chance of selection for the Staff College Course of 1958, and so it proved. As I was to leave Nigeria before Christmas 1957 my family and I would miss recuperation leave but that was no real hardship. We were to return to England by a twin engined Viking aircraft of Eagle Airways, under charter to the Army Movements branch. The journey would take three days with two overnight stops.

One of the more pleasant activities that most of us indulged in was gecko watching. These harmless and engaging little lizards are co-occupants of all permanent buildings in the tropics and watching their antics on the walls of the living room while seated comfortably in an armchair with a cooling drink, became a normal evening habit. It was said that watching them was fine. Talking to them was acceptable, but when they answered back it was time to go home. I had spent six months longer on 'The Coast' without leave than was normal, and having had a distinct impression that the biggest gecko in our household tribe was about to clear its throat and address me, it was undoubtedly time to go home.

My secondment had been lively, sometimes infuriating but packed with incident and never dull. We had made and cemented friendships that endured. I can't say, hand on heart, that I liked the climate much; it was particularly hard on young children. I had no plans to return. The people were OK. The ordinary African is hard working and good-natured and in my view he deserves a better deal than his leaders and politicians have given him in the past half century.

I said goodbye to my Brigadier with genuine regret. For all his eccentricities he was a professional soldier to his fingertips. He had had what we used to call 'a good war', fighting his battalion across Europe until the war's end. I remembered his rages, wonderful to behold, his many kindnesses and his somewhat wolfish sense of humour, reminiscent in some ways of my father. I remembered too, his superb off the cuff talks during officer training days on basic infantry tactics and fieldcraft. He had the gift of bringing dry subjects to life. Patrolling, for instance, the infantry commander's tried and proven method of gaining real time intelligence. His dissertations on this were utterly compelling. Max would be with the patrol commander as though he was sitting on his shoulder from the moment he left his own wire until he returned, giving the correct password. He would liken the patrol commander to a gamekeeper seeking poachers; drawing information from a broken twig, flattened grass or any unusual circumstance along his route. Everyone, however tired, stayed wide awake during the Brigadier's summing-up after an exercise, not because they felt they had to but because it was well nigh impossible to do otherwise if you had any interest in your profession. To my great regret I have not seen him since. Rumour had it that he retired to South America as the riding master and manager of a string of polo ponies for a rich Argentinian rancher.

The Eagle Viking was a small, propellor driven aircraft comfortably fitted out and seating four abreast in rows divided by a central aisle. There were about forty passengers on our trip. We flew at something under 10,000 feet with frequent refuelling stops northwards along the West African coast. This allowed us to see more of Africa than would have been possible had we been flying BOAC direct from Lagos to London Airport and stopping only at Kaduna. Our first stop was at Sierra Leone, still a British colony, where we refuelled and had a meal, courtesy of the local RWAFF units. The gossip centred around Illicit Diamond Buying or IDB, which was of pressing concern to the local Colonial Service administrators. Then on to the Gambia where we stayed overnight, again under the wing of the Royal West African Frontier Force. This was a particularly attractive small colony astride the Gambia River and sliced into the territory of Senegal much as one might take a small slice out of a melon. The Officers' Mess Annexe where we spent the night, sat upon a cliff overlooking the sea where the cool breeze on a magical evening gave us doubts about the wisdom of going home to face an English December.

Next day the interminable mangrove swamp and inland palms slowly gave place to bare and stony desert until we reached the next refuelling stop at Rio de Oro, a Spanish penal settlement where the prisoners, dressed in grey flannel uniform, seemed to have the run of the place without much supervision. We supposed that this was because that there was simply nowhere to go – with trackless desert on one side and the Atlantic Ocean on the other – a sort of mainland Devil's Island. It was quite depressing and we were glad to get out of it. A further refuelling stop was made in Morocco at the pleasant little seaside settlement of Agadir, shortly afterwards to be the scene of a disastrous earthquake with widespread destruction and loss of life. Now rebuilt, it is a well patronised holiday spot for tourists from Europe.

As we flew northwards, signs of civilisation became more frequent. The cabin staff kept us well informed. The Atlas Mountains, snowcapped and impressive to our right; The cities of Marrakesh, Casablanca, Rabat and Tangier appeared below us and then unmistakeably, Gibraltar slipped into view. We made a wide circle to the north west and landed for a night stop at the famous Rock Hotel. The temperature had dropped considerably and warm clothing was worn for the first time in many months.

Our two small girls had an early meal and were bedded down for the night with a nanny to be arranged by the hotel while we went to dinner. They were in a room next to ours with a communicating door but there was also a door leading to the corridor. Helen, at six years old, was bidden to read to her younger sister while we changed and waited for the nanny to appear. Suddenly Heather heard what appeared to be an adult female voice from the childrens' room. I rushed in half-dressed, and saw a very beautiful woman sitting on Helen's bed reading to the children. This vision rose at my appearance and apologised gracefully, explaining that she had been passing in the corridor and the children looked so lovely that she had to talk to them, gave each of the girls a peck on the cheek and vanished.

Later on we were dining with Robert Lyle and his wife in the hotel restaurant when my vision appeared with a distinguished looking man and took a table quite close to us.

"Know who that is?" said Robert, and without giving me a chance to say what had happened earlier, he went on, "Anna Neagle with her husband, Herbert Wilcox."

In the nineteen fifties she was a famous British film star. I had seen her in such blockbusters as *Spring in Park Lane* and equally famously in period dramas – a screen legend of the day. Something to tell the girls when they grew older.

We took off early next morning and to our disappointment skipped the planned refuelling stop at Biarritz, the pilot having decided that he had enough fuel to make Stanstead without stopping. We landed there in early afternoon on a cold and miserable December day and spent our disembarkation leave and Christmas visiting our families.

12

Staff College

A Year at Camberley

It was, and to a much lesser extent still is, unusual for professional service officers to be house owners. We were nomads, liable to be moved elsewhere, often abroad, for two or three years at a time. It therefore made little sense to be saddled with a mortgage for bricks and mortar when it would rarely, if ever, be occupied by its owner during his service career: also in our case, boarding school fees loomed in the not too distant future. The Service provided comfortable married quarters at a reasonable cost and when there were not enough to go round there was an efficient system that hired suitable properties for which the serviceman paid the standard Service rent.

Problems arose when there was a long gap between an officer and his family arriving home and a quarter in his new station becoming available. This was the case for us at this juncture for the first time. We had about a month before I was due to report to the Staff College at Camberley and in the interim I was held on the paper strength of a faceless and unvisited establishment somewhere in north London. Heather had two elderly maiden aunts who owned a large house on the outskirts of Salisbury that had plenty of spare space, more than enough to accommodate our family. They loved children and were genuinely delighted that we agreed to stay with them until we could take up our married quarter at Camberley. We were lucky. The aunts made it plain that they would consider it a privilege to have us when we were in between postings and of course I insisted that we should pay our way. We stayed with them many times; the girls adored them and when we were in Germany or at a distance not too far for them to travel, they visited and stayed with us from time to time.

Arriving in Camberley in January 1958, we were given a married quarter within walking distance of the Staff College in the 'patch' located outside the College grounds reserved for those with at least two children. Camberley in the late fifties was still a smallish town with a distinctly Betjemanish flavour in that it still had a high proportion of retired Service officers among its citizens, although Miss Joan Hunter Dunn would have been getting on a bit by then.

The main road to London before the arrival of the M3 was the A30 that ran through the northern edge of Camberley dividing the built up areas neatly from the extensive grounds that contained the Royal Military Academy, Sandhurst and the adjoining Army Staff College. Our wives shopped in the town and found it attractive in those pre-supermarket days of small shops and personal attention, but if asked, many of us would choose Miss Ward and her dogs as one of our most abiding memories of Camberley's civilian face. 'Kate', as she was known to us, was a grey haired lady of mature years, invariably dressed in black two-piece garments down to her ankles. She had made it her purpose in life to look after stray dogs and she could be seen every day taking her dogs for a walk around the town. It was more of a procession than a walk. She pushed a large contrivance made of scrap wood and mounted on four perambulator wheels around Camberley's pavements: this was full of smallish dogs, perhaps five or six. Tied to the 'pram' handles were at least five bigger dogs, the whole ensemble kicking up a barking and yapping chorus that could be heard streets away. She had obviously become a 'character' and was shown a great deal of indulgence from all quarters.

It was the start of an enjoyable albeit high pressure year. We, the students, were in the main senior captains. The instructors, or DS (Directing Staff) as they were known, were not much older than the students; they were senior majors given the local (unpaid) rank of lieutenant colonels either to enhance their power as a disciplinary force or to increase the distance in rank and so add enchantment to the view – we were never quite sure which. They were, however, old enough to have been through at least part of the Second world War and often at more senior rank, so they were well suited to teach those students, and there were many, who had not yet heard a gun fired in anger. They were also intelligent, observant and articulate. They had to be; the students they were dealing with had cleared many hurdles in order to get to the Staff College and so were at least reasonably sharp and quick witted.

The hierarchy of the College was impressively senior. Looming over all was the Commandant, a major general. In my year as a student it was General Poett, an eminent gunner; as a brigadier he was one of the first senior officers to have parachuted into Normandy on D-Day. He was a benign and somewhat avuncular figure. He had no need to be a whip cracker. He presided over an establishment that was a headmaster's dream. Every member of the student body would be keen to put up a performance impressive enough to collar a good final report and grading. The Commandant was supported by a deputy who was a brigadier and effectively his chief executive, and three colonels, each responsible for one of the College's three divisions. It was an efficient and tightly controlled training organisation that had survived a century's wars and campaigns. 1958 was the Staff College Centenary year and we were to be honoured by a visit from the Queen and Prince Philip.

The College, its administration and two of its three divisions, A and B, were located in a purpose built Victorian building in the grounds of the Royal Military Academy at Sandhurst. Its wartime expansion had necessitated the establishment of a third division and C Division was located at Minley Manor a few miles to the west along the A30. Although I was in B Division and thus based in the Staff College main building at Camberley, I got to know Minley quite well because Heather's two maiden aunts, Winifred and Dorothy, had been nurses – VADs – there when it had been a military hospital in the First World War. They had each become engaged to young officers who had returned to their units in France and been killed in action. They had never married and they loved to visit Minley to wander round the extensive gardens and reminisce. We took them whenever possible.

The instruction was tutorial, based on syndicates of ten, each presided over by a DS with both students and instructors changing each term. Divisions had about sixty students who stayed within that division for the whole year. About one third of the student body of 180 officers was from outside the United Kingdom. There were six terms dealing with aspects of strife in which the Army may become involved, from police actions to counter insurgency, limited war through to global conflicts. Geo-politics came into it of course, under the generic heading of Current Affairs. Curiously, military history was neglected. We had had to take an examination paper on the subject but little attention was paid to pre Second World War campaigns during the Course. As a firm believer in the well known debating motion 'We learn from history that we do not learn from history', I thought that this was a mistake, particularly in the field of logistics.

As the course progressed down the year with practical exercises, classroom discussions and superb presentations, rounded off by lectures and question and answer sessions from top rank speakers across a wide range of military and civilian subjects, I was seized by a thought that gradually became a conviction. I began to realise that at thirty-two and despite fifteen years of military service across much of the world, before attending this course I had still only scratched the surface of the complexities of my profession. This conviction was enhanced when we attended the traditional Battlefield Tour in Normandy.

The Tour was the highlight of the Course. The complete student body accompanied by the instructors and the College hierarchy decamped to Normandy. Five of us, like-minded small boat sailors, obtained permission to make our own way to France. We planned to sail across the Channel from Southampton Water to Ouistreham at the entrance to the Caen Canal. We hired a converted lifeboat from a retired and aged sapper officer known to one of our number who, because he had hired the boat, was elected skipper. The boat was at least as old as its ancient owner and the gear had seen better days, but the weather was good and despite a broken boom and a false landfall on the French side, we eventually locked into the Caen Canal and joined the rest of the Course, billeted at the College Technique in Caen. It was less than fourteen years since the end of the war in Europe. Most of our instructors had personal experiences to offer us and these were supplemented by a number of guest speakers from both sides, Allied and German. Major John Howard gave us a first-hand account of the glider borne assault at Pegasus Bridge that he had commanded on D Day; Sergeant Major Stan Hollis VC, of 5th Battalion The Green Howards, took us over the beaches to the advance inland and Major Hans von Luck of a German panzer regiment gave us his experience of Operation Goodwood, the battle for Caen, from the enemy side. Our own divisional Colonel, Brian Wyldebore Smith, held us spellbound with an account of the first few days of Goodwood, in which he took part. For me it was the first of several of these tours, all of which I enjoyed and on each of which I learned more about my profession.

We returned to our boat to sail back home. After locking out of the Caen Canal, and setting course for the Nab Tower, the skipper said he anticipated 'a fast passage to the Wight'. Twelve hours later, the wind had dropped, we had drifted well off course with the tide and the lights of the French coast could still be seen astern. 'At this rate', I thought 'We'll hit Omaha Beach in another twelve hours'. Eventually, however, the wind rose, mercifully from the south, and we managed a very oblique broad reach across the Channel with a loose footed mainsail assisted by the small diesel engine, arriving back in the Itchen River nearly a day late.

On the way into the Solent and sailing past Bembridge Ledge, I was on watch at about 5 a.m. when we were hailed from a smart grey painted launch manned by a crew in a naval style of uniform which I did not recognise. We had no radio; signalling between small craft in those days was by Aldis lamp using Morse Code, sometimes by flags which few amateurs had on board, but more usually by shouting through a cone shaped loud hailer. I had no idea what they wanted so I waved cheerfully and gestured in the general direction of the entrance to Southampton Water. When we arrived back at our berth we were boarded by a Customs Officer and duly declared our pitiful purchases. Declarations completed, the customs man pointed to a dinghy which had suddenly appeared alongside us containing four fit looking young men wearing overalls who placed official looking peaked caps on their heads and came aboard without asking permission.

"As a result of your failure to acknowledge the challenge of the Customs pinnace crew this morning," he said portentously. "It has been decided that your craft will be subject to search."

We attempted to explain that we were penurious Army officers with neither time, funds nor inclination to do any smuggling but he was adamant. They went through every inch of the boat with rods and mirrors, watched by us with great interest. Had we been potential smugglers it would have been an object lesson in how to avoid places that 'rummage teams' would check. Of course they didn't find anything and the team leader was so disconsolate that the Brigade of Guards' yacht *Gladeye* which followed us in later crewed by Guards' officers and allegedly crammed to the 'gunnels' with nylons and scent, didn't suffer a visit from customs at all.

It was customary for each commandant at the Staff College to exploit his opportunity to influence the rising generation of staff officers by releasing at least one bee from his bonnet. In my student year it was public speaking. Our Commandant was convinced that army officers in general and British Army officers in particular, lacked the ability to speak without notes in public. Accordingly we were told that at some time during the year and without prior warning, each student from the British Army, together with students from nations where English was their first language, would be required to speak without notes for fifteen minutes on a subject of his choice. This of course brought in the Old Commonwealth nations and the USA as well as the Royal Navy and the RAF. The result was that each of us prepared and typed a 'lecturette'. This was carefully and painstakingly memorised and accompanied us wherever we went. The DS joined in the fun and kept us on tenterhooks with broad hints, seldom realised.

One morning with Mr Soames, the Army Minister in 1958, sitting in on a plenary session of our Division, Brian Wyldebore Smith, presiding, suddenly said:

"We've got a bit of space before the next session Minister, would you like to sit in on a couple of lecturettes?" The minister said he'd be delighted.

"Right," said the Colonel. He fished a piece of paper out of his pocket, "Who haven't we had? Pollard? No, he's ticked. Plaskett – front and centre!"

I had been hoping to escape but rose resignedly to my feet and addressed over sixty of my contemporaries and superiors on the subject of Nigeria, the nation and its politics, conscious all the while that there was at least one African member of my audience who knew more about it than I did – Captain Sam Ademulegan, a fellow member of the Royal West African Frontier Force. Without at that stage much experience of public speaking it was impossible to tell if I was making an impression or indeed whether or not anyone was actually listening.

Confirmation that they were alert came when I referred to a recent population census in Nigeria as something of a 'cockshy' because of poor administration, my words being drowned in a howl of raucous laughter led by the Minister. That sort of thing works wonders for morale, although few of my friends would believe that the joke was unintentional.

The course included at least one officer per division from each of the other two armed services and several from the Royal Marines. They made invaluable contributions during syndicate discussions when any form of joint service activity was being discussed, but apart from that they could well have been chosen for their personalities for they were all humorists. I am indebted to an RAF student for the following tale; it is a true story, later confirmed by others present.

Each year the army medics of the Aldershot area arranged a demonstration of field hospital activity for the students during the course. They were experts at lending realism to the most gory sights – amputations, sucking wounds, blood all over the place. These exhibitions took place in the grounds of Minley Manor, home to the College 'C' Division, presided over in my student year by a fiery colonel from an old army family. He spoke in brief barks and had a short way with anything that displeased him. During the medical demonstration one of the DS approached the colonel and asked if one of his syndicate students, a naval officer as it happened, could be excused as he was feeling faint.

"Why?" asked the colonel.

"Well, to be honest, sir, I don't think he's too happy about all the blood around."

"What! Doesn't like blood! Doesn't like blood! Good God. What does the feller like!"

Most of us looked back on our year as students at Camberley with nostalgia. To begin with we were all about the same age. In the main we were married with young children and there was a comprehensive social programme. Our wives had similar interests and we made friendships that lasted throughout our service years and beyond. There was an astonishing amount of talent compressed into each course of about 180 students. Owl Pie, the Staff College annual journal, edited and written by the students, contained much high grade satire of the Private Eye variety. Although designed for course consumption and thus full of 'in' gossip it was nevertheless a good read. In my student year, the annual pantomime was written by an officer who later became a successful playwright.

As on most high pressure courses there had been some casualties, those who in the opinion of our seniors would not, for one reason or another, benefit sufficiently from the course to become effective staff officers. They were few and they vanished overnight without fuss. There was a report on each of us but we did not see it. It was one of the few unseen reports on individuals in an Army career. Our normal annual assessment reports were, seen, initialled and subject to appeal.

For us the main result from the Course was a new posting; the list, pinned up on a notice board, was eagerly awaited and greeted with mixed reactions. Groans from those posted to the War Office in London. Disappointment from those going to major UK formations – Command and District Headquarters. Satisfaction from those posted to field formations in Germany. Elation from those going to active formations, divisions and brigades outside Europe. I, or rather we, for it was an 'accompanied' posting that included one's family, came into the elated category. I was posted to a General Staff appointment with 17th Gurkha Division in Malaya, where there was still a major counter insurgency action, officially known as an 'Emergency' but sometimes more correctly described as a guerrilla war, going on. Heather was very pleased. The girls were still young enough to go with us and we could get through the three year tour without needing to send them home to boarding school.

13

By Trooper to Singapore

We embarked on the troopship *Empire Fowey* at Southampton in January 1959 for a three week journey to Singapore. The old ship had started life as a 'strength through joy' vessel during the Nazi era and had been 'liberated' by the British at the end of the war to be put to work as a troopship. By now she was showing her age although we had no complaints about our accommodation. We were in a four berth cabin; the girls, aged eight and five respectively, viewed the whole experience as an extended holiday as indeed did Heather. It was my fourth and her first journey by troopship and she was determined to enjoy it. For me there were occasional training sessions to organise and spells of ship's duty officer came round at intervals but it was a sheer delight to share such a journey as a family and we made the most of it.

Initially there was one irritation that had to be dispensed with. It was the practice of the Ships' Commandants on troopships to make the best possible use of the officers and warrant officers who were placed for the time being in his charge. Where there were formed units travelling he had to tread carefully as commanding officers kept tight control of their regiments when on board, but individual reinforcements as in my case, were fair game and could be allotted to various duties which may or may not have any relevance to their expertise.

I was made Ship's Messing Officer. This entailed working closely with the Purser on planning menus and dealing with any complaints about the food from the soldiers, sailors and airmen aboard. It should not have been a problem – indeed it should have been a fairly cushy job. The soldiers rarely complained about the food, which was considerably better and more varied than they were used to in those days when regimental cooks held sway and the expertise of the excellent Army Catering Corps had not spread throughout the Army. The sailors too were happy provided that their rum ration was issued daily. There was, however, a large RAF contingent on board and as I knew from my own experience, the RAF were generally better fed and more comfortably accommodated than either the Army or the Navy.

This, I think, was a spin off from the fact that RAF stations by their nature were static and not subject to the gyrations suffered by the other two services, so their administration was more deeply rooted and thus better organised. But the ship's food was wholesome and plentiful and the menus were as varied as the Purser's long experience could make them. Unavoidably, there were long gaps between the places where fresh food could be taken on board and this upset the less easily pleased members of the troopdecks, the RAF being well to the fore in the matter of complaints at the regular mess meetings.

I was no more experienced in the matter of planning menus or dealing constructively with complaints about food than any other regimental officer, and since there was no remedy for these gripes other than a daily air drop of fresh rations, which was out of the question, I began to find the mess meetings both irritating and frustrating and I suggested to the Commandant that I should change jobs halfway through the journey.

"Not a chance," he said. "There are no specialist messing officers aboard and you'll just have to get on with it."

Then I noticed that the bewinged and unduly taciturn RAF squadron leader in the cabin about three doors away from ours looked rather old to be flying. He could, of course, have been an air traffic controller, but it was more likely that he had transferred from flying to some form of administrative work. I made some discreet enquiries. Well, well, well! He was a specialist messing officer who had sensibly kept quiet about it when he came aboard. Moreover he was travelling unaccompanied and had neither family nor job, so far as I could see, to erode his enforced leisure.

The Purser was as irritated as I had been about the higher than usual level of complaints, so I suggested to him that the RAF specialist messing officer who I knew to be aboard might have some useful suggestions. He wondered why he hadn't been told about him and said he would take it up with the Commandant. The upshot was that I was relieved of an unpleasant job just after we cleared Port Said, the Purser apologising profusely but he was sure that I would understand. The Ship's Commandant, however, knew exactly what had happened. Like most of his breed, he was a lieutenant colonel on his last appointment before retiring and wise in the ways of the Service. He told me to emulate Brer Rabbit for the rest of the voyage; I took this to mean 'lie low and say nuffin', which I did.

That was the last troopship voyage we made. For me it was certainly the most pleasant. There was a children's school aboard, organised and run by the several Royal Army Education Corps sergeants on the way to Singapore, so the girls were off our hands until lunchtime. We were not allowed ashore at Port Said or at Suez with the political situation in Egypt still somewhat tricky at that time, but the usual Port Said bumboats came alongside and did a roaring trade with pouffes of coloured leather vying with camel saddles and smaller leather geegaws for popularity. Aden was the first run ashore and the families marvelled at the cheapness of the duty free goods on sale in Crater, the traditional shopping district for visiting liner passengers. German and Japanese cameras, radios and binoculars were the most popular purchases here.

Porpoises and dolphins made their appearance shortly after we left Aden, leaping and gambolling in the bow wave of the ship; early morning walkers on the lower weather decks might find a high altitude member of the flying fish species gasping its last. From time to time an ocean going dhow would appear, tracking across the centuries old trading route from the east coast of Africa to India and beyond, with its enormous lateen sail pulling powerfully and making a splendid photo opportunity for the new cameras bought in Aden. But most of the time it was sunbathing and joining the troops in PT, weapon training and competition rifle firing over the stern of the ship, while voyaging in the warm December sunshine over a sea just slightly rippled by the trade wind.

Colombo was the next port of call and tradition had it that we should repair to the Mount Lavinia Hotel for tea and an opportunity to view and possibly buy moonstones from the gem traders of the Ceylon coast. But luckily Heather's superstitious mother had persuaded her three daughters that both moonstones and the opals for which they were sometimes mistaken, were unlucky; this allowed my usual rocky finances to hold firm against the blandishments of the traders. Regrettably, there was insufficient shore time to visit Kandy, in the centre of the Island and the home of the fabled Temple of the Tooth, a relic reputed to have first erupted from the gums of the true Buddha. Colombo was and is a pleasant city, sadly troubled more recently by ethnic unrest.

On across the Indian Ocean into the Strait of Malacca leaving the Nicobar Islands to the north and the tip of Sumatra to the south, seeing land on both sides as we moved southwards down the Malayan Peninsular into the Harbour of Singapore. I had been there before on my way to and from Korea and so had a vague idea of the geography of the place, but that didn't matter, for we were taken under the wing of the military movements organisation as soon as we arrived there.

14
Malaya. The Emergency.

Not Quite a War

There was no waiting around. On the afternoon of our arrival we were taken to the station for the onward train journey to the Gurkha Division Headquarters. This was located halfway up Malaya on the western side about forty miles south of Kuala Lumpur (KL), the capital city. The train was protected because the war was still going on and some states were still 'Black' and subject to terrorist activity. The Singapore to KL train had been attacked from time to time during previous years and a businesslike platoon of Gurkha infantry was deployed with it for the journey. It had also been delayed from time to time by the presence of wild animals on the line, a fact that the terrorists had not been slow to exploit, and a drill for coping with this situation had been developed and practised down to a slickness that was a pleasure to see.

We arrived without incident at the town of Seremban. This attractive little place, the location of HQ 17 Gurkha Division, was the state capital of Negri Sembilan, where the Sultan, the head of state, lived in his palace – The Istana. It should be explained that Malaya was ruled by a king, the Yang di Pertuan Agong, translated roughly as 'He who is Chosen Lord' and shortened in conversation to the less formal 'Agong'. He was supported by a committee of princes or sultans who were heads of the respective states into which the country was divided. Succession to the throne was decided by this committee after the king had died. Within their home states, the sultans were very important and well respected by the Malay and minority Chinese and Indian population.

As usual there was no married quarter available for us and until one became available we were allotted rooms in the military hostel that rejoiced in the name of 'Purity Lodge' – for reasons lost in time. This stood on the side of a hill looking out over the compound of the state game warden. When we arrived one of the compound cages was occupied by a sick tiger with a very bad cough. He was a noisy beast and a coughing fit would frequently end in a bad tempered roar, allowing my elder daughters to be able to boast with truth that they had often been woken up in their youth by a roaring tiger only feet away from their beds. We lived there for several weeks and it was impossible not to make comparisons with West Africa. Although we were new to Malaya and there were active offensive operations in progress, there was an alluring feel to the country and we felt that we would like it. For a start, although warm and humid, it was considerably less so than Lagos and the evenings were sometimes quite cool. Then, instead of smelly mangrove swamps, the jungle was well drained but very dense in parts. Also, it was quite well stocked with wildlife ranging from elephants in the south through tigers and monkeys to several varieties of poisonous snakes and dangerous hornets, centipedes and the like. Long trousers, rolled down sleeves and two watchful eyes were essential equipment for a jungle trek. Withal, it was a civilised place and many civilian planters had spent their working lives there. Seremban had an excellent and well patronised civilian club – the Sungei Ujong – thoroughly multi-racial with European, Malay and Chinese members. The coastal town of Port Dixon with good sailing facilities and an active yacht club was only a few miles to the west of us.

I was to take over my new appointment from a British Gurkha officer, John Cross, recently promoted to major and very well known throughout the Brigade of Gurkhas. He spoke fluent, almost colloquial Gurkhali and had published books on the subject of English for Gurkha soldiers. He made the handover an easy task and although a bachelor, he was kindness itself to Heather and our children, showing them round the town and introducing the girls to the 'coughing tiger' through the good offices of his friend, the game warden. John, also quite fluent in Mandarin Chinese, held a party for his friends before his departure to which Heather and I were invited. It took the form of a Chinese banquet at the principal Chinese restaurant in Seremban It was explained to us that tradition dictated that there would be as many courses as there were to be guests and that beer or brandy would be served between each course. It would therefore be sensible to eat sparingly because politeness dictated that guests should eat something from each dish placed before them. There were about fifteen guests.

We took this advice but the standard of the cuisine was unmatched by the many Chinese restaurants that I had previously visited and I rather overdid it, with the result that by the time that the Chinese gourmet dish of 'hundred day old' eggs came round, I was totally unable to cope. My resourceful wife, who ate sparingly but couldn't face a dish of whole blackened eggs, quietly slipped one from each of our plates into her handbag, thus saving face. When last I heard of him John Cross was living a happy and fulfilled retirement in Nepal among his beloved Gurkhas.

After weathering the acclimatisation and settling in processes that always follow arrival with a family in a tropical station, we finally fetched up in our new married quarter close to a rubber plantation on Limbok Hill on the outskirts of Seremban. We had only one near neighbour, John, a friendly and likeable major of the Royal Army Ordnance Corps – he was a supply specialist in the Gurkha Division Headquarters. From the back verandah of our square and rather unlovely dwelling, we had a distant view of the Istana, also on the outskirts of the town. We were lucky enough to recruit two Cantonese women as servants (amahs) doubling up as nannies. Cantonese amahs were traditionally garbed in black trousers and white tops; they were known as 'black and whites' and were generally regarded as by far the best available – clean, hardworking and scrupulously honest. Ah Phun, the senior and Ah Yih, her assistant, were spinsters, both mature women in their late thirties; between them they made our three year tour in Malaya a pleasure. They loved children and we could leave them to look after the girls with no qualms. We also employed a 'kebun', a Malay gardener who came every four days – his idea, not mine; presumably he had a personal calender that discounted weeks and months. None of us could wrap our tongues round his name so we called him Harry Ampat, Hari being the Malay word for day and Ampat being the word for four. He was a cheerful old chap and a competent gardener.

The omens were all good. I had benefited professionally from the Staff College course to the extent that I now felt that I knew what I was about as a staff officer on an operational Headquarters and I enjoyed my job. 17th Gurkha Division was descended in a direct line from the celebrated 17th Indian Division of Second World War fame although the black cat and palm tree shoulder flash had been replaced by crossed kukris to signify its new Gurkha parentage. It had three brigades under command. 28th Commonwealth Brigade operated out of Taiping in northern Malaya with one Australian and two British battalions and there were two Gurkha brigades, one in Johore Bahru, to the north of the Strait Causeway to Singapore, and one on Singapore Island itself. The Divisional Commander when I arrived there was Major General Robertson, a distinguished officer who had spent his career with Gurkha soldiers, having been commissioned from Sandhurst into 6th Gurkhas well before the war. He was easy to get on with which was just as well because my job dictated that I worked directly to him for much of the time. I had been posted in as a captain GSO3 Staff Duties and Training with an indication that the job was likely to be upgraded. This happened a few months later and I became a Temporary Major GSO2. The temporary rank meant that I got paid as a major and wore the badges of rank but that if I fell down on the job I could be sacked and reverted to my substantive rank of captain without fuss. It was not possible to achieve the substantive rank of major before the age of thirty-four, a matter of eighteen months hence. The Army abounded with such dodges to keep you on your toes and no one really minded; it was as much a vocation as a profession, particularly when on active service.

My immediate superior was the Division's GSO 1, a Rifle Brigade lieutenant colonel, soon to be relieved. I reported to him on my first morning for duty, suffused with keenness and anxious to learn about the state of the Emergency as it was known, 'war' in the opinion of the politicians being a bit too heavy for what had been going on even though we were deploying as many fighting troops as we had had in Korea. On the G1's office wall there was a large map of Malaya with red and green flags stuck in it seemingly all over the country.

"Are those the locations of recent incidents?" I asked. He looked at me strangely.

"Recent incidents?" He pointed. "The red ones are eighteen hole courses. The green ones are nine hole courses. We don't advertise our incidents. They're kept under wraps in the Ops Room."

Not a good start. Deflated, I saluted and went to seek my new office. Later I discovered that Malaya was riddled with golf courses The General did a good deal of travelling all over Malaya and Singapore. It was usually a case of inspecting or just visiting units and on these occasions I often accompanied him to take notes and write them up on return. In consequence I saw a good deal of the country by air and by road and became familiar with the conditions that units lived under in the jungle.

During the Emergency the states within Malaya were graded by degrees of terrorist activity. Black was the highest grade, necessitating a strong military presence and high security measures for vulnerable points and critical installations. All vehicles moved in convoy with military escorts within Black states. Grey was an intermediate grade and meant that terrorist activity was either light to start with or was decreasing due to pressure from the security forces. White meant a relaxation of security measures down as far as simple surveillance, and in white states it was not necessary for vehicles to move in convoy. Nevertheless, long after Negri Sembilan achieved white status, several of the wives of planter friends living on rubber estates around Seremban kept loaded pistols in their trug baskets when picking flowers in their gardens. Towards the end of 1959, however, large areas of the Peninsular were steadily achieving white status. The Communist Terrorists (CTs) retreated into deeper jungle, the main body, controlled by their leader Chin Peng, being driven daily northwards.

Much of our travelling on duty was done by light aircraft, the workhorse being the Auster, a small three or four seat high wing monoplane. Our Headquarters at Seremban had its own communication flight located at Paroi airstrip on the jungle's edge a few miles from the HQ. Coincidentally, Paroi Camp had been the Headquarters of Subhas Chandra Bose and his desperadoes of the INA when they were allies of the Japanese during the Second World War and before my battalion encountered them in Calcutta in the mid nineteen forties.

Flying over the jungle canopy it was easy to see why navigation was so important. There were very few reference points or landmarks in the sea of green that stretched through a three hundred and sixty degree horizon – bearing in mind that the Auster flew at no more than a few hundred feet. Not long after I arrived in Seremban a visiting pilot on a short test flight with one of the aircraft technicians from Paroi crashed somewhere in the jungle, obviously not far from the airstrip, but an exhaustive air and ground search over five days failed to find them. They did not emerge and radio contact had been severed indicating that they were either dead or injured. There was no sign of the aircraft.

About eighteen months later a Chinese contractor searching for usable timber in primary forest found the wreckage of the Auster close to a small stream at a distance of nine miles as the crow – or aircraft – flies from Paroi strip. The passenger was still strapped in his seat, probably killed on impact. The pilot's remains were found near to the stream; he had obviously managed to crawl a short distance from the aircraft. The body bore signs of attention from wild animals. This somewhat grisly tale underlines the truth of the title of Spencer Chapman's book about Malaya, that 'the jungle is neutral'. In that case neither the pilot nor his passenger had much of a chance as their means of communication were inoperable and the survivor was clearly badly injured, but it underlined for us the fact that jungle trekking on foot was no jaunt. Not only was it necessary to stay alert at all times, it was also necessary to know exactly where you are and to travel with some non electronic means of communication such as a verey pistol.

There were less serious incidents when travelling by light aircraft that could be laughed about later. Sergeant Pilot Wastell of the Army Air Corps with whom I travelled from time to time was flying alone (or so he thought) on one occasion when from the instrument panel in front of him the head of a large snake slowly emerged. He had no idea if it was dangerous or not and by his own account remained open mouthed for seconds before jabbering into his voice transmitter. Austers, like most small aircraft, needed hands on attention. There was no automatic pilot that would have let him take a back seat and of course we flew without parachutes. In any case only a fool would prefer jumping into the trackless jungle in preference to staying in the aircraft if there was an option. When he had managed to convince his ground controller that he was serious – having initially been told to 'take more water with it'- he was instructed to fly as quietly and gently as possible in the circumstances to the nearest airstrip, then land and 'evacuate the aircraft'. He landed safely with the snake sunning itself on the console and the incident received some coverage in the local papers.

There was a sequel. Years later in the late sixties when I was stationed in Germany I had to undertake a reconnaissance for an exercise that I was organising in France. I booked a light aircraft from the communication flight at Rheindahlen on the Dutch border and to my surprise I found that my pilot was to be Sergeant Major Wastell, he of the cockpit snake, now promoted to a higher dignity. Unsurprisingly, he didn't remember me after ten years, for his job was piloting staff officers with whom he had a necessarily fleeting aquaintance, but of course I remembered him because of the snake incident, which I mentioned. His reaction was surprising.

"Sir," he said excitedly, "I've been waiting for someone like you to come along. We've got a few minutes before I file the flight plan. Would you please come with me?" He led me to the pilots' rest room where there were several NCOs and warrant officers reading and gossiping. Calling for quiet, he turned to me.

"Sir," he said again. "You will raise my morale enormously if you would now tell these disbelieving gits about the snake in Malaya." Apparently no one had believed his story and he had been ribbed unmercifully for making it up. I was happy to confirm the truth of it, leaving one contented warrant officer and several bemused pilots.

The job of a GSO 2 (SD) in a divisional headquarters embraces just about anything his superiors want it to embrace. The bulk of it entails examining and reporting on unit and lower formation establishments, accompanying the general on his visits and inspections, organising programmes for visiting notables, including senior Service officers and politicians and taking the minutes at high level and usually security classified conferences. While it was by no means a sinecure because there were so many opportunities for mistakes, it was interesting and varied. I was lucky enough during our three years in Malaya to have three incumbents of the 'head of branch' GSO1 appointment who, while always available with sound advice or direction when asked for it, generally let me get on with what I had to do with the minimum interference. Nevertheless, odd jobs with a General Staff flavour usually landed in SD.

It therefore fell naturally to me to organise and escort the party of very senior visitors from the Imperial Defence College (IDC) in London during their brief visit to 17 Division as part of their Far East Tour. The IDC, still in existence but now renamed the Royal College of Defence Studies, was and is a 'finishing school' for the officers of all three armed services as well as a much prized course for senior civil servants, top policemen and rising diplomats. Its students, who were generally of brigadier or equivalent rank, were drawn from across the Commonwealth, the USA and other allies. Its directing staff comprised admirals, generals, air marshals and senior civil servants. On international air journeys the IDC travelled first class; this gives an indication of its importance in the eyes of a normally parsimonious authority.

The IDC Course lasted a full calendar year and during the autumn months the course divided into groups, each of which was required to study social, political and military aspects of a designated area of the free world. The group visiting Malaya that year was about fifteen strong.

So it was with some trepidation that I found myself acting as 'conducting officer' to the IDC Group during its visit to 17 Gurkha Division. The High Commission in Kuala Lumpur, responsible for sponsoring the visit, had arranged for the party to travel in a dedicated coach as this was easier to protect and control than a group of staff cars. The party arrived in Seremban for a briefing by the General followed by an audience and short discussion with the Sultan at the Istana, then back to their accommodation in Kuala Lumpur forty miles to the north of us. This first day passed without incident. The next day the party was to visit military units in the Malacca area to the south of us. An armed escort would not normally have been necessary as Malacca was classified as 'Grey' at that time but no chances were taken for such an illustrious gathering and the coach travelled sandwiched between an escort of lorry borne Gurkha soldiers.

I picked up the coach at Kuala Lumpur and we staged at Seremban for coffee before moving southwards to Malacca, a distance of about forty miles. My passengers were mainly in their mid to late forties but a few were a little older. About twenty-five miles along the road and travelling through dense rubber on either side, there were several requests for a 'sanitary halt'. At first I demurred, pointing out that we hadn't long to wait before proper facilities would be available and that 'with great respect' the armed escort was there for a reason. I was promptly overruled by the crusty admiral in charge of the group who pointed out in turn that they weren't asking to stop for fun and that when I got to his age I would realise that when nature called urgently it had to be answered 'or else!'

We stopped, the escort dismounted and deployed into the rubber. I stayed close to the escort platoon commander within sight of the coach. We watched with our hearts in our mouths as the precious cargo dispersed behind various trees to relieve themselves. One by one they got back on the coach and when I judged that all had reappeared I asked the admiral if they were all present to which he replied, "Yes, yes. Drive on young man." The platoon commander blew his whistle on my signal, the Gurkhas reappeared from nowhere in that magical fashion they had made their own and we were just about to resume the journey when an American brigadier (in US parlance a 'one star general') with camera in hand reappeared from the jungle. The admiral said mildly, "I must have missed one," and resumed his study of the road from the coach window. The brigadier got on the coach remarking genially to me that he would have had one hell of a walk if we'd gone off without him, and we moved off.

This was a never to be forgotten lesson to me. The escort platoon commander and I both knew that dense rubber provides classic cover for an ambush – a prime feature of CT tactics – a fact that I had not disclosed to the IDC group. Despite the seniority of my passengers, I was in charge of the coach and its escort and given the medium risk security rating of the location, I had taken what I still consider to be a reasonable decision to stop, reckoning on the ability of a full platoon of seasoned Gurkha soldiers to cope with anything that might occur. The admiral had misled me but the responsibility was mine. The repercussions of leaving a senior foreign officer alone and unarmed in what to the rest of the world was a terrorist infested jungle were too ghastly to contemplate. I closed and bolted the stable door for the rest of the journey by counting heads off and on the coach with painstaking deliberation, deaf to the protestations of the admiral who said I was wasting time. On return I made a full verbal report to my GSO1 who said:

"You were lucky. Napoleon always maintained that he preferred officers who were lucky to those who were clever. I hope you've learned the lesson that no matter how senior they are, officers on courses being shepherded around tend to abrogate full responsibility to the shepherd, regardless of his rank."

Despite the hot and humid climate, working hours in Malaya were much longer than those in West Africa. We worked a full day except for Wednesday afternoons; these were set aside for 'sport'. Saturdays and Sundays, however, were free for those not on duty. Heather and I made full use of this free time by becoming members of the Port Dixon Yacht Club situated on the coast about twelve miles away. I volunteered to run the 17 Gurkha Division Sailing Club. This owned several GP 14 foot dinghies and we sailed regularly against the civilian Yacht Club team that consisted entirely of local expatriate rubber planters. We made some good friends and even managed to win a race or two. We were outclassed in anything of a blow, however, by the local boats; these carried more sail than the GP 14. They were built strictly to a One Design specification and were known as the Idlealong Class with its origin in New Zealand. They were 16 feet long with a broader beam than our boats. I hankered after one of these but they were very rarely for sale and the planters passed them among themselves whenever they were.

Walking along the beach one day when visiting the site for the new brigade complex to be built at Bukit Terendak just north of Malacca, I came across the skeleton of an abandoned boat that had familiar lines. All that was left was the remnants of a keel and the curved ribs but the shape was preserved and I surmised that the whole boat could be re-created. A few measurements at the PD Yacht Club proved that the wreck had indeed been an Idlealong and I resolved to rebuild her. The remnants had long been abandoned and there was no prospect of finding the owner so I borrowed a trailer and towed the wreck to our quarter in Seremban behind our old Ford Zephyr. I ordered a suit of sails from Nelson on the South Island of New Zealand and with the willing help of a brilliant Chinese carpenter who was more than happy to work by the hour, the new boat, for she was virtually new, with her mast, ribs and keel copied in new wood, was planked and completed within six months. More by luck than by judgement she sailed like a dream, well balanced and with her new suit of sails more than a match for most of the existing Idlealongs at the PD Yacht Club. We won a tableful of beautiful cups; these we were allowed to keep for a year only but nice miniatures were provided and we were able to take home several beer mug trophies that were competed for on a quarterly points basis.

The boat was also a substantial social asset. A few miles to the south of Port Dixon was Cape Rachado; in its lea was a rocky outcrop making up a reef in about twelve feet of water that was home to myriads of coloured fish. It became our custom to return hospitality by sailing to Rachado and anchoring offshore; we provided our guests with plastic snorkel tubes, masks and flippers so that they could swim over the reef and watch the goings on in the gin clear water below. We all then returned to the boat for a curry lunch under the awning before sailing back to the Yacht Club. It was a popular outing and much appreciated. We often went there by ourselves of course; the girls loved it. But we made sure that we were back in the boat by teatime as it was the custom of several of the fresh water crocodiles that lived in the creek a mile or two along the coast, to swim into the sea in the late afternoon for the purpose of getting rid of their parasites in the salt water.

At first we worried about sharks, but we were assured by the locals that although they were present in the Malacca Straits in considerable numbers, they all stayed well offshore to take advantage of the waste food thrown overboard from the large number of ships moving up and down the Straits all day and night. In three years of sailing in those waters with the inevitable capsize from time to time, there was no hint of a shark alarm – except on one occasion!

We were at Rachado one weekend as a family with no guests. Heather and the children were in the boat organising lunch and I was snorkelling over the reef. It was a lovely morning, the sea calm but ruffled in places by a faint cooling breeze; the sky a cloudless blue. There was a sudden shudder among the small, brightly coloured fish below me and I saw out of the corner of my eye a long and menacing black shape about four feet down and moving slowly in my direction. I must have done the eighty yards or so to the boat at near Olympic speed. I can see myself now in my mind's eye spluttering and shouting,

"Shark! Shark!" to an aghast wife as I hauled myself over the side and fell gasping to the bottom boards. Raising my head, I peered over the side of the boat to the approximate position where the shark had appeared in the corner of my vision – to see a black wet-suited swimmer waving to a companion on the shore and holding triumphantly aloft a small fish on the end of his spear gun bolt. Thankfully, that was my only shark fright in many years of swimming in tropical waters. Believe me, the fact that it proved to be bogus didn't lessen the surge of adrenalin when it was thought to be genuine.

Sharks were to be seen in Port Dixon. Massive hammerheads and other species – but stone dead on slabs in the fish market. We were told that they had all been dredged up from the deep in the shipping lanes. On one occasion, while meandering round the fish market we saw a smallish turtle for sale. It was alive, trussed up and having buckets of water thrown over it from time to time. It looked at us with sad and uncomprehending eyes; my wife was close to tears. Knowing that I was doing something both silly and illogical but somehow urged on by the situation, I did the customary haggling, bought it and we hastened to the boat. We sailed well out to sea off Cape Rachado, slipped the turtle's bonds and slid it into the sea. After half a minute or so, it realised that it was once more in its natural habitat and vanished into the depths. We knew it was unlikely to survive the attentions of the fishing fleet, but we both felt better for having given it a chance.

We socialised quite a lot with the planter friends we made through the Yacht Club and we were both surprised at the richness and quantity of ghost stories that long serving planters could come up with. It seemed to be a feature of civilian life in Malaya. Most planters had started their working lives as rubber estate assistants employed by the major Far East trading companies such as Guthries. They had lived a lonely life before becoming senior enough to go home on leave and take a wife, and perhaps the deep gloom of dense rubber had affected them. Additionally, a number of them had been prisoners of the Japanese during the Second World War, although being acclimatised and speaking the local languages fluently, their survival rate was higher than that of the majority of captives. It was evident, however, that Malaya was heavily populated by ghosts and the stories we heard were complete with all the paraphernalia of mysterious bloodstains, destructive poltergeists and shadowy figures – most recounted as personal experiences.

There was a variation on the usual ghost story that was grimmer than the others. Now and then we drove down to Singapore, staying the night en route at the government guest house at Segamat, near enough halfway. On the hill above the guest house stood a well constructed and quite handsome house, larger than usual and the first time we stayed at Segamat an evening stroll took us past it. The house seemed in good condition but was shuttered and seemingly abandoned, with what had once been a nice garden allowed to run wild. I asked the Malay staff about it on our return, but their normally passable English seemed to have deserted them. I could get nothing out of them. I persisted and someone brought the Eurasian manager who said:

"I'm sorry sir, but the Malays will never talk about that house."

"Why ever not?" Recalling planter tales, a thought struck me.

"Is it haunted?"

"Yes," he said "But seriously and in a special way." I urged him to continue.

"You will know about the Kempei Tai?"

I nodded. This was the name of the infamous Japanese Gestapo, renowned for their ferocity to their victims, who rarely survived their interrogations.

"That house was their headquarters during the war and where they did their torturing. The Malays say that they can still hear the screams of their victims if they go near to it."

The war had been over for fifteen years and the local people would neither approach the place nor even talk about it.

We made a particular friend of Mr Perkins, known throughout the expatriate community as 'Perky' He was a keen sailor and was the captain of the Port Dixon Yacht Club racing team, who were rubber planters to a man. Perky lived in a lovely house overlooking Cape Rachado called 'Bukit Tersenyum' translated from Malay as 'Smiling Hill.' He was a bachelor and had long retired from commerce; he had owned his rubber estate and on retirement he had taken Malayan nationality. From time to time he advised the Government at their request on matters pertaining to the management of rubber, their primary natural resource – the secondary being tin.

I suppose that when we knew Perky he was in his sixties. He had been a prisoner of the Japanese on the notorious Thai/Burma Railway and was the only person I have ever known who had not been to some degree traumatised by the experience. He said that to be sure, he had been immensely sorry for the unacclimatised white soldiers in the camps and he had done his best to alleviate their sufferings whenever possible, but that he had lived in a climate similar to that of Thailand for most of his life and was able to supplement the almost non existent rations with natural produce from the jungle as well as being au fait with the local language and customs. Most of the privation, he said, resulted from a lack of ability to cope with the climate and total reliance on the starvation diet offered by the Japanese. Result – disease and eventually death. The work was demanding but not more than fit, well-fed young bodies could have coped with. I had heard this theory advanced before but not from such an authoritative source. We shall probably never know the truth.

We stayed with Perky at his comfortable house several times, usually before an early start to weekend racing and by doing so we met a wide variety of civilian guests. He was a charming host and was happy to have our girls to stay, when they were thoroughly spoiled by his house staff. Red hair must have some significance to the Asian mind as they were popular wherever they went in Malaya; both Chinese and Malays would often cross the road to touch their hair, at the same time muttering an untranslatable mantra. Perky became a considerable celebrity at home later on; his lifestyle was the subject of a feature article in one of the Sunday papers. There was a private path leading from his house down to the sea and the appearance from time to time of a certain signal light in an upstairs window of his house invited the officers of ships lying at anchor in Rachado Bay to take a small boat to his private jetty and join him for a drink.

The Sungei Ujong Club, mentioned earlier, was the focus of most day-to-day social activity for the European military and civilian element in Seremban. Apart from a well laid out and cool clubhouse it had a large and well patronised swimming pool, a great boon to those of us with children. Most Divisional HQ officers together with prominent Asian public servants and businessmen were members.

We became friendly with several of the Asian members, particularly Jimmy Lim, a Chinese businessman who owned several shops in the town. Jimmy had a lively sense of humour characteristically displayed on one occasion when a rather pompous brigadier asked him if he'd seen his tennis partner.

"I wouldn't know, Brigadier," said Jimmy, looking up from his paper. "All you Europeans look alike to me."

I am indebted to Jimmy for the tale of Mary's Urn. The wife of one of our mutual friends, Mary, well known to be rather scatty, took a liking to two immense urns outside one of Jimmy's shops in the town one morning. We all knew the shop and its purpose and most of us knew what the urns were for, but not Mary of course. She met Jimmy at the Club one evening and asked the price of the urns as she would like to buy them if they were reasonably priced. Jimmy looked at her curiously.

"Before I tell you, Mary, would you please say what you have in mind for them?"

"Well," said Mary. "I thought they would look rather nice filled with flowers either side of my verandah."

"How original," replied Jimmy. "We use them for storing the bones of our ancestors."

It was noticed that the Malay policeman on point duty at the crossroads near to Mary's house quietly moved to the side of the road to signal his instructions when Mary came round the corner in her car. But she was one of those delightful, bubbly girls, adored by all. Life would be infinitely duller without them.

In March 1960, our third daughter, Kate, was born at the British Military Hospital, Kinrara, a suburb of Kuala Lumpur. Another redhead or 'auburn' to her mother. We were both delighted. After this event, with over a year's back leave entitlement due, we decided to take a break.

There were two popular hill stations to the north of Kuala Lumpur called respectively Fraser's Hill and the Cameron Highlands. They had long given the expatriate community a chance to escape the sticky heat of the lowlands. During the Emergency they became no-go areas for troops not on duty as the winding roads leading to these havens provided good ambush positions for the CTs. Earlier in the 1950s a British High Commissioner had been ambushed and killed while travelling by road to the Cameron Highlands. By the middle of 1960, however, the area had been declared white and we decided to take a fortnight's holiday there. It wasn't difficult to arrange. Some of the state rulers had second homes in the Highlands and they were happy to let them out to Service officers and their families for short periods. We rented the 'country retreat' of the Sultan of the northern state of Kedah for two weeks at a very reasonable sum. It was delightful. The air was cool and bracing at six thousand feet above sea level and there were country walks with familiar European flowers and foliage everywhere. We needed fires in the evening to warm our thin blood. Kate, our new baby, was a great hit with the Sultan's house staff – who were part of the deal – and spent her time in a raffia type rocking hammock on the verandah of the residence being paid court to and coo'd over by the female element. At no time did we have the slightest qualms about leaving children in the charge of either Malay or Chinese servants.

There were many tiger sightings in the Camerons' English language newspaper, but we rambled all over the place and apart from a goodly assortment of exotic birdlife we saw no game at all. When we got back to Seremban I met our local game warden in the Club one evening and asked him what one should do in the unlikely event of meeting a tiger on a jungle path.

He said, "The last thing you should do is follow your natural inclination to turn and run. You'd have no chance. The tiger is just a large but lethal domestic cat with similar instincts and as soon as you turn your back and run you become prey. You should sit down with your back against a tree so that you are lower than he is and stay quite still without making eye contact. At the same time pray that he isn't hungry. There is then a good chance that he'll simply snarl at you and walk away." He swore he wasn't kidding.

"What are you having?" I said, resolving to make sure that I would never have to put his advice to the test.

Several tribes of aborigine type natives lived in the Camerons; they eked out a subsistence living supplemented by selling primitive artefacts to visitors. Walking sticks, salad bowls and other wooden tableware and ornaments were quite popular. We bought a walking stick that was beautifully carved and at a cursory glance a most suitable present to take home. It was only when the carvings were studied carefully that they were found to be quite graphically obscene. We still have it but not on general view.

By late 1960 the 'protected village' strategy, that had the effect of denying food to the enemy, was paying major dividends. Growing numbers of CTs were surrendering to the security forces and Chin Peng and his relatively few remaining followers were being penned into an area close to the Thai border in the north east corner of the Malayan Peninsular. Units engaged in the deep penetration operations aimed at forcing the terrorists further and further away from human habitation were relying increasingly on supply by air for replenishment of their needs. This was carried out by aircraft from a joint Army/RAF organisation based near Kuala Lumpur with RAF aircrew and RASC soldier 'air despatchers' who were responsible for packing and dropping the stores from the aircraft. Sadly, there were some aircraft casualties with no survivors, resulting in the RASC holding the dubious honour of suffering more deaths on active service during the ten years of the Malayan Emergency than any other non Gurkha British unit.

Towards the end of 1960 there was a diversion from operations on the Malayan Peninsular. The small oil rich kingdom of Brunei on the north coast of the vast island of Borneo and traditionally a close ally of Britain, began to suffer political unrest. The workers at the Shell oilfields that provided the wealth of the kingdom and additionally were important to the economy of the whole of South East Asia, were being influenced by dissidents to the extent that the workers were threatening to strike. There were contingency plans for such situations and it became necessary to dig them out and warn units that might be involved if they had to be activated.

The balloon went up over one weekend when the oil platform workers were reported to have downed tools, and a small Gurkha force from our division amounting to a reinforced rifle company with logistic support was despatched to the oilfields which ring the shallow waters near the town of Seria. This lies on the extreme western border of this small country at the opposite end from the capital and seat of the Sultan, Bandar Seri Begawan, the name so difficult to remember and pronounce that it is generally known as BSB. My neighbour and the occupant with his wife of the other of our two isolated married quarters, the Royal Army Ordnance Corps major John, was detailed to accompany the force as Supply Replenishment Officer. He asked Heather and me if we would 'look out for' his wife while he was away and of course we agreed to do so.

One evening while he was away his wife rang up to tell us that there was a large and aggressive looking snake hissing and spitting at their glass verandah doors. The form in these cases as in Britain was to ring the fire brigade, and having told her to go to her bedroom and lock her door, this is what I did. I then took a torch and a large stick, for with the Emergency almost wound down we were no longer armed, and I made my way to their house without much idea about what I was going to do.

As luck would have it the brave lads of the brigade arrived at their gate at the same time as I did. They were obviously familiar with the situation for they rushed up the garden path with steel rods with hooks on the end and despatched the snake in short order. For good measure they picked up a set of golf clubs on the verandah and pounded the snake to mush with them. It turned out to be a large spitting cobra and very dangerous; its party piece is to rear to eye height and spit venom into the eyes of its prey; thus blinded, the victim can be dealt with at leisure, the venom being lethal when injected by bite into the bloodstream. The Malay firemen, their religion forbidding alcohol, couldn't have a celebratory drink but we saw to it that they were suitably rewarded.

John came back shortly afterwards and having given me a piece of his mind for not protecting his golf clubs, told me what had happened during his foray to Brunei. It is relevant to the story that John, a shortish man of middle age, must have weighed at least seventeen stones.

In his own words,

"We arrived at Seria and to our surprise the landing strip appeared to be deserted so we had no trouble getting down. As soon as we'd landed the little Gurkhas began to deploy behind any cover they could find, having expected some sort of opposition. I found a large steel oil drum I could get behind so I lay down behind it in my olive green field kit and a loaded rifle feeling more ridiculous than vulnerable. The young Gurkha officer nearest to me had established his platoon HQ about two hundred yards away and was chattering into his radio. It was late afternoon. Then nothing happened for a bit. I was quite close to the road that skirted the strip and I saw a car approaching. It stopped near to me and two chaps in white shorts, long white socks and white bush jackets strolled across and looked down at me.

'I say,' said one of them. 'How good of you to come so quickly. But it's all over and we've laid on tea at the Club. Do join us.' It was like something out of an Ealing comedy or a Carry On film, but they did a rare bara peg (large whisky soda) at their club."

We learned later that with the intervention of the Ruler and major concessions to the strikers by the oil company, the strike was over quickly but not quite quick enough for our operation to be aborted.

As the Emergency diminished, so troop levels began to be reduced creating pressure on those levels of staff that were adjustable within the theatre. Divisional and brigade headquarters together with their operational units under command are established with set levels of staff wherever they serve. They are known collectively as field force establishments with their numbers of officers, soldiers and levels of weapons, equipment and vehicles set on very high authority, usually outside the theatre of operations. Inevitably, however, in an operation the size of the Malayan Emergency, nearly ten years old in 1960, 'in theatre' units that were not part of the field force had been created to provide facilities and services that were not otherwise available for the troops. Pressure for the reduction of staff in these 'non field force' establishments began to be applied, led by the civil service financial department at GHQ in Singapore.

At Divisional HQ in Malaya, thankfully a field force establishment and thus only marginally adjustable, the backing and 'legwork' for the general to help him make his decisions on the adjustments to non field force units is provided by SD branch. This became a large part of my job in the second half of my tour in Malaya.

Gurkha soldiers were trained at the Gurkha Depot located at Sungei Petani in the northern state of Kedah. Their establishment was in the sights of the 'pruners' at GHQ in Singapore and I made several visits to it. I acted in the capacity of a 'friendly adversary' for my general was not only the Commander of the 17th Gurkha Division but also the Major General Brigade of Gurkhas. Wearing that hat he was responsible for the well-being of Gurkha soldiers wherever they were stationed and he had strong views on the maintenance of a properly established training depot for them. It was a case of plotting a surviveable course between the Scylla of GHQ's pruning ambitions and the Charybdis of the General's wrath if the cuts went too deep.

Fortunately Chris Pulley, the Colonel Brigade of Gurkhas who worked directly to the General on specifically Gurkha matters from his small HQ at Seremban, was a friend from staff college days when our eldest girl, Helen, had been at prep school with his daughter Rosemary in Camberley. Chris and Betty Pulley were happy to look after our girls when there was a chance for Heather to accompany me on my trips to Singapore and elsewhere and we reciprocated. Helen and Rosemary are lifelong friends and still meet regularly.

The spin off for me was an opportunity to discuss the suggested cuts to the Depot establishment with Chris before a visit and work out what we could get away with. Usually, in this period of diminishing establishments, visiting a non field force unit was not a happy experience. The Gurkha Depot, however, was an exception to the rule. They felt, not without reason, that they had powerful friends at court and I had little doubt that tactics to deal with the proposed GHQ cuts had been discussed within closed Gurkha channels before my visits. To enter the Depot was to step back in time; it was particularly evocative for me, having been commissioned in India. Although Gurkhali was their language, most of the soldiers and certainly the Indian servants understood Urdu and I was able to dredge up from memory a good deal of vocabulary and a number of useful phrases.

An abiding memory is walking into the officers' mess at breakfast time and seeing in the lobby a row of hooks with Sam Browne belts and Gurkha Stetson type hats hanging from them. Below each hook stood, and I mean stood, a pair of perfectly pressed, heavily starched and very wide jungle green shorts. Inside the mess several officers were eating breakfast clad in bush shirts and green issue underpants. I watched them go into the lobby one by one as they finished breakfast; they stepped into the shorts, an orderly pulled them up, Sam Browne belts were fitted and they were off to parade.

Arriving back at Seremban after one of these visits, I reported to my GSO1, John Hardy, who said, "Do you realise that you have become the head of the richest staff branch in Asia?"

Apparently in my absence the syndicate in my branch had come up with first prize in the Malayan national lottery. Each member had contributed a dollar a week to net a sum giving them each a total of about ten thousand pounds, a vast fortune to Indian and Chinese clerks and typists in 1960. The saddest person in the branch was my staff sergeant chief clerk who had given up his contribution, feeling that it was a waste of money; the happiest was the Chinese civilian supervisor who had taken the chief clerk's place and doubled his stake to two dollars. Neither I nor my staff captain had been approached by the organiser, Bessie Phun, our Chinese typist. A pity; we would have jumped at it, but Bessie clearly thought we were above the mundane considerations of money.

The win received wide publicity and shortly afterwards, Mr Narayan, the senior Indian clerk asked to see me on a private matter. It had to do with Villoo, our Peon, or runner, who delivered urgent messages around the HQ by hand in those days of dodgy telephones, operating in the great tradition of the Straits Settlements' 'fast running coolies' of long ago. He was a young Indian boy, still a teenager and a hardworking lad of somewhat limited brainpower. He hailed from Calcutta and we had often chatted about his city. His parents had both worked for the British Army in the days of the Raj and he had sought employment with us in Malaya armed with a sheaf of 'chits' acquired by his father and grandfather. He lived in basic accommodation among the Indian community and Narayan's message was that he was now in fear of his life from a gang of villains attempting to part him from his money. I suggested contacting the police but that had been ruled out by suspicions that they were being paid to look the other way and nothing could convince the Indian community that it was not so.

Together we hatched a plan. Narayan was still holding Villoo's cheque so he opened an account for him with an international bank in Singapore and after coaching him carefully in the use and purpose of a cheque book, Narayan then arranged for him to buy an air ticket from Singapore to Calcutta after transferring the bulk of his funds to the Bank of India in Calcutta. We then shipped him covertly and rapidly to Payar Leba Airport in Singapore in the clothes he stood up in and Narayan saw him off to India. The operation took thirty six hours with Narayan taking care of Villoo and making sure he didn't attempt to collect any of his belongings from his quarters. The payback came when Villoo's father wrote to Narayan thanking him for his part in the boy's rescue and asking him to thank 'the major sahib' also. The poor lad's head must have been swimming during the course of this cloak and dagger operation but there is no doubt that had he not been smuggled out quickly he would have lost his money and probably also his life.

Early in 1961 we had a new divisional commander, Major General Walter Walker, a professional Gurkha officer and a very professional soldier. He was a veteran of the Far East, where at that time he had spent most of his service, with three DSOs and innumerable mentions in despatches to his credit. He had the reputation of a man who gets things done – a stickler for discipline and an eye for detail, and so it proved. On his initial tour of the headquarters he was kind enough to say, "I've done this job," and fixed me with a beady eye. The message went home and when it became time for me to prepare his thirty two page programme for a five day initial visit to divisional units throughout the Peninsular, I was very careful about getting the details right.

This slavish attention to the small print did not, however, prevent me being carpeted for a one letter typing error. The programme had column headings of serial, date/time, name of unit, name of CO and a wide column at the end for notes on the interests or achievements of those being introduced to the new GOC.

The tour was a success according to the ADC who accompanied the General and I thought no more about it until a note appeared on my desk in the General's trademark green ink. This read 'The CO of the Kuala Lumpur Military Hospital is NOT Lieutenant Colonel H.O.P. Mc Sheeny, MC. See me!' I called for the list of personalities that had been sent in by units being visited and sure enough the name of the military hospital CO was down as McSheeny. I then phoned the adjutant of the hospital who apologised for a typing error and told me that his CO's name should have read McSheehy.

Treatment of this obviously minor nonsense needed careful thought. Our new general was clearly in the process of stamping his personality on the Headquarters and from what I already knew of him he would not take kindly to the rather wet explanation of a typing error made by someone outside his headquarters. Also the ADC had told me that the GOC had known Colonel McSheehy from times past and did not appreciate an incorrect spelling of his name. I therefore made an appointment to see the general but before doing so I told the GSO1, my immediate boss, the whole story. John Hardy, a wise and impeturbable infantryman, agreed with my proposed treatment of this staff duties (SD) slip up.

"Well?" said the General as I stood before him trying desperately to adopt the stance and demeanour of a penitent. I said I had checked with the Hospital and discovered that the name was incorrect and that I had no explanation for the mistake, given that the full 32 page tour programme had been checked exhaustively. I apologised and would ensure that there would be no future SD errors of this nature. I achieved a dismissive grunt and left. Some time later the G1 told me that he had told the GOC what had actually happened and he too had received the grunt.

There is no doubt that our new GOC added snap and fizz to our Division. The Emergency, in which he had taken a considerable part as a lower formation and unit commander, was virtually over and training, which had taken a back seat during the heat of active operations, could now be resumed. The GOC was here, there and everywhere. In the cloying heat of Malaya, his energy, for a man of his years, was prodigious. He missed nothing and much of the follow up landed with

SD. It was for me an enjoyably steep learning curve involving a lot more travel all around the peninsular and quite often to GHQ in Singapore to argue the Division's case for establishment strengths and, incidentally, to enjoy a large draught Tiger beer at Tanglin Barracks in the only air conditioned officers' mess bar in the whole Malaya/Singapore command.

Normally, when I or my new staff captain, a young infantryman and staff college contender, arrived at a unit to discuss and report on establishment strengths, it was a pretty stressful business. We were greeted with all the enthusiasm of an undertaker visiting to discuss a family bereavement. Jobs and ranks could be at stake and unit commanders, usually senior to the inspecting staff officer, could be and often were resentful of the process.

To mix metaphors, the air was full of the sound of grinding axes and it was necessary to walk on eggshells. There was one establishment, however, that was a positive pleasure to visit and report on. This was the Runnymede Hotel on Penang Island. It had been taken over as a leave centre early in the Emergency and the moneymen at GHQ in Singapore had decreed that it had to be inspected and staff levels assessed because of the reduction in troop levels attending the imminent ending of the Emergency. I made an appointment to visit.

The WRAC officer administering the Runnymede Leave Centre was a tactician of some skill. She found out that I was married and I received a phone call inviting my wife to accompany me during the visit so that 'she could express a family view of the facilities.' What a good idea! One of the nice things about serving in Malaya was that it was easy to take a short break together knowing that the children would be well looked after. They, for their part positively enjoyed being farmed out to friends.

We drove up the Peninsular to Butterworth on the north west coast and the embarkation point for Penang Island that was then only accessible by air or ferry from the mainland. I'm told that a road bridge has since been built across the narrow strait. The Leave Centre lived up to its reputation. It was clean, comfortable and extremely well run. The lady 'manager' was anxious to keep her staff and before I had seen the place properly she counter attacked with a proposal to increase it. She needn't have worried. My brief, had she known it, was to do my best to ensure that every member of staff was gainfully employed and to say so. The Leave Centre was a valuable morale maintaining asset that the Division was loath to lose. There was no question of any extra staff but the bid to increase it was useful. It provided me with a proposal that could be rejected in my report while recommending maintenance of the existing staff levels. As I was later to discover, these are tactics not unknown to large companies in the commercial world.

Penang Island was a gem, largely untouched by the troubles of the mainland. Its ancient harbour bore echoes of its colonial past with old iron cannon pointing out to sea against pirates, whose descendants even during the nineteen fifties were still active from time to time in the Strait of Malacca. The Island had a small mountain – or a tall hill – in its centre, accessed by a rack and pinion single track railway. The top provided matchless views. The capital, Georgetown, was picturesque and Indian, Chinese and Malay temples were scattered around with no particular reference to specific ethnic areas, reflecting the comfortable ethnic mix of the Peninsular. The beaches were a disappointment, largely because bathing in the sea was totally out of bounds for us. This was because a particularly venomous species of sea snake infested those waters. There was no reliable antidote for its bite. The situation was made worse by the fact that the local fishermen believed that the snakes harboured evil spirits. They refused to kill them when they were caught in their nets and they routinely released them close to the shore. Bathing for us was therefore restricted to the Runnymede pool, which was pleasant enough.

Apart from the cool breezes and balmy evenings, the beauty of the Island was amplified by its flowers. These surely outclassed even the wide profusion and colour of those to be seen on the mainland. Bougainvillea, hibiscus, frangipani, cannas, tuber roses and even the humble hydrangea, – although 'not as we know it,' – vied for attention with many species of orchid lining all the roads and filling the gardens of the prosperous merchants on the coastal road that skirted the Island. Orchids grew like weeds on the Malayan Peninsular and its islands. To describe it as a riot of colour was not only hackneyed, but also a considerable understatement.

An uneventful drive back to Seremban along almost empty main roads completed one of the most pleasant duty trips of my service.

Not long afterwards, and with a considerable flourish, the Emergency was declared to be at an end and the King decided, or more likely was persuaded, to call for a victory parade. This took place in Kuala Lumpur, with units of 17 Gurkha Division, the Malayan Military Forces and the Malayan Police marching through the City with the King, the Yang Di Pertuan Agong, taking the salute. It was a splendid spectacle and a great success. We all turned up bemedalled and clad in our white tropical dress uniforms to watch our battalions and regiments, each led by its band and marching past to its regimental march. We took the two older girls and we were allotted a prime spot close to the saluting dais. Everyone wanted to be as near as possible to the King, however, and the children were a bit crowded out by local dignitaries. A bachelor friend took them by the hand and said he would get them a less crowded place a few yards to the left.

The parade was at its height and the Sherwood Foresters were moving towards the saluting dais; their band struck up their regimental march and I heard a familiar and very clear childish treble give voice in time to the music, "The 45th are a dozy lot; they left their colours in Aldershot." This was a soldiers' ditty from the mid nineteenth century when the Sherwood Foresters – previously the 45th Foot – travelled on the first railway train from Nottingham to Aldershot complete with their regimental colours. The subaltern in charge of the colours, presumably overwhelmed by the occasion, failed in his duty and they were left in Aldershot. The culprit in this case was my bachelor friend who had carefully coached Helen, our nine year old, in the words and prompted her to sing just as the band struck up and the order 'eyes right' was given. I knew the Commanding Officer and met his frozen eye as he passed. He tried and failed to pinpoint the adult hand that had caused his embarrassment and of course I could not possibly reveal the name, but if you are reading this, Richard, I still think it was a dirty trick.

A major civil engineering project, the construction of a road in the northern state of Kedah, had recently been completed by an independent plant troop of the Royal Engineers. It was to be opened by the King and our GOC together with a few of his senior staff officers attended the ceremony. I was not there but the unofficial story of the opening was widely circulated. The engineer plant troop was scheduled to take part in the force reductions towards the end of the Emergency. It was an unaccompanied unit and its soldiers were due to leave for the UK by a certain date; they were not at all pleased to be delayed in order to make the necessary preparations for the grand opening.

Someone had decided that the age of the dignitaries might argue a degree of incontinence so a five star wooden loo befitting their status had to be built. This was located in a specially cleared space on the side of a hill overlooking the area of the speeches and the tape to be cut by the King. At the time there was successful and well publicised show in London called *The Teahouse of the August Moon* based on the life of the Chinese community in San Francisco.

The day for the opening arrived with the early mist gradually being dispersed by the morning sun. The King arrived and the speeches commenced as the mist lifted to reveal the special loo in all its pristine newness with painted on the side in stark white letters 'The Peehouse of the August Tuan'. There was no coverage of the incident in the Press. I wondered if the story was apocryphal – a case of the old journalistic maxim of never let the facts get in the way of a good story – but I was assured by several of those who were there that it was genuine.

A few months later with the end of my three year tour of duty looming, I received my next posting. We were to fly home in January 1962 and after a month's disembarkation leave in England, I was to travel unaccompanied to Germany to take over my new unit, an independent company – a major's command. I would be able in the jargon, to 'call forward' my wife after taking over the married quarter that went with the job.

We had all enjoyed our time in Malaya, a happy posting. We would miss the social life of the charming little town we had lived in. The Sungei Ujong Club with its swimming pool and friendly multi-racial membership. The Sultan's baby elephant who, when out for his constitutional with his keeper, delighted in knocking the locals off their bicycles with his trunk to roars of laughter. Even the satay parties that became fashionable for a while. The satay man would appear on his tricycle with his mobile cooking contraption to cook the kebab type offerings which were usually so tough that they were disposed of under bushes in the gardens where these parties were usually held. The attraction always lay in the gossip and the get togethers.

Our two older girls had loved it. They had become very attached to the two Chinese amahs, Ah Phun in particular, and were distressed to have to say goodbye to them. They would also miss the heavy social life that the young enjoyed within the garrison. Birthday parties produced novelties that you didn't see at home. European conjurers were replaced by Indian snake charmers and Chinese professional magicians providing wonderful magic learned over many generations. Kate, our baby girl, was eighteen months old when we left and had a fairly wide Chinese vocabulary, soon lost at home.

We would not miss the Durian time. The Durian is a tree fruit to which the Malay population was generally addicted. It appeared at a certain time of year and the people couldn't get enough of it. To us, that is to say to Europeans generally, it smelled and tasted foul. Taken in quantity it differs in its effects on individuals. With most it has a narcotic effect inducing a mild form of stupor. With some it appears to create a sense of well-being. A few lose their reason and sometimes become dangerous. Amok is one of the few Malay words that are familiar in English. Occasionally the cry of Amok! Amok! would be heard, perhaps while shopping in Seremban. Shops would close, car doors would be slammed and a clearly deranged person would be seen pirouetting down the street, perhaps wielding a heavy stick, a kris, the snake knife of Malaya, or even a machete. It was like an extreme form of drunkenness and the police, who soon appeared, had little trouble in subduing the man; I didn't hear of anyone being hurt by an amok during my three years in Malaya although I saw several of those who had lost their reason, invariably during the Durian time when the country roads are slippery with the reddish mush from the fruit and small villages were best avoided.

We would miss the yacht club and our planter friends, supportive to the last. Because we were travelling back by air we had to despatch our heavy baggage to go by sea some weeks before we departed for Payar Lebah Airport at Singapore for the flight home and we were issued with an 'air loan' to tide us over our last few weeks in Seremban. This consisted of Army white crockery and other basic equipment not normally provided by the Army, but of course our pictures and ornaments had gone. We chatted about this at the yacht club the weekend after our heavy baggage had left, while lamenting the demise of the troopships that had by now been completely replaced by air trooping. Nothing was said at the time but on the following Monday a small van appeared at our house and a grinning Malay driver unloaded an enormous heap of fresh orchids of all types, sizes and colours, accompanied by a note suggesting that they might be a suitable temporary replacement for our ornaments and pictures. Best wishes from our planter friends, led by Perky, accompanied the note.

A week later we embarked on the train for Singapore accompanied by the usual send off party of friends. I had sold my boat to the senior military policeman of the Division with a strong exhortation to look after it. I'd made a profit but not when sweat and labour were taken into account. I learned years later that in due course he, too, had sold it at a profit.

We travelled home by a chartered Britannia aircraft. It had four turbo prop engines and was popularly known at the time as the 'whispering giant'. It certainly lived up to its name; it was quiet and comfortable and leg room was ample. Refuelling stops were Bombay and Istanbul. There was no overnight staging and we seemed to be home in no time. Air trooping had progressed by leaps and bounds.

Nigeria 1955. Umaru and Mo with piccans.

Malaya 1960. Snake charmer's demo before a children's party.

171

Malaya. Our 'square and unlovely' married quarter at Seremban.

Malaya. A light aircraft pilot's view of deep jungle.

15

Wuppertal. Plus Rockets.

Although we had achieved our usual trick of returning from the tropics in midwinter, it was nice to be at home with a tour of duty on the Continent and the great pleasure of commanding a unit to look forward to. At that time I must have been one of the few regular officers of field rank (major and above) in the Army not to have served in Germany when I took over my new command in 1962.

We found that for the first time in our lives we were able to afford a brand new car provided we bought it on the Continent and used it for no more than six months in the UK. This would allow us to get it duty and tax free, a very considerable saving. We chose a Peugeot estate and I went to Paris to collect it and drive it home before leaving shortly afterwards to report to my new unit in Germany. Until I could get the British Forces Germany (BFG) number plates fitted, the car bore a Paris registration. Heather and the children could not join me until my married quarter was signed over so I was alone in the car. I managed to miss a turning in Belgium and on a long lonely road with only a lone cyclist in sight I stopped, got out of the car, and asked the attractive young lady rider if she could direct me to the Dutch border. I was driving a French car with Paris number plates and I spoke in French.

She answered in fluent English. I thanked her and asked, "How did you know I am English?" She looked at my tan leather shoes, grey flannels and sports coat and gave a dismissive gesture.

"Don't be silly. Of course you are English! What else could you be?"

6 Company (GW) was a guided weapons transport company and unique to my Corps. Our job was to transport the rocket missiles together with their propellants to their up country deployment positions in the event of a war threat. The missile was a big beast, not unlike the Thunderbird rocket of children's fiction in appearance, about thirty feet tall when it was placed on the ground. Its propellants were liquid and hypergolic in nature; that is to say they burned ferociously when allowed to be in contact with each other and thus provided the motive force for the rockets. My unit was part of a Royal Artillery

brigade for operational purposes and my vehicles were large and powerful road tractors each towing a forty foot trailer containing the carcases of two missiles side by side. We also had cranes to unload the missiles from the vehicles and special trucks fitted with mountings for the propellant containers. When on the road we could easily have been mistaken for an oil drilling expedition.

The nature of the appointment meant that I had to learn a good deal about rocketry and the missile world in general if only to be able to brief the various high powered visitors who came to see us, largely out of curiosity. This had considerable advantages for an independent unit wishing only to be left alone to get on with its job. It was possible to include enough technical rocketry jargon to make the average high level 'curiosity' visitor's eyes glaze over and after the first few visits we tended to be avoided except for those with a genuine technical interest in our task. We were located on the heights above the pleasant town of Wuppertal to the south of the Ruhr and to the east of the major city of Dusseldorf. The Artillery Brigade HQ and its two missile regiments were located about forty miles away. We were part of a small garrison comprising an infantry battalion, an anti-aircraft gunner regiment and my company, our barracks dating from the Hitler era. The garrison commander, in keeping with the cat's cradle chain of command in Germany, was the CO of the infantry battalion, the Prince of Wales Own Regiment of Yorkshire (PWO).

There was also a German Army (Bundeswehr) battalion near us – its entrance directly opposite my house. It gave us a strange feeling to see their armoured personnel carriers leaving their barracks with large black crosses on their sides, so reminiscent of those not so far off days when they represented our main enemy. In fact we got to know their CO, Oberst Hans Clausem, well; there was a small training area within the garrison that we shared with the Germans. When we held minor exercises to refresh our soldiers in tactics and weaponry we provided men for each other to act as enemy. They would all end up fraternising with a mug of tea and a bun at the NAAFI wagon when the exercise ended. We got on well with our German neighbours.

As an independent company commander I had a 'tied' quarter; this meant that Heather and the children could come out as soon as my takeover from the incumbent, Denis Blackburn, was completed and he had vacated the house. This was accomplished without difficulty and we settled down as a family in what was to prove a pleasant if demanding two years. Denis had left me a 'tight ship'. He had been a highly trained technical staff officer and as such, he had forgotten more about the missile business than I was likely to learn. But he did an efficient teaching job in the short time we had together and he left me knowing more about rocketry than most of my Corps were ever likely to want to know. This was an excellent foundation for the new job and I was left strictly to my own devices so long as I kept the gunners happy. Both my gunner brigadiers, John Cordingley when I arrived but shortly afterwards to be replaced by Harry Langstaff, were pleasant and helpful to me and with the honour and professional competence of my Corps at stake, we did our best to keep them on our side.

Soldiering in Germany was different to anything I had hitherto encountered. The scene was obviously set for full scale conventional war with its panoply of heavy armour, artillery and air support incorporated into an all embracing plan. By the early 1960s the plan, equally obviously, had to take account of the existence of both strategic and tactical nuclear weapons; scenarios ranged from the merely desperate to ultimate doomsday, the latter epitomised by the aptly named MAD theory – Mutually Assured Destruction – that began to feature in serious speculative articles in the quality media.

The Cold War was at its height. The Berlin Wall, started in August 1961 on a barbed wire and hurdle basis, was being upgraded to concrete while we were in Wuppertal.

Military exercises in a Germany increasingly edging towards full post-war independence and undergoing the 'economic miracle' much admired throughout the free world, had reverted to a centuries old pattern based on the changing seasons. Early in the year and shortly after the Christmas break, minor unit and sub unit training would begin on training areas usually near to unit locations, thus leaving the main roads and autobahns fairly free from military traffic. Also at this time all units had to classify as competent on their personal weapons on the numerous weapons ranges dotting the countryside. In the spring and early summer, company, squadron and battery training would take place in preparation for formation training. This was always planned to occur during autumn after the harvest had been gathered and brigade, division and even Army Corps exercises could operate with no fear of damage to crops. After this and leading up to the Christmas break, all units were subject to inspections. Weapons, vehicles and various administrative functions such as documentation, fire precautions and catering were examined by specialist teams of staff officers. After they had submitted their reports to superior headquarters the whole process culminated in an Annual Administrative Inspection of every unit by a brigade or divisional commander. The military year was then complete and the training cycle for the following year could commence.

Serving, as I did, for a number of years in Germany during the next twelve years and visiting units stationed there as a more senior officer for many years afterwards, this annual pattern hardly varied. The area of Germany occupied by the 1st British Corps encompassed invasion routes down the centuries. The commanding heights and the forests of the Teutoberger Wald had to receive as much attention from the compilers of the latest strategic defence plan as did its Roman occupiers in the first century AD, when the Commander of the then Rhine Army, Quintilius Varus, lost his Emperor, Augustus Caesar, three fully armed legions to the irregular fighters of the German tribes on its slopes because of sloppy reactions and an imperfectly thought out plan.

There was a unique perk to my new command that I relished greatly. As the senior professional logistician in the brigade, I was the Brigadier's transport adviser as well as a unit commander and this gave me a place on the annual field firing trip to the Scottish Islands. Our brigade was allowed to test its missiles live only once each year and for this we used the NATO Range on the island of Benbecula sandwiched between North and South Uist in the Outer Hebrides. My unit carried the missiles to and on the ships and I had to see that they were delivered to the range undamaged and on time. Our gunner regiments took it in turn to assemble and erect the missiles, fuel them, set up the electronics for targeting and then firing into the Atlantic. This gave the missile teams vital practice in setting up and firing live, which no amount of inert practice can replace.

It was a most impressive performance – a sort of mini Cape Canaveral, particularly at night. The dramatic countdown, the great ball of light, the deafening roar as the great beast rises slowly and evermore rapidly into the gloaming, its tail light of rocket fuel eventually disappearing; all this in itself made the trip worthwhile. But since the Brigadier, his brigade major and I, comprising the brigade headquarters team, were all passionately keen game fishermen, just being there was an additional pleasure. There was lots of free time because we had no commitment to the nuts and bolts of the operation. Once the missiles and their accompanying telemetry had been delivered; the rest was down to the regiments.

To be sure, we had to be there at the firing and the Brigadier conducted the post-mortems but that didn't take long. So we walked the lochs and fished for the small and very tasty loch trout while breathing the clear island air and realising that the lifestyle of the islands had a lot to do with the fact that the gravestones in the small island cemetery reflected a final age for most of those resting there of between eighty-five and one hundred years. Later on in my service I had a good deal more to do with the Benbecula ranges. The maritime element of my Corps was responsible for crewing and operating the ships that ferried the stores, equipment and vehicles from the mainland and it became one of my responsibilities.

Back to Germany. Heather and I found that we enjoyed living on the Continent. Wuppertal translates into English as 'Valley of the Wupper' the river from which the town takes its name. The military barracks were on the heights above the valley and most of our married quarters on Hermannshohe, or 'Herman's Heights' offered magnificent views. The people were quite friendly and it certainly paid dividends to make an effort to learn enough German to get by. My unit strength including dependants was above four hundred with soldier strength about two hundred and fifty, the remainder being wives, families and certain supernumeries not part of my unit but occupying accommodation in the barracks.

I was very fortunate in inheriting a first class company sergeant major, Freddie Finch. He was young, keen, highly intelligent and always one jump ahead of the minor villainies that young soldiers tend to get up to, even when properly supervised. I learned with amusement that his nickname within the unit was 'Cousin Fred', but my amusement was modified when I found out some time later that one of mine – there are always others, less repeatable – was 'Uncle Fred'.

I had a hardworking second in command and some keen and very promising subalterns. One of these innocently foiled a little ploy that the sergeant major had adopted with my full knowledge. The early 1960s marked the rundown of National Service but we still had a number of these young men in our unit. Most served uncomplainingly and played to the rules, but there were one or two who tended to stretch them. At the time the rules still demanded that off duty soldiers not living in married quarters should return to barracks by 2359 hours – or one minute to midnight.

It was an out of date rule in the 'enlightened' sixties and we all knew it, but it was still policy and had to be observed. So it was enshrined in Unit Standing Orders – the unit bye-laws. There was a wire perimeter fence surrounding the unit location but as the critical equipment and vehicles were separately guarded by twenty-four hour patrols, it didn't have much security value. I had been puzzled soon after my arrival in the unit at the seemingly perfect behaviour of my single soldiers in the matter of returning to barracks before the midnight deadline and I suspected that there was something I didn't know about. I did a close inspection of the perimeter fence and sure enough, there was a man sized hole in one corner screened by a bush. I turned to the sergeant major, who was with me.

"You knew about this, didn't you?"

He looked embarrassed. "We, that is the senior ranks and me, keep a close eye on it, sir."

"Well," I said. "You can continue to do so. But you can also let it be known that any abuse of this cunning little ploy will be stamped on, hard!"

Shortly afterwards a newly arrived subaltern, clearly capable of putting clues together, also did a quiet tour of the perimeter fence, and on his next duty officer stint he waited patiently beside the fence like a fox beside a hen run, and collared two miscreants returning to barracks in the small hours. I had to deal with them and did so; they had broken the eleventh commandment and had to suffer for it, but not painfully. I praised the keen young man who had caught them, but also gave him a short lecture on judgement when in command. I hope it stuck with him; he commanded his own unit with distinction in later years. Shortly afterwards the out of date rules on returning to barracks, along with other unnecessary hangovers from the war, were dispensed with by a decree from on high.

Walking to the barracks each morning, a matter of two hundred yards or so, it wasn't long before I noticed that my attached Royal Army Pay Corps sergeant, who was responsible for accounting for public funds – the soldiers' pay among other things, was driving to work in an almost new top of the range Mercedes. This sort of thing couldn't fail to raise a spike of doubt in the mind of the average CO and I was no exception. He was a nice fellow, highly intelligent and the life and soul of sergeants' mess functions with his attractive German wife who was a supporter of the unit wives' club and according to Heather, always expensively and fashionably dressed. But a new Mercedes was well beyond the pocket of practically every serving officer I knew – and a Pay Corps sergeant – well?

I rang the chief paymaster at my higher HQ, who laughed. "Cease worrying," he said. "Have you met the girl he's married to?"

I said I had.

"Well not only is she very attractive. She has also quite recently inherited a hairdressing empire of several shops in Berlin and elsewhere around Germany. She'll eventually succeed in her campaign to get Sergeant X out of the army, so enjoy his services while you can. They can afford a garage full of Mercedes."

Heather, for the first time in her life, became the chatelaine of the company wives' club. It is a foolish unit commander who neglects or undervalues his wives' club. Apart from the importance of keeping the wives of his soldiers happy and community minded, it is among the most valuable sources of intelligence he will ever have. Frequently, soldiers' wives, for whom I have the greatest admiration and respect, will 'open up' to the CO's wife and reveal the true reason for a married soldier's behaviour problem that has baffled his officers and senior NCOs. It can be a two way traffic. COs of units realise quickly that their soldiers are poor conduits for matters affecting their families. Wives simply don't get told. Announcements at the wives' club, however, are absorbed and acted on. Similarly, complaints on domestic matters are best transmitted through the sergeant major's wife, who normally acts as a sidekick to the CO's wife, and the complaint will be swiftly transmitted to the quartermaster.

In the Ruhr area of Germany, the wives did well. Social functions were frequent and outings for them to places of interest in or around the surrounding and fashionable cities of Cologne and Dusseldorf were organised on a regular basis. On the other hand, husbands were away on exercise very often during the summer and autumn and they were left looking after the children in the married quarters. It was easy for boredom to take hold and an active wives' club could serve as a useful antidote.

Security was something of a problem. When we were away the 'married patch' suffered from occasional prowlers and there were one or two attempts at forced entry.

We didn't think the offenders were locals. The economic miracle had spawned much building work and a great deal of 'guest labour' had been imported, mainly from Italy and Turkey. We minimised, but never really solved this problem by regular patrolling of the quarters by our own regimental policemen with the tacit agreement of the German civil police.

On one occasion I was on an exercise in the East/West German border area when I was recalled to my unit urgently to deal with a pressing legal matter. I arrived back in Wuppertal very late at night and having dealt with the business I had returned for, I decided to stay overnight and return to the exercise next morning. Our quarter, adjoining the schoolteachers' mess, had suffered from prowlers and while I was away Heather spent the nights with the children locked in the main bedroom with an upstairs telephone handy. It was a rule that wives left alone would not answer the door until sure of the identity of any caller. I phoned her from the barracks and arranged to throw pebbles at the window and then give a coded knock at the door. I was duly let in. A few days later my second in command's wife was discussing security with two of the lady schoolteachers and mentioned that we had had a problem with prowlers. The two ladies looked at each other.

"We know," said one of them. "We saw one only a few nights ago while the men were away on exercise. It was very late and he threw stones at the Major's bedroom window."

"Good heavens" said the second in commnd's wife. "Did you phone the guardroom?"

They looked at each other again.

"We didn't like to. You see, he was let in!" Heather said she could never work out after that whether the teachers regarded her with envy or dislike.

We fraternised regularly with the other units in our small garrison. Colonel Taylor, the CO of the Prince of Wales Own Regiment of Yorkshire (PWO) and an experienced regimental soldier, was always there for advice and support when I needed to consult him as our garrison Commander. We had a good deal of social contact because I had known two of his company commanders at the Staff College. One Sunday morning while we were having an after church drink and gossip in our mess, Peter Taylor phoned me and said abruptly.

"Are your officers there? All of them?"

"Yes," I said. "Why?"

"No time now. I'll tell you later. Meanwhile I want you all down here to my mess dressed in Blues as soon as you can make it."

He rang off. Whatever it was, it was urgent. We all went home and changed into the blue, high necked tunic and trousers known officially as Number One Dress but colloquially as blue patrols or just Blues and used for ceremonial or social occasions. We went to the PWO Mess in a body.

We arrived to find all the Battalion officers in Blues together with as many other supporters as the CO could muster at very short notice and all was made clear. The Battalion, with an intention to foster Anglo-German relations, had created a display of its regimental silver in the gymnasium and had advertised in the local paper inviting the population at large to come and see it. They had expected a fairly small attendance, certainly no more than could be coped with by their own officers. They had not reckoned with the Teutonic fascination with all things military; half the town had turned up and we were required to become instant experts on the regimental history and explain how and where the exhibits had been presented or acquired.

The display was truly magnificent. The PWO are an amalgamation of the old East and West Yorkshire regiments with a long and glorious regimental history; they had seen service in most parts of the globe. There were silver gilt pieces, silver soldiers down the generations in regimental dress, silver mountains, silver soldiers carrying silver muskets and placing flags atop buildings and other artefacts, all in silver or silver gilt, too numerous to record. We had a crash course on the exhibits and were thrown in at the deep end. But it was not possible to go wrong. Goodwill was so much in evidence that whatever we said, however inventive, became the gospel truth so far as the visitors were concerned. It was a great day for the PWO, indeed for the Brits in general and very much appreciated by the local population.

The town of Wuppertal had a feature found nowhere else. This was an overhead railway known as the Schwaberbahn, a forerunner of the modern monorail. I believe it still survives. It runs over the river down the valley for about ten miles and is supported by steel beams forming an inverted 'V' with the legs on either bank and an overhead rail secured under the apex. The cars are suspended from the rail and a regular service is maintained. The installation was manufactured in nearby Solingen, Germany's famous steel town. It was, so the story goes, made before the First World War for South Shields on Tyneside, but when completed, the town couldn't afford it and Wuppertal stepped in. The local population used it to commute along the long, meandering valley but for us, and particularly the children, it was a splendid joyride. Most Saturday mornings there were British families travelling to and fro on the Schwaberbahn.

The population of Wuppertal at large was well disposed towards us but I never quite worked out the depth of enthusiasm on the part of officialdom. The commanding officers of the military garrison were entertained formally each year by the town officials, headed by the Burgermeister – the Mayor. Although commanding a minor unit, I was included in this invitation because my company was an independent command and housed in a major barracks because of its size. The German commander, Hans Clausem, was also included and it was very noticeable that he was 'one of us' and not one of them at these functions. I knew him well enough to remark on this and he told me that Wuppertal was well known to be doubtful about the military in general, possibly because it had suffered so badly in the war from the RAF fire bombing raids. The prevailing wind that swept down the narrow, high-sided valley had caused much of the town to go up in flames. Nevertheless the Mayor was an affable host and spoke near perfect English. We were entertained in the very impressive opera house and on my first visit I remarked to him on the quality of its design and the beauty of its internal decoration.

Deadpan, he replied, "Yes, we are very proud of it. We were very lucky. The old one was burned to the ground by your Royal Air Force and the rebuild has only recently been completed."

It is said that most of those who are of an age to recall November 22nd 1963 can remember with clarity exactly what they were doing on that fateful day. I can remember that we were organising an All Ranks Dance at our barracks in Wuppertal. The event was to take place that evening. It had become a tradition, initiated by one of my predecessors, to hold a social function for all ranks on the run-up to Christmas, I was happy to keep it up. The dance had always been a lavish affair and was eagerly looked forward to, particularly by the single men. We imported from the BAOR headquarters at Rheindahlen as many lorryloads of WRAC girls as we could persuade to come and they were supplemented by the unattached friends of the numerous German wives of our soldiers. Spirits were banned but beer and soft drinks were available. The presence of the girls normally ensured that we had no serious drink problems.

Realising that there would be fierce competition from other units in BAOR for the attendance of the WRAC girls at our dance, I thought it would be a good idea to 'make my number' with their officer at the Rheindahlen HQ. I went to see her a week or so before the dance. The WRAC officer, however, immediately handed me over to her RSM who proved to be a petite and initially rather forbidding woman. On hearing my request she sighed and opened a drawer in her desk to show a pile of invitations from units all over Germany.

"The girls are spoiled for choice," she said.

"I'll see that they're properly looked after," I replied.

"You needn't worry too much about that Major," tapping her forehead. "My girls are pretty sensible. They've got it up here."

I looked at her seriously. "I'm sure both you and I know, RSM, that it doesn't matter where the girls have got it. The boys will always find it."

She giggled, rather becomingly. I'd never heard an RSM giggle before. A small dimple appeared. Not so forbidding after all.

"I set that up for you, didn't I? An old joke Major; I've heard it before. But that doesn't lessen its truth. I'm sure you'll see that the girls are looked after. I'll do the best I can for you. It helps that you're not all that far away."

We parted amicably. The RSM was as good as her word. We had a bigger contingent of English girls than usual at the dance.

Preparations were well in hand and there were only a few hours to go before the dance was due to start when my second in command came into my office with a serious face and told me that President Kennedy had been shot and killed that very day.

There are times in the life of every career officer when the expression 'the loneliness of command' comes to mind. This was one of them. You didn't have to be a military genius to realise that a missile unit would deploy at an early alert state in any impending crisis and all we knew was that the leader of the free world – who had so recently proved himself in an eyeball to eyeball confrontation with President Khrushchev – had been killed, allegedly murdered. The prospect of my unit being called out with the drivers 'half cut' could not be contemplated. On the other hand the cancellation of our major annual social function would not only be a blow to morale but it would also generate unwelcome rumours and harm our deliberate and carefully nurtured low profile.

I decided to trust my soldiers but at the same time to take appropriate precautions. All officers and NCOs were assembled and told that despite the sad news the All Ranks Dance would go ahead as planned but would end at an earlier hour than was usual. They were instructed to brief their men on the reason for these limitations and to keep a close eye on alcohol consumption generally, but they were bidden particularly to make sure that the drivers of each missile tractor were and remained in a fit condition to drive. In the event the precautions were unnecessary. My soldiers proved themselves to be intelligent professionals. We enjoyed the evening and there were no instances of drunkenness.

It turned out that the order to deploy was not given as it became apparent that there was no sinister 'Red Plot' behind the assassination of the President. Shortly afterwards I thanked all ranks of my unit for their praiseworthy reaction to this potential crisis.

16

JSSC

An eventful first tour in Germany was cut short by a few months by a sudden posting to the Joint Services Staff College (JSSC). This was located at a country house in the village of Latimer in Buckinghamshire and was due to last six months. As its name implied, it received officers from all three armed services together with a number of Commonwealth and foreign students. There were married quarters for instructors only and students had to negotiate their own family accommodation from a list of houses and flats that had been graded as acceptable hirings by the College quartering organisation. We found a small cottage in the grounds of a large house overlooking the River Chess, which flowed past our back door. It had been the gardener's cottage, the central one of a terrace of three. On one side of us, in the chauffer's cottage, was Major Peter Sibbald of the Yorkshire Light Infantry (KOYLI) and wife Maureen and on the other side was Colonel Rahim Khan of Pakistan and his doctor wife, Mali, occupying an under-gardener's cottage.

It was a tight squeeze with three children. Although Helen, our eldest, had started boarding school, she was home for much of the summer and the course started in late spring. But it was a case of all being in the same boat and our neighbours became firm friends. Most of our free daylight hours in summer were spent in the communal garden. The Chess was a trout stream and I received permission from our lady landlord to fish at will. Sadly, it was heavily polluted by a detergent factory upstream and clumps of coloured foam drifted down past us all day. I caught plenty of fish and they seemed lively and healthy, but we were warned against eating them; the dog having done so after stealing one had been violently sick so it was prudent to adopt the technique of catch and release from then on.

The course could not be described as intensive, but there was plenty to learn. It concentrated on inter-service discussion and instruction. Although there had been an increasing degree of inter-service co-operation since the last major war, it had seemed to reach a plateau at fairly high levels; the JSSC set out to increase the degree of inter-service thinking at lower levels and I think that this aim was achieved. In the main the students were of equivalent rank – we were lieutenant commanders, majors and squadron leaders, and our directing staff instructors were naval captains, lieutenant colonels and wing commanders, one rank higher. The commandant rotated through the three armed services; during my course he was Major General Deakin of the Brigade of Guards, an approachable gentleman of infinite humour.

Much of the value of the course lay in the visits we made to various establishments and units across the three services. Literally seeing how the other two thirds operated and lived. We had a 'Seaday' with the Royal Navy and Royal Marines embarking at Portsmouth and sailing out to an area some miles south of St Catherine's Point – reminiscent of my time in HMS Pretoria Castle as a young rating. We visited several RAF units and watched flying demonstrations followed by a chance to talk to aircrew and ground staff. All this was useful to the soldiers and when we were hosts at the School of Infantry demonstration on Salisbury Plain, the sailors and airmen said they were suitably impressed.

A good deal of course time was spent studying events behind the Iron Curtain and I recall spending a couple of weeks attempting to analyse a long and immensely abstruse Communist Party Congress speech by Kruschev and then being required to write a three thousand word treatise on it.

During a short break in the course, Heather and I took the children with us to Scotland for a few days fishing. We booked five days at a B and B in Glen Rogart near Lairg in Sutherland and because of the shortage of time we travelled with the car by Motorail to Inverness. The days were spent fishing for the tiny trout on the inland lochs, attempting to lift sea trout out of the Kyle of Fleet and drinking in the matchless scenery of the northern highlands. The two old ladies who owned the B and B were enchanted with the children and spoiled them thoroughly.

Considerably refreshed, we drove to Inverness to put the car on the train for the journey south. We arrived at the station to be told that we were early and would have to wait a few hours before loading. I suddenly remembered that Culloden was not far from Inverness but my map gave no clue to its actual position. There was an oldish man sweeping the railway station forecourt. I asked him if he could direct me to the battlefield. He leaned on his brush and looked mystified.

"You know," I said, "Culloden," and added – in retrospect unnecessarily pompously, "the graveyard of the Clans." Enlightenment dawned.

"Aye," he said in that pure highland lilt. "The Forty-Five. It's on the lower road to Nean." He looked into the car. "Ye'll be showing the bairns? Ye'll mind to tell them there's one or two English lying there as well!"

17

3rd Division. The 'Fire Brigade'.

Arctic Circle to the Desert

After the JSSC course it was perhaps appropriate that my subsequent staff appointment was to the Third Division at Bulford Camp on Salisbury Plain as DAQMG (Operations), effectively the logistician responsible for planning and organising logistic support for brigade and divisional operations and exercises. The Division had been nominated as the United Kingdom Strategic Reserve – the UK's military fire brigade – and as such would be working in concert with 38 Group RAF operating from Upavon Airfield across the Plain and within sight of Bulford. When I arrived there to take up my new job, the divisional HQ was in Cyprus operating as part of the UN Force there. They were due back in the UK within weeks and I stayed in Bulford until the Division returned. We were allotted a married quarter in nearby Tidworth.

I took over the job from Major Bill Allen of my Corps who was and is a friend, now retired and a vintner in the South of France. I inherited a great pile of contingency plans relating to possible operations and of course these had to be kept up to date. One or two were activated during my tenure, but as every soldier knows, 'no plan survives contact' (with the enemy) and when a plan was occasionally extracted from the safe for activation, it was always subject to radical revision.

My immediate boss was the Division's Assistant Quartermaster General (AQMG) Lieutenant Colonel Bryan Watkins of the Royal Tank Regiment, a tall man of great enthusiasms, a powerful voice and a good sense of humour. We got on very well. He was kept busy with the day-to-day logistic problems of a field force division spread around the United Kingdom with brigades in Colchester, Aldershot and Tidworth. There was also a vast Territorial Army order of battle to be activated as necessary, but meanwhile to be kept supplied with vehicles, weapons and training assistance. He was therefore happy to let his several subordinates get on with what they were there for.

Our higher headquarters was the recently established HQ United

Kingdom Land Forces, located in nearby Wilton just north of Salisbury. It was said that when the decision was made to place all UK land forces under one rusticated HQ, the inevitable committee discussing nomenclature among other things, called in the future Commander in Chief to sit in with them at the decision making session. The army has long been wedded to acronyms and it was decided to call the new Headquarters Land Forces United Kingdom (LFUK). The chairman looked towards the new C in C, a senior general, and asked if he was happy with that. The C in C elect, who had been doodling on his pad, flung down his pencil and said.

"No. I'm not." Consternation among the Committee.

"Why not?" said the Chairman politely.

"Because I am not prepared to travel around my command being called 'Kinkelfuk'!"

When the laughter had died down LFUK quickly became UKLF and existed as such for many years until recently renamed UK Land Command.

Major General Michael Carver commanded the Division when I arrived but very shortly afterwards he handed over to Major General Blacker – or Monkey Blacker as he was known throughout the army and the world associated with horses. He was a cavalryman, late of The Royal Inniskilling Dragoon Guards. He descended on us whirlwind style. He was super fit for his years and was reputed to have boxed for his regiment in his forties. He decided that his staff needed more organised exercise and soon had all officers from his headquarters out of doors twice a week for exercise sessions. The senior doctor, worried about the effect on people in a hitherto rather sedentary existence being required to throw telegraph poles around and run long distances to a timed programme, managed to persuade the General to divide these sessions into 'under thirty-fives' and 'over thirty-fives', but Monkey, although by then in his late forties, joined the under thirty-fives. He had a delightful wife, known as Zulu and one would get Christmas cards from 'Monkey and Zulu'. He was a charismatic and effective GOC and had the unconscious but priceless gift of inspiring affection and respect, particularly among his headquarters staff. General Monkey ran a happy ship, one of the happiest I can recall during my service.

He was, however, by no means a pushover and a 'rocket' from the

GOC tended to bite deeply. There were two military gymnasiums in Tidworth quite near the general's quarter and he spent a good deal of time in them. I think I was the only member of his immediate staff who also lived in Tidworth and he made me their unofficial custodian. I was told to make absolutely sure that at least one gym was to be kept open at all times. I duly passed this instruction to the civilian works officer of the Tidworth Garrison and he promised to see that it was strictly adhered to.

One morning the ADC came in to my office with a troubled face and said, "The General wants to see you – now! I don't know what it's about but he's not at all happy."

Mentally reviewing all the things that could have gone wrong but unable to think of anything that could have attracted such high level annoyance, I went into the GOC's office to be met with an icy stare and, "Didn't I tell you to see that at least one of the gymnasiums in Tidworth is to be kept open?"

"Yes sir, you did."

"Then why was I locked out of both this morning, with workmen all over the place? If you don't know, go and find out – now."

Thoroughly chastened, I spoke to the civilian works officer who said he didn't know either but he would investigate and ring me back. He didn't do so and I rang him an hour or so later to be told by his lady clerk that he had driven to Bulford to see me, or so she thought. He didn't do this either and in a fine fury I was about to ring his office again when the ADC came into my office and said, "Flap over. The works man, who is apparently an ex-member of your Corps, has been to see the General and explained that it was no fault of either his or yours, just a contractor cock-up. He'd had your instructions and passed them on, but the contractor had ignored them in the interests of saving a bob or two by doing both jobs at the same time. One of the gymnasiums is open again and the general says you can go back to sleep!"

It turned out that the works officer was a retired RASC quartermaster officer, a fact that I had not known. When I rang him to thank him for his action he said that for him it was all water off a duck's back and if he had a pound for all the irate generals he had placated in his service he'd be a rich man. The incident was not mentioned again.

At last we were in the helicopter era. We actually had a liaison flight close by at the Army Air Corps HQ at Middle Wallop. Fourteen years after Korea we had no longer to look enviously at the US Army's ability to field helicopters for casualty evacuation and staff liaison. A phone call to Middle Wallop, the Army Air Corps nearby HQ, could instantly bring a 'bubble' type chopper to our helicopter pad for a quick trip to a brigade or unit headquarters to settle something that needed map study or was otherwise too complicated to be settled on the phone. This was very useful and it didn't take us long to exploit the facility fully for planning purposes. 16 Parachute Brigade, based at Aldershot, was one of the formations under command of our GOC. It was led by firebrand and man of action Brigadier Tony Farrar-Hockley. The super fit paras were impatient of staff procedures and wanted everything done yesterday. This was fine and we did our best to accommodate them, sometimes to the annoyance of more pedestrian superior headquarters, but I have to say that they were a 'can do' bunch and despite all the bombast and corner cutting that they were so adept at, it was a pleasure to work with them.

It was a very active job and we didn't spend a great deal of time in our offices. I had to be away a good deal, visiting our units throughout the UK and taking part in joint reconnaissance trips with the RAF. There were numerous exercises to plan, many of them overseas, necessitating planning and liaison visits, in particular to Cyprus, Malta and Libya. We organised at least one major exercise a year jointly with the RAF and at least one jointly with the Royal Navy, making use of the assault ships, *Fearless* and *Intrepid* that were designed to accommodate enough troops for a seaborne assault.

The major joint exercises in the Libyan Desert entailed a vast amount of logistic planning. My task was to activate the strategic stockpiles of equipment and vehicles that we maintained in Cyprus, get them loaded on the landing craft for transmission to the harbour of Tobruk, then get them unloaded and delivered to the units flying in for the exercise from the UK.

Then it was on to Malta to arrange in liaison with the RAF for airdrops of supplies at pre-arranged points in the desert, the aircraft for this task being based at RAF Luqa on the island of Malta. Sometimes there would be an airborne assault exercise using VC10 aircraft to carry the troops to Luqa, staging overnight at Malta and then re-embarking the paras at Luqa to drop from smaller aircraft into the desert. The General Staff planning for this was pretty complicated, the logistic planning even more so because liaison was not only necessary with the RAF, it also involved the 'Q' staffs of Malta and Cyprus and activation of a sea tail to get the stores from the strategic stockpiles to the exercise area.

Inevitably, I got to know my opposite numbers on the staffs of the overseas headquarters that we dealt with quite well, as I had to stay there sometimes for a week or so, sometimes at both ends of the exercises. A number of the staff officers in Cyprus in particular, were women – (WRAC), always as efficient as their male counterparts, but often also more practical and thoughtful, as women tend to be. They occupied separate quarters to the male officers but shared the same mess. I left Cyprus when the stores and vehicles had been sent over to the desert exercise and I went directly to RAF El Adem in Libya where I became a staff officer in the joint Army/RAF tented headquarters set up there. I manned a radio set beside my RAF opposite number, a wing commander from 38 Group RAF.

Army movements was one of my staff responsibilities in the field and a Royal Engineer 'mover', Douglas Harding, later to be known as Old Douglas, worked to me on this.

One day, while giving instructions by radio for the recovery of some specialist fuel containers that the roving Bedouin had stolen from the dropping zone in the desert, there was a tap on my shoulder and Colonel Ken Lomax, the divisional RASC commander, appeared by my side accompanied by his second in command, Major Sid Pledger, a great practical joker known to his intimates as El Sid. Ken Lomax offered a serious face.

He said, "I have something to tell you that may or may not be disturbing. Did you realise that you'd left your pyjamas behind in Cyprus?"

I said I had realised and had signalled back to Cyprus to get them sent over.

"Well," said Lomax, "they arrived in a parcel on an aircraft yesterday en route to UK and the young despatcher, not realising that you were here in the Joint Force HQ showed enough initiative to get your home address and sent them on."

"That's all right," I said. "Heather will realise what's happened and they'll be all nicely washed and clean when I get back." There was a pause.

"That's not all," said Lomax. "The parcel was damaged. There was a note, unsealed, that fell out. The lad replaced it and mended the parcel but confessed that he'd read the note before he sent the parcel home."

I began to feel a sense of disquiet. "What did it say?"

Sid broke in. "It was from a woman. Name of Linda. Obviously one of your WRAC friends. He couldn't remember exactly but he could recall that it ended with 'Love, and two Xs'."

They looked at me with expressionless faces.

I said airily, but with a sinking heart, "Well, they're all nice girls and we've become good friends in a strictly business sense of course. Linda is the staff captain to my opposite number in Cyprus, but that sounds a bit over the top."

They nodded sympathetically. A further pause while they regarded me intently and then Sid produced the parcel and the unsealed note from behind his back. Across the years, I can remember the words almost precisely. It read, 'Dear Freddie, We had your signal and found your pyjamas, enclosed. You'll never become a success in the Service if you scatter your kit across the Med like this. Take care. Linda.' Nothing more – the addition of love and Xs characteristically down to Sid.

"Do you know," said Lomax conversationally, "all the world passed across your face just then. You looked positively hunted." Back at home, knowing the small world I inhabited, I lost no time in showing Heather the note before the inevitably embellished story reached her.

RAF El Adem was about fourteen miles inland along an arrow straight desert road from Tobruk, that famously contested lynch pin seaport town during the Second World War. It had a couple of decent beaches that the RAF used during their free time but little of interest to visitors other than the row of British Army regimental badges that greeted you on entering the town from the desert and the enormous, fortress-like, German Africa Korps war memorial on a hilltop across the harbour. El Adem, a non-families' posting, must have vied with the memorable Habbaniyah of my youth as one of the most boring RAF stations on earth.

Yet the desert itself could, on occasion, be almost sublime. The Libyan coastal plain is not the Beau Geste type desert of rolling sand dunes and oases. It's all a mixture of very sparse and intermittent scrub scattered on a limitless expanse of small stones and sand. The Great

Sand Sea that is the desert of song and fable starts miles inland. The nature of the coastal plain offers reasonable going for both wheeled and tracked vehicles and this is where our joint force training took place. We operated across the territory that had seen the British Eighth Army and the German Afrika Korps play a deadly game of military ping pong for nearly three years.

And desert living is not at all unpleasant, certainly for short periods of time. The air is as clean and fresh as one could ever know it in these days of almost universal pollution. It is also dry enough to clean up the 'tubes' of the most bronchially inclined or catarrhal person; in my experience hangovers were almost unknown. While the attractions of the daytime climate for sun worshippers are obvious, the nights were clear and cold and the stars, free of manufactured light, more sharp and bright even than at sea, or so it seemed. From a professional point of view there was very little habitation, no crops to be accused of despoiling and no civilian traffic to worry about; in all a perfect place for military exercises and indeed for a war if there has to be one.

Between the end of a major overseas exercise and a return to UK, there is always a delay for Headquarters staffs while units operating in the field, who naturally have priority for air passages, are embarked and flown home when they have delivered their heavy equipment to the ports. This is an opportunity for those not heavily involved in the winding down operations to visit nearby places of interest. From El Adem, other than a tour of wartime battlefields for which there was not enough time, there were only two places accessible by road, that were worth bothering about. These were the ancient settlements of Cyrene and Appolonia, important trading places in their day, that had lain virtually untouched since they were laid waste centuries ago after the Carthaginians had made the desert bloom. Mass tourism had not yet reached them in the nineteen sixties. Very little rots or rusts in the clear desert air and ancient artefacts were clearly visible in the clear water of Appolonia, the coastal town and port that was devastated by an earthquake and sank into the sea in Roman times and there were mosaic floors and graceful columns at Cyrene. The round trip of four hundred miles entailed an overnight stay but the visit was the highlight of an otherwise pretty dull 'winding down' time.

One of the peripheral tasks of 3rd Division was to find a battalion for the NATO flank protection force, formally designated the Allied

Command (Europe) Mobile Force but shortened in conversation to Ace Mobile. Its task was to guard the western and eastern extremities of NATO against attempts by a potential aggressor to turn the flanks. All NATO nations could be required to provide elements for the Force but in 1965 it was the first time that the UK Third Division had been detailed for it. The Force western deployment area was Finnmark in northern Norway, well up within the Arctic Circle and well to the north of the northernmost Norwegian brigade. A winter exercise was due and it was clearly going to be exceptionally cold. We did some research on winter living conditions in the field and found that snow holes and reindeer skins were key items for the maintenance of body heat at night. Apparently Norwegian troops wound reindeer skins round their sleeping bags and were experts at digging snow holes to sleep in.

"We'd better get some advice," said the General. "You must go and have a look and find out how we get our hands on them."

I was sent to see the Norwegian brigadier for advice on the purchase of these skins and sundry other matters.

My first stop was Headquarters Armed Forces Northern Europe (AFNORTH) in Oslo to consult the staff. I had known that the Green Howards had been heavily involved in Churchill's ill-fated attempt to liberate Norway in the early stages of the Second World War and that there was a 'special relationship' between the Regiment and that country – the King of Norway was and is Colonel in Chief of the Regiment. I was therefore not surprised to note an unusual number of Green Howards officers on the Oslo staff. Although it was nearly twenty years since I had been part of the Regiment and my primary loyalty now rested elsewhere, early connections never completely vanish and it was easy to 'make my number' and gain staff support for my trip to the northern brigade HQ. It was September and Norway was at its best. Long days were still in evidence and it was cool with a strong hint of an autumn chill. Everywhere was spotlessly clean.

I set off in a Scandanavian Air Services twin engined aircraft for the flight north. There was a stop halfway up at the small coastal town and fishing port of Bodo, itself well inside the Arctic Circle, followed by an hour long hop to the airfield of Bardufoss, one of the two most northerly airfields in Norway, the other being Tromso slightly to the north and west at the edge of the sea. I was met by a young officer of the Norwegian brigade and driven to his headquarters, where I was ushered in to the presence of his brigadier, a jolly gentleman who, I was pleased to see, wore British medal ribbons on his tunic. He became even jollier when I presented him with two bottles of Scotch, extremely expensive in Norway even then; he told me that he had escaped the Germans during the war in a small boat and landed in Scotland where he promptly joined the Norwegian Free Forces and had stayed in the Army after the war.

I asked about the use and value of reindeer skins.

"They are absolutely vital in winter," he said. "We simply couldn't do without them. We can teach your battalion the techniques of winter living, snow holes etcetera, but you must have the skins or you will take casualties from the cold."

I asked how we could get hold of them.

"We buy them from the Lapps," he said. "At certain times of the year they cull and skin their herds and then they come down here and we barter for the skins. They would normally be here by now but there's no accounting for them. They know no frontiers and their lives are regulated by the seasons. I think the thing to do is to go home after your port recce and I'll signal your Headquarters when the arrival of the Lapps is imminent.

"One other thing," he went on. "They will sell both cured and uncured skins. I strongly recommend that you buy the cured skins. They are twice the price of the uncured ones, but they store very well if you want to use them again."

It had become very cold despite fact that it was only late September and I was glad of my British Warm greatcoat that had so pleased the Brigadier. Reminded him of old times, he said. Dressed as I was in Service Dress with Sam Browne belt while my Norwegian friends were clad in woollens and parkas, I blessed the impulse to take the heavy coat with me. My final job there was to visit the port of Soreissa to the south of Finnmark and assess its ability to meet the needs of our ships – that 'sea tail' essential to the operational competence of airlanded troops, in that it carries their vehicles and heavy equipment.

The Port had been chosen on Norwegian advice as being reasonably ice free in the winter months and provided that it had deep enough water at the wharves and good road access it would serve for us. Our logistic ships carried their own gantries and handling equipment. My young Norwegian escorting officer travelled to Soreissa with me in a heated Volvo jeep. I was relieved to note that the access road was quite adequate for our vehicles. We stood on the wharf with a keen wind whistling across the water and I suddenly realised that my feet and legs had become numb up to my knees. "Pretty chilly isn't it?" I said, conversationally.

"Oh, I don't know," he replied. "Can't be much more than a few degrees below." I conducted the remainder of the recce in the jeep with the heater at full blast.

The journey home via Oslo produced its own drama. The flight to Heathrow had been cancelled and with the first snowstorm of the year impending it made sense to accept whatever was on offer. I got a seat on a commuter aircraft bound for Copenhagen and before we took off from Oslo I had a grandstand view of the Norwegians' short way with nature. The threatened snowstorm duly arrived as we moved along the perimeter track to the runway. Immediately four enormous snow blowers moved down the runway in echelon and in a trice it was cleared and we were able to take off. I said how impressed I was to the Danish passenger sitting next to me.

He laughed. "It gets much, much worse than this" he said "from now on it will very often be closed for days. We were lucky."

I managed to avoid an overnight stay in Copenhagen and caught an evening flight to Heathrow.

My report on my Norwegian recce complete with appropriate recommendations about the purchase of reindeer skins found its way to the Ministry of Defence as did all things involving expenditure on any scale. It spawned a meeting that I was bidden to attend to represent the Division. Fortunately this was chaired by Colonel Robert Lisle, an 'Old Coaster' from West Africa days who I knew well. It was recommended and subsequently agreed by General Monkey that I should go out to buy the skins when my Norwegian brigadier friend signalled to let us know that the Lapps were selling. The Ministry insisted, however, that their representative should be present, presumably to ensure that I didn't spend too much. Their representative was a pleasant young civilian moneyman.

True to his word, the brigadier signalled that the Lapps had put in an appearance and were selling skins. We retraced my journey to Northern Norway. At Bodo, on the way up, the aircraft filled with ladies travelling to Tromso, its final destination. We were told that they were the wives of oil rig technicians returning from a day's outing.

By now it was quite late in the year and, flying at about twenty-five thousand feet, the snow covered central range of mountains could be seen far beneath us, a majestic sight. Suddenly the cabin of the aircraft started to fill with acrid smoke. My companion and I looked at each other, frozen to our seats. The Tromso women started to scream; I had a fleeting thought 'is this how it all ends?' It is a curious feeling. Your first instinct is to run through the options; then realisation that nothing can be done is followed by a suspension of belief – 'this can't be happening to me!' The jagged, snow covered peaks below suddenly looked ominous and my companion and I, discussing it afterwards, agreed that we were thinking seriously about joining in the screaming when the aircraft captain said something in Norwegian that calmed the ladies considerably.

He then said in English, "I understand that we have British passengers on board. Do not be alarmed. The pressurisation plant has failed and I must descend very quickly. You may feel some discomfort in your ears and it will get very cold. The cabin staff will give you blankets and something to keep you warm."

With that the aircraft virtually stood on its head and zoomed down to what I was told afterwards was eight thousand feet. As it pulled out of its dive I felt a bang in my left ear and went completely deaf on that side. We were then given blankets and more than a sufficiency of a potent Scandanavian spirit drink. The aircraft was grounded at Bardufoss until a replacement could be provided but we were collected by our Norwegian friends and taken to the Brigade HQ.

My civilian companion, although not very senior, had a hotline to the Treasury. He was persuaded by the Norwegian brigadier that buying uncured skins was a false economy and frantic signals passed back and forth to London. He was told, however, that he was to undertake to buy the cheapest available and so we ended up with a battalion's worth of uncured skins that the Norwegians agreed to store for us free of charge. The battalion – so far as I can remember it was the Somerset and Cornwall Light Infantry – went to Norway and carried out the exercise successfully, using the uncured skins. They were placed in store for use on the winter exercise the following year. When the store was opened for the next battalion, nobody could go near it because of the smell of the rotting skins and as an emergency measure, very expensive cold weather kit had to be bought from Canada with scarce hard currency. Our Treasury mandarins always know best even when presented with expert local knowledge.

The sequel for me was a visit to the doctor for lasting deafness in one ear.

He examined me and said, "This is very curious. Have you had a flying accident recently?" I recounted the tale of the aircraft in Norway.

"Ah," he said. "I thought so. You have a burst eardrum. We used to get this with fighter pilots in the war when they pulled out of a too steep dive. It will mend in time, but it will leave a recognisable scar and it might have some effect on your long term hearing."

How right he was. Incurable tinnitus occurred a few years later followed by impaired hearing in later years. After expert examination all were pronounced to be 'of service origin' so that the expensive hearing aid I now wear was at least paid for by the State.

There followed other training exercises, one at home with the Division deployed around the United Kingdom from Castle Martin on the tip of Pembrokeshire to Otterburn in the North and as far West as Ulster. This was some years before the Troubles erupted. There was no hint of them when one brigade of our Division deployed in the Antrim Mountains operating against a mythical enemy. All three brigades were controlled from a tented Joint Force HQ set up with 38 Group RAF and our Divisional HQ and located on spare land at Greenham Common that was not at that time being used by its American occupants. As time went by we became quite skilled in the field of 'jointery', perhaps more so with the RAF than with the Royal Navy

Towards the end of my tour of duty with 3rd Division our fourth daughter, Lucy, was born at Tidworth Military Hospital. A gorgeous blonde to add to our three lovely redheads. Mother and daughter hale and hearty. Particularly good grounds for a celebration. Although our new addition was very much wanted, Heather had worried slightly that at thirty-eight she may have been a little old to produce another one.

As my third staff tour drew to a close, I pondered the possibilities for the future. I knew that I was due for a job with soldiers – at regimental duty. I would be very lucky indeed to get yet another posting outside Europe. Our overseas stations had shrunk to a handful with the loss of most of the Far East and Africa. Hong Kong, Cyprus and Gibraltar were virtually all the accompanied possibilities left. We maintained a tenuous hold on Aden but that was rapidly reaching boiling point and it was likely that families would be sent home in the near future, leaving units scaled down to active service status. The best I could hope for would be a job with an armoured divisional transport regiment in the Rhine Army.

One morning during this critical period, Peter Upton, a red-trousered 11th Hussar, and the Division's staff officer looking after discipline, postings and the 'people' side of logistics, strolled into my office. We chatted for a bit – a daily ritual – and he said as he was leaving:

"Oh, by the way, you've been posted."

He got his reaction. "What! Where? When? As what?"

His face cracked – almost a leer. "You're going to be a GSO1 Instructor, a DS, at the Staff College."

"Pull the other one Peter. Now give me the real news."

"Pukka," he said. "General Monkey and the A/Q (Bryan Watkins had been succeeded by Robin Carnegie, a cavalryman) both know about it and are pleased for you. Also, you'll be promoted. They're no longer local lieutenant colonels as in our day at Camberley. Someone has persuaded the Treasury that the job is worth the pay, so you get the paid temporary rank until you become substantive."

I sat back, stunned. I would have laid very long odds against this happening; indeed it had never entered my mind as a possibility. I would be happy to have a go, but like most of my contemporaries, I had regarded the DS at the Staff College as rare beings hovering above the rest of us on an intellectual plane to which few could aspire. Stuff and nonsense of course and a tribute to a painstaking build up of the Staff College at Camberley as a difficult hurdle to be surmounted before promotion could be achieved. It followed, however, that success as an instructor at that hallowed establishment should further enhance one's career chances and I was both surprised and grateful to be given the opportunity.

18

Camberley Again and Henley

I was to take over from Ian Hodder of my Corps who was leaving to take command of a regiment in Germany. We had both been students on the 1958 Staff College course and were therefore well acquainted. Heather and I were also pleased to be able to take over his detached married quarter in the Staff College grounds midway between the nineteenth century building housing the Staff College and the complex of buildings that housed the Royal Military Academy Sandhurst. The combined grounds, secured by guarded entrance gates at the eastern and western ends, were both extensive and attractive – very safe for children to roam in and complete with an assault course that became an unofficial play area after Sandhurst's normal training hours were over. It would be a pleasure to be able to walk to work in two or three minutes. The quarters we had lived in when I was a student there had been located well outside the grounds.

The town hadn't changed much. Camberley Kate was still exercising her dogs and the rapid expansion sparked off by the construction of the M3 Motorway had yet to happen. By now both our older girls were at boarding schools in the south of England and easy to reach on 'out' weekends so all things considered, we were well satisfied with the domestic arrangements.

By this time Commandants and staff had changed several times since my student days but most of the civilian staff members were still there and used to seeing harassed students returning as even more harassed instructors. DS were organised for writing and exercise setting in specialist teams of two or three. There was a tactics team, a joint warfare team and others devoted to organising and applying instruction in the art and techniques of warfare in all its aspects from full scale operations through limited war to internal security tasks and aid to the civil power. All formal instruction through exercises and presentations was written and presented by the directing staff, sometimes on a tutorial basis in syndicates of ten and sometimes in plenary sessions either with the whole college attending or in divisions presided over by the divisional colonel, who was one rank up from the 'dull, brutish mass' of DS.

I took Ian Hodder's place as the team leader of the Administrative Team, as it was known. At that time every activity in the British Army connected with replenishment of supplies and ammunition, transport and repair, casualty evacuation and movement of troops came under the heading of 'administration', partly because no one could be bothered to come up with a more descriptive term to describe these vital activities and partly because the front line element of the Army led by the main 'blood letters' or 'teeth arms', the cavalry and infantry, had traditionally preferred not to know what went on behind them.

There were more enlightened exceptions to this attitude and in my team I had a gunner officer who later reached four star general rank as Commander in Chief British Army of the Rhine and Northern Army Group and later still was appointed by the Queen as the Master Gunner at St James's Park. It helped that we knew each other well. Martin Farndale had been the Brigade Major Royal Artillery in 17th Gurkha Division in Malaya when I had been GSO 2 SD there. He had a keen interest in 'admin' as it was colloquially known and supported my contention that we should encourage the Army to embrace the Greek word 'logistics' to describe what we did. This was already in vogue in the US Army and it was not difficult to persuade the Deputy Commandant of the College, who acted as Director of Studies, that we should change the name of our team. A short paper was submitted, agreed, and we became the Logistics Team, shortened in conversation to the Log Team. Terminology matters.

The set-up was exactly similar to my student days of 1958, eight years earlier, only this time I was viewing it from a different side. I was no longer 'one of us'. I was now 'one of them!' albeit on a learning curve as a new member of the directing staff. While students had to undergo six terms of instruction during the course, the system for DS was based on teaching and 'swinging'. You would be teaching a syndicate of ten for a term of six weeks and then 'swing' for a term, when you would be occupied preparing and writing exercises and presentations for the following terms. We were given great licence to expand our ideas for fulfilling our general brief. The brief for the Log Team was simply to educate the students in the logistics of operations past, present and projected. Thus we had an input and a part to play in all exercises and presentations, both on paper and on the ground. Ideas were welcomed, indeed encouraged. It was a golden opportunity to indulge our opinions by incorporating them in the 'pinks' – the instructors' notes on every discussion topic; these were given to the DS but denied to the students. We could also write the scripts for presentations and act onstage the parts that we considered most suitable for us.

There was a drawing office at our disposal with several excellent civilian draughtsmen. I had always wanted to make a cartoon film, an ambition that was shared, I discovered, with the head draughtsman but I had never had either the time or the facilities and he said he had never had a script to work to. So I wrote a script entitled 'Limited War Logistics' – a title hardly likely to send Steven Spielberg singing to the bank, but based on the Cyprus problems of the 1960s with Archbishop Makarios and General Grivas as the villains. My draughtsman friend did a superb job and it went down well at its premiere, a plenary session; I hope it imparted a bit of logistical instruction into the bargain. Also, giving rein to my penchant for military history, I managed to slip into the programme a presentation with voiceovers and music that reviewed the progress of modern military logistics from the shambles of the Crimea to the birth of computer dominated supply, transport, warehousing and distribution.

While engaged in scripting this presentation I needed an older voice to quote extracts from some of the despatches from William Howard Russell, *The Times* newspaper's famed special correspondent during the middle and latter part of the nineteenth century, so I went down to the college library and asked Colonel Young, the retired officer librarian, if he would be prepared to help.

"Why me?" he asked keenly.

"Because sir," I said tactfully, "I need a voice with gravitas and authority nicely mixed and yours would be perfect for the task."

He laughed. "Flattery wins the day again. I'll do it. But there's a price. You're going to have to help me reorganise and tidy up the library shelves in your spare time."

I didn't need to think. "Gladly. I've been meaning to browse down here more often, but other things have got in the way."

I managed an hour or so each day until the librarian was satisfied that the condition of his stock was up to his exacting standards and it was while rummaging in a dark corner that I came across several copies of a small red bound book entitled *The Soldiers' Pocket Book for Field Service*. It was obviously old and the author was one Colonel Garnet Wolseley.

I sat back, seized with a sense of discovery. Garnet Wolseley! A name to conjure with. In Victorian and into early Edwardian times his name was a byword for military organisation and efficiency. The Corps of Royal Engineers has always been noted for its deep reservoir of extraordinarily talented officers – not a few of whom have been genuine eccentrics. Chinese Gordon instantly springs to mind, but there have been many others, unsung but sufficiently plentiful to credit the Corps' officers with being collectively 'mad, married or Methodist'.

Garnet Wolseley was a sapper, eccentric, fiery and unamiable by turns, but blessed with that 'infinite capacity for taking pains' that is held to be the hallmark of genius. The small square book I held in my hands, all five hundred and fifty small type pages of it, was written not at the height of his career but in his forties when he was Deputy Quartermaster General in Canada. He published it at his own expense because he saw a need for it, the War Office being too mean to provide money for the purpose. Much of the advice he offers is as fresh and true today as it was when it was written in 1869.

Sir Garnet Wolseley became far and away Britain's most popular soldier, the living model for W.S. Gilbert's 'modern major general' satirised in the Pirates of Penzance. In late Victorian times, 'shipshape and Bristol fashion' gave place to 'all Sir Garnet' for anything done properly. He died as Field Marshal the Viscount Wolseley in 1913, a year before the Army he had helped to fashion was to meet its greatest challenge. Colonel Young generously allowed me to borrow a copy of Sir Garnet's Little Red Book; it became the subject of an article published elsewhere for which I received the princely sum of fifty pounds.

We were all enjoying the luxury of grinding our own particular axes and to some extent our students acted in the capacity of critics for they were very much on the ball. Many went on to higher things. During my three years as a teacher with B Division of the College, I can recall many future generals as students, at least one president of an African state, one or two future MPs and a junior minister as well as a high-level knee breeched functionary at the Palace of Westminster. It was very unusual for members of the directing staff to leave because of shortcomings; I can recall only one officer who was 'ploughed' but several decided that they had a vocation for teaching and retired from the service to pursue an academic career.

There were one or two perks, not many. For us it tended to be a relentless if enjoyable grind. But the annual Battlefield Tour was entertaining as well as educational. The job of administering it naturally fell to the Log Team and Martin Farndale became the expert. He hit on the idea of taking over the hotels of a small holiday resort in Normandy just before it opened for the annual summer season. We fixed on Cabourg, not far from the Second World War landing beaches and with the enthusiastic co-operation of the mayor and the town's hoteliers, our students, instructional staff and guest artists descended on the small town for a full working week.

The first year was a great success and we repeated the arrangements for the following year. This was slightly marred by an incident reminiscent of a French farce, hilarious in retrospect like so many of these things, but a bit tricky at the time. There was a regimental sergeant major and a small soldier staff at the College to provide drivers, clerks and general tasks that could not be done by civilians. Before the Battlefield Tour got under way an advance party commanded by the RSM and augmented by soldier labour from Aldershot went to France to set up the administration for the Tour. They were accommodated in one of the Cabourg hotels and by all accounts had an enjoyable time when off duty. It was a popular chore.

It was part of the job of the duty NCO to root them out of bed each morning at an early hour. One morning an imported corporal who did not know all the men, was performing this task when he entered one of the soldiers' rooms to find the man in bed with a young woman. On such occasions NCOs tend to be somewhat peremptory and with a cry of, "Up you get you lucky bastard", he hoicked the man out of bed then went round to the other side, dragged the young woman out, slapped her behind and said, "And as for you, blossom, you'd better get off home before your mum finds out."

It was only when he was assailed by a torrent of French from both of them that he realised that something was wrong. They turned out to be not only man and wife but also young relatives of the proprietor's wife;

they had arrived late at night and been given accommodation in the half of the hotel that had been opened for the Staff College. Sense of humour failure on the part of Madame, but the proprietor himself eventually saw the funny side of it. Bottles of scotch changed hands and the incident went no further.

Now and then there was another much sought after perk when overseas commanders asked for observers from the Staff College to attend and comment on their in-theatre tours and exercises. Competition for places was strong and I vied with fellow DS inventing profoundly specious reasons to justify nomination as an observer on this or that overseas enterprise. The Tactics Team naturally collared the lion's share of these outings but I managed to get myself included on one memorable jaunt because of my recent experience of the Libyan desert.

General Johnny Frost of Arnhem fame was commanding our land forces in the Middle East from his HQ in Malta and had planned a three day study of the 8th Army's operations against Rommel's Afrika Korps in the desert war. I was chosen to be an observer for this along with John Graham, an Argyll and Sutherland Highlander turned parachutist. We flew to Malta and were accommodated in style there before flying to RAF El Adem with General Frost in his small communication aircraft.

We were based at RAF El Adem for the study and left there each morning in a procession of Land Rovers, raising a dust storm that must have been reminiscent of those created by wartime vehicle convoys and so beloved of the Luftwaffe's Stukas and the fighter bombers of the RAF. The study concentrated on the Gazala Line battles and both British and German brigade commanders were there as guest artists. We visited the Knightsbridge Box on a windswept plain, the empty cartridge cases still evident under the desert dust, and of course we travelled the length of the Gazala escarpment itself. We were organised in syndicates and General Frost's staff had prepared problem questions along the lines of a Staff College exercise. Brigadier Pip Roberts, who had commanded a brigade in the Gazala battles, gave a moving account of the action and following the account by the German side, General Frost called for questions and comments. When asked what intelligence his radios had provided, the German commander laughed.

"Radio? We didn't have any. We used runners when necessary, but mostly we fought the battle visually."

It was another example of the undoubted fact that the Germans make superb soldiers but it doesn't tell us why, if that is so, they have not won a war since 1870.

Perhaps the most poignant sight was the Free French brigade position on the southern flank of the feature at Bir Hachim. Of course the abandoned hardware had long gone, dragged away by scrap merchants. But the bone dry air of the desert is a great preserver and the empty wine bottles still lay in profusion around the slit trenches of the defenders; the wire was still there and the spent cartridge cases crunched underfoot. The Bir Hachim battle was particularly bitter. The French, dug in, fought a valiant action against great odds but were eventually overwhelmed by enemy mechanised troops.

Particularly interesting was an account of the activities of the Long Range Desert Group by David Lloyd Owen who served with them at this time. "While this was going on," he said. "We were miles to the south west playing havoc with enemy supply lines." The desert exploits of the LRDG, forerunners of the SAS, have passed into military legend.

I went back to Camberley with the satisfying feeling of achieving a long-term ambition. During those exercises in the desert with 3rd Division I had tried without success to create time for a tour of the battlefields but had to be content with one trip to ancient settlements and short tours around the immediate area of Tobruk. General Frost's study had presented me with what I had wanted to do. The emergence of Colonel Gadaffi and the Libyan coup shortly afterwards would have closed the country to any possibility of battlefield tours for many years.

It had become a tradition for Field Marshal Montgomery to address the students towards the end of each course. On these occasions 'Monty' let his hair down, feeling correctly that he was among fellow soldiers and could express his views freely on contemporary events as well as past ones. He demonstrated that he was master of several lecturers' tricks. One of these was to tell students that the Americans had been mistaken in being drawn into a war in Vietnam.

"My second rule of war," he said. "Is never to get involved in hostilities in South East Asia. There's nowhere to go." He then went on with his talk and invited questions. The students had been pondering on the conundrum raised by his answer to the previous question as Monty knew perfectly well and he was ready when someone inevitably got to his feet and asked what his first rule of war was.

"Don't march on Moscow," replied the Field Marshal to a roar of laughter.

He also had a fund of good Churchill stories. On one occasion in 1945 not long after the breakthrough into Germany, he was accompanying the Prime Minister on a trip to the front by car. It was a long journey and Churchill was an old man.

"Would you like a sanitary halt, Prime Minister?"

Churchill took his cigar out of his mouth. "How far is the Siegfried Line?"

"About ten miles from here," said Monty. "But why do you ask?"

"That's all right", replied Churchill. "I'll wait."

Camberley offered the students a full social life but the DS were more constrained by their heavier workload. Those students who did not go back later as DS probably wouldn't agree with this, but it was a fact. Keeping ahead of the student body entailed a good deal of midnight oil, particularly when teaching. But everything stopped for the Staff College Summer Ball. This was normally held at Minley Manor, still the home to C Division of the College about six miles from the main College building along the main A30, not far from Blackbushe airfield. The Ball was a lavish affair. The ladies rose to the occasion with a display of gorgeous dresses and eye-catching jewellery and the polyglot nature of the student body was reflected in the multicoloured styles and patterns of foreign dress uniforms. As always on these occasions however, the Oscar for spectacle went to the British Army. Almost every regiment and corps was represented in formal, multicoloured mess dress, in many cases dating back through three hundred years of history.

The setting was superb; the old country house seemed to preen on occasions such as this and the discreetly lit garden in high summer was rich in the heavy scents of lavender, old-fashioned roses and night scented stock. The warm late July nights were sometimes offset by cool breezes and between dances there were gentle walks down to a Ha Ha wall. The dance section of a regimental band in full regalia played until the early hours followed by breakfast at about five am.

Times were changing and an MOD sponsored study had

recommended that there should be a major shake-up and reorganisation of the Army's logistic services. The RASC was to be disbanded and its responsibilities were to be split between a new Corps to be dedicated to all forms of military transport, and the Royal Army Ordnance Corps, which was to take over the responsibility for supplies and barrack services. The Royal Engineers were to lose their responsibility for railways and movement services to the new Corps which was to control road, rail, sea and air transport – this in liaison with the RAF. The new Corps was to be known as the Royal Corps of Transport, (RCT). The vesting of the RCT took place just before I became a teacher at the Staff College and I had been rebadged and formally transferred to it.

Thus the Royal Army Service Corps, the 'Jam Stealers', marched – or they would perhaps prefer rode – into history. They had provided the sinews of war to generations of the British Army in peace and in war. They bequeathed to their successors not only their regimental silver and trappings, but also the 'Buller Collection', well known in numismatic circles as a matchless medal collection of honours, campaign medals and gallantry awards won by members of the Corps and its predecessors over two centuries; it included nine VCs. It was an honourable dissolution.

Movements, one of the Army's most important logistics functions, provided the RCT with a second 'tied' major general appointment, that of Director of Movements at the Ministry of Defence. With the disbandment of the RASC, the titles of units and sub units for the new transport corps changed to revert to those of a mounted corps, reflecting the history of military transport and movements. Divisional transport columns became regiments, their companies became squadrons and the smallest sub units became troops.

We lived life in two or three year bursts in the Service and the time for a posting was looming. I could justifiably expect command of a regiment of the new Corps, hopefully in Germany, and I was not disappointed. I received news that I was to take over as Commanding Officer of the 4th Armoured Division Transport Regiment RCT in Duisburg, a major inland port and steel town on the Rhine. This was to take place in June 1969 but my replacement at Camberley, Bill Allan, from whom I had taken over at 3rd Division, was posted in to the Staff College in January, a full six months before I was to take command of my regiment. The Army rarely gives out six month holidays with pay – something was afoot and needed to be looked into. Enlightenment came when I learned that I was to be a student on the main Management Course at the Henley Management College.

I did not like the idea of this at all. Bill Allen had already said that he wanted the house that went with the job at Camberley and it was clear that he should have it. The civilian Henley course was residential. I had no house of my own and I would have to find accommodation for my wife and two small children – the two older girls were at boarding school. I doubted if the Army would help. Apart from domestic problems, however, I had had enough of staff colleges and I wanted to get back to what I had joined the Service to achieve – command of a major field force unit.

The Commandant at Camberley at this time was General 'Tubby' Butler, a no nonsense parachutist well known for strong and pithy views and for calling a spade just what it is. I resolved to go and see him and requested a formal interview. Dressed in Service Dress with Sam Browne belt and hat I presented myself to General Tubby who was lying back in his swivel chair reading *The Times* with his coat unbuttoned. He looked up as I entered his office.

"What's this all about Fred?" With Tubby you laid it on the line without frills. He was never interested in elegant variation.

"General," I said. "I've heard about this plan to send me to the civilian management college and I am not happy about it. The long and short of it is, I've had a bellyful of staff colleges and courses and it's about time I was allowed to do what I joined the Army for and command a unit without having to become a student again. I suggest you send someone else to Henley. It's a high powered course and there would be plenty of volunteers."

Tubby sighed. "It's all down to Solly," he said. Sir Solly Zuckerman was the chief scientist to the Army.

"He went to the States recently and toured the Harvard Business School. Came back and persuaded the Army Board that our middle piece officers need management training. I've been told to provide one on the next Henley course. You just happen to fit the slot timewise."

He buttoned his coat, carefully folded his newspaper and sat up in his chair. "Colonel Plaskett, I've listened carefully to your proposal and I have explained to you why it is not possible to meet your wishes. Now (with acerbity) go away and do as you're told!" Except that he didn't say 'go away'.

The next step was an interview with the Principal of the Henley Management College with a view to slotting me into a syndicate. The system was tutorial along the lines of the Camberley course. I couldn't help but be impressed with Greenlands, the home of the Management College. It was a handsome white stone Georgian type building, formerly the residence of Lord Tweedsmuir of W.H. Smith fame and located alongside a beautiful reach of the Thames above Henley town. Student accomodation and facilities seemed to be first class, but I still had a problem to solve. As I had suspected, the quartering people at Camberley made my family and me non-persons as soon as I was struck off the strength of the Staff College to attend the Henley course. I was once again on the paper strength of some faceless military 'sump' organisation that had little interest in me and no interest in my family's accommodation, so I had to find somewhere for my wife and two younger children to live for the duration of the Henley course before going to Germany. Our former standby, Salisbury, although not completely out of the question, would be difficult. Both the maiden aunts had died; Heather's parents and mine were old and although willing to help, I had a conscience about saddling them with two lively young children.

Help was at hand from a friend, however. Brigadier Pat Claxton of my Corps had a spare unoccupied quarter in the middle of his training area at Bordon in Hampshire and offered it to us for as long as we needed it.

"There are snags," he said. "No one wants it because it's big, it's old and it's reputed to be haunted."

It was called Louisburg House after a nineteenth century battle and it was both big and old as he had said. As for the haunting we'd have to wait and see. Heather, like most Army wives who follow the drum, had an inner core of forged metal. She arranged to teach our two younger girls at home since enrolment at school for five months would be silly, and with my family deposited, but certainly not settled, in our temporary quarter I departed for Henley. I would be officially permitted two weekends at home during the next four months.

Despite my initial mutinous reluctance to attend the Henley course, I couldn't help being fascinated by my first exposure to this large sample of the UK's civilian middle management. I suppose the Course was about sixty strong; I was the only servicemen and indeed there had only been two previously – well spaced apart. It was an expensive and highly regarded course and the other students were a mixture of rising executives from the clearing banks and other large companies, leavened by a few from the public service. There was one trade unionist, Roland Bull from the AEU who did an excellent job keeping his end up in a thoroughly capitalist atmosphere.

I had seen the course syllabus and had blanched at the entry and the reading list for the first week – management mathematics! This pre-course instruction was conducted as revision on the assumption that we would all have at least some knowledge of the abstruse jargon relating to the details of balance sheets, yields and other complicated financial subjects. At the end of the first day I approached the lecturer taking the session and explained that half the time I hadn't the least idea of what he was talking about.

He laughed. "I saw that there was a soldier on the course and assumed he was from the pay corps. Full marks for coming clean. You won't get far here without a basic grasp of accountancy. Who's in your syndicate?"

I told him. "Let's see. You'd better sit next to a banker and when you're unsure ask his advice."

He put me next to Jim Poland, a rising star in the old National Provincial Bank from whom I shamelessly cribbed and who helped me enormously. At the end of that week I was able to read a balance sheet like a book, was well versed in yields, profit margins, price earnings ratios and such arcane practices as discounted cash flows. I possessed skills that although they were only occasionally useful to me during the rest of my Army career, were to stand me in very good stead after retirement from the Service.

I found to my surprise that I began to enjoy Henley. Many of the subjects we studied, operational research, resource management, behavioural science, the art of leadership, the 'Directing Authority', were similar to those I had studied and indeed taught at Camberley under other titles. The exercises or war games familiar to me became business games, the military aim of holding or gaining ground being replaced by the elusive goal of enhancing profit. Years of command and staff work followed by teaching had banished any reluctance to speak in public, something that was noticeably absent from the skills of most of the students who were, in the main, experts in their own specific fields who had been singled out for higher management within their companies. They had therefore had little chance to speak in public and I later learned that many had been sent on the course to improve their skill at this necessary attribute of senior management.

Hours of work were unusual. We started at nine a.m. with syndicate discussions on a subject that had been selected and notified a few days previously and on which a controversial paper had been written and distributed. We were expected to read it and to turn up prepared to discuss it. Our tutor was a management academic, long on theory and very articulate. There might be a plenary discussion session on the subject of the day after the morning break clearly designed, as days went by, to draw out those who were reluctant to get to their feet and give their views. An hour's lunch break was followed by 'compulsory exercise' until the late afternoon. We had to choose a mode or modes of exercise. I chose walking and rowing and spent many happy afternoons rowing the College's excellent skiffs on the Thames and sometimes walking in the woods on the slopes above Greenlands. A period of 'private study' led up to dinner and afterwards there would be a lecture or presentation by the chairman of chief executive of a major company, or perhaps a politician or 'high gee' in the City. Michael Heseltine, the MP for Henley, visited frequently and was good value.

There is a theory sometimes quoted in military circles and attributed to one of those early nineteenth century Prussian military savants. It holds that army officers fall generally into one of four categories. These are firstly, the stupid and industrious, then the stupid and lazy, followed by the clever and industrious and finally the clever and lazy. The theory goes on to suggest that the first category, the stupid and industrious, are the bane of an army; they constantly foul things up with the best intentions and as staff officers they are responsible for most minor and major military cock-ups. The stupid and lazy present no problems; they are often high born low achievers and in not so very distant former times they were bought commissions by parents glad to get rid of them. They were then able to strut around in gorgeous uniforms until ultimately being fed into the cannon in some convenient war. The clever and industrious were an army's chiefs of staff, responsible for planning operations and sparing the commander from unessential detail. The clever and lazy were able instinctively to grasp the main issues and became commanders of formations and high level military strategists.

Of course the theory is somewhat specious and more relevant to previous centuries than this one when clever and industrious technicians increasingly dominate our lives with more and more advanced consumer goods and technical devices. But I floated it into a plenary session at Henley and wondered if it was at all relevant to the civilian business world. I was surprised at the reaction.

The general view was that the theory was as much applicable to civilian life as to an army. Obviously many of the students had applied the theory to their own organisations and found viable parallels with its four categories. It created a great deal of discussion and I was glad I had aired it.

In fact it was supported in a strange way by a visiting mogul – the chairman of Imperial Chemical Industries. ICI was at that time, the late nineteen sixties, the bellweather of British industry and it was a coup on the part of the Henley course planners to get their top man to address us. He was a large man, reflective, slow spoken and totally in command of his audience. He spoke for about forty minutes without notes and then invited questions.

Someone said, "You've given us the aims of your company. Can you tell us what are your personal ambitions – if indeed you have anything left to aim for?" This to general laughter. He surveyed his audience seriously.

"My personal ambition is and always has been to delegate sensibly to the maximum possible degree, to sweat as little as possible and always to leave time to think ahead." A shining and brilliantly successful example of the clever and lazy – if he was to be believed.

John Adams, my syndicate tutor, had discovered my interest in military history, which he shared, and one day mentioned that he often went to tea with a friend who lived on the hill above Greenlands. Perhaps I had heard of him and would I like to meet him?

His name, he said, is Sir Basil Liddell Hart! He was not a well man but he enjoyed meeting serving officers; in his youth he had been one himself. Having read most of his books I said I would be greatly honoured to meet the man whose ideas had been advanced well before our military establishment had been prepared to adopt them, and whose published works had been credited with presenting the Germans with ideas for the Blitzkreig tactics that had served them so well at the start of the Second World War.

Captain Liddell Hart, although obviously ailing when I met him, was clear of mind and very interested in the recent changes to the Army's logistic set-up. He said he hoped we'd got it right this time. He died a year later, much mourned by his wide following.

Throughout all this I was mindful of the situation of my wife, stuck in the middle of a wooded training area with two small children and in a supposedly haunted house. Determined to join her as often as possible I played hooky from the course regularly. Saturday was a full working day but I found I could turn up to breakfast on Sunday mornings and vanish until the evening session without comment – there was often a Sunday evening lecture; time was money in civilian life and senior people could often only spare a Sunday evening to visit us. I was aided in my furtive Sunday visits to Bordon by the fact that our friends Peter and Maureen Sibbald were abroad together and had left us in charge of their VW Beetle while they were away. In those days very few Service people had two cars and obviously Heather had to have ours. Thus I had Peter's Beetle at Henley.

The haunting had played no part in Heather's experience of Louisburg House. She was not a fanciful person nor given to the vapours. Had the ghost turned up she would probably have greeted it politely, expecting to be subjected to an insurance or double glazing pitch. There were no untoward incidents until the second of my authorised weekend absences from the course when we were sitting in the drawing room having an evening drink before dinner. The front and back doors were closed and bolted, there were no open windows and our two younger children were fast asleep upstairs. Suddenly, without warning there was the sound of running feet, heavy feet, up the stairs outside the drawing room door and along the upstairs landing. Burglar, I thought and grabbed the poker from the fireplace shouting to Heather to get the police on the phone. She ignored this, saying afterwards that her first thought was for the children and ran after me with a heavy cut glass vase.

We looked in on the children, still sound asleep and then went from room to room upstairs and then downstairs. Nothing. No sign of an intruder. Both doors still firmly secured and no sign of forced entry to windows. I even searched the loft for a break in the roof covering, or missing slates. Still nothing. A complete mystery. But we had both heard it clearly and our stories tallied exactly. There is no explanation but I discussed it with Pat Claxton and he said that over the years there had been similar reports. No one had ever been hurt or molested and there had been no manifestations, evil or otherwise. Just strange incidents along the lines I had described. As a result the house had acquired an unpleasant reputation and would only be occupied as last resort.

I gave Heather the option of moving out and going into lodgings for the short period of time the course at Henley had to run, but she declined and said she would stick it out. In fact there were no further incidents, but I remain baffled to this day.

The main social event of the Henley course was the Course Dinner, held just prior to the departure of the students. It was a stag affair, with each student asked to bring one guest connected with his work. Most asked their chairman, managing director or chief executive, many of whom were previous Henley 'graduates' as the college was pleased to describe those who completed the course. The senior guest, invited by the Principal of the college, would make a speech and propose a toast to which a student, nominated by the course, would reply. The guest speaker was a high official of the Bank of England and the nominated student speaker, who was expected to speak without notes, was also required to offer several apposite jokes about the course. I was approached to do this but demurred on grounds that as a soldier and alien to the commercial world before the course I could hardly be expected to stand up and speak sensibly and critically about it. Under pressure I said I'd do it if they couldn't find anyone else. Of course they professed to be unable to find anyone else. "We've already tried!" they said, implying that no one else was mug enough to take it on. So I was landed with the job.

In fact it went quite well. The Bank of England man was as cautious as his appointment would indicate, allowing me to say when my turn came that I'd heard about the Bank of England buying sterling. Perhaps he would be able to tell a simple soldier what the Bank was using for money? I had invited Martin Farndale as my guest, not only as a friend, but also because he was a bona fide businessman who managed a road haulage business in the Isle of Wight that his wife had inherited from her father. It was an enjoyable evening. There was no course report or grading. At least that was the official line but I couldn't believe, knowing what I then knew about the ways of business, that any large enterprise would be prepared to spend thousands of pounds on an expensive course for one of its managers without being given some idea of his progress.

Back to Louisburg House. I had been considering for some time how I could make it up to Heather for the rotten time she must have had by herself in the woods at Bordon looking after two small children with only the occasional armoured personnel carrier racing past the house for company. We had nearly two months to wait before leaving for Germany and it occurred to both of us that we were substantially mobile. We could up sticks and move to wherever we liked – or could afford. The older girls had gone back to boarding school after the Easter break and when they returned for the summer we would be in Duisburg. Why not find somewhere to stay on the Continent, preferably in the sun?

We scanned the Sunday papers and found a promising spot on the Adriatic just round the corner from Venice at Jesolo Pineta. It was a self-catering apartment just about within our budget and allegedly almost on the beach. The two younger children were still being educated at home on a correspondence course designed for families stuck in the bush without access to a school, so they could be anywhere. We packed up, consigned our heavy baggage to store and drove over the Brenner Pass to Italy for a pleasant six weeks without responsibilities We were able to pursue our joint love affair with Verona, Padua, Vicenza and those other delightful towns of the Veneto Region on day trips by car. We also got to know Venice quite well. It was a short train ride, emerging from the station to face that elegant sweep of steps down to the Grand Canal shimmering in the sunshine with the vaporettos at the station landing stage waiting to take travellers to St Mark's. I would always try to arrive in Venice by train. It is probably the most splendid scene to be offered when emerging from a railway station anywhere in Europe. We also found out very quickly that two coffees and two ice creams in that central Square cost nearly the whole of our spending money for the day and could be undercut by eighty per cent in any one of the charming little squares encountered on the walk from St Mark's back to the station. Nevertheless, to be tired of Venice is, as Dr Johnson said of London, to be tired of life.

All too soon, our Venetian Idyll came to an end and we drove back over the Dolomites and through Austria to the workaday world.

19

Commanding the Regiment

Duisburg

I had learned from the incumbent CO at my new regiment that he was reluctant to hand over the CO's quarter in Duisburg as he had not yet been allotted a quarter at Rheindahlen, the Rhine Army HQ to which he had been posted. I was not happy about this. It is neither pleasant nor proper for a new CO to have his predecessor occupying the CO's quarter after the unit had been handed over, for obvious reasons. But there was a considerable wait until Heather and our two younger girls could be 'called forward' and she had to move in with her increasingly ageing parents; their house had ample accommodation but the presence of two lively grandchildren for any extended period was certainly inconvenient for them. There were no spare quarters in Duisburg and I lived in a flat over the officers' mess while efforts were made to sort this problem out.

The difficulty was eventually disposed of, however, and some time after I became the Commanding Officer of the 4th Armoured Division Regiment, Royal Corps of Transport, we moved into the CO's house only a few hundred yards from the barracks.

Ask any retired professional soldier of senior rank what he enjoyed most in his service and it's a safe bet that if he is one of those privileged persons who has done so he will tell you that it was commanding his regiment. It is, after all, the summit of ambition for most, and in the days when numbers of officers had estates or businesses to inherit, many used to retire after their 'ration' of regimental command. It is also the only time in the Army when one has real power in close contact with one's men – and in some cases these days, women, I suppose, although even in my day, command – for in Germany such it was legally – of the regimental wives provided social contact with quite enough ladies to be going on with.

One of the first jobs for a CO when new to a unit command is to check the unit standing orders. These provide the framework for unit administration; they govern the conduct of officers, other ranks and all families by supplementing the Army Act and the Queen's Regulations that give them force of law. They act in a similar manner to bye-laws for a local community and are normally contained in a fairly thick book signed by the commanding officer. Quite frequently they have been built up over years by successive commanding officers based on empirical knowledge of the peccadillos of unit members over time. There was no doubt that my new Regiment had been well administered. My predecessor's standing orders were superb. Nothing had been left out and all I had to do was replace his name on the front with mine. This I did on the first day.

There is always a 'honeymoon' period when command of a unit changes; the new CO sizes up his officers, warrant officers and senior NCOs and absorbs the unit's general ambience. This cuts both ways for his officers and other ranks are doing the same thing in reverse. If you fail to stamp your personality on your new command in the first sixty days, there is a danger of allowing your impact to become stale. This is not to suggest that everything has to change. The American expression 'If it ain't broke, don't fix it', should apply. Nor does being popular matter. No good CO ever gave a damn about it. For popularity wears a false face. It vanishes when the dice roll against you. All a CO should strive for is respect and loyalty and this will be achieved by generating a perception that he is just and fair in dealings with his subordinates. If they happen to like him as well, then he – or she – should be grateful.

Having said that, however, new commanding officers tend to have ideas, formed well in advance of achieving command, on how their regiment should function were they lucky enough to be allowed to command one. I was no exception.

So there was much to do. One or two of the officers and one warrant officer, a squadron sergeant major, I had known previously. This is not a good score for a new CO commanding a large field force regiment of his Corps. It was due to my long absences from my Corps as a staff officer. It meant, however, that although I didn't know many of them, they, by the same token, didn't know me, giving me the useful advantage of being an unknown quantity. Nevertheless, it was evident that there was a great deal of goodwill.

I decided right away to get rid of the coloured pullovers worn as uniform by the officers. A fashion had grown up among commanding officers in BAOR to ditch the olive green pullovers issued by the army to all ranks and worn as barrack dress in cold weather and replace them with pullovers in the standard pattern dyed in a different colour – usually for officers only. This practice had been adopted by my predecessor and the colour he chose was, I recall, orange. It was a fashion that I abhorred. I firmly believed that officers, NCOs and soldiers should be uniformly dressed when on duty, distinguished in the field and in barracks only by their badges of rank. The coloured pullovers had to go and on day two of my new command, they went.

There was some unrest. The coloured 'woolly pullies' had had to be bought by individuals; junior officers in particular, perennially hard up as ever, were upset. But banned they were and that was that. The fad had become ridiculous. At NATO rifle meetings, for instance, when most member nations contributed teams, the Brits stood out like something out of a musical comedy. An American friend told me that his people fell about laughing at us and his soldiers actually took pictures of our teams to send home. He even had the cheek to suggest that our C-in-C was probably related to Sigmund Romberg. As time passed, the coloured pullover fad declined almost to extinction.

Our barracks at Duisburg, officially 'Glamorgan Barracks', was known locally as the 'Flak Kaserne', having been the home of the two Wehrmacht anti-aircraft regiments assigned to protect Duisburg Port during the Hitler war. The Wermacht became the Bundeswehr in post-war Germany. As a newcomer to that part of Germany you didn't have to engage a local German long in conversation to be told that you lived in the biggest inland port in Europe, fed by the mighty Rhine River.

Relations with the city authorities (The Stadt) were excellent, all credit to my predecessor. They were helped along by the fact that the Burgermeister, Herr Auguste Seeling, had been a prominent anti-Nazi and as such had been interned during the war in a monastery in the Eifel region located above the Mosel Valley. One of my bounden duties was to preserve and enhance this amity; with goodwill on both sides and numerous German born wives among the regiment's families, this wasn't hard to achieve. It was also helped by the fact that the Germans, despite the hammering that they had had in the war, do not have the deep-rooted suspicion of soldiers and armies in general that has been healthily endemic in Britain since Cromwell's day.

Duisburg was also a major steel town that had grown into a go ahead city. Some of the senior men (stahlmeisters) of the steelworks had served in the flak regiments during the war and competition for invitations to our mess functions was quite intense. This was a two way traffic. They were all immensely rich and most of them had estates either on the Rhine or in the Dutch border area which meant that invitations to shoot during the season came thick and fast. These I accepted whenever I could, accompanied by my HQ Squadron captain, Roy Garside, who was also a keen shot. Roy was a fluent German speaker and with his supportive German born wife Gerda, had been a tower of strength as my sergeant major for a while in Wuppertal before he was commissioned. The soldiers profited from this association too. During the grape picking season many unattached young men from the Regiment spent their summer leave allocation working alongside the villagers in the stahlmeisters' vineyards on the lower Rhine where, if the stories were to be believed, the local girls were friendly and they had the time of their lives on generous pay.

Our barracks were quite close to the steelworks that lined the river bank, with their chimneys looming over our main parade ground and issuing clouds of coloured and evil smelling smoke. Because of this Duisburg was not regarded by other units in BAOR as a pleasant station and helicopter pilots said that the city was always easily recognised from a distance because of the black cloud that hovered over it for six days of the week Shortly after my arrival, however, the West German authorities passed a Clean Air Act and the situation was magically transformed. No longer were cars left in the open covered in a film of grey dust each morning and the faint but all pervading smell of sulphur vanished from the air.

The 4th Armoured Division was one of the three armoured divisions in Germany that, with supporting units, made up the 1st (British) Corps of the British Army of the Rhine (BAOR). Our Division was organised along standard lines with three armoured brigades under command, one of which was the Guards' Brigade. This meant that the Division was often commanded by a guardsman; on my arrival it was Major General Vernon Erskine Crum, an immensely tall man, late of the Scots Guards. He had heard that I was fresh from a civilian management course and his Division being the one chosen to be the target of management consultants for a soldiers' pay structure examination, I was summoned to join the General for lunch with the consultant from Hays MSL, the firm chosen to conduct the study.

The General had decreed that the consultation was to take place in the field while on a divisional HQ exercise. I arrived for a briefing before the consultant turned up. The message to me from my General was that he expected me to interpret any 'management jargon' spouted by the consultant and, he said, "I'll make damned sure that he's made aware of the conditions our soldiers have to endure, particularly in the field. It would help," added the General, surveying the lowering sky, "if it rained."

I responded, to a wintry smile, that the course hadn't covered rainmaking, but the fates were on his side and sure enough the consultant, a slight and apologetic young man, arrived in a passable downpour. The ADC had suggested that in view of the weather conditions, it would perhaps be advisable for the consultant to be given lunch in the mess tent, rather than on the log in the woods previously suggested as a venue.

"Not on your life," said the General. "Colonel Plaskett and I will entertain him for luncheon sitting on a tree stump in a wet wood and we will dine on Army stew out of mess tins as arranged. You may, however," he added generously, "provide him with a hat and a poncho" – the soldiers' issue waterproof cape that doubled as a bivouac cover.

And so it happened. There was little doubt that the young man, who took it all in good part, realised that he was part of a demonstration. Having been told that I had recently completed the long management course at Henley, he did spout a bit of management jargon and we parted amicably.

The General was happy with the outcome of his staged tableau but sadly, he failed to see the result of the study for shortly afterwards he was posted to command in Northern Ireland and died of a heart attack before he could take up his new appointment. His replacement in command of 4th Armoured Division was Major General David Fraser, a Grenadier, known within the Brigade of Guards I understand, as 'Fraser the Razor'. If the aspect of his character implied by this existed, neither I nor my Regiment ever came across it, for to us, and particularly to me, he was affability itself. He was and is an extremely erudite man with a dry sense of humour. He reached the commanding heights of the Army and is now a well known writer of note. He inspired great respect in all of us and helped to make my command tour a pleasure.

My Regiment was organised on a standard field unit establishment of a regimental headquarters and three transport squadrons, each supporting one of the Division's three brigades. We operated a menagerie of vehicles ranging from the armoured amphibious Alvis Stalwart designed to keep up with armoured vehicles across country, through ten tonners down to three tonners plus a large clutch of Land Rovers, all with the object of keeping our Division provided in the field with the paraphernalia of modern war. For the first time I had a fully established radio troop, allowing me to communicate with my squadrons in the field while on the move – a great boon. It actually worked, with few breakdowns and my officers became thoroughly proficient in radio procedure.

The Cold War was still exercising the minds of our political and military masters. The training pattern for BAOR, described previously, was still in existence and I had arrived in early summer during brigade and squadron exercises. This meant a good deal of moving round the brigades with not much time in barracks. It also meant renewing acquaintance with numerous friends from my years on the staff and at Camberley because they too had reached the regimental command stage of their careers. Networking oils the wheels in the Service just as it does in civil life; favours are given and returned and it all enhances the efficiency of the organisation.

As soon as possible I took my regimental headquarters into the field for a working up exercise. It was a mutual necessity. The HQ complement and I had to find out about each other, particularly as there were some important new arrivals, the regimental sergeant major being foremost among them. The RSM, a Warrant Officer, Class 1 and the senior soldier in the regiment, leader of the sergeants mess, is a key man. A good one is a pearl beyond price; a bad one can make the CO's job more difficult than it should be and if found to be so, then the CO must harden his heart and dispense with his services. I had no such problem. RSM Stanley Gould should have been Stanley Gold. Five feet six inches of fire and movement. Smart as a whip, a hard man on the football field and very well respected. I could not have been more loyally supported.

We moved out for a week to several locations close to the east/west German border to test our communications, working practices and movement drills. The choice of the exercise area was no accident. The closer you got to the border the fewer problems you had moving on the roads and using farmland. The farmers and the population in general liked to see us there, conscious as they were of Big Brother Bear lurking only a few miles to the east. Farmers were particularly generous with offers of accommodation for the officers in the farmhouse if wanted or needed, but I can't recall hearing of anyone who accepted these offers. The object was to live and operate in the field, under canvas when necessary. We did, however, occasionally accept covered accommodation for our vehicles in those huge Saxon barns so plentiful in Germany, mainly to avoid the chore of putting up and pulling down camouflage every time a vehicle moved.

On one occasion this gave me a hitherto unsuspected insight into animal behaviour. We had set up our HQ in a copse close to a large piggery; there must have been about four hundred pigs in residence, all blessed with five star accommodation in a huge shed. The night before we moved to the next location I arranged with the farmer that we could sleep in the central aisle of the pig shed with the enclosed pig pens on either side of us. This was to allow us to move quickly at dawn without having to take down and stow canvas. The floor was concrete and perfectly clean; there was a noticeable but by no means unbearable animal smell and the pigs were making very little noise – just a soothing snuffling. We settled down early in our sleeping bags conscious of the dawn start. The pigs settled to sleep a little later on. There was some light snoring, mainly from us.

Suddenly there was an almighty racket, not easy to describe. It was perhaps as though we had been awakened by an almighty belch. I looked at my watch. We had been asleep for three hours. The pigs were clearly the culprits but they were now silent. Three hours later, almost to the minute, it happened again. This time we managed about an hour and a half before being roused by the guard for the early start. I discussed this shortly afterwards with a pig farmer who said, "They were just turning over in their sleep. I'd never sleep in a shed with a lot of pigs. When one turns over they all do and they clear their throats at the same time." A useful lesson in field living and something to be avoided in future.

The Regiment's Transport Co-ordinator, an important appointment filled by a major, was Noel Maguire of the Royal Australian Corps of Transport on secondment to us for a year and living in married quarters with his family. He took to the job like a duck to water and his efficiency was such that I wasn't in the least surprised to learn years later that he had become the head of his Corps as Director RACT. His wife, Susy, became a stalwart of our wives' club and we were all sorry to see them go when they had to return home.

I had inherited an excellent and high spirited bunch of young officers. In the tradition of subalterns they got up to all sorts of antics. There was little evidence that they realised that their elders had once been young themselves but my recollections tell me that that is standard. They were all young enough to know everything about everything with no need for their wisdom to be tempered by experience, so naturally they regarded their seniors in today's vernacular of youth as a menagerie of 'old farts'. We were refugees from Dad's Army attempting to curb their natural exuberance and obstructing their secure knowledge that given half a chance they could run the Regiment and its squadrons much better than we could. I doubt if they realised it at the time but they afforded me great pleasure and it is nice to recall that almost without exception they have gone on to successful careers.

But it was sometimes necessary to apply restraint. We were located not far from Dusseldorf Airport, a matter of forty minutes drive. Newly comissioned officers fresh from Sandhurst and destined for the Regiment were picked up there and brought to the barracks by Land Rover. The Adjutant normally detailed a senior subaltern to meet these young men, introduce them to our Mess and generally show them the ropes for the first few days. I was aware that they were always the victims of spoofs on their first night – being bamboozled into wearing full mess dress on a normal supper night when suits are worn by everyone else, for instance. Or more elaborately, one of the older officers acting as the padre, feigning falldown drunkenness and foully blaspheming. My eldest daughter Helen, now eighteen and living at home, was sometimes roped in as the drunken and amorous schoolmistress. All this was acceptable because it was done within the Regiment and no offence was taken.

But fertile minds spawned more complicated and less acceptable tricks. I always insisted that those meeting newly commissioned officers from Sandhurst arriving at the airport were properly attired in their best parade uniform with highly polished Sam Browne belt, to ensure that the right impression of the Regiment was given. It was therefore with some surprise that sitting in the airport coffee shop one morning dressed in plain clothes and waiting for a flight to England for a two day study period, I saw one of my Land Rovers draw up and disgorge an immaculately dressed subaltern, leaving another subaltern in the back very scruffily dressed in dirty overalls and no beret. The driver, a third subaltern, but clad in barrack dress and soldier's beret and wearing the badges of rank of a corporal, then got out and sat in the back of the vehicle. Just at that moment my flight was called so I had no chance to investigate.

Returning to Duisburg two days later, I learned of what proved to be an elaborate 'sting'. The immaculate subaltern greeting the new young officer off the plane appeared harassed and apologetic.

"Welcome to the Regiment," he said. "And I'm sorry that on your first day I have to saddle you with an unpleasant job, here at the airport. The thing is that as we arrived here the military police handed over an apprehended deserter we've been trying to get our hands on for ages. He's in the back of the Land Rover being guarded by my corporal driver and I'd like to get him back to the Regiment in custody as quickly as possible. I have to stay here to complete the paper work for the military police. I've phoned the Adjutant and he says you are to take custody of the prisoner and get him back to barracks right away."

Whereupon he handed the bemused young man a piece of paper – a receipt for 'one live body', the Army's own prose for this situation – and asked him to sign it. They both returned to the Land Rover where, with more profuse apologies, the greeter departed. The 'corporal' driver saluted smartly and having thrown the new subaltern's kit in the back of the Land Rover, suggested to him that he should sit in the back for the short drive to the Regiment so that the prisoner, well known to be a desperate character, could remain guarded.

They left the airport and drove through Dusseldorf city. While stopped at traffic lights in a densely populated area, the 'prisoner', hitherto sitting hangdog with his head bowed, without warning vaulted over the tailboard and vanished into the crowds, leaving a newly commissioned young officer about to embark on his first posting to report to his Regiment with a receipt for a reputedly villainous prisoner and no live body to back it up. The adjutant, of course, had no inkling of all this but immediately smelt a rat to the extent that the mystery was almost unravelled when I returned, followed by a full confession from the culprits.

There was considerable admiration around the Regiment for this enterprise, but it was too much. The three perpetrators suffered their 'rocket'; each did his ration of extra orderly officer duties with good grace and the victim quickly recovered from his somewhat unkind introduction to his new career. But future scams inflicted on new arrivals would be conducted 'in house'.

Like most of the young, they were into old cars, being able to afford nothing better. The Officers' Mess, occupied exclusively by members of my Regiment, was located across the main road outside the barracks. There was a rather smart paved car park in front of it and very little other than a high wall behind it. Thus the car park was in full view of passing traffic. I became irritated by the number of 'old bangers' in front of the Mess, some showing signs of rust; others on wooden blocks bereft of wheels. When off duty the subaltern owners could be seen working on these rust buckets in overalls.

The RSM, a man of tidy mind, was much more upset about this than I was and it was a matter of great rejoicing to him when I decreed that vehicles incapable of movement, i.e. without wheels, would not be countenanced on the Mess forecourt. From then on, all was well. The cars were still there, but complete with wheels and they proved their mobility by being parked in different places. It was not until years later when I met one of my former young officers, by then a major and an instructor at Sandhurst, that I was told that they remained rust buckets, that the wheels were bogus and that each evening parties of four or five subalterns would bodily lift the wheelless vehicles to a different place on the car park, then place the wheels against the protruding axles. My loyal daughter, Helen, knew about this but was persuaded that in the interests of her father's blood pressure, it was better that he remained ignorant of the deception.

Having an eighteen-year old daughter living at home while commanding a regiment on the Continent could, I suppose, have presented problems. It is to Helen's lasting credit that it did not and it was a great joy to her mother and me to have her with us again. She had travelled widely with us until boarding school in Hampshire had claimed her. She had turned down an opportunity to go to university and had instead attended a year's residential course at St James' secretarial college at Bridport in Dorset. Armed with this qualification and passable spoken and written German, she had no difficulty in getting a job as a translator and general secretary with a major import/export firm in Duisburg. Of course she was much in demand by the young officers as a dancing and disco partner and it became necessary to impose a curfew. Like Cinderella, she had to be home by midnight, thus giving rise to the only embarrassing incident we experienced while Helen was with us in Germany and indirectly caused by me at that.

As with all fathers I fretted if she wasn't back by the curfew hour and on this particular evening she had gone to a disco in Dusseldorf with a thoroughly trustworthy young man. But midnight came and went and Heather and I began to get worried. At two a.m. I was on the brink of getting in touch with the RMP at Dusseldorf when there was a scrape of a key in the front door lock and a whispered, "Would you like to come in for a cup of coffee John?" By this time I was on the landing bellowing, "It's two o'clock in the morning! What do you mean by etc!" A muttered, "No thank you. Goodnight Helen." Then a curse and the sound of a fall outside. John had forgotten that workmen had been digging a cable trench across the front gardens of the officers' married quarters and in his haste to get away had fallen into it. He spent some days hobbling round on two sticks while the nasty sprain to his ankle healed – to unkind hilarity from his contemporaries, who quickly found out what had happened.

Individual brigade exercises were taking place in June and July and with my squadrons away supporting the brigades that they were assigned to, I decided to enrol myself on the short residential German course that took place at Sennelager in Northern Westphalia at the southern end of the Teutoberger Forest. Accommodation was in the Sennelager Training Area Mess, which had a transitory membership. The course was based on a language laboratory and instruction was mainly done with tapes and earphones. This offered standard pronunciation and a true feel for the language. It didn't go deeply into grammar; there wasn't time and anyway I had no desire to discuss Goethe in the original. But I came away from it much more confident of 'getting by' in German.

There was a battalion of Foot Guards in the Sennelager Mess while I was there. They were obviously using the training area. I forget which regiment but I recall that their commanding officer was a tremendous swell and much too grand to commune with lesser mortals, especially at breakfast, when he strode in and immersed himself in his newspaper, oblivious even of requests to pass the salt. One morning, when I was about halfway through the course, the Mess unaccountably filled with Guards subalterns at breakfast time. This was unusual because they normally preferred to have a cup of tea and something saved from the night before in their rooms while dressing for first parade. There was an air of suppressed anticipation when a Mess servant appeared and handed a package in the form of a large, thick envelope to the Guards' commanding officer.

"This came addressed to you, sir."

He looked up, surprised, weighed it gingerly in his hand, then curiosity got the better of him. He opened the envelope with a breakfast knife and pamphlets, photographs and curious objects fell to the table. He looked mystified then he picked up a photograph and a pamphlet. His eyes widened, his face crimsoned, then became puce with anger.

"Disgraceful! Disgraceful!" he thundered, pushed his chair back and strode from the room. Suppressed merriment from the Guards' subalterns.

The major instructor on the permanent staff sitting next to me, laughed.

"He's not a popular gentleman and he's given them a hard time. I heard that some of them had got together and planned something special for him." He leaned across and picked up some of the material. "They must have written to a sex publisher, probably in Holland, and using his name, asked for a selection of their wares and publications. He'll never manage to run the culprits to earth."

The year dwindled down to autumn and higher formation exercises which meant that we took the field as a full division with its three brigades deployed. For me this was an opportunity to test my newly acquired regimental radio net and I spent a good few days and nights on the road visiting my squadrons in the field and liaising with their assigned brigade commanders and staffs. It was a great opportunity to get to know the personalities of the Division. I was also able to renew contact with those of my friends from my teaching stint at Camberley who were also commanding regiments within the 4th Division.

On divisional exercises the RCT regimental commander became the GOC's transport adviser in the field and established his regimental HQ at divisional HQ along with those of other supporting arms and services. We were usually located near to the medics who were always good value because they were invariably cheerful characters with an inexhaustible fund of medical jokes of the 'Doctor in the House' variety. Major exercises tended to mirror war conditions to the extent that they often consisted of long periods of near boredom punctuated by bursts of frenzied activity – paraphrasing a well known description of active service. High grade and cheerful gossip was thus a big plus factor when living in the field.

The dreary late autumn months when my Regiment prepared for and suffered most of its annual inspections were livened up a little by several civic events in Duisburg that we were expected to take part in. To the local German population we were 'their' soldiers living in their city's only military barracks. It seemed to matter not at all that we had been sworn enemies in two world wars. Ceremonies that had taken place since before the Kaiser's day were still observed annually and we took part in them gladly.

The postal address of our barracks was the Duisburg suburb of Wedau that boasted a comic opera type military force known as Der Roten Funken or in English 'The Red Sparks'. They came to the fore during Karnival time. Dressed in red costumes and sporting a genuine ancient cannon loaded with black powder they attacked the closed steel gates to the barracks in late evening, having first traded insults with a selected band of our German speaking soldiers, firing their cannon and ersatz weapons. They eventually 'forced' the gates and with nearly all the Regiment and our wives looking on they negotiated a ransom of a large barrel of beer before handing the barracks back to my control. The Karnival Princess – a pretty local girl in her late teens then gave yours truly, the blushing Oberst, a big kiss and the Prinz of Karnival, a rich local businessman who was paying for it all, shook hands all round and invited the CO and his wife to the Prince's Breakfast, held in the Stadthalle or Town Hall.

Karnival was a big annual event on the Rhine. Supposedly having its origins in the Roman Saturnalia, though no longer necessarily held in December, it went on for days. The Red Sparks affair was a minor happening in the calendar: the main event was a parade in the centre of the city complete with numerous floats, dancing men and girls and high stepping 'majorettes' twirling batons and wearing short, short skirts. As a regiment we were expected to provide a float and add a specifically British flavour to the proceedings. Never slow to delegate, I gave the task of organising the Karnival float to the wives' club and our wives responded with a will to the challenge, Captain Ken Adey, our attached REME officer, supervising the construction of the float.

They decided to produce a replica of Tower Bridge with the children dressed up as Yeomen of the Guard and City of London Policemen. As a finishing touch they asked me to produce two Scottish pipers. Fortunately we had a Scots Guards battalion serving in the Division and their CO cheerfully loaned me a brace of very large and suitably hairy-kneed pipers from his regimental pipe band.

Came the day and Heather and I attended the Prince's Breakfast before the float parade. We sat down with all the city dignitaries, linked arms and swayed from side to side during breakfast singing the Karnival song which translated into English runs something like 'Who will pay for all this? Who has so much money?' repeated over and over for about fifteen minutes. It sounds better in German and anyway even at that time in the morning we were all very merry on the Hock provided in quantity from our host's personal vineyard.

After this we repaired to the balcony to watch the parade. We both swelled with pride as our float passed mounted on a trailer and looking magnificent – instantly recognisable as Tower Bridge with children waving, blowing kisses to the crowd and drawing gasps and loud cheers from the townsfolk who thronged the road on both sides five or six deep. The pipers were a great attraction: they were in full Highland regalia and their bearskins made them look about seven feet tall. They received a special cheer. To our surprise and great pleasure, our float won a substantial cash prize – to be put by for next year's effort.

Afterwards and back in barracks I made a point of personally thanking all those who had helped to make our contribution such a success but when I asked the RSM to produce the pipers he shuffled his feet and said with some rancour that he had a party still out looking for them. Night followed day and they were nowhere to be seen. I phoned their CO and apologised for the delay in sending them back but said that they were still engaged in the process of cementing Anglo German relations. He didn't seem too bothered. Further investigations were made without success so I phoned the office of the Prince of Karnival and asked politely if they knew of the whereabouts of my 'Doodlesac Pfeifers', the charming German name for them. They said they had no idea where they were but added comfortingly that they were sure they would turn up.

The frisson of amusement in the voice of the lady I spoke to carried an unmistakeable message.

Two days later they turned up at the entrance to the barracks – dropped from a very large Mercedes car according to our regimental policeman at the gate. It zoomed away and he didn't get the number. The RSM was very cross, to put it mildly. He charged them with absence without leave and they were paraded before me at a special CO's orders session. They were both sweating with embarrassment and fear of what their own CO might say, let alone my probable punishment.

I asked them where they had been. They said they didn't know because after the parade they were approached by a German lady in a big car who had said she had permission from 'the Oberst' for them to play at her private party and so they went with her to a very large house on the river where they played their pipes for a succession of parties for about 48 hours.

"We kept asking to be taken back to barracks, sir," they said. "But they took no notice. Then we realised we'd been kidnapped, sir. It was terrible!"

All this in that soft Highland burr well nigh impossible to reproduce in print... a likely story.

What they didn't know – unless they had been told by their kidnappers – was that the day after the parade was Ladies Day when the women were traditionally entitled to pick any male they fancied from the street and invite him to entertain them. The mind boggled at the thought of what these poor six foot three Scotsmen had had to endure! Even the RSM was staring at the ceiling with twitching lips.

I did not have their conduct sheets in front of me and without those I could not legally punish them; they didn't know that either. But of course I had no intention of doing so. They received a wigging and the RSM was instructed to march them out.

Before he could do so, one of the guardsmen said swiftly, "Permission to speak, sir?"

"Yes, what is it?"

"Excuse me sir. If you're calling for volunteers next year sir, would you bear us in mind!"

It is often said that the Germans lack a sense of humour. This is a not so; they simply laugh at different things. In the round, their perception of events is not much different to ours. Living amongst them and in close contact with them, that is how I found them.

What I certainly found to be true, however, is their habit of rigid obedience to rules, particularly written instructions. An instance comes to mind. It had become a tradition for our Division, 4th Armoured, to hold a military tattoo each year at Divisional HQ near Herford, situated to the east of the Teuterburger Wald in Lower Saxony. All commanding officers within the Division together with their wives were invited and as it was a pleasant evening and a chance to socialise with friends from around a wide area, all those who could manage to be there accepted the invitation. There were many German guests with their wives.

The function took the form of a drinks party in the Divisional HQ Officers' Mess then transport to the tattoo ground followed by the show. The programme was printed in both English and German. The signal to leave the Mess and get on to the coaches standing outside was to be a trumpet fanfare from the minstrels' gallery that was a feature of most nineteenth century German officers' messes. We chatted to our friends and our guests and in due course the fanfare sounded. This of course was the signal for the less disciplined British to visit the loo and then return to the party for a short chat before getting on to the coaches. The first year we attended we did this and having returned to the party I suddenly noticed that there were no Germans present. "Where are they?" I asked friends who had been in Germany for some years.

"Look outside," they said. I did so and saw that our German guests were sitting in the coaches, arms folded and waiting patiently to move off.

They had responded with perfect discipline to the trumpet call. It happened every year and I can recall similar instances in different circumstances. Discussing this with a wise German friend, he said, "We are both inherently Saxon races and we are similar in many ways. But you have a leavening of the Latin. This causes you sometimes to regard rules as flexible while our people are happier to regard them as rigid." No offence was ever taken at our later arrival and the Tattoo itself, featuring bands from most of the major units in the Division, was always a much admired spectacle.

When the shooting season came round I relished the frequent invitations to weekend shooting trips and took advantage of them whenever possible. It was important to understand the instructions of the chief huntsman, issued in rapid German. There were many pitfalls for the unwary and no allowance was given for the insufficiently fluent guest who may have misunderstood the instructions. Rule breaking was punished by a round of drinks for the whole field, both guns and shoot servants and could be expensive. But Roy Garside, my companion on these occasions, had colloquial German and he translated accurately and swiftly. At the end of each shoot the huntsman would lay out the bag and read out the totals by type of game shot. The guns would stand round in a half-circle and as the bag of each species was read out all the guns would raise their hats and shout Weitmannsheil! (Hail to the Fallen!) There would be flying game – pheasants, partridge, perhaps a few snipe; ground game – rabbits, hares; and perhaps at the end a couple of cats. This surprised me until I learned that cats at large are treated as feral. It is not permitted to shoot them within 200 metres of a dwelling but I once saw a domestic moggie blasted off a garden fence with no comeback, probably because the owners were estate servants. Should the unwary guest or shoot member step over any of the laid out game it is an instant penalty and he is hit hard in the pocket for showing disrespect to the fallen.

The shoots we attended were usually covert shoots with marked stands and beaters. I was strongly advised against attending any walking up shoots with gatherings of jolly German gentlemen. The reason for this is that although the start of the shoot until mid-morning strict gun discipline is observed and on reaching an obstacle guns are broken and unloaded, bean soup and schnapps are invariably brought out at about 11 a.m. and after this gun discipline tends to slacken – considerably. Enough said on that subject. But our hosts on all these occasions were both hospitable and friendly.

Twice a year we were invited to a town vermin shoot. This was fun. It took place on the thickly wooded outskirts of Duisburg and most of the town dignitaries took part. There was always an abundance of vermin. Crows, jays and the occasional grey squirrel were the real quarry. I didn't see any foxes; M'sieur Reynard clearly used his loaf on these occasions. Competence varied widely; some of the participants had obviously borrowed their weapons and had attended to be close to their civic bosses; others were superb shots. From our point of view we were happy that the guns were always pointed high even after the morning's lavish refreshment because on this occasion there was no stigma attached to shooting sitting birds – the tighter they perched the better!

After Karnival it was the turn of our Regiment to entertain – on Guy Fawkes Night. Early November is intensely cold in Westphalia and our barrack square, where we located the bonfire and the firework display, needed to be heavily salted. The whole Regiment, wives and children not at school were there, well wrapped up against the dry cold, and each mess, officers, sergeants, corporals and drivers, laid on a party. They were encouraged to entertain as many of the townsfolk as they could fit in, as repayment for hospitality that we had received during the year. The police were there in force together with the fire brigade (just in case). I made a point of 'pushing the boat out' on Bonfire Night, using regimental funds quite lavishly.

I had invitations printed for the officers' mess party firmly rounded off at the bottom with the now old fashioned legend 'Carriages at 2300' or whatever time appeared to be seemly. This was as a result of experience from my previous tour of duty in Germany. Although the Germans play strictly to the rules, if no rules are laid out they will feel free to interpret the situation according to their inclinations. Having failed to lay down a time for a dinner party to be over on one occasion in Wuppertal, we had had to entertain my bibulous local bank manager and several other German friends until four in the morning; perhaps not untoward at a weekend when a morning lie-in is possible, but on a weekday evening with a mandatory early working parade next day, not good for morale.

The firework display was, as ever, superb. We had an attached officer from the Royal Army Ordnance Corps whose job was to liaise with the providers of the various types of ammunition and stores that we carried in our vehicles; he happened also to be an explosives specialist, the ideal person to take charge of the fireworks. He planned the display precisely to a timed programme and it went off to great effect. I recall explaining the historical background to a newly arrived official from the City Hall who combined good English with a keen sense of humour.

"You mean you celebrate this fellow's failure to blow up your seat of Government? We would have planned it better and would be celebrating his success!"

Hot dogs, mulled wine and the inevitable Coke and other fizzy drinks were available during the display and it was nice to see both policemen and firemen holding sparklers for the children.

There were bonuses attached to being the only British troops – or indeed troops of any nationality – for miles around. Our nearest neighbours in a military sense were a motley collection of small units at Mulheim an der Ruhr, some fifteen or so miles away. As CO of the only major unit in the area I was also the Garrison Commander for Mulheim and I had a retired officer as Station Staff Officer there to administer the polyglot units in that small garrison. Our nearest large garrison was at Dusseldorf, about sixteen miles distant in another direction and beyond that Rheindahlen, the Headquarters of the British Army of the Rhine, a small piece of England located near to Munchen Gladbach on the Dutch/German border and about forty miles away from us.

Next to Duisburg itself, within walking distance of the barracks, our favourite place to visit was Dusseldorf, a lovely city which was fond of calling itself 'The Paris of the Ruhr'. For us it was a very easy to get there. The 'Schnell Tram', a fast and comfortable tram that contained a bar serving light refreshments ran from Duisburg to the centre of Dusseldorf and passed quite close to our barracks. It operated from early morning until late at night. The Wedau tram stop was on the route and was a two minute walk from the barrack gates and also from the main married quarter 'patch'. It was used extensively by all members of the Regiment and their families. We often took the children to Dusseldorf on Saturday mornings to watch the small boys turning cartwheels in the Koenigsallee, a broad tree lined boulevard lined with outdoor cafes and smart shops: then lunch in the Old Town and perhaps a film show at the British Army Cinema. On a fine day, Dusseldorf was a delight to visit.

The RSM had to liaise with the local police as part of his job, and had done so to such effect that some of the senior policemen had been made honorary members of our sergeants' mess, a situation that they relished. The spin-off for us was that the regiment rated low in the disciplinary statistics published quarterly by the Dusseldorf Provost Marshal. Clearly he didn't believe that I had a barracks full of sober plaster saints as of course I didn't. But the RSM had arranged with his local police friends for any soldier arrested for a misdemeanour or simply found falling down drunk within the jurisdiction of the Duisburg Police, to be brought straight to our guardroom instead of having to be booked in at the police station and the Provost Marshal's staff then notified. This didn't apply of course, to offences committed elsewhere and we featured just as prominently as other units in the statistics related to Dusseldorf and Rheindahlen.

Early December and the series of inspections covering the functions of the Regiment had been completed by visiting teams of specialists and reports sent to Divisional HQ . They were not too bad but they had highlighted corrective action to be taken, which was after all their primary purpose.

We found that we suddenly became very popular at about this time. Most units in the Division had substantial holdings of wheeled transport to help them carry out their specific functions and these vehicles were inspected by specialist teams each year. Transport not being their primary purpose in life, we, as the Division's transport professionals, were often approached for help with updating maintenance records – usually urgently – under the Old Pals Act. They couldn't seek help from the Royal Electrical and Mechanical Engineers (REME) because they were actually carrying out the vehicle and equipment inspections. I was always happy to oblige on these occasions; goodwill is a valuable commodity and it sometimes becomes necessary to draw on it in return.

Our own annual vehicle inspection was of particular importance to us bearing in mind our role and I was at pains to negotiate a truce in the 'friendly' war we waged with the higher formation REME Workshops while we were preparing for the inspection. My drivers became very attached to their vehicles and fretted considerably when they were held in Base Workshops for repair longer than their drivers thought necessary. Now and then I had to deflect complaints that Driver X or Lance Corporal Y had sent a 'Get Well' card to the workshops CO on behalf of vehicle number so and so while lower down the pecking order his mechanics had been heckled aggressively.

This was usually due to a shortage of spares and no fault of the mechanics. It helped that the REME brigadier in 1st British Corps, Mike Kneen, was a just man who realised the frustrations on both sides and his reports were invariably fair.

Each year the GOC picked out several units of his Division to be subjected to his personal formal inspection. We were honoured with a GOC's inspection on my first year in command. Any CO who fails to keep in mind the fact that his General has been through this himself is missing a trick. We were a big regiment with hundreds of vehicles and pieces of equipment; our General was a highly intelligent and astute professional soldier so normal military 'flannel' was out of the question. There were bound to be shortcomings. The day – for it took a whole day, went quite well. Just a few minor horrors surfaced. Once again the troops had turned up trumps.

I had one bad moment. We were visiting the main cookhouse: it shone in places it should have shone. The cooks were in spotless whites; the warrant officer chef was articulate but not too plausible – then as we were talking to the General, the RSM, by my side as ever, could not forbear to stiffen visibly. Fortunately the General was deep in conversation with the chef and didn't notice but I followed the RSM's eyes and watched, transfixed, as the biggest cockroach I have ever seen crawled idly over the General's polished boot. German cockroaches are a special species. Ineradicable, short of complete demolition of their habitat, they haunt cookhouses and clubs, defeating all attempts to exterminate them. This one sauntered off without attracting attention.

Most of us can recall bad moments on annual inspections. My favourite is the true story of one general famous for being determined to root out the domestic horrors which experience told him were hidden in even the best run units. At the CO's brisk "This way sir", he was notorious for replying, "No. We'll go this way".

On the day of this particular inspection he caught out one of the squadron offices by insisting on going 'the other way' and arrived a few minutes before the time appointed on his programme for inspection. The soldier detailed to give warning of the inspecting party's approach gave the signal, causing confusion in the office where the sergeant chief clerk and his staff had almost completed the smartening up process. There was an old German civilian lady cleaner just finishing mopping the floor and with no chance to get her clear before the great man arrived, the sergeant opened the door of an empty broom cupboard and shoved her in, upturning her bucket and saying, "Sit on this and be quiet till I let you out."

The inspecting party arrived and the General went through the office like a terrier, barking questions and hardly waiting for the answers. The sergeant, with his squadron OC at his shoulder, showed the general round his small domain, ignoring the broom cupboard.

"What's in there?" said the General, and without giving the sergeant time to reply he wrenched open the door, to be confronted with a seated old lady apparently performing a natural function.

"Oh, my God. I'm terribly sorry. I do apologise," closing the door and turning to the CO with a crimson face. Apologising again for his hasty behaviour, the General left the office quickly and for the rest of the day stuck rigidly to his timed and structured programme. The grinning CO was later heard to say, "I couldn't have planned that better if I'd tried. I must remember that one for future use on a different inquisitor."

We all know about graveyards being full of indispensable people, but as a CO, taking the full six weeks annual leave entitlement at one go was really not on. Apart from the practical consideration that finding six consecutive weeks clear in a busy calendar of events was well nigh impossible, there was always the haunting conviction that while you were away, Murphy's Law would snap into action and cause something dramatically ghastly to occur either within the Regiment or within the Garrison. So we tried to take a fortnight as a family to a warm and sunny spot during the school summer holidays and take two or three days' break during the spring holiday when Wendy, our second daughter and still boarding, often invited a school friend to visit us. For this we had a couple of set outings. These were either the ever popular visit to Amsterdam about two hours' drive away, for a trip on the canals, or a day trip down the autobahn to Koblenz at the confluence of the Rhine and the Mosel Rivers, then along the Mosel Valley to Trier, where it became the Moselle, and back to Duisburg through Belgium and Holland.

The great attractions of the Mosel trip for the visiting girls were the border crossings. Normally our distinctive British Forces Germany (BFG) car number plates were instantly recognised by the border police and customs and we were waved through, but this was never good enough for our teenage schoolgirl guests. Armed with their passports they would leap out of the car at the crossing points into Belgium, then into Holland and back into Germany. At each border they would sweet talk both customs and border police into stamping every rubber stamp available into their passports. Very valuable back at school for esteem purposes apparently, and years later I learned that one or two 'lookalike' young ladies I had never even met had benefited from a probably indictable deception, having provided their passports to be stamped while still at home in England.

In common with all major units, we had several extra regimental tasks set by Divisional HQ. One of these was to provide a patrol from time to time for duty on the East/West German border. This was set at an officer, a sergeant and the equivalent of two infantry sections – about sixteen men. All the patrols were much photographed by the Russians and East Germans. They aimed their cameras quite blatantly from the border wall's watchtowers. Making a surprise visit to one of my patrols one day I was surprised to find the patrol sergeant wearing a subaltern's badges of rank on his combat dress.

"What's going on and where is your officer?" I asked.

At that moment the officer in command of the patrol appeared from the woods, wearing sergeants' badges of rank. He apologised and said that they had all got so fed up with the continual photography they had decided to give the other side something to think about. So they changed jackets on a regular basis between watchtowers to confuse the photographic interpreters. It wasn't a bad idea and certainly did no harm so I let them get on with it. I later learned that it was a ploy adopted quite regularly by patrols, partly to relieve the boredom of patrolling in peacetime and partly to confuse our putative enemy.

Duisburg was, and perhaps still is, twinned with Portsmouth and it was the custom of the Burgermeister to visit the barracks with some of his senior officials around Christmastime to greet and present all those soldiers hailing from Portsmouth with gifts and a large Christmas cake. We made a ceremony of it. The Christmas twinning presentation featured annually and at length in the local papers and often on the TV news. All ranks of the Regiment were also invited by the townspeople of Duisburg to join them in singing Christmas carols on the steps of the Cathedral. We did this with pleasure and with all the children at home for the holiday we attended in force. Our two older girls at twenty and seventeen respectively wore long coats covering the fashionable miniskirts of the late nineteen sixties and along with some of the similarly dressed younger wives of our soldiers this also attracted press comment. Pressure was always on to maintain and enhance Anglo-German relations and this gave me the germ of an idea.

Our Corps Band, long reputed to be one of the best in the Army, was doing a BAOR tour in the spring of 1970, the following year. The Germans love military music; why not combine a band concert in the Mercatorhalle, the main concert hall for the city, with a charitable appeal for Anglo German good causes? I secured my bid for the Band and discussed the proposition with the Burgermeister who readily agreed to let us have the Hall free for the evening provided that there would be no further expense to the Stadt. We set up an Anglo German committee. After very little deliberation this proposed that any profits made by the concert should be divided equally between the German Red Cross and the RCT Benevolent Fund. Sadly, for he was a strong supporter of Anglo-German relations, the date chosen conflicted with another commitment for our General, who had to decline, but we managed a goodly selection of VIPs and strong support from the German fraternity.

Mercator – the celebrated mapmaker, he of the Projection we used to learn in school, had been a teacher in Duisburg and the Hall named for his memory and fame is enormous. For the concert it was packed, standing room only at the back. Our Band, dressed in Blues with Victorian style shakos as headgear, looked suitably impressive on the vast stage and I redeemed my promise to my doubting officers by making a speech in both German and English, having been carefully coached as to accent and delivery by the charming and invaluable Gerda Garside.

The concert was a great success, so much so that the band had repeated curtain calls and couldn't get away until eventually the Director of Music had to call to his rescue the orchestral piece that allows the musicians to leave the orchestra in ones and twos leaving a lone brass player to vacate the stage. We raised a considerable sum for the two charities and again managed substantial media coverage. The spin-off from this could have proved my undoing.

Not long after the concert and its attendant publicity, I received an invitation from a local German Old Comrades Association to attend with some of my soldiers a memorial service at a Reichswald military cemetery to commemorate the fallen in the Second World War. The Reichswald battle towards the end of the war was a particularly vicious affair with little quarter asked or given on either side. The Reichswald itself is a thick forest in northern Germany just across the Rhine. The invitation looked innocuous and twenty-five years after the end of the war, relations with our German allies were probably sufficiently relaxed to look with favour on a joint commemoration of the fallen.

But it paid to be cautious in these matters and before replying I resolved to consult the PR people at HQ BAOR. Before doing so I showed the invitation casually to my fluent German speaker and shooting companion, Roy Garside. He blanched, "Don't touch it. That chap, the person signing the invitation, is a prominent member of the Neo Nazi Party!" The PR section at Rheindahlen confirmed his assessment. The consequences of accepting this invitation had I not checked could have been serious. The media wolf pack would have had a field day had it become known that we had attended a memorial service as the honoured guests of a bunch of Neo Nazis; my Regiment would have been pilloried and I would have been deservedly in deep trouble for lacking judgement, that essential attribute for commanders at all levels.

The attitude of commanding officers in BAOR to the British press generally at that time is worth comment. Most of us tended to avoid contact, preferring to hand enquiries to the PR people at higher formation HQs. Still strong in the memory was the recollection of the distasteful episode centred on the garrison at Minden when so called 'investigative journalists' descended on the town and pilloried a battalion of a famous regiment that was alleged to have upset the townspeople by creating trouble on Saturday nights. The stories that appeared in the Sunday papers at home were lurid and probably exaggerated, but within BAOR, supposedly true tales abounded of journalists bribing the alleged troublemakers to get drunk and create mayhem. Whether these stories were true or not, it was certainly unfair and unreasonable to saddle a whole battalion of fighting soldiers with the nickname 'Poison Dwarfs'. This created a climate of distaste for journalists among commanders in BAOR jealous of the reputation of their regiments. This did not apply to the local media: they took a more balanced attitude to our activities, although when criticism was called for they did not hesitate to voice it.

It was in the nature of operations that the three squadrons comprising my Regiment were dispersed to the brigades they supported in war when we took the field as the 4th Armoured Division, while our regimental HQ became part of Division HQ with a co-ordinating radio net monitoring their activities. But I was keen to take the regiment into the field as an entity at least once in my tour in command in order to spruce up convoy disciplines, defence and emergency drills, radio procedures and simply give the soldiers an opportunity to get out of barracks and do what they enjoyed most – field work at all times of the year – even in the depths of a German winter.

So with approval from Divisional HQ, Dick Chinn, our second in command, clothed the bones of a blueprint for a major exercise that involved deployment into Sleschwig Holstein on the Jutland Peninsular – the Danish border area – followed by redeployment to the southern part of the British sector, crossing the Weser River on a pontoon bridge built by a field engineer regiment commanded by a friend who just happened to be engaged on a bridge building exercise at that time.

While our ten tonners and domestic vehicles crossed John Groom's bridge without incident, our Stalwart armoured amphibious vehicles swam across the river without any leaks or sinkings. The exercise took place in spring and involved considerable planning, bearing in mind the fact that Germany was hard at work and our activities inevitably caused some inconvenience to the civilian population. It went well; there were a few breakdowns, quickly recovered and one or two traffic accidents rapidly dealt with. Rusty radio procedures were smartened up, convoy and close protection drills were tightened and new arrivals to the Regiment learned about field living in BAOR.

The visit to Schleswig Holstein to the north of Hamburg was particularly memorable. It took place at a time when the storks were nesting and in every village there was at least one occupied nest at the highest possible point. All you could see was the long beak of a stork protruding perhaps from the top of a tall chimney or from a high flat roof. The villagers were very protective; we were told that it was a harbinger of ill fortune if the storks missed their village while neighbouring villages were honoured. I stood down the exercise on Sundays, partly to give the drivers a rest but also because the German authorities regarded heavy vehicles on the road on the Sabbath as bad news. Special permission was required for heavy military vehicles to travel at weekends and was rarely given for anything less than an emergency.

During the Schleswig weekend my regimental HQ, consisting of a couple of light radio vehicles, an office truck and a domestic 3 tonner, was located by invitation on the land of an elderly widow who clearly relished the company afforded by the young soldiers and she supplemented their rations by all sorts of delicacies. They responded by setting to with a will to mend her gates and fix anything that needed fixing on her somewhat rundown property.

As we were preparing to leave on Monday morning the old lady asked to see the Oberst. She showered thanks on me, praised the soldiers to high heaven and handed me a parcel wrapped in bright paper.

"This is for you," she said. "It is not much for I do not have much. But it has been in my family a long time and I would like you to accept it."

I thanked her and said that while she was very kind, presents were not necessary. But I opened the parcel to find a porcelain plant pot container beautifully hand painted and obviously old. I happen to have an interest in old porcelain and I am acquainted with the German marks. I looked underneath the pot container and saw the mark of the Keil factory that had closed down some years before.

"I really can't accept this." I said. "You must realise that it is a collectors' item and worth some money. I don't know how much in Germany, but a considerable sum in England." All this with the help of one of my sergeants who was married to a German girl.

"Well," said the old lady "I have another one which I'm sure is not valuable because it is slightly cracked." She went away then reappeared with another pot cover, also from the Kiel factory. This one was indeed visibly cracked and therefore of little use to a collector, although very pretty. It was clear that we were not going to get away without accepting her kind gesture in one form or another so I thanked her gracefully and we moved off. Although still cracked, the old porcelain pot must have been very well put together; it has survived several house moves and is with me still.

Duisburg was near enough to HQ BAOR for the Regiment to be

allotted many visits both from senior officers of our own Corps and from officers of Commonwealth and other armies. This was usually a pleasure, very occasionally a bore and now and then a delight. For visiting individuals we had compiled a standard programme comprising a tour of the barracks to allow the visitor to talk to the soldiers and see the unit at work, followed by a briefing on our war role if the security classification of the visitor warranted it, lunch in mess and in the afternoon the high point of the visit – a trip on the Rhine in one of our amphibious Stalwart vehicles. In fact they swam well and clearance with the port authorities was never a problem as the drivers stayed well clear of barge traffic which was heavy but kept within defined lanes in the wide river. Somewhat cynically, I suppose, I regarded a full day and a full belly as the key to a successful visit from someone outside our Division.

In the delight category came a two week attachment to us of a small unit of the Danish Army commanded by a young major who was built like an oak door. He was also a very agreeable character and determined to enjoy his spell with us. Like most Scandanavians, he, his officers and most of his NCOs and men spoke excellent English and they all got on with us like the proverbial house on fire. I think we have school and Shakespeare's 'Gloomy Dane' to thank for our abiding impression of the Danes as a dour people but that certainly didn't apply to this bunch. They had their own training programme; I had agreed to provide accommodation and messing only but they were such a cheerful and friendly lot that we were rather sorry to see them go.

I recall Harald, their major, telling me that his father was a civil servant during the German occupation and employed at a port on the Danish west coast. Part of his duty was to liaise with the occupying Germans and in 1943 in company with a German officer he was viewing the remains of a newly discovered Viking ship in the silt of the harbour when the German officer spoke disparagingly of the 'idiot Vikings' attempting to mount an invasion of Britain in such flimsy craft. Harald's father responded by saying something along the lines of 'Maybe so, but they managed it a damn sight more successfully than you did' – for which he was hauled before the German port commander and threatened with transfer to a forced labour squad if he didn't show more respect to the Third Reich.

Later in the year as a guest at a drinks party I met an English speaking German officer who was the commanding officer of a Bundeswehr regiment stationed, he told me, in the Allgau region bordering the German Tyrol.

"Ah," I said, "Sound of Music country."

He understood the reference but replied, "It's all very well for you to say that but my soldiers are bored silly. Most of them come from the Ruhr and quite a few from Duisburg itself. They're mainly National Servicemen and when the military elastic is released, they're back here like a shot. Where we are stationed is, I admit, beautiful countryside, but relieving the boredom of young man brought up in a swinging industrial area is not easy. You wouldn't like to swap for a bit?"

I laughed and said I'd take a raincheck – which threw him completely until I translated from the original American.

Mulling this over later, however, I thought if he was serious, why not? We could do with somewhere pleasant to do our annual live firing classification and the fitness tests involving route marches that we all had to do to confirm our medical grading each year, and where better to do that than the fabled countryside of Southern Bavaria.

I got in touch with my German friend again. He said he had certainly been serious and leaped at the chance to occupy our barracks for a month, leaving us his hutted camp outside the Bavarian country town of Kempten.

We took with us as few vehicles as possible, using our three tonners as troop carriers. The object of the trip after all, was to concentrate on weapon and fitness training and we needed to be able to get back quickly in any emergency. We left a substantial rear party in Duisburg and the unit quartermaster stayed behind to liaise with our German 'barracks swappers' and look after the families. I insisted that both our padre and our doctor accompanied the Regiment to the great delight of the doctor, but I wasn't sure that the padre was all that happy. Stand-ins were easily arranged. There were numerous TA doctors in England who would welcome an invitation to a month in Germany ministering to the families of a large barracks, and the spiritual needs of those left behind could be catered for by the Mulheim Garrison padre.

So in due course we found ourselves occupying a Bundeswehr hutted camp in the Allgau Region of Southern Bavaria and enjoying the autumn colours of one of the most beautiful and unspoilt areas of Europe. The camp was located in the depths of the countryside midway between the town of Kempten and the village of Bad Oberstdorf which lay at the foot of the Allgauer Alps in the shadow of the mighty Nebelhorn at 7500 feet. To the east and not many miles away was the town of Fussen, quite close to Hohenschwangau, the castle of the mad King Ludwig of Bavaria.

The countryside was truly glorious and a marked contrast to the dust and activity of a thriving Ruhr steel town. Nevertheless I could see the point made by the German CO we had swapped with. I would have to organise things so that my soldiers were active almost until they dropped. Even great beauty palls eventually if there is no sense of purpose, and fit young men need to be kept busy. We made our number with the local Stadt in Kempten and in no time we had organised a football match with the town team. There was a well equipped rifle range for practice and inter-squadron competition shoots and daily route marches took place – working towards the annual fitness test. This entailed a five mile 'bash' over mixed country with rifle and full equipment followed by a requirement to carry a man of one's own approximate weight for one hundred yards and culminating in five rounds rapid fire at a pop up target – all within a time envelope. Fitness tests had to be monitored by a doctor – hence my insistence on having ours with us.

The time passed in a flash and there was little chance to become tourists and see the sights for which the region is famous, although some of us did manage to take the cable car from Oberstdorf to the top of the Nebelhorn. It was a clear day and the Austrian Alps presented a magnificent Alpine snowscape. I resolved to go back with my family and over the years I have done so several times, mainly in the spring to hike over the fields and foothills carpeted in wild flowers and stay at the country inns that abound in the area – where the north German 'Guten Tag' gives place to the Bavarian salutation of 'Gruss Got' or 'Greetings to God'.

All too soon my next posting was on the cards – the blow softened by the surprising news that I was to be promoted to Colonel, my Corps mess kit of black jacket with white facings to be replaced by the staff officers' standard scarlet jacket with black facings. I would not have much of a chance to wear it though, for my next appointment was to be Colonel Movements (Plans) at the Ministry of Defence in Whitehall. I would be sad to leave the Regiment, but fortunately the Military

Secretary's branch gives you a few months to get used to the idea and make the necessary domestic arrangements prior to leaving for the UK and home.

These months passed quickly. I learned that my replacement was to be one Ben Harrold who I did not know, but in the event he turned out to be a very nice fellow and supremely capable; he got in touch and was clearly delighted with his new appointment. It would be a pleasure to hand over to him secure in the knowledge that the Regiment would be in good hands.

Not long before we were due to leave Duisburg, Heather noticed a lump in her breast and although she was reluctant to 'make a fuss' at this critical time, I persuaded her to see our MO, who lived only a few doors away. He said it was probably fibrous and of no consequence but insisted that she attend the RAF hospital at Wegburg, some miles away, for a biopsy. This entailed cutting the lump out and checking to see if there were any sinister indications. She stayed in hospital for two days and on the third day when I was due to bring her back in the evening, I received a call from the Wing Commander CO who asked if I could see him right away; he would give no reason over the phone, which I took to be ominous.

The interview was brief and to the point; the lump had turned out to be malignant and Heather was to be evacuated medically to England right away for a mastectomy – at that time the standard treatment for breast cancer. I was shattered. This was certainly the worst thing ever to have hit our close-knit family. The Wing Commander said that if I didn't feel up to telling her, then he would do it but of course there was no question of ducking that task; it was down to me.

Germany. The Regiment's winning float for the Duisburg Karnival.

A troop of our Stalwart armoured amphibians entering the Rhine.

They swam well in deep water. Reaching the other side.

Regimental athletics. He won the father's race!

20

A Year at the Madhouse

Heather bore up well but it was clear that she was mortally afraid. The Wing Commander doctor had said that the prognosis was promising and advised us not to cancel any long-term arrangements we might have made. Heather was evacuated by air to the Army Millbank Hospital adjacent to the Tate Gallery in London; I handed over the Regiment more hastily than I had planned and with the two younger girls in tow, drove to Ostend and then to Salisbury. I was rudderless; we operated as a team with the domestic arrangements normally out of my hands. But Heather's very elderly mother was marvellous with the younger girls and Wendy, our second daughter, at seventeen had just reached her school leaving age. She left her boarding school in Dorset and joined me in Salisbury.

The operation, conducted by Colonel Kevin Coakley, our old friend from West Africa days, and now senior surgeon at the Millbank Hospital, was successful but they kept Heather in for some weeks before she was allowed home.

We were once again in that military limbo between postings. It was late 1971 and on the cards that I would eventually be allotted a quarter in the London area, but in conversation with a solicitor friend in Salisbury, I was urged to buy a house as soon as possible.

"There's a boom coming," he said. "And if you don't act now you'll regret it." I had to agree.

"There's one small problem," I said. "It's called money and I haven't got enough of it. I need at least four bedrooms and it must be within reasonable reach of London." To my great surprise he waved the problem aside.

"Find the property that suits you, manage somehow or other to rake up a ten per cent deposit and I'll get you a mortgage for the rest on reasonable terms. I happen to have a strong line into two prominent building societies and on my recommendation they'll advance you anything within reason."

I discussed this proposition with Heather, by now convalescing in hospital and she agreed that I should get on with it although I suspected that she had reservations about my competence in this sort of transaction. So during the few weeks before I had to report to the MOD, Wendy and I prospected for houses in the Winchester area, about an hour's train journey from London. As I had suspected there was little available that met my minimum specification and was also within our budget. What there was for sale was either too cramped or in a shocking state of repair, or had so much 'character' – a favourite estate agents' euphemism for outlandish properties – that it would only have suited owners ranging from the highly eccentric to the plain barking.

Disappointed and disillusioned, we stopped at a village shop one afternoon to buy a jar of jam. The middle-aged lady serving behind the counter was deep in conversation with a customer obviously well known to her and I heard her say, "I'm afraid he's no better; it's too much for him so we have to move and we're putting it on the market next week." My ears twitched. Wendy had obviously heard it too and frowned at me in surmise. I shook my head; we made our purchase and went outside.

We hadn't really noticed the place other than to identify it as the village shop but on closer inspection it was a detached double gabled house as well. In addition it had a substantial two storey brick built extension at the rear – part of the house but for a purpose not evident to the casual eye. Judging from the upstairs windows of the house there were four bedrooms although one may have been a bathroom. There was a fair sized garden and it was a very pretty village.

What had we got to lose? We went back inside the shop and explained our situation. The lady was indeed the wife of the owner and said that they had decided to sell with great reluctance because her husband had had a severe heart attack and could no longer follow his trade as a baker. We had stumbled upon the village bakery now operating solely as a shop only because of the owner's indisposition. The extension to the house was the defunct bakery on two floors with ovens downstairs and flour store above. There were in fact four bedrooms and a bathroom that had been carved out of the massive flour store. The owners had had the property valued but had not yet made a deal with an agent to advertise it for sale. The valuation was above our maximum but not excessively so because the valuer had appreciated that there would be substantial conversion costs.

We were offered an instant informal viewing that we accepted. Wendy liked it and was convinced that her mother would too. *Carpe Diem*! I made an offer within our budget, stressing that we had no house to sell and could exchange contracts and complete the transaction quickly with a friendly solicitor to do the conveyancing. The husband came out, displaying symptoms of ill health even to my untrained eye, and we shook hands on a deal subject to the usual caveats of survey and mortgage.

The owners confessed to us later that they were very relieved. Apart from the saving on agents' fees and commission, they felt that they needed to get inside the city limits quickly to be nearer the hospital and they moved out as soon as they could to a flat in Winchester. The survey was good, the mortgage and conveyancing went through in double quick time and before Heather came out of hospital we took possession of our new house. When she did leave hospital she took one look at the house, with shop windows and a side window bearing the legend 'deliveries throughout the district' and said, "My God! What have you done while I was out of commission?"

In fact, the house part of the bakery was quite adequate for us to live in until we could complete the conversion of the place to a five bedroom, two bathroom dwelling with the shop eventually serving as a large drawing room. I pointed out that at that time developers all over the south of England and elsewhere, were snapping up old bakeries, old forges, old schoolhouses and in some cases even deconsecrated churches and chapels to turn into desirable residences to meet the insatiable demand for housing. I would, of course, have to do a lot myself and I looked forward to it as a change from being a Whitehall Warrior in my day job. In fact, it was a somewhat daunting prospect; I was more heavily in debt than ever before and could see little prospect of raising the money needed to pay the builders for necessary alterations to the structure of the house. Fortunately, school fees were in abeyance. Our third daughter, Kate, did not need to board and could travel daily on the bus to school in Winchester. This suited Heather and me well as we felt that we had missed much of the growing up of the older girls who, because of our circumstances, had to board.

I had taken little account of the fact that locked away in safe keeping were two insurance policies that I had taken out at the urging of a TA officer we had sponsored years earlier during a staff college study. He was a financial adviser in civilian life and, grateful for our hospitality, he had offered to review my insurance and finances, waiving his normal fee. In fact, living from hand to mouth as I and most of my contemporaries in the Service did, I hadn't at that stage bothered much about the future and he persuaded me to set an affordable amount aside each month for two endowment policies which, he said, could be used as security for a loan, should I ever need one. I remembered this and I was able to raise enough for the conversion of our bakery by assigning the policies to a building society through the good offices of my solicitor friend.

All this took place at breakneck speed and I took up my new job in Movements at the MOD with a buzzing head. I had been lucky to escape the 'Madhouse' as the MOD was known, until I was fairly senior. Nevertheless my life there could be compared without too much exaggeration to that of a pit pony. I left home at about seven in the morning to catch the train for a one hour journey to Waterloo. The train was usually full on leaving Southampton so there was little chance of a seat for those getting on at Winchester and beyond, and so like many others I carried a small folding wire and canvas seat in my briefcase for use in the corridor. A brisk walk across Hungerford Bridge to the Ministry to reach the office slightly before nine a.m. followed by a daily telephone and paper battle until it was time to catch the evening train for an hour dozing, until seven p.m., then home for three hours DIY or decorating until exhaustion took over. I did this for a year and consoled myself with the thought that for many, commuting is a life sentence – rumour has it that some even enjoy it, but they're probably institutionalised like old lags to whom prison has become home.

But there were three things to cheer about. The first was that Heather had quickly regained her strength, although it took some time for her to get over what she thought of as her 'mutilation' and she would have to undergo three monthly examinations for a long time. The second was that my boss, to whom I worked directly, was General Bill Bate of my Corps, the Army's Director of Movements and a brilliant staff officer who seemed, without trying, to keep at least one thought ahead of most of us. The third cheerful circumstance was being able to see our house conversion develop under the hands of competent builders. I didn't have enough confidence in my DIY skills to undertake structural alterations; these had to be done by professionals. Plumbing, wiring and internal decorating, however, could be self-taught.

We couldn't run to an architect so I did the drawings for planning permission and building regulation applications myself. Although I thought they were OK, my confidence wasn't shared by the Winchester planning authorities. I still treasure the letter from an obviously exasperated but very polite official who wrote to thank me for the application for a conversion of bakery space to a second bathroom but said that he could not quite follow the drawings. He had therefore had them done by his draughtsmen to what he thought were my ideas and would I please confirm that this was what I wanted? The accompanying impeccable drawings were a perfect representation of what I had in mind. A truly civil servant!

In the early seventies I was one of many converting buildings on a largely DIY basis. They were not by any means all Service people. You could spot them in the train – men in city suits with a tired, hangdog look, often dozing over their morning papers and sometimes with traces of paint in their hair. Our reward came in the late seventies and the early eighties when to everyone's astonishment, properties bought for what later turned out to be a song, had increased in value sometimes tenfold.

I hadn't much cared for the planning job; it was a big letdown from commanding a unit and as I was an anchor man, with the Director doing most of the travelling, the pit pony simile was quite apt. I was therefore delighted to be promoted to Brigadier after only a year in the Ministry and appointed Commander 2 Transport Group based at Bulford Camp on Salisbury Plain with my HQ adjacent to 3rd Division of happy memory. Just before I left the Ministry, Derek, a friend and fellow student at the Staff College in the nineteen fifties visited to say goodbye. An infantryman and bachelor, Derek had volunteered for Intelligence work. At the height of the Cold War, he had to have at least a nodding acquaintance with Russian. He was sent on a 'deep immersion' course involving intensive study at a language laboratory. This was followed by several months living with a Russian émigré family in Paris. The family had a daughter in her early twenties – we shall call her Natasha – who spoke reasonable English but was keen to deepen her knowledge of our idioms. She was a nice girl according to Derek, who was happy to squire her around Paris and he also took her occasionally to regimental functions. He told her that a 'Horse's Neck' in the Service had nothing to do with horses and he explained the mixes of the gin based drinks such as John Collins and Tom Collins.

He told me that one very warm evening in summer he had taken her to the ceremony of 'Retreat' performed by his Regiment in Germany. After the ceremony, the Regiment's officers, their ladies and their guests repaired to their Mess for drinks. Natasha, determined to impress with her colloquial English, threw herself into a chair and said in her carrying voice, "I am so hot, Derek. What could I not do to a nice, long, cool John Thomas!"

Having then observed that he had heard that the selection board had been drinking again, my generous friend said, "You do realise of course that your new appointment has nothing to do with you having done well here? It's merely the application of bureaucratic practices being carried over to the Services."

"What can you mean?" I asked.

"Well," he replied. "Everybody here knows that the only way to get rid of an unsatisfactory civil servant is to recommend him for promotion. Congratulations anyway for beating the rap."

21

Two Group

My new appointment meant that our family would be able to move into the smart quarter available to us at Bulford complete with a staff of three, but Heather now loved our converted bakery and turned down the opportunity to move. We had made many friends, both service and civilian, in our adopted village and we were both happy to stay there. Bulford was only a half hour drive from us and getting there would be no problem with the dedicated staff car and driver that went with the job. Also, I would be doing a great deal of travelling round the four major units under my command as I didn't intend to spend any more time in the office than I had to.

My compact HQ was established on almost identical lines to the one in Lagos all those years ago. I had a major GSO2, a captain GSO3, a major DAA&QMG and a staff captain – the Army needs initials as babies need milk. The difference from West Africa was that the staff captain was a re-employed retired officer (RO). Sometimes inelegantly but affectionately known as 'retreads', these officers gave good service to the Army and their situation allowed them to stay close to the lifestyle they had enjoyed for many years. They were required to retire again at sixty-five, thus giving them ten years extra full employment from their Service retirement date of fifty-five. My RO was Bill Wynn – Wernick, late of the RCT. He had served for many years in the maritime wing of the Corps and was well known in the wider world as a maritime artist. It was an efficient and happy set-up.

Someone had described my new command as the Corps 'funnies', meaning the units outside the conventional field force establishments. The Group had four major units and one minor unit. There was a very much oversize transport regiment with a wide range of vehicles and equipment. It had tank transporters, Volvo oversnow vehicles for logistic support on the Norwegian flank of NATO, plus a substantial ration of ten tonners and three tonners as well as radio and domestic vehicles. Because of its size and diverse tasks this was commanded by a colonel, Danny Cardle, who had, like me, started his career in the

Fleet Air Arm. He had a lieutenant colonel second in command. Also part of my Group was the RCT air despatch regiment located with the RAF at the several strategic reserve airfields in the south of England.

In addition I had the maritime regiment of seagoing tank landing craft crewed by soldiers, based on Portsmouth Harbour and operating mainly in support of the Army'establishment in the Outer Hebrides. Finally, there was Marchwood Military Port on Southampton Water with its ocean going logistic ships crewed by the Royal Fleet Auxiliary but bought with funds from the Army Vote and 'owned' and tasked by the Army Movements directorate at MOD. The port had an establishment of soldiers and equipment sufficient to warrant a lieutenant colonel in command. It also had a troop of DUKWS commanded by a warrant officer. These amphibious wheeled vehicles, operating extensively in the Second World War for landings and resupply over beaches, had last been used in Korea by the Americans, where I had seen them employed as lighters conveying stores from ships lying offshore in Pusan. So far as I knew they had not been gainfully employed since. They were the remnants of the army's holdings and were kept alive by cannibilisation of parts. There were about eighteen left road and seaworthy and they were shortly to be phased out.

Our one minor unit was constantly under threat of disbandment. This was the Army's only Hovercraft Squadron located close to the Browndown rifle ranges on the Solent and commanded by a major with the craft driven and maintained by soldiers. They were devoted to their strange machines but their survival would depend on the ability of the MOD marketing men to sell hovercraft abroad and much of their activity consisted of exercises and demonstrations of their British built craft to potential foreign military buyers.

Clearly this disparate collection of units could not operate or be used as an entity but all the units were part of my Corps, I knew the COs and many of the officers and my predecessors in command had successfully fostered a 'Group' spirit. The commanding officers knew where to come for advice or instruction and there were regular policy meetings of COs at my HQ. In some ways we had an edge over the field force Army when there were no active operations on the go. My units always had a full-time job to do and this provided a sense of purpose sometimes difficult to maintain as I had learned in Germany when now and then, preparations for inspections had to fill the days and weeks. It was a truly worthwhile command and I counted myself lucky to be once again in direct contact with soldiers at this late stage of my career.

A subsidiary task took up a good deal of time. There was a large Territorial Army logistic establishment that would be embodied in the event of a war or other major emergency and would operate as the Logistic Support Group (LSG) under my command in support of Strategic Reserve operations. It was part of my job to keep it trained for field operations and of course this meant close contact with the GOC and senior staff of the neighbouring 3rd Division. This was now commanded by Major General Dick Worsley, a cavalry officer who I did not know well. Shortly after my arrival, however, Colonel Bill Allan of my Corps was posted in as his senior logistic staff officer, a stroke of luck both for me and for my HQ staff as it was essential that we should get on well with the logistic staff of the Division.

Close contact with the seagoing element of the Corps was a particular pleasure. The maritime regiment's barracks was on the Gosport side of Portsmouth Harbour, only a few hundred yards from HMS *St Vincent*, the 'shore ship' I had reported to as a Fleet Air Arm pilot trainee in 1944. The imposing entrance was still there but peering in as I was driven past, the old parade ground was now a playground with the great mast long dismantled and the place converted to a civilian educational establishment.

After my initial visits to units I set myself to the task of strengthening the Corps case for new ships for the maritime regiment. At that time the Regiment was equipped with old Landing Craft Tank (LCTs) left over from the Second World War. They had given sterling service for many years all over Europe and Asia; we had several in Singapore during the Malayan Emergency, and one or two had only recently been withdrawn from Cyprus, but by the early nineteen seventies they were tired and prone to breakdowns at sea, and if the reports from the ships' captains were to be believed, sometimes in pretty hairy situations. There was a proposal to have two new ships built for the maritime regiment. They were to be known as Landing Craft Logistic (LCLs) with the specific purpose of resupplying the Hebrides ranges with weapons, stores and equipment. I had been in on this proposal in my previous appointment at the MOD and I knew it was dear to the heart of the Director of Movements, Bill Bate. I decided to join a re-supply run to the Northern Isles.

There were two LCTs stationed in Scotland and based at Helensburgh on the Clyde, a short drive from Glasgow. Each had a crew of two officers, a warrant officer and about eighteen NCOs and soldiers. They were flat bottomed and capable of taking the ground, an essential attribute for landing tanks over beaches. There were watertight doors at the bow that when opened, revealed a ramp that could be lowered for this purpose. I had been aboard LCTs several times both at home and abroad but I had not made a long passage in one. For the passage to Uist and St Kilda I joined ship at Helensburgh; it was low tide and the ship lay alongside the wharf on the shingle looking very small to brave the turbulent waters of the Minches and the North Atlantic. I was duly piped aboard and given the best accommodation on the ship. This consisted of a small cabin with a pipe cot, a basin with running water and a chair. Pretty basic but practical and adequate; I had certainly survived much worse and the crew would have considered it luxury. I spent a convivial evening visiting the troops' messdeck, the tiny warrant officers and sergeants' mess and ending with dinner in the wardroom. It was surprising how much accommodation such a small vessel disposed of. The new ships would be much bigger.

We embarked the stores and vehicles for the Hebrides Range early next morning at the tiny port of Rhu, a mile or two upriver from Helensburgh and then set off down river with the tide. We were blessed with calm and dry weather for the crossing and apart from two US submarines making their way on the surface to their base at the Holy Loch we saw little traffic on the Clyde. But the scenery on either side was impressively grand after we cleared the industrial areas around Greenock. It was late afternoon when we cleared the Mull of Kintyre and turned north to the Sound of Islay, a narrow strait between the islands of Islay and Jura and thronged with whisky distilleries reaching down to the water. Then the evening drew in as we made passage through that short stretch of the Atlantic before reaching the shelter of the Northern Isles and the Minches.

We reached the small port of Loch Carnan on the island of South Uist shortly after dawn and tied up alongside an all-weather wharf. So far so good. The ship had shown her age through creaking and groaning during the passage but there had been no testing weather and she had ploughed on gamely. The real test would come tomorrow when we took passage for the detachment at St Kilda, a very small rocky island out in the Atlantic a matter of fifty miles due west of the Hebrides and exposed to the worst that the elements could throw at it.

Stores and equipment for the artillery range at Benbecula were put ashore that afternoon and with no time to cast a fly into one of the numerous island lochs before darkness fell, we turned in early in preparation for a dawn departure for *The Island on the Edge of the World* – the title of the only book I had been able to find on St Kilda's history.

Loch Carnan being on the eastern side of South Uist, the shortest passage to St Kilda necessitated negotiating the Sound of Harris, a narrow channel separating the islands of North Uist and Harris that contained many reefs and rocks just below the surface, making navigation a tricky business even for local fishing vessels. We started at dawn and we were halfway through, moving very slowly, when there was an engine failure, causing the ship to drift towards a rocky reef just visible on the rising tide. On the bridge, the captain and I watched helplessly as the rocks slowly came closer. Obviously we wouldn't be shipwrecked and there was little danger to life and limb but there was likely to be a good deal of damage done if she struck. The engineers below reported that they had identified the problem and were working furiously to correct it. The vagaries of the tide caused the ship to miss the first set of rocks but there were others in sight further along the Sound and if power could not be restored quickly it was inevitable that we would end up with a badly damaged vessel. Fortunately the engineers turned up trumps and we completed our passage through the Sound and into the Atlantic without a collision.

With a further fifty miles to go before we reached St Kilda, the captain confessed that now the danger was passed he was glad that I had been able to experience at first-hand some of the problems that he and his fellow mariners had been complaining about for years. I told him that I would not hold back when compiling my report and would additionally recommend that one of the LCT captains should appear before the committee at MOD that had the task of deciding on the disposal of funds for major equipments. This would at least give the Maritime Regiment a chance to curdle the blood of the committee members.

We reached St Kilda in the early afternoon and had to stand off in Village Bay until the now receding tide had cleared sufficient beach for the bow ramp to be lowered and the vehicles and equipment for the Army detachment to be disembarked. The approach to the Island was fascinating. We passed several enormous rocks rearing from the sea bed. These were uninhabited but home to immense colonies of sea birds. One was the habitat of the largest Gannet colony in Europe and the ship was surrounded by these large yellow beaked birds, folding their wings and diving from a great height into the sea after small fish near the surface. There were also Puffins, Kittiwakes, Skuas and Fulmars in large numbers. The captain said he wouldn't normally disturb them but as I was the new commander of the Group I ought to be able to say that I had seen the result of a blast on the ship's siren and he would make his peace with the bosun later – an odd remark, I thought.

He pulled a rope and the siren gave voice. Immediately about a million seabirds took to the air and whirled around us – an impressive sight and one I had never seen before or since. The air was rent with a banshee screaming. The bosun, a warrant officer responsible among other things for the administration and cleanliness of the ship, immediately appeared on the bridge and with a pained expression said,

"That was unkind, sir." It was only on leaving the bridge that I realised that he wasn't lamenting the discomfort of the birds. The weather decks and the tank deck were covered with white splodges of birdlime. I left the bridge to get a closer look at this amazing happening – to find the bosun on the weather deck below gazing disconsolately at his fouled decks. I said sympathetically, "Now I understand your gloom sar' major. It must take ages to clear this lot up."

Looking grim, he shuffled his feet. "Right sir," he replied. "Every time the skipper does that the birds are scared witless," – at least it sounded like 'witless' above the screaming still echoing round the ship.

Shortly afterwards the environmental authorities ruled that ships' sirens should only be sounded in evident and recorded emergencies in the vicinity of the seabird colonies, a sensible and compassionate decision that most of us agreed with – particularly the Bosuns' Union.

In the nineteenth and early years of the twentieth centuries, St Kilda was inhabited by a colony of hardy Scots living mainly on a diet of fish supplemented by the meat of captured seabirds. All the inhabitants were forcibly evacuated by Act of Parliament in 1928, the colony being considered no longer viable or worth maintaining. The shells of their croft style houses are still there as are the conical cairns of stones in which they stored the carcasses of the birds There is a schoolroom with schoolbooks on display with the names of children who, until recently, occasionally returned from where they had settled around the world to visit their chilhood home. There is also the remains of a village hut and meeting place where the village elders met to hammer out adjustments to their subsistence economy.

The remnants of the village are now maintained by one person from the National Trust of Scotland who lived a lonely life until the Army decided that the island would make a suitable forward observation post for the NATO Range on Benbecula. A small Royal Artillery detachment of soldiers was established there with one young officer in command. Despite the fact that it was often cut off for days, weeks even, in winter when both ships and helicopters were stormbound, I understood that it was a popular job and that there was no lack of volunteers for it. Now and then in summer, a visiting tourist vessel would call in to Village Bay and passengers would be lightered ashore in ships' boats to have a conducted tour of the island. The Army detachment quickly set up a gift shop that did a roaring trade in trinkets and St Kilda neckties to the benefit of the soldiers' funds.

We returned to Helensburgh without further mishap but I was thoroughly convinced by the experience that my maritime soldiers were being sold short and operating under unnecessarily primitive and dangerous conditions for the benefit of the NATO nations. I lobbied strongly for something to be done. So far as the Corps and the Movement organisation were concerned, I was pushing against an open door. The case for two new ships was being pressed strongly at MOD but any further pressure that could be applied in the right quarter would be welcome. Eventually by maintaining that pressure an agreement in principle was obtained, the money was earmarked and specifications for two ships to be known as Landing Craft Logistics (LCLs) were put out to tender. Credit for this triumph could properly be claimed by Generals Bill Bate and John Carpenter, respectively the Director of Movements at MOD and the Director and professional head of the RCT at the time. I realised, however, that the ships could not be designed, built and at sea before my tour of duty in 2 Group was over.

Not long after the Hebrides trip, the CO of the Air Despatch regiment, Keith Davis, told me that he had sent a detachment to work with the RAF at Machrihanish on the west coast of Kintyre and would I like to visit them. I said of course I would but given the time and distance factor, Kintyre being a particularly long journey, I couldn't spare the necessary three days to get there and back. Shortly afterwards I had a 'phone call from Air Vice-Marshal Crowley Milling, the Commander of RAF 46 Group located at RAF Upavon on Salisbury Plain and within sight of my HQ at Bulford. He said he was visiting his detachment at Machrihanish the next day and would I like to accompany him in his C130. We would be back late afternoon. Too good an opportunity to miss. I rolled up to Upavon next day expecting to accompany a fair sized party of people to Kintyre, only to find myself fitted into flying overalls and told that I was to be in the co-pilot's seat next to the air marshal who was flying the aircraft. The only others were a flight engineer and one soldier air despatcher, both of whom remained outside the cockpit. The air marshal, a distinguished and well decorated wartime fighter and fighter bomber pilot, had clearly not let conversion to heavy transport aircraft dampen his skills. He was an urbane and charming conversationalist and made piloting the great aircraft look easy. Starting early, we were in Machrihanish before lunch and I was able to visit my detachment to their evident pleasure, since the RAF also had their boss visiting, then lunch and the purchase of a box of the famous Machrihanish kippers and home for a late tea. As the air marshal said. "There's simply no other way to do it in a day."

One morning, while immersed in the daily ration of paper, my secretary buzzed my phone and said, "I have Lord Mountbatten's secretary on the line. He'd like to speak to you."

"I can think of no conceivable reason why," I replied. "But by all means put him through."

A polite voice appeared on the line.

"Good morning Brigadier. I'm speaking from Broadlands (the Mountbatten house near Romsey) on behalf of Lord Mountbatten. You may know that he introduced the amphibious DUKWS to the British Army when he was C-in-C in the Far East during the war. He has heard that the last unit in the Army, stationed at Marchwood, is being disbanded and he would like to take the disbandment parade. Could you please let me have details, date, time and so on so that I can fit it into his diary?"

This was a fast ball. So far as I knew, there was no disbandment parade planned. "I'm afraid," I murmured, "that details for the parade are not yet finalised. But I will speak to the commanding officer at Marchwood and he'll be in touch with you shortly. Meanwhile will you please thank Lord Louis on behalf of 2 Group for his kind offer to take the parade. We will be honoured to accept."

I then rang Stanley Ball, the CO of the Military Port. "Stanley," I said mischievously. "Do you have details of the disbandment parade for the DUKWS yet?" There was a sharp intake of breath at the other end.

"Disbandment parade?" Stanley was an honest man, devoid of guile or military 'flannel.'

"Actually Brigadier, I wasn't planning to have a parade. We're simply waiting for disposal instructions for the vehicles from Ordnance."

"Think again, Stanley." I told him about my phone call.

"In the circumstances, we can't not have a parade of sorts. It will be good PR for the Port since Lord Louis is certainly the most prominent public figure in your county and the local Press should certainly be interested. Also I suggest you keep it in the family and involve exclusively your unit, its soldiers and families. But if we can persuade Lord Louis to join us for lunch, plan also for a 'nobs luncheon party' to include those Corps senior officers you would like to invite. Please work out some suitable dates well ahead and liaise with his secretary, then we can discuss it."

Stanley rose nobly to the occasion. It was a notable and unusual day. He decided to have a 'drive past' at sea with the inspecting officer taking the parade afloat. He would stand on a Land Rover secured to a Mexefloat – a robust metal raft we used to move stores and vehicles from ship to shore. Lord Louis, a showman to his fingertips, was amused and pleased by the arrangements. He was ferried out to the Mexefloat, moored at a point about one hundred yards offshore in Southampton Water and saluted as the DUKWS drove past, a brave sight with their auxiliary propellers churning and their radio antennae bending in the wind. He then came ashore and charmed the Regiment's assembled families with his informal and unstuffy approach.

I sat next to him at lunch and he asked if we had met before. "No," I said. "But I've been present several times when you've addressed the army staff college and once at the joint services staff college."

"Then you'll have heard most of my stories. Let's talk about the DUKWS."

He proceeded to give me a 'horse's mouth' account of how they were introduced into the Service and their activities in the Far East, together with a few indiscreet comments on the personalities prominent at the time.

"Of course," he added "I was so young when I did those jobs that most of my wartime friends are dead – Winston, Ike," followed by a panoply of famous names. He then went on to despair of the Ulster situation and said how much he loved Ireland, its people and how much he enjoyed his annual visits there. His feelings were obviously not reciprocated by the extremists for they later murdered him together with members of his family and a young local boy during one of those annual visits.

Involvement with 3rd Division in our Logistic Support Force (LSF) role called for several joint Army/RAF reconnaissance trips around Europe. At that time, joint recces with the RAF were five star travel because we travelled in our own aircraft. RAF Thorney Island on the Hampshire coast had a fleet of Andover aircraft that offered sufficient seating for a party of about ten with a few seats to spare and one of these was usually placed at our disposal by our RAF partners. We could spread ourselves, hang up our uniform jackets, hold impromptu meetings and undertake map recces with no worry about security considerations.

We got to know each other well. It was joint service co-operation in practice. As the nominated Commander LSF if it ever had to be deployed, I was the 'Chef de Mission' with a colonel from the 3rd Division as my deputy. The senior RAF officer was normally a group captain. I usually took the GSO2 planner from my HQ, the irrepressible Major Malcolm Allen. The Andover, although a comfortable aircraft, did not have an impressive operating range and we refuelled in Southern France at a military airfield near Istre. The refuelling process was obviously OK but I can't say that any of us were impressed with the facilities for visiting allied officers or with the attitude of the mainly civilian staff which was long on gallic shrugs and short on welcoming smiles.

Italy was a horse of a different colour. Wall-to-wall cheerfulness and eagerness to please was very evident. The first recce we did there involved the Po Valley and the Dolomites including liaison with the Italian Air Force and on the ground the mountain troops – the Alpini. Northern Italy has an abundance of palazzos and similar historic buildings and in an effort to keep them well maintained, many had been taken on by the armed services as officers' messes. So the smallest messes boasted magnificent chandeliers, graceful sculptures and floors of different shades of marble. One evening I had a drink with a veteran fighter pilot who spoke excellent English but was scathing about his Army.

"If we do have another war," he said, waving his arm around. "This lot," meaning his Army colleagues, "are bound to get it wrong." He snorted. "Look what happened last time. They built redoubts and fortifications and laid plans against an attack from the north or through the Balkans. And what did you do? You came up through Sicily. Always happens. The flexibility of air power is the only answer."

Nevertheless, I was impressed with the Alpini soldiers; they were young, tough looking and certainly knew their business on the alpine slopes.

We liaised with the local army HQs, drew up our location plans for a possible deployment and returned to Thorney Island with the comforting feeling that a good reception was to be had in Northern Italy if circumstances dictated that we had to go there.

A few months later we embarked on a second joint recce, this time to Greece. We were briefed that we should be cautious in our approach to our Greek allies and on no account express any hint of criticism of what we saw or heard while we were there.

At this time, the early nineteen seventies, Greece was ruled by 'The Colonels' – the military had taken power and it was evident when we arrived that they ruled with an iron hand. All bridges were guarded by soldiers and identities were checked regularly. There was no suggestion that the population were cowed, but we obtained a distinct impression that they were 'walking softly'. We, however, were greeted warmly as fellow soldiers and no effort was spared help us with our task. We first went to the historic town of Larissa in Thessaly to meet the senior officers at that district HQ.

That first visit to Greece was very special. I could see Mount Olympus clearly from the Greek brigadier's office window. I walked the Drama plain, trod the slopes of Mount Metamorphosus – presumably connected to an incident in Greek mythology rather than to Christ's Transfiguration – and visited Meteora, the site of hilltop monasteries reached only by baskets hauled up the cliffs by machine driven cables and about forty miles west from Larissa, hiking the last five miles over rough country. I recall accidentally kicking a large stone and picking it up I was surprised to find that it was marble. On closer inspection the whole hillside was marble – a marble mountain! Astonishing, and no wonder that marble is such a common building material in Italy and Greece.

In Larissa we were accommodated in a rather indifferent hotel and I had several complaints, particularly from the more junior officers who were two to a room. Before we left to travel north to Macedonia I was asked by the brigadier area commander if our accommodation was satisfactory. I was about to reply that both accommodation (which we had to pay for) and service could have been better when in my mind's eye I saw the manager being led out to the hotel courtyard to be shot. I hastily assured the brigadier that the arrangements had been perfect.

We next flew to Thessaloniki (Salonika) the principal city of Greek Macedonia, en route to the border area after a briefing from the area staff at their Salonika HQ. It turned out to be a modern and attractive town with good restaurants and excellent public transport based on a tram system. I like to make one or two journeys by public transport when visiting an unfamiliar foreign town. By doing so you can get a 'feel' for the place and sometimes have a chat with one of the locals. Travelling by tram in Salonika, I had an interesting conversation with a cultured gentleman sitting next to me; he recognised instantly that I was a foreigner and probably an Englishman and introduced himself as a professor of history at Salonika University. I asked him if he was prepared to talk politics. He said, 'Yes, but only to a limited degree.' He confirmed that the Colonels' rule was strict but held that it was not inhumane and that in his view the country could have slid into anarchy had a dose of strict discipline not been applied.

"They have saved us," he said. "But their rule must be finite," and then proudly. "Greece is where democracy was born, and we will return to it when the task of these soldiers is completed." He then treated me to an enthralling potted history of Macedonia and I was sorry when he had to get off.

That evening we went out to dinner in a body and we were introduced to the Greek custom of visiting the restaurant kitchen to decide on your meal from the array of food being cooked. We were also introduced to the dancing and plate smashing. Malcolm Allen had a wonderful time, joining the dancers and smashing plates. His face was a study when he realised that his bill included the cost of all the plates he and his dancer friends had shattered with such abandon.

The next day we started out journey northwards to the Metaxas Line overlooking the Bulgarian border. We travelled in three land rover type vehicles, four wheel drive being necessary for the unpaved mountain roads. In all our travels in Greece while on duty, we were accompanied, perhaps escorted is a better word, by an officer of the Greek Army; on this trip he was an English language graduate doing his national service as a subaltern. He was an engaging young man but I warned the party not to discuss politics with him because it was apparent that everything we did or said would go back to his seniors verbatim. We were of course travelling an historic route. This was Greek Macedonia. Alexander, son of Philip of Macedon, had set out from here over three centuries before the birth of Christ to conquer the known world; there had been a Greek/Turkish conflict here early in the twentieth century and around thirty years before us the Germans had invaded down this road to take the Greek mainland during the Second World War.

It was majestic countryside with some cultivation towards the slopes of the steep hills, lessening as we travelled northwards and the hills became mountains. We saw little habitation and passed through few villages. The road became steeper and I saw from my seat in the front of the leading vehicle, a donkey approaching us with an old man trying to catch up with it to grab its headrope. He would almost reach the donkey which would then move on a few paces as though it was a game, then stop and wait until its owner had almost caught up before moving on again. We could all see that the old fellow was on his last legs, so without reference to our guard and guide I ordered the driver to stop, then jumped out of the vehicle, caught the donkey and handed the rope to the exhausted ancient. He, clearly terrified that soldiers had even noticed him, took off his cap and muttered something that I took to be an expression of thanks, then moved off. During the whole of this exchange, the old man had not once lifted his eyes to my face. Our Greek subaltern escort said nothing and acted as though he had not seen what had happened.

We reached the Greek/Bulgarian border post, noticing that a soldier dressed in combat clothing stood at the knife rest barrier. Behind him at the entrance to the guardhouse stood a sentry in what I remembered being described as Evzone dress of shoes, white stockings and frilly white skirt with a frilly white tunic topped by coloured headdress. It looked strange to our eyes and perhaps a mite effeminate, but in fact the Evzones are a famous fighting regiment and no one who served with the Greeks in the Second World War or had known them in Korea has ever been known to describe Greek troops as effeminate.

We moved on to the Metaxas Line, a fixed defence line occupying a commanding position on the heights overlooking Bulgaria. There we were met by a major who proceeded to give us a lecture on the history of the fortifications. He was a bit boot faced and humourless, which I took to be a certain nervousness, and he was thoroughly disconcerted when his audience to a man deserted him halfway through his talk and rushed to the edge of the fortifications overlooking the valley. I explained afterwards that we had seen two beautiful golden eagles glide past only feet from the edge and that as it was a sight almost unknown in our country, it was something that we could not miss. He laughed, all nervousness gone, and said that for him it was an almost daily occurrence. The birds seemed to realise that within the military protected zone they were not at the mercy of hunters and they moved around without fear. He then became thoroughly human and finished his talk.

He told us that the fortifications, designed by General Metaxas, had allowed their defenders to hold out so successfully against the Germans, who had invaded Greece through Bulgaria, that they had had to be by passed. When the Germans had secured the Greek mainland, they offered the Metaxas Line defenders, who were still fighting, the honours of war if they would give up. Realising that it was pointless to carry on, the defenders marched out with their weapons and colours still in their possession and rather than being placed in prison camps were allowed to return to their homes on promising no further resistance.

The major was going back to Salonika with us that evening to attend the dinner being held in our honour by the area commander. On the way he asked me if we would like to see a typical Macedonian village and we branched off the road on to a narrow track that led to a village only a few miles from the border.

"This," he said, "is a thriving community but you will see very few young men in their twenties, although, happily we now have plenty of young children."

He went on to explain that the Greeks were at war with the communists for several years after the official end of the Second World War. When they were finally driven out over the Bulgarian border, the communists took with them all the young children they could find in the border villages. The children were indoctrinated as communists and sent back to their villages in Greece during the Cold War, the aim being to subvert the border people and destabilise the area ready for a Moscow backed invasion. The plan failed. The village people were not prepared to be subverted, and those young men and women who would not renounce their enforced ideology were sent back to Bulgaria.

We were taken to the village school where we were met by the mayor, who had obviously been briefed on our visit. There just happens, he said, to be an English class in progress and would the English brigadier please address the children?

I faced a class of about thirty bright-eyed little girls and boys. After managing an introduction along the lines of, "Good afternoon. It is very nice to meet you and we like your country very much. I hope that you are all enjoying your lessons," I corpsed and stood there beaming inanely while the children giggled and beamed back.

One of the RAF officers came to my rescue, "Can you count?" he shouted. "One, two, three…" The children took up the challenge and faultlessly counted up to ten. Survival with honour. We made our farewells and drove back to Salonika.

The dinner that evening was excellent. I sat on the right of the area commander, who turned out to be a Manchester United supporter. In conversation I mentioned that I had been in Malaya with a friend who was of half Greek extraction, one of his parents being Greek. Demetrios, or Dimos as we knew him, was married to a Greek lady. He had left the Army and settled in Athens where he was employed in an administrative job at the British Embassy.

"Will you see him on this trip," said the brigadier.

"Sadly, no." I replied."Athens is not in our programme and we leave tomorrow afternoon." The brigadier looked amused.

"That is not a problem. I can have him here by the time of breakfast and you can have a pleasant meeting with your friend." Visions of Dimos being dragged from his bed at dead of night by the Secret Police came to mind. I had to invent a totally spurious story about him being godfather to one of my daughters and due to visit us in England shortly in order to persuade the brigadier to abandon his kindly gesture.

Speeches followed. In the course of his address the brigadier confirmed my thoughts about our escort by turning to me and saying "We have all heard the story of the peasant man and the donkey. That is an example of the public relations which the British are so good at."

Leaving aside the fact that public relations had nothing to do with it – I was simply doing a small service to an exhausted old man as I am convinced that any of my fellow service officers or indeed most Britons would have done – I suppose it was a plus for us.

On our way back to the UK we staged once again at Istre in the South of France for refuelling. It was Sunday and the skeleton military station staff said they had had no warning of our arrival. Consequently there was a considerable delay before refuelling could be arranged. We had an aircraft full of wine but no food, having assumed that we could obtain lunch during the hour or so taken to refuel the aircraft. But the messes and canteens were all closed and the few people around displayed that implacable disinterest which the French are so good at. We were advised not to leave the airfield so I despatched Malcolm Allen, a passable French speaker, to ask the station duty officer if he knew of anywhere we could buy something to eat. We were all standing on the steps of the control tower out of the keen wind when Malcolm returned and appeared below.

"Gentlemen," he said, with a serious face. "I have to offer you both good and bad news. The bad news first. This area of France appears to be closed on Sundays. There is no food available anywhere. The good news, however, is that as a concession, the authorities have agreed that the British officers may be allowed to graze – senior officers on the right if you please, and junior officers to the left!"

Well I thought it was funny but to most, his joke had all the properties of a lead balloon. Having not eaten since breakfast, we had a stomach rumbling day, arriving back at RAF Thorney Island in the evening. Malcolm left the Service not long afterwards and I was sorry to hear it. Not only was he an irrepressible humorist even in the most dire situations, he was also a good staff officer and that rare being, a lateral thinker, full of ideas. I met him years later at a business conference. He had done well and was a senior executive in industry.

As evidence of their goodwill towards us, our Greek hosts had presented a case of wine to each member of our party before departure. With no wish to denigrate this very generous gift, I have never been a fan of Greek wine, but Brigadier Donald Locke of my Corps and stationed near to Bulford, had been in the British Military Mission to Greece after the Second World War; he professed to enjoy their wine, which I think is probably an acquired taste, and he was happy to accept it as a gift.

Soon after returning from the planning trip to Greece I was told that the Hovercraft Squadron at Browndown was once again under threat of disbandment. The world, the military world at least, had not taken this British invention to its heart. The Americans had bought a few for use on the Mekong River during their war in Vietnam; the Germans had shown some interest for possible use in the marshy country north of Hamburg and I had accompanied the Squadron OC with two of his craft to a demonstration there but the deal had not matured.

We fought hard for retention of the squadron on grounds that air cushion technology had probably emerged before its time and we should retain a capability until its value would be properly recognised. But the MOD was, as usual, up against its financial buffers and it was decided to realise the small saving that disbandment of the Army's hovercraft capability would achieve. I took no pleasure in passing this news to the Squadron, but I felt that I had to do it personally and I drove to Browndown one miserable morning to break the sad tidings to a very disappointed band of enthusiasts. It would be nice to report that the Army Board had subsequently realised that disbandment of the Squadron was a mistake, but this has not happened and, all things considered, an in-house hovercraft capability was probably an expensive luxury.

My time with 2 Group passed all too quickly and the news in May of my second year in command that I was to attend the following year's course at the Royal College of Defence Studies was received with mixed feelings. Earlier in the year I had been approached by a retired senior officer of our Corps with so many business interests that he was domiciled in a tax haven outside the UK; he had asked if I would be interested in applying for a senior executive appointment shortly to become vacant in a major organisation concerned with transport. He intimated that the job was mine if I wanted it and that the pay, perks and prospects were considerably in excess of those I was then receiving. Had I not known about the RCDS posting I would have been seriously tempted, but the lure of the most prestigious course that the defence establishment had to offer was not to be denied. I saw the advert for the proffered post in *The Times* and decided not to apply.

22

RCDS

The Royal College of Defence Studies is housed in the heart of Belgravia, one of London's most fashionable locations. It was formerly the Imperial Defence College mentioned earlier, but the name was changed to reflect the dissolution of Empire, although the quality of the course and its reputation had not suffered from this. Its student body was international, mainly military but with a strong sprinkling of civilians from the UK and from friendly nations across the world. The course lasted a full calendar year and was reputed to be self-financing from the high fees demanded and received from foreign nations for those of their students who were admitted after assessment.

There were seventy-seven students on the 1975 RCDS Course, forty from the UK, eleven from the Old Commonwealth, that is to say Australia, New Zealand and Canada, where the Queen's writ still nominally runs, and six from the USA. The remaining twenty embraced the free world. The military/civilian ratio was about three to one in favour of the military but the civilian element was generally more senior in age and rank, comprising senior policemen of chief constable or equivalent commissioner level, plus diplomats and civil servants on the way to the apex of their careers. The mix was cleverly structured to achieve the maximum value from discussion.

We, the students, were at one star (brigadier or equivalent) level or below. Our instructors (DS) were major generals, rear admirals, air vice-marshals and civil servants of the equivalent two star status. As at the Staff College, the instruction was syndicate based, but we spent much of the year attending lectures and presentations and syndicate discussion was the exception rather than the rule.

The political climate in the UK in 1975 provided a prime subject for heated discussion during the course for it was the year of the great referendum designed to give UK citizens the opportunity to decide whether we wanted to join the Common Market or not. As a confirmed anti-joiner I was in a minority among the UK students and I had a hard row to hoe in both formal and informal discussions on the issue, although since most of the Old Commonwealth was against it, I had a few supporters. I took the view that while I would happily vote for an economic union devoted solely to trade, there was no rock solid assurance that it would stop there, particularly if the long term aim for a common currency was achieved, for it would be followed by a proposal for a political federation as sure as the dustcart follows the Lord Mayor's Show. I wanted no part of a United States of Europe, Winston Churchill's dream notwithstanding, and I still think that had the great man lived he would have drawn back from the brink.

It was not a high pressure course and the more enjoyable for that. We were all ambitious professionals and keen to learn from the experience of others. We were also no strangers to command and well past the knee trembling stage when it came to questioning the views of the very eminent people who came to speak to us. There were several three or four day comprehensive visits to various parts of the UK to study the provincial infrastructure. These were mainly designed for the foreign element but most of the UK students confessed afterwards that they had learned a lot about what went on in their own country as well. We visited Scotland Yard, courtesy of the Commissioner, Sir Robert Mark, who also made a presentation on police activities, and we travelled to the near continent to visit NATO Headquarters. We were required to write a paper of at least 3000 words on a subject of our choice in our own time, but since on most days we were released for private study after lunch, this was not an onerous task.

The Commandant of the College was invariably a four star military man. The appointment rotated across the three armed services In 1975 it was a distinguished airman, Air Chief Marshal Sir John Barraclough, remembered by all with respect and affection for he ran the course on a loose rein, well aware that we were all highly motivated. He and his wife were also charming and generous hosts in the mews house behind the College that went with the job. I recall that one evening when Heather and I dined there, a student who was also a diplomat from a newly oil rich African state was a fellow guest. Sir John told me that this gentleman had tipped the corporal who had opened the door for him a fifty pound note. "I'm thinking of asking him again," said Sir John. "Only this time I'll answer the door and who knows?"

For Heather and me, domestic arrangements were good. We lived in our own house in Hampshire and I travelled by train daily to the

College in Belgrave Square, a ten minute walk from Victoria Station. It was an early drive to the station to be on the London train by seven thirty a.m. but on many days I was able to be home for 'private study' by about four p.m. – an unprecedented situation.

Amid the welter of high level presentations and discussions there was one 'capsule' in the RCDS course worthy of special mention. For too long, service officers had performed less than adequately when confronted with the media – particularly during TV interviews. This was very noticeable in Northern Ireland when commanding officers were often unable to put their side of a disputed case or incident convincingly.

There were of course notable exceptions. A few officers were natural raconteurs; they could think on their feet and marshal their arguments or explanations in a manner that could be readily understood and sympathised with. But something needed to be done to correct the general lack of expertise in dealing with the media and it was decided that the Army education complex at Beaconsfield should sponsor a short course in TV interviewing for senior officers. British officers at the RCDS were required to attend a shortened version of the course and we all did so gladly. It was interesting and to begin with somewhat daunting.

We had been told that the interviews would be hostile and that the interviewer, who was clearly an expert, would have our complete service records in front of him. The interviewing room was a TV studio furnished with the professional TV equipment that I came to be familiar with in later life as a civilian businessman. Assessment was done in Marxist fashion with one's 'friends' – other course members – watching through one-way glass and being invited to criticise the performance of the student in the hot seat when each interview was over.

I recall that I was quizzed on something that I had initiated seventeen years before in Malaya. It was a claim for disturbance allowance and removal expenses that had been turned down, unjustly in my view, so I had pursued the claim through repeated appeals and rejections all the way to the Army Council in London, which I was entitled to do.

The fact that it had finally been turned down had not lessened my sense of grievance. This clearly still clouded my judgement and the interviewer expertly tied me in knots. Others went through a similar process and then we were taught how to avoid the least obvious interviewing pitfalls. For me this was one of the most interesting and valuable things to come out of the RCDS course.

The months sped by towards the high spot of the course. This was a four to six week trip to a region of the globe to study its military and political infrastructure with a specific emphasis on defence. On offer were Europe, the USA, Australasia, Asia, the Far East, and Africa. My choice was Australasia, which took in Australia, New Zealand and Indonesia. I had not been to any of these countries although I had gazed at the Indonesian island of Sumatra across the Straits of Malacca when I had lived in Malaya. The tour allotments were confirmed before we took the summer break in August and I was pleased to see that I had drawn my choice; the tour was to take place in October.

In early September on returning to the College, I was astonished to receive a letter from the Military Secretary (MS) telling me that I was to be removed from the course in early October to fill the appointment of Director of Movements (D.Mov) at the Ministry of Defence in the rank of Major General. – promotion! But at a price, for I had set my heart on visiting and studying a part of the world I had thought I would never get to. The Military Secretary made the point that I had been selected for the appointment in the summer and would not normally have taken it up until the following spring, but the incumbent, John Carpenter of my Corps, had secured a prestigious civilian appointment as a Traffic Commissioner and was keen to retire.

I went to see the Commandant who was sympathetic; he didn't particularly want to lose a student before the course ended: he said he would ask the MS to visit and discuss the situation with him and that I should be there to see him afterwards. A plus point in this affair was that the Colonel Movement Plans at MOD and effectively the second in command to D Mov was Colonel Ronnie Jenkins, an old friend. We had been subalterns together in Korea and had maintained our friendship down the years. I was confident that he would have no problem standing in as D Mov while I was away just as I had done for Bill Bate when I was his Colonel Movement Plans four years earlier. MS, General Sir Patrick Howard Dobson, was kind enough to take this point and agreed that I should take up my new job a month later in November. I asked if he could arrange for Ronnie to have the pay while he was filling the appointment and I believe he did so. A sigh of relief.

It had been in my mind to write for publication, a review of the Australasian scene we were about to witness and I had mentioned this as part of my case. I was now committed to it.

23

Diversion Down Under

Our party of eight led by Rear-Admiral Clayton, the tour DS, left Heathrow in the late afternoon of a cold October day. It was raining. But the promise of a first class air passage to Australia via Singapore did much to lift our spirits. I was pleased to see that the RCDS still travelled first class by air – confirmation if any was needed that the course still paid its way from the fees of overseas students. Jumbo jets in the seventies reserved the upstairs lounge for their first class passengers and we spent a mildly alcoholic evening discussing the pleasures to come. I was assured by my RAF companions that the hump on the Jumbo was designed specifically to enable the pilot to sit on his wallet.

About halfway through the journey the door to the flight deck opened and an important looking man appeared sporting four gold rings on his uniform sleeve. In conversation he admitted to being the captain of the aircraft and producing his pipe said that this was his time for a smoke, the aircraft presumably being looked after by his co-pilot. He found out that our party included two RAF group captains and the three of them had an enjoyable chinwag for about an hour. Leap forward nearly thirty years to the present day and the Jumbo upper level has been handed over to business or economy class, while any suggestion that the aircraft captain, ensconced in his terrorist proof compartment, might emerge for a social chat with his passengers, is out of the question. Progress?

We had a two night stop in Singapore to await the connection to Australia. I knew the city well from Malaya days and marvelled at the changes engineered by Lee Kuan Yew, the Prime Minister. From the raucous, ill disciplined chaos of the late fifties it had become a model of prosperous and well policed good order. I travelled on a tram from our hotel down to Orchard Road to window shop among old haunts. I tendered too much for the fare and the tram conductor, wagging his finger at me, returned the excess. The streets were clean and refuse free; I was told that there was a substantial fine for spitting. Anyone who could stop a city full of Chinese men from spitting on the street just had to be a superman; a mental hat tip to Mr Lee, as he was generally known to his constituents.

My tropical uniforms had worn thin and looked rather shabby but a member of my Corps was the Defence Attaché at the High Commission and arranged for a Chinese tailor to come to our hotel and measure me for two suits of tropical uniform to be delivered within twenty-four hours. While we wore plain clothes on most of the trip, we would need uniform for Indonesia, still under military rule. Bert Laugharne, one of our party and a provincial chief constable in England, knew the Singapore Chief of Police from his course at the Hendon Police College and we spent an evening with him visiting several night clubs that none of us could have afforded had we been on our own.

We were scheduled to arrive at Sydney around dawn so the onward journey from Singapore was by night. Few of us slept; the novelty of first class travel with unlimited champagne had not yet worn off and some of us arrived slightly the worse for wear. Fortunately this passed without comment; I expect the reception committee was used to it. We were assumed to be jet lagged and so we were given time to sleep off our 'travel fatigue.'

Sydney is a splendid city and the Aussie establishment, both civilian and military, literally and figuratively pushed the boat out for the RCDS course. We saw all the sights, the Circular Quay, the Opera House of course, the Harbour Bridge, Bondi Beach – less attractive than we had expected – and on Sunday we were taken down the harbour by boat to a curry lunch as the guests of HMAS *Watson*, a shore ship situated right by the Heads at the harbour entrance, the terrace of its wardroom facing the vast enclosed expanse of water.

It was a beautiful sunny day and the harbour was full of small craft. There was a race in progress featuring Sydney Harbour Skiffs, long, narrow boats with a press of sail that appears to be much too great for the slim hull. In fact it is too great and in anything of a blow the crew has to act as a counterweight, often being tipped into the water when the boat becomes unstable. I asked one of my hosts about sharks.

"The harbour's full of them," he said. "You wouldn't get me into one of those things for love or money," pointing to the Skiff fleet. "But they seem to survive, probably because the sharks are feeding from the holes in the bathing nets on the beaches. There's a damn sight more shark attacks in this harbour than ever appear in the paper, you know."

I glanced at him, knowing the Aussie penchant for deadpan humour, but he seemed serious. His remarks were given point years later when as a businessman I visited Sydney and took time out to see the new harbour aquarium, situated near to the famous Bridge. It had several magnificent specimens of sharks. I was told that they were 'harbour sharks' and that the method of catching them was to sink two forty foot containers to the harbour floor leaving large quantities of meat inside, then when the required numbers of sharks were seen gorging on the meat – and this didn't take long – the doors were closed and the sharks were transferred to the underground display area of the new aquarium. They were quite big and I asked if they were maneaters.

"Too right," said the attendant "They won't go hunting you but if they see a man swimming and they're hungry they'll eat him all right." Maybe my naval officer friend's views were not so far from the truth after all.

We left Sydney by air for a day in Melbourne and a visit to a sheep farm. Arriving at the airport I saw a familiar face. It was Noel McGuire, my attached Aussie major from the Regiment in Germany only now he was a full colonel and a staff officer at the Melbourne military HQ. He had seen my name on the list of RCDS visitors and had volunteered to be the 'greeter' for the Melbourne visit. We enjoyed much reminiscence and good gossip. He had a message from Susie, his wife, now living in their house in Canberra; I was to call on her without fail during our visit to Australian Capital Territories (ACT).

In Melbourne we were entertained to morning tea and a chat by the moguls of the Australian trade unions, several of whom had been immigrants from the UK in their youth. They were pleasant and quite friendly but it couldn't be said we had a meeting of minds. Britain at that time was slowly sinking under the bloody mindedness of our trade union barons who seemed determined to ruin the competitiveness of our industry and to wreck our public services. It was hard to display a polite face to the standard socialist claptrap that we were treated to, although we knew that as guests we had no other option. But we knew also that Australia was still very much a land of opportunity and simply hoped that it would never allow itself to reach the parlous situation that as a nation we found ourselves in at that time.

The visit to the sheep farm was fun. Our host was a twinkling humorist in the style we would now recognise as akin to Barry Humphries' Dame Edna and Les Paterson. He took the Mickey out of the visiting Poms with such style and humour that we simply couldn't take exception. There was hardly a dry eye throughout the visit and we also learned a good deal about rearing sheep and processing wool. His final act at the end of his talk was to unbutton our jackets – a pat on the back if he found the Woolmark and a raspberry if he didn't. Luncheon was first class. Excellent Aussie wine and would you believe roast lamb?

Next stop Canberra, ACT. Australian Capital Territories is a relatively recent innovation along the lines of Washington's Districts of Columbia in that it is a territorial envelope into which they have inserted the nation's capital city. As I understood it, ACT takes care of Canberra's domestic and internal administration while the city of Canberra itself accommodates Australia's Departments of State – dealing with home affairs, foreign policy and defence.

I made good my promise to visit Noel's wife in the house they had just bought on the outskirts of Canberra. Susie picked me up in their car at our hotel and I spent a pleasant evening with Noel's family, their little girl my younger daughters had played with in Duisburg now grown up and seeking a career. Susie told me that they had bought the house because Noel reckoned that he would probably finish his career in Canberra, a prediction that proved to be correct, and because it also enabled them to secure the perks offered by the Australian Government for those government servants who were prepared to settle in this newish territory and very rapidly expanding city.

It was a new house in a new road with open country visible at the end of it and one of the perks was a free garden to order!

"Do you mean," I said, "That they send along an architect to design it and then plant it for you?"

"It doesn't work quite like that," she replied. "They level and grade the plot and build a house to a design that you choose from a number of standard designs offered. Then you plan your garden and order the trees and shrubs from a vast government sponsored garden centre and they come along and plant them for you. You get an allowance for perennials but you have to provide your own annuals and vegetables. For people like us it's a good investment. Even if we're posted away, perhaps to an embassy job, the city will expand and as it does so the facilities – shops, restaurants, bus routes etc, will expand outwards and our house will increase in value as we become less remote from the centre."

I raised my glass. "To you both. That sort of thinking can't be faulted".

We moved on to Adelaide, the City of Light, so called because much of it was designed in the nineteenth century by Colonel Light of the Royal Engineers; there is a statue of him on a tall plinth peering into infinity in the city centre. Adelaide had a gracious and old-fashioned feel to it. As befitted its position as the focus of Australia's most famous wine producing region, we had heard that it boasted several excellent restaurants and we asked our taxi driver to recommend one while driving to our hotel from the airport. He did so and then in that friendly Aussie fashion asked what we were doing there. We told him and when he learned that we were UK Service officers he introduced himself as a reservist major in the Israeli Army. Then learning that his four passengers were respectively a policeman, two RAF officers and a brigadier, he insisted on discussing tactics in the Arab/Israeli Six Day war; he had flown to Israel on recall for it. He offered to pick us up at the hotel that evening to take us to 'the very best restaurant in town'. The upshot was that we had an excellent evening and he returned to take us back, refusing payment.

The following day saw an eagerly anticipated visit to the Barossa Valley vineyards, all part of our study of the commercial infrastructure of Australia. At that time South Australia was the country's most important wine growing region, 60 per cent of all wine production being centred within easy road travelling distance of Adelaide. The fame of vineyards such as Penfolds had already spread worldwide and we were given an insight to the then new methods of production involving stainless steel fermenting and storage vats – techniques that have supplanted many of the age old traditional methods, even in France, which is now host to many young Australian vintners. We visited several vineyards and I recognised in the wines of several with German names, a distinct flavour of the Mosel and Lower Rhine familiar to me from those shooting parties in Germany. The Aussies had also hijacked, apparently quite legally, such generic names as Chablis and Burgundy. Nowadays, of course, Australian wines are among the world leaders.

Our visit to South Australia embraced a weekend and we were asked what we would like to do in the 'free time' marked on our tour programme. Three of us said we'd like to go sailing and a twenty-four foot sloop volunteered by a member of the Port Adelaide Yacht Club was offered to us for the day. Skippered by its owner and crewed by his girlfriend, we set out on a perfect morning in a Force 3 breeze occasionally gusting 4, which meant sailing across a lively but by no means vicious sea.

I had sailed since my teens and hold a Yachtmaster qualification. Although I didn't own a boat then, I had made frequent use of the Corps yachts, the biggest at thirty-four feet. I managed to persuade our host that I knew what I was doing so he let me take the helm of his precious craft. She had been built by her owner, a common practice in Australia and New Zealand, and she handled beautifully. We were all fascinated by predatory fish and the talk turned once again to sharks. The boat was tiller steered and I was in the cockpit steering, with the transom (the stern) about a foot clear of the water. The rest of the party were lounging on the cabin top.

"Aw no," said our skipper "We don't see many. Big Fred's our only worry." Big Fred?

"We think he's either a big Tiger or a Great White. Can't be both because they wouldn't mix. Got to be one or the other." Again, you never know with Aussies; it could easily be a leg-pull. We persuaded him to explain.

"Well, there's been two or three what you might call incidents. Nobody's been lost but one joker had a big chunk of his transom bitten off and someone else lost his dinghy while it was being towed. But it doesn't happen often enough to worry about. Shall I take over now?" – with a deadpan face. Dumbly, I handed over the helm, still not sure whether or not we were being conned.

Later on we asked our Aussie conducting officer and he said that it was unlikely that it was a tall story.

"You've got to understand that we have to be aware of these creatures all our lives. Lethal spiders such as the funnel web and others in the cities, deadly snakes in the open spaces. Nasty jellyfish and killer fish in our seas. Eventually they amount to no big deal if you're careful."

We next visited Tasmania. The RCDS Tour usually visited Queensland but those on high had decided this year to vary the route and Tasmania had been included apparently to the great pleasure of the

Tasmanian establishment. They were certainly very hospitable. We flew from Adelaide to Hobart with Ansett, Australia's major internal airline and were accommodated at the upmarket Wrest Point Hotel overlooking the lower reaches of the Derwent River. Here we lost our supervising DS. Admiral Clayton fell ill with a nasty virus and stayed in hospital in Hobart for some time after we left Tasmania. He nominated a student member of our party, Lord Tom Bridges, a hereditary peer and diplomat, as group shepherd in his absence.

Our hotel contained the biggest and presumably the best casino on the Island. It was well appointed and very well patronised. I wandered into it one evening in company with Bert Laugharne, our policeman and he, from the height of his long experience in these matters, pronounced it honest and 'worth a punt.' But I was more interested in the punters. Their dress was by no means uniform, a mixture of informal gear, suits and evening clothes. Obviously the rule was that anything goes if you can afford the stake. The place was brilliantly lit and a band was playing softly in the background. But I had the weird feeling that here we were, in one of the last outposts of civilisation before reaching the Antarctic land mass, and we might have been in Bournemouth.

We had arrived in Hobart at a difficult time for the locals. The bridge across the Derwent River that connected the west or commercial part of the town to the east or dormitory part had been struck by a big cargo ship and the main span had dropped into the river. There was no other crossing in Hobart but there was a military landing craft ferry service operating and when we went aboard to get to the eastern bank I was surprised and pleased to find that the skipper was an old friend, late of the RCT Fleet. He had left the British Army to emigrate to Australia with his family and had joined the Royal Australian Corps of Transport in the same capacity. He was in quarters with his family in east Hobart and I spent a pleasant evening dining with them.

Our itinerary in Tasmania included a visit to an isolated mine location on the west coast. We spent the night there and we were entertained in a bar where the managers gathered with their wives. In standard Aussie fashion the women had foregathered at one end of the bar with the men at the other. The RAF members and I thought it would be courteous to chat to the ladies for a while and we wandered over to them, to be met with pleased, if rather surprised, smiles. We were not there for longer than about three minutes when two of the mine managers came over and one said:

"You gentlemen don't want to waste your evening talking to the ladies, do you? They like to gather together to chat among themselves." The other one then said:

"Let me refresh your drinks." They led us gently but firmly away. We agreed afterwards that we had probably been the innocent recipients of a dose of frontier law. When women are in short supply, their men tend to guard them carefully.

Before leaving Tasmania we were scheduled to drop in to the city of Launceston where we visited its Returned Servicemen's League (RSL) branch and were later entertained by the Mayor and some of the town's prominent citizens. Launceston was described to us as one of Australia's typical small country towns, and so it proved. It could have been, say, Trowbridge. The weather, the scenery, the small town problems and concerns described to us, were similar. The RSL could have been any branch of the British Legion. We all enjoyed the visit and late at night in his Parlour, the Mayor, in a gush of bonhomie said to everyone's surprise, "Let's make 'em all citizens!"

This, we were later told, had not been planned. Our party comprised Tom Bridges, our temporary leader, a German general, two brigadiers, one British, one Ghanaian, two RAF group captains, a Canadian colonel, a chief constable and our devoted Aussie major conducting officer. In scenes of some jollity we were solemnly sworn in as honorary citizens of the town of Launceston, Tasmania and each presented with a tie to mark this honour. Tom Bridges made a gracious speech of thanks on our behalf and we departed for our hotel. We all agreed it was a pity that the admiral was missing; he would have enjoyed the evening.

We flew back across the Bass Strait to the mainland to change planes for a visit to Alice Springs. This entailed a two hour flight across some of the most arid and desolate country I had seen. A mass of scrub, eucalyptus trees and desert. I was sitting next to our conducting officer and he said longingly, "Just imagine what we could make of this country if there was reachable water under all that."

The Alice, as the area is known by its inhabitants, is in the Northern Territory and is located on the Tod River; this rises in the hills around the town from the springs featured in its name. We were told that the

'Alice' part commemorates the name of the wife of a director of the company providing the telegraph station around which the town grew. When we visited in 1975 it was a thriving centre of communications and of course the nearest habitation to Ayers Rock, an increasingly popular tourist attraction that had not long before been dignified with its own airstrip.

Our visit programme featured a climb to the top of Ayers Rock and a twelve seater light aircraft was hired for a day to take us there. But 'the wet' was still in progress and the strip was rained off so we had to be content with circling round this impressive natural feature. Strangely enough, while everywhere we went we were told that the country's biggest drawback in the interior was a lack of water, the one time we could have done without it, right in the middle of the country there was too much of it. Years later, travelling across Australia with an internal airline I landed at Ayers Rock's all weather airport, very well equipped with all the latest facilities.

Our taxi driver taking us round the town was a Liverpudlian. He told us that he had jumped ship in Sydney and settled as far away as possible from the sea – and possible pursuit, we suspected – most of us having enough command experience to have developed a nose for a rogue. He took us to an aborigine settlement well outside the town where the custodian was at pains to explain to us that the Government was adopting a much more enlightened policy towards its original inhabitants than it was generally given credit for. We were allowed to talk to some of the native members of the settlement and they seemed happy enough. This, incidentally, was the first place we saw kangaroos and wallabies in the wild.

Our last night in Alice Springs was a Saturday and a party night at the local Returned Servicemen's League to which we were invited. Talking to a tall, retired ex-soldier who said he was a farmer 'up country' I suddenly had a feeling I'd met him before. We swapped career notes and he turned out to have been the RSM of one of the battalions of The Royal Australian Regiment and I had indeed met him before when my platoon moved his battalion out of the line in Korea. He told me that he had left the Army in the fifties and had taken advantage of the Australian Government's generous cheap land offers for returned servicemen who were prepared to settle in the unexploited countryside. He farmed 'a few thousand' acres three hundred or so miles to the north east of the Alice.

"The wife didn't mind," he said. "She'd been an Army wife for long enough to be happy when I was there, and eventually we made a fair go of it."

He worked the farm with his two sons and several 'blackfellas' and their families but now that his sons had grown up they were taking an increasing share of the burden leaving him more time to travel with his wife.

"We come here every Saturday night to meet old mates and have a swill," he said.

"It's a long drive every week for a party," I suggested. He looked surprised.

"Drive? My property's got three little planes we use like cars. Wouldn't think of driving to anywhere where there's a usable strip." He told me that his holiday territory tended to be South East Asia – Singapore, Thailand, Hong Kong and as a third generation Aussie he had no hankering to go back to what some still called the Old Country.

At 9 p.m. there was a shout for silence for 'The Ceremony'. Everyone stood motionless, glasses in hand for about one minute, ending at the bugle sound of the Last Post. We had been told about this weekly ceremony. It had not happened at the Tasmanian RSL, probably because that party was specially laid on for us, but our conducting officer said that it was a common occurrence at RSL functions. We thought it moving – akin to the Menin Gate ceremony at Ypres – and we were touched that these tough and self reliant people should take time off at a weekly social function to remember their lost comrades.

On to Sydney to change planes for the flight across the Tasman Sea. I had made copious notes during the Australian leg of the tour knowing that they would come in handy later on, but more importantly I had also made firm mental assessments of the concerns of the people we had met, military and civilian, from all walks of life. I found that a fear of unrestricted immigration was common to all Australians. They knew that to exploit to the full the riches of their vast continent they needed more people – but not just any people. They were happy to take intelligent, well motivated and preferably young, healthy people; possession of a trade or profession was a bonus. So immigration was heavily screened. Their abiding worry, however, was an invasion by the landless hordes of Asians to the north. "Our infrastructure," said a thoughtful government servant I discussed this with, "simply couldn't take it."

Before leaving Sydney we were joined by our admiral, now completely recovered.

After the pace and space of Australia, New Zealand offered a change to a lower gear. Christchurch, the South Island's biggest city, was lovely. It bathed in a cloistered calm. The emphasis wherever we went was on agriculture. I have always thought of 1975 as 'the year of the Second Spring' for we had arrived down under in our late autumn and their early spring. The year's new growth had been evident in Australia but by the time we reached New Zealand spring had thoroughly burst forth and Christchurch was a picture. Clear days, snow capped mountains in the far distance and flower packed gardens everywhere.

Christchurch stands on the edge of the Canterbury Plain and after meeting our new conducting officer our first visit was to a farm on the Plain, the origin of the imported Canterbury Lamb of my youth. It was flat, featureless and the farm was very isolated, but I can't recall ever before seeing so many sheep in one place. We were treated to a demonstration of castration – there was an almost irresistible urge to cross one's legs! All part of a farmer's job but it wasn't pretty.

We then flew to the North Island and Palmerston North University where we were treated to a splendid presentation on New Zealand's history with a reconstruction of the country before the major woodland clearances. In my mind's eye I had New Zealand as a small country of rolling pastures full of sheep but in fact the first settlers had found a thickly forested country with few open spaces on the rich soil. They had to set to work with what to us would be primitive tools to clear immense stretches of land to open it up for farming. There could be no question of failure. Their homeland was a world away and a passage to it was beyond the means of almost all of them. We were shown original sepia prints of the early days of almost superhuman toil and effort to achieve those rolling pastures and produce the enviably high standard of living that today's population enjoys.

The University was dedicated to achieving advances in agricultural practices: there had been notable successes such as the marketing of what we used to call Chinese gooseberries, but we now know as Kiwi Fruit and the popularity of NZ apples. In 1975 the country had yet to achieve today's stunning success of its vineyards, but they were well on the way. Pride in their country and its achievements was very evident.

Problems? Worries? Well, there was evidence of a conscience among officialdom about the situation of the native Maoris, mainly over land distribution. There was absolutely no evidence of racial discrimination. Why should there be? The Maori race, like the Gurkhas in Nepal, had fought the British to a standstill in the days of expanding empire and in both instances an honourable peace had been negotiated. I had had Maori soldiers in my platoon in Korea; I had been at staff colleges with Maori officers and had sailed small boats many times with a particular Maori friend, Brian Poananga, who later became a major general in the New Zealand Army and NZ High Commissioner to Papua New Guinea. But there was still some dissatisfaction and press comment on ancient rights and land issues. During a visit to New Zealand as a businessman a few years ago this was still rumbling on.

A more pressing but probably transient problem was put to us by the Chief of Police during our visit to Auckland later. Light industry had grown round the rim of Auckland and had created a shortage of labour. This had been solved by importing labour from the nearer Polynesian islands and these temporary labourers, without their families, suddenly found themselves rich by their standards with little to spend their money on but beer and the favours of Auckland's prostitutes. Ordinarily they were unsophisticated but gentle giants. In drink, however, they became wild and dangerous. "It's not unusual," said one of the beat policemen in conversation, "to see them sitting in a corner of a bar with a crate of beer in front of them just swigging it back, bottle by bottle. The barman then gets worried and refuses any more and you end up with a wrecked bar and several broken heads. It's a real problem."

We ended our visit to NZ with a trip to Rotorua. Before that we had a free day and we were asked what we would like to do. Our two RAF officers and I, keen fishermen all, said we would like to achieve a life's ambition and catch at least one fish on the legendary Lake Taupo, not far from our hotel. We were embarked on a large cabin cruiser equipped with a wide 'stern walk' and taken to the middle of this great lake. Taupo is reputed to be up to two miles deep in places and is certainly home to massive trout.

We were then equipped with rods and trolling reels and having each attached a large spinner to our line with perhaps three hundred yards of nylon line reeled out, we trolled slowly backwards and forwards; it was mid-afternoon and not an auspicious time for catching game fish – not in England anyway. Suddenly my neighbour's line sang and I saw the nylon being ripped off the reel. It gave all the signs of being a monster, but when he reeled it in it weighed only about three pounds. We each achieved our ambition of catching a Taupo fish that day; the professional fishermen handling the boat said they were never in any doubt. The hotel cooked all three for our evening meal. This little interlude had to be recorded. The lake is world famous and for game fishermen not native to New Zealand, catching a trout on Taupo is the equivalent of playing a round at St Andrews for a golfing fanatic.

The presentation at Rotarua, a place of great significance to the Maori race, gave us an insight into their history and their concerns about heritage and ancient rights, but the hot sulphur springs and the mud geysers were also a great attraction. We walked over a landscape pitted with steaming holes from which without any warning, showers of boiling mud erupted from the earth accompanied by a strong whiff of sulphur. As someone said at the time, if you were either very religious or very superstitious, a visit to this place would put you on your best behaviour for a long time to come.

It would be hard not to be seduced by New Zealand's unruffled lifestyle and quiet charm. Our visit gave us the impression that the country is devoted almost wholly to the exploitation of its agriculture. There was little evidence of great riches among the population yet everyone seemed happy and satisfied with his lot. Your average artisan had his own house, car and in most cases a boat as well. There was every type of team sport available for the young and for those inclined to fishing, sailing or field activities the place was a paradise We all thought it was a pity it was so far away, although on reflection, this probably has a great deal to do with its happy situation.

We returned to Australia to stage and change planes at the fair city of Perth en route to Indonesia. The city overlooks the upper navigable reaches of the Swan River that flows into the sea at Freemantle, a short distance away, a major port and one of the earliest penal settlements. We had two nights there to meet Perth's dignitaries and get a flavour of Western Australia. Sitting on a grassy bank in King's Park with a backdrop of the tall buildings of the impressive business district and the river glinting in the sun below, I thought that Perth is without doubt, and with apologies to my macho Aussie friends, Australia's prettiest city.

24

Indonesia

After just over three weeks of travelling, listening to presentations and lectures without number and meeting an unconscionable number of people, the programme compilers had decided that we would be due for a break. So before the start of our formal and official visit to Indonesia we were flown from Australia to the island of Bali for a three day interlude and accommodated at the five star Bali Beach Hotel, then the last word in western style and luxury.

We were pleased to find that for once the Treasury watchdogs had fallen short of their normally penny pinching standards. The usual procedure for accommodating servicemen on courses overseas where there is no publicly funded accommodation is for the UK Defence Attaché to visit local hotels, assess their suitability and cost and recommend a rate for an official daily allowance for visiting officers and other ranks. This is invariably less than it costs to stay in anything more than a three star hotel.

The Bali Beach Hotel, chosen for us by the Indonesian military authorities, was extremely expensive and way beyond anything most of us could have normally afforded. We were told that messages raced back and forward between the Embassy in Jakarta and London but eventually the authorities had no alternative but to instruct our admiral to send the bill, whatever it was, to the Embassy when we left. The Admiral told us this with a broad grin on his face and then said that we should all join each other for a drink at different locations on each of the three nights we were there.

The Balinese are mainly Hindu with a smattering of Christians and presumably also a leavening of Muslims as Indonesia is officially a Muslim nation. The hotel, to which we travelled by coach, was completely divorced from the town with a knife rest barrier operated by an armed guard preventing access from the only road in.

There was, however, a 'native village' adjacent to the hotel. Its near-perfect rattan roofed houses were occupied by handsome young Balinese men with their attractive and lissom wives and beautiful children. It faced a picture postcard palm fringed bay with curved prahu – type boats drawn up on the beach, their lateen sails drying in the trade winds. The earth 'street' was spotlessly clean. There were no rooting piglets, scraggy chickens, snotty nosed children or pariah dogs to be seen. We all wondered why it was there. It was, in a way, an insult to the intelligence of the hotel's patrons for no one who had seen a real Balinese village could be in any doubt that this one had been manufactured to present an as yet unattainable ideal. But then, many of this Hotel's patrons arrived by helicopter directly from the airport; they would leave the same way, so perhaps they would be seduced into believing that they had encountered an earthly paradise where every prospect pleases and not even man is vile.

But the accommodation was excellent, the swimming pool superb, with a fully stocked bar at one end at water level to save the swimmers the bother of leaving the water to get a drink. This arrangement is commonplace today but it was new to us thirty years ago. Each evening before dinner there was an 'entertainment' with a Balinese flavour. The performances were good; the dancing was attractively choreographed and the choral singing was first class.

We were taken into the town to buy Batiks from the state shop. For those who have not encountered it, the Batik serves as formal evening wear in Indonesia. It is a bush jacket type garment tailored in silk or heavy cotton and in variegated and attractive colours and patterns. We were told that we would each need one to wear at evening functions during our Indonesian visit. Day wear would be tropical uniform for serving officers.

All too soon we left Bali by air for Jakarta and officialdom. On our arrival we were poured into a plush coach for the journey to our hotel. We had known that Indonesia was in the grip of a military government, but we had not expected to be accompanied by military outriders with screaming sirens clearing the streets of traffic. The hotel, in the centre of Jakarta, was pleasantly modern without being garish.

Next day, attired in tropical uniform, we were greeted by a covey of senior military officers and allotted a conducting officer. The defence attaché from the British Embassy was also there, presumably to keep us up to speed on local manners and customs and to see that these RCDS visitors didn't put up any black marks, bearing in mind that until quite recently Britain had been fighting Indonesia over land issues. We were then taken to pay our respects at the memorial to the unknown soldier where I managed to put up the first black without realising it until it was pointed out by the attaché. I am left-handed and I was in a country where the left hand is often used for unsavoury purposes. We each had to take a handful of rose petals from a large bowl and scatter them on the memorial. I did so with my left hand, causing our faithful attaché to hiss at me like a snake about to strike. But it was too late. Fortunately our Indonesian conducting officer had either not noticed or was too well mannered to make an issue of my lapse, but the lesson, learned many years earlier but forgotten, once again sank in.

We were treated as fellow servicemen by our hosts; it was clear that the military grip on the country was tight but we were encouraged to question anything we saw that called for comment. They said they assumed that as fellow professionals we had a similar mindset to theirs and they welcomed constructive criticism. It was a beguiling approach and we warmed to it, but we were advised by our attaché not to take it too far.

That said, the Indonesian military were very friendly and they looked after us extremely well. Their hospitality was faultless. Wherever we went we were treated as honoured and important visitors. I had experienced the status of an honoured guest in Greece under the Colonels' regime but this went far beyond that. Road travel was routinely accompanied either by motor cycle outriders or by military police vehicles clearing the streets for us and those we met and those who addressed us had obviously been well briefed on our respective backgrounds. But there was no free time and practically no contact with the public. No chance at all of travelling on public transport. Jakarta was an interesting city; its centre appeared to be well laid out and adorned with statues in the heroic mould favoured by states of a totalitarian nature, but there was no chance of getting closer to it. I can't speak for my fellow course members but I found the situation curiously unsettling.

We were there to learn and observe though, and our hosts certainly did their best to enlighten us on their country's situation and their plans to modernise it. We were introduced to their Panca Sila philosophy described to us as 'The five principles of the Republic of Indonesia' – a series of social and economic targets not dissimilar to the five and ten year plans adopted by some of the world's economies, although my notes, taken during the visit, do not reveal a projected timescale.

We left the island of Java by air to visit Sumatra and a tour of rubber and palm oil plantations so important to Indonesia's economy. For me, nostalgia emerged as I surveyed upcountry Malaya from the aircraft across the narrow Strait of Malacca. I persuaded myself that I could see Port Dixon of happy memory but it was probably wishful thinking as we flew quite high. Then back to Jakarta and a tour of the Freedom Museum where the British took the stage with the Dutch for a while as the villainous occupying forces after the Second World War. But it was all accepted with the benevolence brought on by thirty years distance from those events and no sensibilities were offended on either side.

Our final evening was marked by a charming show of Indonesian singing and dancing put on by the wives and daughters of the officers of the Jakarta military establishment. At the end of the show the ladies and teenage girls left the impromptu stage and we didn't see them again. As someone said afterwards – a clever way of preserving Muslim customs by letting us see their families without actually meeting them.

Throughout our official time in Indonesia there was little mention of defence arrangements. We didn't press the issue because we were conscious of the short passage of time since we had been at odds with the country. Our hosts were predominantly serving or retired officers and this probably mirrored their feelings. It would therefore have been tactless to raise the fears of the Australians that the vast arsenal of weapons left behind by the Americans in Vietnam might have seeped southwards, creating a danger of instability in the South East Asian economies.

One thing that did become evident in discussion was that they were aware that they still faced a serious internal security problem. They governed a notoriously volatile multi-ethnic community spread over a country made up of a string of islands and therefore very difficult to administer. We gained an overall impression that they were intensely inward looking and unlikely to be a short or long term threat to their neighbours. Leaving aside a few nasty internal eruptions and border disputes, this has proved to be the case in the ensuing thirty years.

Back to Singapore to change planes for the journey home and a landing at Heathrow to the usual foul November weather.

25

Return to the Madhouse

In 1976, not long after my 49th birthday, I was staring at the Pacific Ocean deep in thought, indeed surmise, at least as wild as that of stout Cortez, but this was no peak in Darien. I was standing on a flattish, very slippery rock armed with a six pack of Canadian beer, a bucket and a small claw hammer. My perch had only recently been uncovered by the tide. The flat Canadian coastline was just in sight on the low horizon across a calm and empty ocean. The Alaskan border was about fifteen miles to the north, no distance at all. My companion, Old Douglas, was perched on a similar rock about a quarter of a mile away. There were no vessels of any sort in sight. A strange situation, of which more later.

Shortly after I had re-appeared at the Ministry of Defence in Whitehall as the new Army Director of Movements, D Mov (A) to the initiated, I was visited in my office by my old boss, General Monkey – now the Adjutant General and elevated to a new dignity as General Sir Cecil Blacker. He plonked himself into a chair and said, "Thought I'd greet you. Have you been here before?"

"Briefly," I said.

"Did you enjoy it?"

"Not much."

"Well," he said. "That's a healthy sign. But you get used to it and a lot depends on the job. I think yours will keep you pretty active, which is all to the good."

Wise words. You don't join the Service to work in Whitehall but in fact my new job proved to be remarkably fulfilling. For a start I was very well supported. I had inherited four staff branches, three military and one civilian. The military ones were each headed by a serving colonel and staffed by soldiers. They dealt respectively with movement planning, worldwide air movement and worldwide surface movement.

The civilian branch, Movements Finance, managed my budget and was wholly civilian headed by a civil servant at equivalent colonel rank.

My immediate office staff consisted of a personal staff officer who was a young infantry captain, and a civil service secretary, an efficient and hardworking spinster lady named Barbara. The three colonel heads of department I had served with previously and knew well. Ron Jenkins, movements planning, has been mentioned earlier as has Wally Burnett, surface movement, a very old friend from infantry days and Korea. John Bidmead, air movement, had commanded one of the squadrons of my regiment in Duisburg. They were all quick thinkers, an essential attribute for a movements job, and I found the military side to be a comfortable set-up from the start.

The finance side was an unknown quantity. The senior civil servant initially appeared to be a stuffy individual, almost lugubrious. I put this down to an element of unhappiness at having to report to a military officer who he clearly suspected was intent on spending public money like a drunken sailor on a Saturday night. Had I been of that mind, with the annual movements budget at nearly seventy million pounds, I could have had a memorably good time. But he proved to be a competent moneyman and it is nice to be able to record that as time went by he appreciated that my actual aim for his 'part of ship' was to do my best to strike a good deal for the taxpayer with the many commercial organisations that we had to deal with. He gradually released his tight grip on the dotted line in the chain of command that gave him a right to appeal to his civil service superiors when he disagreed with my financial decisions, and we maintained an amicable, if not warm working relationship.

One of the things that all 'movers' across the three services know is that their function only assumes importance in the eyes of their contemporaries and superiors when something goes wrong, either collectively or when an individual believes he or she has a grievance. On paper the D Mov (A)'s responsibilities are vast and his terms of reference stretch to pages of print. In practice they boil down to a responsibility for the efficient and cost effective movement of military people and things across the globe, plus the planning of movement for projected or contingency operations.

I reported directly to the Quartermaster General for the Army. At that time it was General Bill Jackson, well respected and serious minded. I can't recall seeing him smile although on one occasion he became extremely animated and indulged in a good deal of whip cracking. This was when his mess, the sapper HQ Officers' Mess at Chatham, was seriously damaged in a fire and in his capacity as the overseer of army quartering, he was able to ensure that it was repaired at top speed. He was a distinguished and gallant Royal Engineer and a well-known modern military historian. He was also a prolific author and essayist. We got on well professionally and I admired his achievements enormously but he came over as a somewhat Olympian personality.

General Jackson was in the mould of the 'clever sapper' epitomised by, among others, Garnet Wolseley. During his stewardship of the Army's logistics he presided over a farsighted and effective reorganisation. He 'rusticated' the professional heads of the major logistic corps to an old RAF airfield near Andover, forming in the process something that came to be known as the Logistic Executive. It worked well, as I have reason to know, and I believe that an up-to-date version of it is there still.

Early in my tenure of the movements appointment General Jackson became the Military Historian at the Cabinet Office and later Governor and C-in-C Gibraltar. He was replaced as QMG by General Pat Howard – Dobson, a completely different type of person. He maintained an 'open door' policy for discussion and advice and he never professed to know more about what I was doing than I did. He was also satisfyingly relaxed about things provided that they were maintained on an even keel. I had been grateful to him when he was the Military Secretary for his forbearance over my request to stay at the RCDS for the overseas tour and did my best to see that he was not unduly bothered by 'events' from my branch.

Contacts with commercial enterprises were important For instance it was my annual job to negotiate with British Rail's Director of Operations on the volume discounts for Forces' passenger and freight movement. It helped that the BR negotiator during my time was Bobby Lawrence, a wartime Movements specialist still with strong military connections. Bobby, although a tough adversary in the strictly commercial sense, undoubtedly gave us a fair deal to the extent that the 2nd Permanent Secretary at MOD who was our budget watcher, confessed himself satisfied.

I also had to deal with Hogg Robinson, the Government Freight Agents; they operated under a charter granted by Queen Victoria and proudly displayed on the wall of the managing director's office in the

City. This allowed me occasional visits to the Baltic Exchange, a sort of stock market for shipping in the City where I was warned to be anonymous in case my appearance generated rumours that the Services were about to make a major bid for shipping and thus drive up the hire rates.

Contacts with road transport firms were also frequent. The National Freight Company, the biggest, had been an offshoot of British Rail and because of this was favoured for freight movement by road until it severed ties with Government and became completely independent. I noticed that civilian road and rail management, while in keen competition with each other commercially, were quite incestuous socially. Many of them were Members or Fellows of the Chartered Institute of Transport and members of The Worshipful Company of Carmen, a livery company in the City of London founded in the 15th century and closely associated with the transport industry.

The Army's D Mov, because he outranked the movements chiefs of the other two services, also held the appointment of Chairman of the Defence Movements Co-ordinating Committee, the senior movements forum for Whitehall. Its members included D Mov (RAF) an air commodore, a naval representative from 2nd Sea Lord's Department and a senior man from the Whitehall Sea Transport Branch. The Committee met about once monthly, more often during a tri-Service 'flap'. Its most important 'perk' was a seat for its Chairman at the Joint Service Chiefs of Staff table, albeit very much at the bottom end, but privy to the highest levels of tri-service thought.

I had hardly settled in and updated myself from my stint in MOD Movements four years earlier when we had a burgeoning problem in Canada. A bi-lateral agreement with the Canadian government had allowed the British Army the summer use of the remote and enormous Suffield training area near to the town of Medicine Hat in the prairie province of Alberta. Suffield permitted live firing for both infantry and armour. We shipped the tanks and all the ammunition over in our logistic ships (LSLs), manned by Royal Fleet Auxiliary officers and Chinese crews and tasked by my surface movements branch. Vancouver was the arrival port and both tanks and ammunition moved onwards by rail. Troops were moved by air in RAF VC10s to Calgary and onwards to the training area by road.

For several years everything had gone smoothly, no hitches at all.

Until early in 1976 when our Vancouver agent visited us and told us about growing unease in that city about the shipment of ammunition through its Port.

"We hear," he said, "that demonstrations are planned and the authorities in British Columbia and perhaps even the national government in Ottawa will have to take notice of them."

He also told us that a port that may well be acceptable for the shipment of ammunition was being developed in Northern Canada close to the Alaskan border at the small town of Prince Rupert. We asked our High Commission in Ottawa to investigate and they confirmed that sooner or later and probably sooner, Vancouver Port would be denied to us for the movement of ammunition.

The last thing we wanted was to upset or embarrass our friendly Canadians so it was important to review possible solutions to this situation and if possible pre-empt any problems. On reviewing the situation it seemed at first sight that we could save much needed shipping time by sending the tanks and ammunition overland from the Canadian east coast. Our six LSLs were fully employed on moving ammunition, vehicles and stores to BAOR, to Cyprus and to NATO bases elsewhere. It was obvious that the option of rail movement across Canada would avoid the long trip through the Panama Canal and northwards up the North American coast and ease the pressure on our ships.

I asked the High Commission in Ottawa to investigate the possibility of using an east coast port and onward rail movement. They came back very quickly and told us that we would be well advised to stick to our present arrangements if possible because the French Canadian port of Quebec had the only suitable east coast facilities and that if Vancouver was unhappy about the movement of ammunition there was no guarantee that the French Canadians would react differently. Also the Canadian Government had been approached and had indicated that they too were uneasy about the situation and that their preferred solution was to move the ammunition through the new port in northern British Columbia.

As a result of this research we abandoned the possible east coast option. We would seek to modify our existing arrangements.

This would allow us to keep our experienced and efficient agents in British Columbia but first we had to be sure that the Port of Prince

Rupert had the depth and handling facilities to accept our four thousand ton ships and that suitable rail links were available and adequate. Our Vancouver agent had checked and they appeared to be suitable but I wanted to be sure. So we arranged for the first LSL trip of the year to discharge in Vancouver then travel up the Inner Passage between Vancouver Island and the mainland to Prince Rupert to assess the port's suitability. The QMG had been kept well informed of this affair and agreed that I had to go and have an extended look.

I timed my arrival at Prince Rupert to coincide with the LSL. Lieutenant Colonel Douglas Harding, an ex-sapper movements specialist, had been looking after surface movement to Canada and he came with me as he would have to do the detailed work on any modifications to the arrangements. It helped that we were friends from 3 Div days when we had wandered the Med together on recces for joint service exercises. He was known to me as Old Douglas to distinguish him from another Douglas Harding, Young Douglas, a less senior RCT officer also in the movements business.

There was no question of picking up the perk of first class air travel allowed to major generals and above on duty because there was a regular RAF VC10 service to Calgary twice weekly during the training season. I flew on the Tuesday flight to meet our Calgary agent and discuss the rail adjustment. He was a cheerful third generation Canadian not in the least put out by the projected new arrangements, although he foresaw some problems. At some point in its journey from the north the ammunition would have to be transferred from Canadian Pacific Railway metals to those owned and operated by Canadian National Railways. These two enterprises were in keen competition with each other.

"There'll be fireworks," he said. "But nothing I can't handle."

Next day we lunched at the revolving restaurant at the top of Calgary's highest tower.

"Pity you couldn't come on Saturday, General," he said, "Me and a few friends flew down to Vegas for the day in my Cessna. You'd have enjoyed it."

He went on to point out Calgary's landmarks.

"That's the Stampede Ground and over there is Scotsman's Hill. Years ago after they introduced payment to watch, the Scots used to gather there to see the Stampede for free. If you hadn't got a Mac to your name you got thrown off."

He was an effervescent character and I was left with a comforting feeling that he would cope rapidly and effectively with whatever problems might be thrown up by the major shift in our movement arrangements.

I had arranged a two day trip to the training area at Suffield to check on reception arrangements for vehicles and stores. Douglas Harding had travelled separately to Prince Rupert by air and I was to travel there by rail over the weekend. My visit to Suffield happened to coincide with that of the GOC 3rd Division, Michael Walsh. We knew each other well and we teamed up to watch his troops live firing on a night exercise. It was a film set affair with the infantry flares illuminating the area and the flashes of live rounds being fired – a totally different sound to blanks. Natural gas had recently been found near to the small town of Medicine Hat some miles away and the gas flares provided a backdrop on the horizon giving the impression of a distant battle on another part of the front. All that separated it from the real thing was the absence of a background orchestra of field artillery and that essential ingredient, a real enemy!

At one stage we had to run across a flat, stony expanse of scrub to a viewing stand. "If you feel a sharp pain in your lower leg," said our Canadian conducting officer mysteriously. "Don't assume it's a small stone. Tell me right away."

Our party was quite large. A number of 3 Div officers had turned up to accompany their General. When we got to the stand the conducting officer turned to us and said, quite seriously, "Great. No rattlers tonight." Apparently the piece of land we had crossed was notorious for rattlesnakes and there had been several casualties among visitors from bites. We were told that although painful, there was little harm done if a serum was administered quickly.

On the Friday afternoon I embarked on Canadian National Train Number One for the overnight journey to Prince Rupert. This had been a subject of some contention with my staff who had assumed that I would fly from Calgary.

"Not on your life." I said. "I'm not going to miss the only chance I'll ever get to travel through the Rockies by train and furthermore it's a weekend and I'll only be an embarrassment to my hosts if I arrive late on Friday. Book me from Edmonton to Prince Rupert by rail."

I 'entrained' on a Friday afternoon. Two locos pulled the train. We started in early evening and travelled upwards for several hours. There was an observation car with a Perspex roof of the type familiar to my generation from picture books. The high Rockies were visible in the distance but the car attendant said that sadly, we would miss most of the spectacle because we would travel through it at night. On hearing that I was travelling to Prince Rupert, however, he said that there would be plenty to look at in the morning as the train would divide during the night, one half going to Vancouver.

After a drink before the evening meal in company with a number of hefty Canadians who announced themselves as lumberjacks, I found myself sitting opposite an oldish gentleman with an English accent. We introduced ourselves and he said he been a British Army officer attached to Canadian forces, but was now a Canadian citizen. He said that he had found the country to his liking; he had no ties and had wanted to retire there. I looked at him curiously.

"With due respect I would have thought you would come up against the age barrier. How did you manage to get over it?" He smiled.

"Wheels within wheels. I knew I was over age for citizenship and I didn't want to do anything dodgy like lying about my age, so I consulted a policeman friend who told me to take my retirement leave here, which I could do quite legally. Then when my time as a visitor was up I was to vanish and let him know how to get in touch with me. He knew there was an amnesty coming up and he'd tell me when I was to give myself up to him as an 'overstay'. He'd then be able to class me as a surrendering 'illegal' of otherwise good character, a suitable applicant for the amnesty and citizenship. I never made a better decision in my life. It's a wonderful country and I'm happy to salute my new flag."

I turned in and slept the sleep of the just – and tired – in the sleeping compartment allotted to me.

There were two stops during the night. Jasper and McBride I think, but I don't know where the train divided. Next morning dawned bright and clear and the train rambled through glorious and unspoilt scenery. There were frequent stops in developed places with names like Prince George, Vanderhoof, Telkwa, Smitrers, Hazelton. Also many small halts that were obviously logging camps where the lumberjacks got on and off. I saw no four legged wildlife but there was abundant birdlife and I wished that I'd taken the trouble to learn more about Canadian species. The slopes were thickly forested below the snow line. The trees were almost exclusively fir and pine although within the settlements attempts had been made to introduce broad leafed deciduous varieties. But it was obviously frontier-type living. The smaller settlements were little more than camps relying mainly on the railway for outside contact.

The train arrived at Prince Rupert on Saturday afternoon and I was astonished to be met by a deputation. Old Douglas was there together with the Mayor, the stationmaster and several other functionaries. Douglas made the introductions, I concealed my surprise at this unlooked for civility and we were whisked away to the Crest Hotel overlooking the harbour to be guests of the town for the evening meal.

The mayor said, "We've heard that you like fishing and as you may know, our area is famous for salmon. We won't be working tomorrow, Sunday, so I've arranged for Pete Murot, who runs a sports shop here, to take you both out in his boat on a fishing trip. I hope that's OK?"

I said, "Very good of you. Delighted."

Afterwards I quizzed Douglas on the reasons for the reception committee. He said:

"I was as surprised as you are but I've discovered that the British Army contract is regarded as the key to an expanding commercial future for this town and you, as its representative, will be unable to do any wrong. Mr Murot will be here to collect us at nine thirty tomorrow morning with the necessary kit for salmon trolling so I suggest we both accept their hospitality with good grace. We don't start work until we do the port recce on Monday morning and we can't assess its suitability until the LSL arrives on Tuesday. Incidentally the mayor has arranged for the forest ranger to take us to the town tip on Monday afternoon to see the bears!"

Pete Murot and his driver duly turned up next day and we embarked on his thirty foot motor cruiser berthed in a creek about half a mile from the sea. Pete was a short, round, cheerful and extrovert character perfectly happy to entertain us and pleased that he had been chosen by no less a person than the mayor to do so. His crew and helmsman was a second generation Irish Canadian who had clearly been itching to find out from a British General why we were in Ulster 'against the will and wishes of its rightful citizens.'

I did my best to explain that soldiers go where they are sent. Also that they are bound to obey lawful commands issued by their democratically elected government. And that government, irrespective of its political colour, had no alternative but to oppose violence within its territory from whatever source.

But I was pushing at a closed door; there was no rancour but my Irish Canuck, a nice fellow, could not accept my explanation. I had to admit that I hadn't served in Ireland and it was obvious that so far as he was concerned that meant I didn't know what I was talking about. I changed the subject as soon as possible.

We trolled all over the bay outside Prince Rupert Port, going out to sea about five miles, but nary a salmon came near us. "Aw Hell," said Pete, a man of quick decision. "It's half tide. We'll get some abalone."

We cruised over to some flat rocks emerging from the ocean. He jumped over from the boat, sure footed, and gave me a hand on to the rock. He called for a 'pick' that to me looked like a claw hammer and explained how to recognise and prise abalone from the rock. For those who do not know this bivalve, it clings to the sea rocks like a whelk except that its shell is flat rather than conical and it is easily prised loose. It is a seafood delicacy and highly prized. The abalone were large and numerous and I quite enjoyed the quest. Up to this point I had assumed that this was to be a joint enterprise until I heard a hail from Pete, the boat now drifting away from the rock.

He pointed to a sixpack of beer and a small bucket.

"The beer's for if you get thirsty," he said. "And try to fill the bucket with abalone. We're gonna do some crabbing. Be back before the tide gets over your head."

With a great laugh and a wave they roared off to another rock where the hapless Douglas was deposited with similar equipment and the boat sped off towards the coast and vanished from sight.

Although I was in no doubt of Pete's goodwill, it was a fact that his driver had neither grasped nor accepted my explanation for the problems of Northern Ireland and there was no doubt where his sympathies lay. Also motor cruisers are prone to breakdown and it would have been impossible to get to the shore in the event of an emergency. Hence the wild surmise. It would have been a long, cold swim to shore. So it was with some relief that we watched Pete reappear after about an hour with a netful of crab and acting as though nothing out of the ordinary had happened, which for them was probably the case. He was delighted with our joint haul – two buckets full of shellfish and we dined that night on crab, abalone and chips, prepared for us at our hotel and washed down with excellent Canadian beer.

Next morning we drove to the port. We were both old hands at port recces and knew what we were looking for. Prince Rupert was the Canadian ferry port for Alaska and the new commercial port was being developed adjacent to the established ferry terminal. It was clear that a great deal of money was being spent. Massive rock groynes protected the harbour, the wharves were certainly sufficient in length for our LSLs and they were rail served. The handling facilities were probably adequate but since our ships were equipped to handle goods both offshore and alongside with their own gantries if necessary, that was not a critical factor. We met the port manager, an Englishman, by name Kitching.

"That's not a common name," I said. "And you bear some resemblance to a John Kitching who was in one of my syndicates when I was instructing at the Staff College. Any relation?"

"My brother," he said. "He told me you were a fisherman. I hope you enjoyed the trip yesterday."

They were obviously very keen to secure the military contract, but since they held all the cards it was good of them to take the trouble to find out about us.

Our recce prior to the LSL's arrival completed, we were picked up by the forest ranger in his truck and driven to the town tip to be confronted with a similar scene to any municipal rubbish tip at home. But with one essential difference. Although the place was surrounded with a wire fence, it contained about eight bears happily rooting about among the rubbish. There was also a substantial colony of bald eagles, the noble bird of the American presidential insignia, also scratching and pecking in the rubbish like vultures, any pretensions of nobility thoroughly cast aside. Of course they were all protected species. The ranger told us that the problem was protecting the bears and birds from the people rather than the reverse.

He said, "Believe me, I've seen some weird things go on here. Before we had the fence I once saw a young couple drive up in a pickup. The girl got out, rushed over to the nearest bear, the man took a quick photograph and they were back in the truck and away before the bear realised what was happening. On someone's mantelpiece there's a picture of a pretty girl standing right up close to a bear holding a can of trash in his paws and looking over his shoulder with a puzzled expression on his face. I chased after them and gave them a piece of my mind. They didn't realise that they'd been dangerously stupid but they'd done nothing illegal so that was the best I could do."

Our ship, the LSL, arrived next day. She drew no more water than the larger ferries so the harbour bar was no problem and she berthed alongside quite happily. The plan was for me to travel with the LSL down to Vancouver; Douglas was to fly down and set up my meeting with the agents to discuss any necessary adjustments to the contract before returning home to ratify the changes.

It was an important part of my job to get to know the captains and crews of the LSLs who worked for us and the trip down to Vancouver was part of the process. The captains were all career master mariners and they travelled the seas of the world on our behalf. The Army was keen to retain its stewardship of the LSLs, vital links in our lines of communication not only with NATO but also with the middle and far east, where we still had commitments even in the nineteen seventies. The six ships were named after King Arthur's Knights of the Round Table. I recall that I sailed in *Sir Geraint* on this occasion. Her Master was pleased to have sailed the Inner Passage, a first for many of his officers and crew and certainly for the six young RFA cadets on board and under training, although his purser was unhappy about the rapid reduction of ship's rations.

"We'll all starve before Vancouver at this rate. These young lads get through a sack of spuds a day!"

Before we left Prince Rupert I asked the Captain if he would mind if I invited the Mayor, the Port Manager and one or two other officials who had been kind to us to join us in a drink aboard the ship.

"Delighted," he said. "I was going to do that anyway but you've saved me the job of making contacts here, and since we have a fund to cover entertainment of that nature under the heading of social liaison in new ports, your kind offer to pay for the drinks isn't necessary."

We had a pleasant evening with our new friends before Douglas left to fly to Vancouver.

Next morning we left with the tide for our trip down the Inner

Passage to Vancouver. It was a splendid trip and has since become a star tourist attraction, but travelling southwards it didn't really become interesting until about halfway down the chain of islands when the ship passed through Queen Charlotte Sound and entered the narrow strait that separates Vancouver Island from the mainland. This is about five hundred statute miles long, a two day journey with land close on either side for most of it. We passed many small coastal communities on the landward side. They lived in the inlets and were obviously logging settlements, their only means of transport to wider civilisation being boats or floatplanes as there were no roads to the interior. The logs were felled on the steep slopes leading to the sea, stripped of their foliage then allowed to gravitate to the water, to be 'knitted' into great rafts and towed down to Vancouver behind powerful tugs. The ship's Master told me that it was vital to keep a sharp watch for 'deadheads' – when a log gets free of the raft, then becomes waterlogged and upends itself so that it rides vertically in the deep channel and can do serious damage even to big ships under way, since all that can be seen is one end sticking perhaps a foot out of the water. The bridge had a permanent lookout on either side throughout the whole trip.

I was met on arrival at Vancouver by Old Douglas and Mervyn, the representative of our agents there. Mervyn was British born, having settled in Canada after his National Service. It was the second Friday of our trip. The agents had booked us into the Pacific Palisades hotel, close to the harbour and rather upmarket. I found myself in a suite with a magnificent harbour view, overlooking the seaplane base with the little floatplanes moving in and out like taxis. Looking at the back of the door I was appalled at the nightly rate shown there – more than three times the cost of my daily MOD allowance for meals and accommodation. I rang down to reception and said there had been some mistake and could I have a less expensive room. The girl at the desk seemed to be anticipating my enquiry. "No mistake sir. You are booked in at our commercial rate, thirty nine dollars a night."

"But it says a hundred and sixty on the door." "Ignore that sir. Your rate is thirty nine dollars a night. Trust me!"

What else could I do? But I did take the matter up with the agents when they invited us to join them on their company boat later that weekend. They said that they pushed so much business towards the local hotels that they had managed to negotiate a super deal for their clients. We had no idea, they said, that our full board 'commercial' rate at the hotel is similar to your MOD daily allowance.

Vancouver is a busy and attractive town and this was the first of many visits both as a tourist and a businessman. One of the nicest things about it is the evident pride that the inhabitants have in their city. As soon as they realise that you are a visitor their aim is to make sure you know about all its attractive features and offer advice on how to see them. The climate is less extreme than that in the rest of Canada because the Rockies protect it from the worst excesses of the icy blasts from the east.

We had a satisfactory conference with the agents and then I made for home. Douglas stayed behind for a day or two to finalise the paperwork. I boarded a British Airways Jumbo and we flew quite low over the top of the Rockies. The snow slopes were visible only about fifteen hundred feet below, a magnificent sight.

There was one stop – at Calgary, where the vacant seat next to me was occupied by a youngish man who appeared to have an expensive thirst. Whiskies vanished down his throat at an alarming rate. I buried my nose in my book, but after about thirty minutes he turned to me and said, "I expect you think I'm a drunk."

I replied that it was no business of mine how much he drank, but he put his hand on my arm and said, "I've had a terrible shock and I have to tell someone about it. Please!"

I sighed. "OK. If it makes you feel any better."

"I should explain," he went on. "I'm a banker, a merchant banker in the city." He mentioned an old and well-known firm.

"My job is to seek out major projects for possible investment and if, when we've looked at them, they come up to our standards we lend them money at a negotiated rate of interest. Two days ago, with a colleague and incidentally, a good friend, I came to Calgary to look at a site for a major building project some way out of the city. Travel was to be by helicopter. There were quite a lot of us with the city engineer and his planners and we needed two helicopters to get to the site. I was in one and my friend was in the other one. We circled round twice before landing and his helicopter suddenly dived nose first to the ground." He drained his scotch. "Everyone was killed. My friend is in a wooden box below us in the cargo hold."

He looked hunted. "That's tragic enough, but his wife and children are meeting him at Heathrow; they live well outside London and I don't think my message to the office will have got there soon enough for one of the partners to get to her and tell her. It'll be down to me and I don't know how I'm going to face her."

"Have another scotch – or two," I said. "At least it'll make you sleep and you should wake up in better shape to see them." He eventually faded to sleep and I left the aircraft before he woke up. One of life's unsung tragedies. I heard no more and often wondered what had happened but of course any enquiries would have been prurient.

When the sums had been done and the new arrangements for the movement of ammunition had been put in place, we found somewhat to our surprise that the adjustments had had much less impact on the costs than we had feared. Our reward was enhanced goodwill in Canada, well worth the small extra expenditure.

About three weeks after I got back to Whitehall the Master of the LSL rang me.

"As you'll know," he said. "We arrived back at Marchwood a few days ago. I was told not to tell you until we got back, but the Mayor of Prince Rupert left a salmon in our deep freeze for you. It's a big one – the cook says over twenty pounds. I suggest you collect it soon as we're off again in a few days time. You'll need a sizeable cold box."

This needed some thought. The rules relating to gifts in the public service are strict. Unless you can prove that the donor would be outraged at the thought of his or her gift has not been received and enjoyed or appreciated by the donee, all gifts have to be handed over to the authorities. In our case this was one of the Whitehall civilian management branches (CM something or other). I had had tussles with them before. It was impossible to persuade some of the business organisations we dealt with that there was no point in sending us gifts, and so my practice was to ensure that when, for instance, our civilian contractors sent us bottles of booze at Christmas, I made sure that they were fed into one or other of the office parties to be consumed by those on the 'shop floor' who actually did the work; usually the CM people accepted this, albeit somewhat grudgingly. This time, however, I was resigned to being told that I would have to give up my salmon, but I would be damned if I would provide the necessary refrigeration for it to be transported to the faceless beneficiaries at the MOD.

I wrote to the Mayor thanking him for his gift and told him that it would be enjoyed by my large family, then I rang the Senior Principal of the CM branch and told him about the Mayor's gift.

"Hard luck General," he said. "I'm afraid you'll have to give it up." I gave a sigh of resignation. "OK. Will you arrange to collect it?" I knew his answer before he gave it.

"Good gracious, no. We have no facilities for that sort of thing. You must arrange that. After all, you are the Director of Movements." His voice betrayed a smirk.

"Very well," I said. "I'll arrange collection. But unless you authorise me to hire suitable refrigeration facilities I can give no guarantee as to its condition by the time it gets to you." Long pause.

"OK. You win. Enjoy your salmon."

"I'll need written confirmation of your decision," I replied.

"That's worth at least a salmon sandwich," he said.

It was nice to know he had a sense of humour. Regrettably we didn't enjoy the salmon. Heather sent it to be smoked, but when thawed out it was found to be unsuitable for smoking; because of the length of time it had been frozen it crumbled and had to be fed to the smoker's cats. I suppose it was a just outcome, all things considered.

Marchwood Military Port on Southampton Water was still part of 2 Transport Group and was the home port for our LSLs. High up on their list of tasks was the replenishment of ammunition for the UK's land and air contribution to NATO. Standardisation of weapons and equipment, much talked about over the years, had not progressed very far and the armies of most of the NATO nations still operated some weapons or weapon systems that needed replenishment from their homelands. The UK was no exception.

But the Port was showing signs of age; it had been developed piecemeal from its origin as one of the sites for sections of the Mulberry Harbour used to support the invasion forces on the Normandy beaches in the Second World War – a facelift was long overdue. It became evident that without renovation it might fall foul of the new regulations for health and safety at work and we simply could not afford to countenance the loss of a secure line of communication (L of C) to the Continent for our ammunition. The key word was 'secure'. With the country in the grip of the union barons and the Labour government seemingly unable to resist their demands, a request for the twenty five million pounds needed to bring the port up-to-date was going to be difficult to navigate through the necessary layers of bureaucracy, although it was not hard to justify.

I did a complete review and rewrite of the modernisation proposals for the Port that had been mooted and rejected for some years. The resulting paper was approved by the QMG, and I was then sent in to bat to get the money. The L of C was already as secure as we could make it. Although much of the ammunition was moved from the ordnance depots to the port by rail, we had sufficient military manned vehicles to dispense with rail movement in an emergency.

On arrival at the port the ammunition was handled by soldier stevedores. It was then transported by our own ships to the military depots in Belgium. So the unions were not involved and didn't need to be consulted. No civilian jobs were at stake in the proposed modernisation of the port. The problem was to extract the money from a government perennially strapped for funds. It took two years. Between overseas visits and other enterprises the Marchwood bid for funds lasted for the majority of my tour as D Mov. It circulated around the Ministry, was rejected, resurrected and finally reached the desk of the Permanent Secretary, Sir Frank Cooper, a wartime RAF pilot and a wholly admirable man who could be relied on to be sympathetic to the main argument of the need for a 'secure L of C'.

It was decided that I was to accompany the Permanent Secretary to make the case for the money to the Secretary of State for Defence. The choice of Fred Mulley as the political supremo at the MOD was a happy one. Unfortunately he had been pilloried by the press for dozing at a Royal Air Force demonstration on a hot day, a variation on something we have all done occasionally when seated at a lecture or presentation, but Mr Mulley had the cameras on him at the time and he was not allowed to forget his lapse.

A pity, for he had been a soldiers' soldier. Volunteering in the early stages of the Second World War, he had served in the ranks and been captured in North West Europe in 1940. He had then spent five years in a prison camp, obtaining a degree in economics and qualifying as a chartered secretary while a prisoner of war. When he emerged from the camp in 1945 and had gone up to Oxford as an adult student, he took first class honours in PPE, after which he became a barrister and had then succumbed to an interest in politics. It pays to know your man and I had researched his impressive background before making my presentation. I found him to be a quietly spoken and modestly charming person, but he gave nothing away. I was thanked politely and left. As I went out of the door I heard the Permanent Secretary say quietly, "They're right, you know. We can't afford to let this go and it isn't a lot of money."

The result was success – to be exploited instantly before minds were changed. A project officer was appointed and told to pursue the renovation of the port relentlessly.

Four years after I had left the Army and become a businessman, I was invited to the 'vesting' of the now updated port, with new and elongated jetties, warehouses and handling equipment. Chatting to the CO, we were approached by a uniformed major who was vaguely familiar but I couldn't for the life of me remember where I had seen him before. He turned to me, saluted smartly and said:

"Five years ago, General, you told me to go away and eat, sleep and live the upgrading of Marchwood until it was completed, then to report to you that the job was done. I'm doing this now." It was the project officer. I was happy to buy him a drink. Marchwood Military Port has repaid the money spent on it many times since then. It was used in the build up to the Falklands War, extensively used before and during the Gulf War and continues to support our military commitments worldwide. We should all be thankful that both the Secretary of State and the Permanent Secretary at the MOD when the key decisions were made, whatever their personal politics, were first and foremost patriots.

Six months into my stint as D Mov (Army) I realised that I had never been more gainfully employed. It was a very active job. So much so that I had to find a pad in London because unplanned 'events', most of which affected Movements, almost always happened at about four p.m. and usually on a Thursday or Friday which meant an overnight stay in the capital.

There was a Deputy Secretary, a very agreeable fellow. He was at the end of my financier's dotted line and was in effect his last court of appeal against any dodgy financial decisions I might make. Deputy Secretary is a high rank in the civil service and my friend had been a wartime soldier who had lost an arm, I think at Monte Cassino. He dropped in to see me occasionally, usually in the evening when over a drink in my office we mapped out a line on anything complex involving finance. One evening, after a good moan from me about the expense of finding somewhere in London to stay overnight when it was too late to get down to Hampshire, he said, "But haven't you applied to be put on the Lodging List?"

"Fat chance," I replied. "Isn't that a civil service closed shop?"

"Well yes, mainly," he said. "It was designed for those of us who regularly get caught in London overnight. But it can be applied in exceptional circumstances to Service people in Whitehall who have to work unsocial hours and in this job you must be a prime contender. Put up a case through me and I'll do my best for you."

This would be a great bit of luck if it came off. The Lodging List offered a very generous and untaxed allowance to civil servants and, I think, MPs who lived out in the country but found that they had to stay in London regularly because of unexpected emergencies. I knew of no service officers who had managed to get on to it but I later found out that there were several. Access to the List, however, was jealously guarded and I had not thought that I had a chance. To my surprise, my application went through without comment. Ken Morris, A retired officer of my Corps, was the General Manager of the Dolphin Square complex at the time; he was kind enough to offer me a small apartment that had recently become vacant. The rent being well within my untaxed allowance, I took it, buying the carpets, curtains and sundry other household items from the previous tenant at the same time.

Gone were the heady days of command when a staff car with driver was provided. Travel 'from residence to place of duty' at MOD was on foot or by public transport. This was no hardship in London, where public transport is always available if not always on time. Also, when there was no 'flap' on, Whitehall is quite slow to get going in the mornings. Senior people in most departments of state arrive at their desks something after nine a.m. This is held, not always in jest, to be a hangover from the days when the start of the day's business was based on the time it took for the horses to gallop from the first morning Channel packet at Dover with the continental mail!

A small part of my job was to oversee the MOD staff car pool, a task performed in detail by my surface movement branch. I had to spend a disproportionate amount of time explaining to senior officers fresh from command appointments that they were simply no longer important enough to warrant a dedicated staff car. I told particular friends that it was good for the soul and doubtless designed to make sure that we didn't 'get above ourselves' in Whitehall's only military Department of State.

The car pool was equipped mainly with Rovers – the late and lamented comfortable model that allowed you to wear a peaked cap in the back. But we also had four Daimlers for VIP visitors and one Rolls for special occasions. Shortly after Mrs Thatcher became Prime Minister I had a call from one of her advisers in the Cabinet Office. I don't remember who he was, but he scored fifteen out of ten for pomposity.

"The Prime Minister saw a civilian woman leaving the Ministry of Defence in a Daimler car this afternoon. She requires to know who it was and on whose authority this lady was occupying a Government vehicle (the driver was in uniform). The Prime Minister requires an answer by close of business today." The phone was replaced without giving me a chance to reply.

Action this day! Very Churchillian. At that time Colonel Alan Gidley was head of surface movements and had a ready answer. The lady was the wife of a visiting senior NATO Commander and thus entitled to a top grade car under the rules laid down by Government. She had been returning from an official function with her husband and had dropped him at the Ministry before returning to their hotel. It didn't help on these occasions that the Richmond Terrace end of the MOD is almost directly opposite the entrance to Downing Street and the Prime Minister's minions seemed to watch our comings and goings like hawks, alert to any transgressions of 'The Rules for the Control and Use of MOD Transport', our car pool bible.

Dolphin Square was a twenty minute stroll from Whitehall or a ten minute ride on the number twenty-four bus in bad weather. The small London pad proved to be a boon to Heather and me. Our two older girls, now free of school, lived in London and Heather was able to see much more of them than she would otherwise have been able to. The two younger girls, Kate and Lucy, were still at day school in Winchester, but we had close friends they could stay with overnight when we were both in London. Also the regular medical checkups that Heather had to undergo at the Millbank military hospital were made much easier with a local 'pad' to stage at.

The London pad also allowed me to honour an outstanding commitment; just as well because I had made it to my MOD immediate boss, the QMG, Pat Howard Dobson, when he had been the Military Secretary. In my plea to him to be allowed to go on the RCDS tour, I had said that I planned to write a review of the Australian defence scene and during the tour I had made masses of notes to that end. It was completed in the Dolphin Square flat in the form of an article and submitted for publication to the Royal United Services Institute Journal. I called it 'Dilemma Down Under'. It was accepted, published and I was paid for it. I mention it because there was a follow-up. I keep the copyrights of my scribblings whenever I can and not long after the RUSI Journal bearing my article was published, I had a letter from the publisher of the Australian United Services Institute Journal asking permission for it to be republished 'down under'. Naturally I agreed and I asked him to send any honorarium to the RSL at Alice Springs to have a drink on the travelling Poms of the 1975 RCDS Course in gratitude for their lavish hospitality when we had visited them there. The result was a copy of the edition that contained my article and a note to say he had done what I had asked in the matter of payment.

It was not long before another movements crisis loomed, this time in the Far East. There were two unrelated problems, one concerned with surface movement and one with air – to be specific, the Gurkha Airlift. It had long been the task of the RAF to move Gurkha units and leave parties by VC 10 aircraft from Khatmandu to and from Hong Kong where we maintained a substantial Gurkha force. By 1976, however, it became clear that the Nepalese authorities had decided that the Royal Nepalese Aircraft Corporation (RNAC) was ready to undertake the task under contract to the British Government.

The RAF wanted to keep the Gurkha commitment and our Government was not keen to be saddled with a financial outlay that was seen to be unnecessary since we already had the means to do the job 'in house'. There was much diplomatic activity with long messages flying back and forth between our Ambassador to Nepal and the Nepalese specialists at the Foreign Office. But to no avail. The King of Nepal was determined to take over the Gurkha Airlift and operate it with his own aircraft.

Alongside this was the fact that we were losing an enormous quantity of stores consigned by sea to Nepal through the Port of Calcutta. This was surprising because the World Bank had recently advanced a great deal of money to India to build a state of the art container port on the Hooghly River to the south of Calcutta. This was said to be completed but we were still shipping goods on a 'break bulk' basis to Calcutta and beyond by sea. Break bulk is the term used by freight forwarders for goods not shipped in containers. Compared to containerised traffic it is obviously insecure.

There is no substitute for the Mark One Eyeball and once again I had to go and have a look. On this occasion I was additionally charged with the pre-contract negotiations with the RNAC over the knotty problem of the Gurkha Airlift.

I left London well before the onset of the autumn monsoon. I was to spend two days with the Defence Attache in Delhi to be briefed on the up-to-date situation in India. It became clear that they knew I had lived in India during the last days of the Raj and I had to be brainwashed to ensure that I didn't bruise any delicate sensibilities during my dealings with the Indian authorities. It wasn't really necessary. I had always liked Asians and had got on well with them, but it was good to renew acquaintance with Delhi. I had visited the city briefly while stationed in Calcutta in the nineteen forties and from what I could see it hadn't changed much. Most of the rickshaw wallahs were now riding trishaws – three wheeled bicycles fitted with a rickshaw type passenger compartment – and the streets were filled with hordes of Morris Oxfords – or Ambassadors as they were known in India, the Morris Oxford moulds having been sold to India some years previously. But the Red Fort still dominated the city and the old and beautiful British colonial buildings were still standing and being used by the country's administrators.

I met our local representative, Colonel Jim Boyles of the RCT, stationed with his family in Hong Kong but responsible for Army movements throughout our Far East commitment. As soon as we could get away we made for Calcutta by Indian Airways. We flew in a Caravelle; one of the fleet that the Indians had bought from the French when they had finished with them. It was still an impressive performer with a particularly steep rate of climb after take-off. As is the custom in India, there was plenty of livestock accompanying the passengers, but I was pleased to see that the aviation authorities had banned the use of those small paraffin stoves that you see on the trains in India. We were treated to a series of curry flavoured small eats during the journey by pretty, sari-clad young air hostesses. It was all quite euphoric.

We landed at Dum Dum, transformed from the US Army Graves Commission airstrip of my youth to a large international airport fully endowed with the bedlam inseparable from any transport terminal in any large city in India. We were met by a representative of the firm of James Warren, our agents in Calcutta and driven to our hotel, the Oberoi Grand in Chowringee, Calcutta's main thoroughfare. It was clean and comfortable and had survived the years almost unchanged from when I had known it thirty years earlier as the principal watering hole for officers on leave from almost anywhere in India and Burma.

A session with the British Consul was on the cards for next morning, after which we would be taken over by our agents to discuss our freight losses. Meanwhile, having lived in India, I made an elementary mistake for which I deserved no sympathy. My room servant was an upright old man who had been a soldier and I conversed with him in my fractured Urdu interspersed with mime. We seemed to get on well. He left me a chagal (earthenware jar) of cool water to drink and I assumed, stupidly, that in a five star hotel it would have been boiled as indeed it should have been. So I didn't bother to use my stock of water purification tablets and took a deep draught. Jim and I had a pleasant dinner and comfortably tired, I returned to my room and fell asleep.

In the middle of the night I woke up writhing in agony, only alleviated by a session in the loo followed by a couple of hours vomiting after which I passed out. Next morning, still out, I was shaken awake by the old bearer and weak as a kitten, I managed to shave and dress for the visit to the Consul.

The visit was unfruitful; I was unable to concentrate and after a while I had to excuse myself and return to the hotel where an Indian doctor gave me some 'cement mixture' that seemed to work. I was convinced that I had a mild attack of cholera, made less serious than it would otherwise have been by the cholera jab I had had before leaving home. But perhaps it was a particularly vicious attack of 'Calcutta Belly', although uncommonly long lasting.

Next day I had recovered sufficiently to meet the local director of our agents, Messrs James Warren. He was introduced as Mr Smith, a European. He was a pleasant fellow and told me he had spent many years in India – "since the war, actually." A few sentences later he said "Haven't we met before?"

And I said, "Malcolm Smith. Of course!" We had both been

commissioned at Bangalore in 1946. This was a plus. Our overseas agents were important to us and to be able to establish personal contact was a considerable advantage over an impersonal relationship. Malcolm Smith had taken a job as a junior with James Warren shortly after he left the Service and had stayed with them for thirty years reaching the top of their tree in India. There wasn't much he didn't know about freight movement on the subcontinent. We lunched at the Bengal Club, altered from the forties only in that it had installed air conditioning in the dining room. The sepia photographs and etchings dating from the early days of the Raj were still there and most of the public rooms were still cooled by the old slow moving 'punkah' fans. Sadly I was in no fit state to assault my stomach with one of its world famous curries but Jim Boyles tucked in handsomely.

I brought up the subject of theft from our break bulk cargoes, to be met with a shrug of the shoulders from Malcolm. "The port authorities do their best and we have watchmen, but as you know, a roll of roofing felt or a sheet of corrugated iron is a very valuable item here and all we can do is keep the rate of theft as low as possible."

On the question of containers he would only say, "Tomorrow morning we visit the container port down the river and you'll see for yourself."

Later on that day I took a short walk across the Maidan (equating to a common) in the centre of the city to the old Fort William – in 1946 the home of the East Lancashires with whom we were brigaded. Entry was barred, however, because it was still a military post so I changed tack and walked to the Victoria Memorial. This monument had remained untouched from colonial days, evidence if any were needed of the goodwill and good sense of the Indian population.

As usual, I was followed by a horde of small boys chanting "Backsheesh sahib." A handful of annas – a coin worth a fraction of a penny – scattered them and a demonstration of empty pockets together with a burst of soldiers' Urdu for 'go away' persuaded them that they were wasting their time so with flashing grins they vanished. At no time did I feel in the least threatened; the life of the city went on around me and apart from the attentions of an occasional mendicant I could have been an ordinary inhabitant.

The visit to the container port was an eye opener. We drove about ten miles southwards to the Hooghly ferry where we boarded a hired launch to cross the river to the site of the new port. From a distance it looked good. The new container cranes had been installed and reared impressively over the site. Entering the dock between the concrete caissons, however, it was evident that there was no traffic and one of the cranes had toppled into the water Even so, the port should have been usable with one crane out of action.

I asked Malcolm what had gone wrong.

"You may well ask," he said gloomily. "In their haste to get the money and build the port, nobody thought about road access. We've recently had the monsoon and the only access road capable of taking commercial traffic, of laterite, as country roads are here, has been washed away. There's talk of restoring it but it's doubtful if there'll be enough money to make it all weather, so we're stuck with break bulk traffic and a high degree of theft until they can get their act together."

Next morning we flew from Dum Dum to a small airfield close to the Nepalese border and from there embarked on a bumpy journey along unmade roads in a landrover driven by a cheerful Gurkha soldier to the Gurkha Depot at Dharan. The Depot, commanded by a British brigadier and bigger than its now defunct sister establishment I had known at Sungei Patani in Malaya, trained recruits for the Brigade of Gurkhas and also provided its central administration. In the same location there was a British military hospital, necessary for the medical examination of recruits since tuberculosis, conquered in the developed world, was still rife in mountainous Nepal: the hospital also acted as a useful medical centre for the local population – local was anywhere within walking distance, fifty miles being no distance for a Nepalese, whether ill or not.

The Depot commander and his wife kindly entertained Jim Boyles and me to dinner on the first evening. I was still in the delicate stage and left most of my meal, a fact not lost on another guest, the CO of the hospital who said in an aside:

"Come and see me in the morning." I told him what had happened and he said, "Shame on you. An old India hand should have known better. But we'll fix you up."

And fix me up he did. I don't know what he gave me but it did the trick and from then on I regained my appetite and full awareness of what was going on around me. Just as well because the tricky part of the tour was coming up.

We spent a day at the Depot – long enough to assure the brigadier that the RAF would not abandon the airlift until the authorities were satisfied that the RNAC could safely take it over, then we departed for Khatmandhu, the capital city of Nepal and the seat of its administration. I was to stay with the Ambassador, Mr Scott, who, with his charming American wife, was very hospitable. I would have had to negotiate with Mr Rana, the Chairman of RNAC and a relative of the King. At that time the Rana family occupied most of the top positions in Nepalese commerce and the public services. The Ambassador was in no doubt that they were determined to collar the Gurkha Airlift contract; he thought it would be in our best interests to let them have it on the most favourable terms for us that we could negotiate. I explained that my brief was to find out precisely what they wanted and what they had to offer, then to return and report. If and when the decision in principle to let them have the contract was made, there would be a full scale negotiating team including aviation experts to take the matter forward on the spot.

My hosts were committed to social engagements on both evenings that I stayed with them. This is not in the least unusual in overseas diplomatic posts. During my movements travelling I occasionally stayed in 'embassy quarters' around the world. The incumbents just have to like social life; even the defence attachés find that most of their evenings are taken up with social events of one sort or another, and nearly always with the same people attending – mainly from other embassies. It must be unutterably boring for them but they have to pretend to enjoy it. There's always the chance of hearing something commercially or diplomatically useful.

I excused myself and grasped the chance of walking round Khatmandhu. I was to see Mr Rana the following day and during my walk, in the late afternoon, my mind was so taken up with the airlift problem that I found to my great surprise that I was mixed up in a near riot – only this time on the wrong side. It was impossible to walk around Khatmandhu in the late nineteen seventies and not be aware of the hippy population from all over Western Europe and America. Something to do with the easy availability of drugs before they had spread throughout the western world. These people had become a pain in the neck to the Nepalese authorities and the police had become impatient with their antics.

Walking along a road near to the main temple in the heart of the city I was overtaken by something akin to a scene from Jurassic Park. In this case it was a large herd of colourfully dressed young people of European appearance who were obviously fleeing from someone or something. This turned out to be the police. One of the pursuing policemen fetched up alongside me and said something in rapid Gurkhali that I didn't understand but his attitude and his upraised baton said it all quite clearly. It is unwise to take issue with armed and angry Gurkhas. I replied in fractured Urdu that I was a visiting British officer on the way to visit the nearby temple and realising that I was a bit old and obviously too 'square' to pass as a hippy, he shouted something to his passing companions and they vanished into the distance.

The following morning saw one of those days that make Khatmandhu one of the most magical cities in the world. It dawned clear and bright with a semicircle of the snow covered Himalayan range glinting in the sunshine and seemingly not far away. You only realise how high they are when you have to look up to see the peaks. Conditions like these don't happen all the time. Khatmandhu all too often offers only limited visibility for days on end and visitors sometimes miss what they have come to see, but when the weather clears, the fabulous views emerge, the air is clear, cold and heady and the spirit is uplifted.

So morale was high when I went to see Mr Rana. I was received with great courtesy but I was left in no doubt that he was determined that his airline should take over the Gurkha Airlift from the RAF. I made it clear that I was there to scout the ground and asked what he had in mind. He said that the Royal Nepalese Aircraft Corporation (RNAC) should take over the flying task completely as well as the ground administration at the Nepal end, providing transit arrangements as well as the terminal, while the ground administration at the Hong Kong end could remain with the British Army. This was not good news. Our transit arrangements had been carefully put together in liaison with the Gurkha Depot and HQ Brigade of Gurkhas in Dharan and we reckoned that we had at last got it right. Much of the Gurkha Airlift centred around leave arrangements. Gurkhas serve without leave for longer than British troops but when they do go on leave they get a much longer spell. The reason is that when arriving back in Nepal, it often takes them days, weeks even, to get to their villages in remote areas of Nepal.

I explained this to Mr Rana and pointed out tactfully that divorcing the ground arrangements from the British Army movements organisation in Nepal would certainly cost him more than he could achieve by introducing alternatives into the contract costings. It was clear that he had no intention of adjusting his position although he promised to bear my remarks in mind.

Mr Rana then asked me if I was empowered to negotiate a contract. I replied that I could certainly hear what terms he envisaged and I would convey them to London, after which a full negotiating team would be assembled to discuss the issues, either in Khatmandhu or, if he so wished, in the United Kingdom. The meeting ended with expressions of goodwill but I felt that I hadn't accomplished a great deal. It had become clear that commercial interests dominated the minds of my hosts and that the issue would go no further until someone appeared who was able to talk contract terms in detail. I spent the rest of the morning at the airport with the RAF and Army movements staff before travelling on to Hong Kong in a VC10 freighter.

The pilot invited me to sit beside him for the approach and landing at Kai Tak airport late that afternoon. I had previously visited Hong Kong twice, but never before by air. As we flew low over the apartment buildings of Kowloon with the Chinese inhabitants hanging out their washing on the flat roofs a couple of hundred feet below us, I was alarmed to note that the side of the mountain ahead of us was getting very close. I looked sharply at the pilot who was calmly speaking into his radio mike and I was just about to grasp his arm and point out the mountain when the aircraft suddenly did a ninety degree turn to the right and the lone runway and bright landing lights of Kai Tak airport appeared right in front of us.

Because I was visiting the Far East as a joint service staff officer and not as head of my Corps, I didn't get heavily involved with regimental work in Hong Kong this time, although I was accommodated at Gun Club Barracks, home to the Gurkha Transport Regiment and I enjoyed the hospitality of their Mess. It was a short visit, mainly to brief the Commander British Forces on the state of play of the RNAC bid for the Airlift and to see the joint service movements staffs in the colony. A certain degree of gloom was evident when the news that RNAC would probably succeed in their bid was passed, but no one doubted their ability to fly the planes. It was mainly because the Hong Kong Gurkha establishment didn't relish the thought that transit arrangements might end up in the hands of RNAC, these having been fashioned over years of trial and error. It was alleviated somewhat when I assured them that the MOD would want to retain them and would seek a solution that kept them in our hands.

Before I left Hong Kong for home, I renewed acquaintance with Sam The Tailor in Nathan Road and had two high speed suits made. I had lost about fifteen pounds as a result of the Calcutta gastric episode and they fitted me perfectly. Alas, after a month at home I found that my lost weight had crept back again and the expansion margin in the suits having been taken up, they had to go to the Salvation Army. Sam made good suits and I hope whoever got them appreciated them for they were nearly new.

The Gurkha Airlift saga progressed for some time and the Nepalese wishes were satisfied so far as the movement of troops and freight was concerned. We kept tabs on the transit arrangements at both ends though, and of course as I write, the whole issue has passed into history.

Back home again it became obvious that some attention needed to be paid to the military rail network for which I was financially responsible. Rail movement expenditure was met by funds from the Movements Vote. Clearly we were spending too much money on demurrage. The OED defines this as 'stay, delay, hesitation, pause.' In our case it was a charge raised by British Rail for the detention of their railway trucks and it was costing us thousands of pounds on military sidings all over the country. Using the 'management mathematics' techniques learned years earlier, I discussed the books with my civil service financier, much to his surprise, I think, although I didn't tell him that my ability to do so rested almost entirely on cribbing from my mentor on the Henley course.

The Mark One Eyeball to the fore again. I toured the MOD sidings at several supply depots and found that a good deal of the money was being spent for the convenience of the railways, who were not collecting empty wagons when they were ready for collection. They were happy to leave them on the MOD's metals until it was convenient to collect them, at the same time raising a charge for 'denial of use'. Easy money! It had to stop and with a grin the railway moguls realised the game was up. It was a useful lesson to me for commercial life later. When a scam is rumbled in business, provided there are no sinister or illegal connotations, there is little breast beating or recrimination. You just bend your mind to stealing a march on the competition in another direction. Relations with our BR friends remained on an even keel.

During this welcome spell at home I was invited to several after hours farewell drinks sessions at the MOD. It probably isn't generally known that the offices of state in Whitehall possess quite a few historic rooms and places. The Ministry's Main Building in Whitehall for instance, is built on the site of an old royal palace that contained Henry VIIIth's wine cellar. This has been preserved and access to it is from the ground floor of the Ministry. It is available to MOD staff for functions and is a regular venue for farewell gatherings. You leave the stark, fluorescent corridors of the Ministry and go down ancient stone steps to a large space walled with obviously handmade Tudor period bricks set on lime mortar and supported by recognisably mediaeval stone arches. It offers a perfect 'atmosphere' for a party. It used to be open to the public by appointment for visiting as an ancient monument, but I imagine that the demands of security in recent years have made this less likely.

Equally impressive but in a different way was the War Ministers' office suite in the Old War Office, a step along Whitehall from the present MOD Main Building. In the late seventies this was reputed to have last been decorated to a design set out by Valerie Hobson, the actress wife of John Profumo, a War Minister during the early sixties. It was a perfect blend of pastels and set off by the classic Victorian furniture, the effect was quite stunning. You could stand there nursing a drink and admiring the decor while snatches of drinks party conversation drift by – "He's a right pain in the backside. If I could have found someone else to do his job, I'd have got rid of him long ago."

"Yes, of course I know what a divorce is, but what's a 'quickie' divorce?"

"It's what happens after your wife reads the map on a long continental road journey!"

Belize, an ex-British colony to the north of the central American isthmus, formerly British Honduras, had been having problems for some time with neighbouring Guatemala and feared invasion by its bigger and more powerful neighbour. It was agreed that a joint service force would be despatched to 'beef up' the local defences and counter the Guatemalan threat. An infantry battalion was sent to monitor the frontier with Guatemala and several Harrier fighter ground attack aircraft were sent to Belize Airport with an RAF Regiment element for close protection. Belize was also placed on the list of suitable jungle training areas; this ensured that the area would be used by British troops not actually stationed there, but often enough to give the Guatemalans pause for thought. Someone, God knows why, had sent several Stalwart armoured amphibious vehicles to Belize. These load carriers had been designed specifically for use in North West Europe to resupply armoured columns and keep pace with tanks travelling across country. I had had them in my regiment in Germany. They were totally unsuitable for use in tropical conditions so it was no surprise when they suffered from the heat and finally expired. Belize had spawned several seemingly intractable movement problems and at the request of the Commander British Forces there for a 'transport and movements specialist' to visit, I packed my bags and flew civil via Miami, there being no convenient VC10 flight.

There was an RCT movements officer at the Belize HQ; he signalled me with a reminder that I could travel through the States on a NATO travel order, obviating the need for a visa, otherwise necessary at that time. I had one prepared and arriving at Miami airport to stage overnight before moving on to Belize next day, I presented myself at the immigration desk and offered my passport together with the NATO travel order. The immigration officer looked at it and said, "Natto. What the hell's Natto?"

I had come face to face with the inability of a certain type of American to understand or have the slightest interest in anything that went on outside his own country. Unusual in an immigration official but I later came to realise that these individuals are common to all walks of life in the US. I explained as best I could in a short time with a queue of people waiting impatiently to get through immigration but he cut me short.

"You, sir, are a very lucky man. This beautiful young lady will escort you to a place where we will be able to sort this out for you."

The young lady, wordless and possibly beautiful to the extremely shortsighted, duly escorted me to a caged compound, ushered me through the wire gate, then swiftly locked it and departed. I looked round. The other occupants were a small group of disconsolate looking men of Central American appearance. I stared through the wire on to the busy concourse feeling like Guy the Gorilla on show at London Zoo.

Eventually two men wearing identity tags and looking quite important passed nearby and I hailed them. They came over to me and I explained the situation.

"You're telling us you are a British general passing through on an authorised NATO travel order and the immigration officer didn't know what NATO means?" They looked at each other.

"Yes I am. Also he took my passport and travel order and I haven't seen them since. But just let me phone the British Embassy in Washington and then we'll let events take their course," I said.

"No need for that sir," said one hurriedly. "I'll deal with this right away," and the evidently more senior official went away, leaving me chatting with his companion who was an anglophile, knew London well and apologised profusely on behalf of the airport authority.

His companion returned with my travel order and my passport stamped, also apologising profusely. This, he said, is not how we normally treat our allies but the immigration organisation is 'something else' and he shook his head and shrugged. Their evident goodwill had banished any feelings of grievance; I was no stranger to untouchable bureaucracy, so I let it go. They did, however, provide me with transport to a good airport hotel.

Next morning I reported with my bags to the airport.

"I'm booked to Belize with Silver Star Airways," I said.

The official looked at my ticket, smiled, raised an eyebrow and lifted the flap of his counter. "Come this way please."

I followed him to a door behind the reception desk on to the tarmac where stood a small, twin-engined, propellor driven aeroplane bearing the legend Silver Star on the side of its fuselage. I climbed the steps to be met by our air hostess, a pleasant and smiling young lady. The aircraft was long and narrow and carried about twenty passengers. The pilot was visible in his leather flying jacket through the open cockpit door. It reminded me of those Biggles-type journeys to the Channel Islands years before.

Settled in a seat, I had a glass of champagne thrust into my hand and as soon as the baggage had been loaded we were off without formality, although I can recall our little craft being in a queue for take-off with a jumbo jet in front and several behind. The pilot was a young man, reassuringly serious.

We crossed a good deal of sea. Cuba became visible below us to the south and I think we landed once on the Yucatan Peninsular of Mexico to refuel and discharge a couple of passengers, but since the ambition of our hostess seemed to be to get us all smashed on quite bibbable champagne, an enterprise enthusiastically supported by her mostly male charges, most were beyond caring when we eventually reached Belize 'International Airport' – a small building with its roof steaming gently from the tropical rain as it dried in the emerging sun. Angus, Colonel commanding British Troops and a fellow DS from staff college days, was there to meet me.

"I see," he said, "that you travelled by White Knuckle Airways. Thank you for coming, nice to see you and we're putting you up with us at Flagstaff House."

"Sounds pretty grand," I said. Angus gave a short laugh. "Wait till you see it before passing judgement."

On the way to his house we passed the weapon pits manned by the RAF Regiment on either side of the single runway. The Harriers were under their monsoon covers at one end. The climate was hot and sticky, reminiscent of Malaya, with similar jungle type foliage stretching down to the wire fence around the airport.

Flagstaff House turned out to be a smallish married quarter standing in its own compound. It had a corrugated tin roof like most of the buildings I had seen on my way there. A union flag on a long pole in the garden gave respectability to its name. Angus's wife met us at the door and we gossiped into the night. I slept the sleep of the very tired, not even stirring to the noise of the monsoon rain on the tin roof that was such a feature of the place.

There was no hope for the Stalwart vehicles. The engines were totally unsuited to the climate and operating conditions. They needed a complete overhaul and arrangements were made to ship them back to UK.

A visit to our shipping agent in Belize City was on the agenda. The City, a few miles from the airport, was pure Graham Greene. Deep storm drains lined both sides of the main street and I was even hailed by a European drunk in a soiled white suit; he just had to be a 'remittance man', one of those sad characters regularly featured in the reading material of my youth. The locals were extremely friendly and it was evident that the support we were giving them in their quarrel with their bellicose neighbour was much appreciated.

I had asked to visit the RCT landing craft detachment that moved the supplies and ammunition from the coastal town of Punta Gorda to the Gurkha battalion at that time protecting the southern border of Belize with Guatemala. I could make the trip inland by river to the Gurkha regimental HQ. The journey to Punta Gorda entailed a helicopter trip of about two hundred miles and Angus made one available to me, piloted by a pleasant young Army Air Corps officer.

We left the helipad in the cool of the early morning. The pilot asked if I had ever seen a Caribbean Cay, an offshore coral island.

"No," I said. "But I'd like to if it isn't too far out of our way." He said we'd have to fly down the coast anyway and the cays were only a few miles offshore.

Along the coast perhaps forty miles south of Belize City an astonishing sight appeared below us. The dense jungle had been quite literally knocked flat across a strip about five miles wide. It was as though a giant steamroller had rolled over it. Immense trees, secondary growth of all types, everything was as flat as a pancake. The margins of the strip were unaffected; the jungle grew up to its ruler straight edge as though nothing had happened. I didn't see any habitation.

"Oh that," said the pilot. "A common sight here. You get these mini hurricanes that race across, knocking down everything in their path. Hard luck if your house is in the way, I suppose, but you can't legislate against freaks of nature."

We made a short detour seawards and he said:

"Keep an eye out for pelicans on your side," as a large flock took to the air just in front of us.

We landed on a genuine Caribbean island. Sand, pellucid sea and waving palms just as featured in the tourist brochures and all made more attractive by the cool trade winds. There were few off duty attractions for the soldiers and airmen in Belize and the pilot told me that the sappers had set to and organised a primitive 'leave centre' on one of the more northern cays, using assault boats for sea bathing and fishing. This one and those in sight from it seemed devoid of life except for pelicans and land crabs.

My visit to Punta Gorda had been arranged to coincide with a supply run to the up-country battalion and I was made welcome by the RCT detachment commander who was also one of the landing craft skippers. We embarked on his craft, a Ramp Powered Lighter (RPL), a powerful little day vessel without much accommodation but hardy, reliable, and a very practical load carrier, particularly useful in places where roads were at a premium.

The jungle hemmed us in closely on either side as the slow flowing and opaque river twisted and turned into the interior. There were few difficult shoals or other hazards to speak of, which was just as well, since navigation appeared to be largely a matter of empirical judgement. A close watch was kept on the encroaching jungle, however; for one of the problems faced by the Belizean population had been the incursion of well-armed Guatemalan bandits into their territory.

Access to the resident infantry battalion was by air or river craft; there were no useable roads to their location and had my Corps not been providing a maritime detachment, I would have landed at their helipad in the jungle. I was met by the Gurkha battalion CO and his Gurkha Major – or RSM. The CO had no complaints about the efficiency of the supply arrangements but confessed that he was grateful for visits from senior people as they felt that they were 'a bit on the fringe' as he put it. I was invited to have a look at Guatemala from a forward observation post and trekked into the jungle with an escorting subaltern to an escarpment overlooking a Guatemalan military post on the border.

We crawled the last few yards into a 'hide' manned by two Gurkha soldiers and gazed down on a neat little complex of huts and laterite tracks carved out of the jungle below us. I was told that we were only a couple of miles from a small Guatemalan border town and this was its military detachment.

"There are two platoons," said my escort. "It could be our army. On Saturday nights the off duty men go into town and come back about midnight the worse for wear. There are quarrels, drunken laughter, songs and sometimes fights. On Sunday you see the Padre all in black and doing his best to round up sinners for a church service followed by COs orderly room parade on Monday with the culpable sinners being marched in and out."

"Do they know we're here?"

"Oh yes. They know we're around, but I don't think they've sussed out this particular OP yet. Our people are well used to covert jungle surveillance as you will know from your Malayan days."

"Full marks for research," I said. He smiled.

"The CO likes to know a bit about our visitors." We returned to battalion HQ for an excellent Gurkha curry in their field mess.

Next day at Belize City, Angus had laid on a drinks party at his house to be attended by some of the local dignitaries. I met the Premier, Mr Price, an experienced and long serving politician who had steered Belize through many pitfalls towards the independence that it shortly afterwards achieved. He was a jovial and interesting conversationalist; love of his small country shone out of him and it is nice to note as I write, twenty-five years later, that both Mr Price and his country are still thriving. I also met the senior RAF officer, Belize and asked him how the RAF Regiment men manning the weapon pits at the airfield avoided being bored out of their skulls with nothing to do but prepare for a virtually non-existent threat. It was improbable bordering on the impossible that the Guatemalan air force would tangle with the Rapier ground to air missiles guarding the airport, let alone the waiting Harriers that far outclassed anything the Guatemalans could put up against them.

He agreed with this, but said:

"In these situations agile minds find things to do. For instance, when the VC10 flights come in from UK they're met by a reception committee as they land and a departure party when they take off. The lads study the landings and take-offs and the pilot who's landed well gets a row of airmen standing on the top of their weapons pits holding up cards forming the word MAGIC!"

"What if he's landed badly?" I asked.

"Well, then he gets cards forming, you've guessed it – CRAP! Of course it doesn't stop there. Someone is running a book. I've yet to find the bookie, but in the interests of morale, I'm not looking very hard."

Leaving Belize next day by VC10, I was interested to note that the pilot's spirits must have been buoyed by a MAGIC as he landed on the inward flight from UK. It was supposed to be a direct flight home but there was a technical hitch and we landed in Bermuda at about seven p.m. The few families returning home would have liked an overnight stay, but as Belize for most was an unaccompanied posting, the majority were pleased that we were confined to the airport while the small technical irregularity was sorted out by the airport ground staff and we re–embarked after a couple of hours' delay.

Shortly after I returned to London, Major General Sam Cockerham, the US Army's Director of Movements, made a liaison visit to MOD. Sam was a cheerful character; he was travelling with his wife, Alice. It became my task to look after him during his visit to us and Heather and I entertained them both at our house near Winchester. Heather looked after Alice and I arranged an official tour programme for Sam that he seemed to enjoy and professed himself grateful. The US Army's movements set-up mirrored ours although theirs was a vastly bigger organisation. Their D Mov appointment, located like ours, close to their seat of government in Washington's Pentagon, was 'tied' to the US Army Transportation Corps, the US equivalent to the RCT. Before he left, Sam said he would like to arrange a return match to show me some of their installations. I made suitably polite noises, not expecting anything to come of it, but we had both liked the Cockerhams and had enjoyed their company.

The Quartermaster General, meanwhile, was visiting installations and units in the Far East. We had arranged a comprehensive programme for him. On his return he reported to our weekly Q Directors' meeting that his tour had been successful, but when the meeting ended he asked me to stay behind. He fixed me with an expressionless eye and said, "I didn't enjoy my visit to Moscow!" I smiled, wondering what he meant, and suspecting a joke.

"No," he said. "It wasn't funny. Having finished our meeting with the Defence Attaché at the High Commision in Delhi, Roger (his military assistant, a young major) and I were routed to London by Air India. It wasn't until we were airborne that our flight time to Moscow was announced by the pilot. Obviously when we landed I couldn't leave the aircraft and we both spent an uncomfortable hour being sprayed with insecticide and watching the babushkas cleaning up the passenger compartments. Find out what went wrong!"

This was a serious business. The QMG was a member of the Army Board and privy to many of NATO's great secrets. The Cold War was still very much in session and the presence in the Russian capital uninvited of a British Army general could have been a severe embarrassment to our government. I checked the QMG's itinerary.

Sure enough he had been routed British Airways to London from Delhi. Something had gone very wrong. Air Commodore John Stevenson, Director of Movements RAF and my air force opposite number, agreed to investigate. Our movements detachments around the world were manned on a joint service basis and the one in Delhi had a flight sergeant RAF as its detachment commander.

Signals flashed back and forth and the mystery was unravelled. Mrs Gandhi, the Indian Prime Minister at the time, had suddenly needed to fly to London for an urgent meeting. The BA flight was first away but all first class seats were booked. It was unthinkable to send the PM business or tourist so the British movements detachment was approached and asked if they would swap the two BA seats booked for the QMG for two seats on a later Air India flight. The flight sergeant had agreed and explained the situation to the QMG's assistant, but neither knew that the Air India flight stopped in Moscow. Everyone knew that India at that time was friendly to Russia, but it didn't occur to anyone that Air India flights to London might make a Moscow stop. An understandable cock-up but worthy of a cautionary signal to our detachments round the world.

Things were now moving on the domestic front. Helen, our eldest girl, announced her engagement to a young land agent. We heartily approved – not that it made all that much difference whether you did or not in the seventies, but Mark played it by the book and asked for my approval. It was a bonus that he was and is a keen sailor and an accomplished navigator on the cross channel passages we have made together since.

Wendy, our second daughter, was also getting serious with Fergus, who was the assistant to Michael Croft, founder and prime mover of the National Youth Theatre. Fergus, having given up his original ambition to be an actor, had gone into theatre administration and conducted the auditions for the NYT. This resulted in our house at weekends being thronged with young aspiring actors, mainly men but now and then a young woman was included, for lunch and free beer. I solved the problem of looming bankruptcy by buying a 'pin', or small barrel, of beer whenever an invasion threatened. Placed on the seat of the outside loo, the young were invited to help themselves on the understanding that when the barrel was empty it was time to go home. The system worked well and I can recommend it. Some of these young people have since become familiar faces on our television screens and Wendy and Fergus, now long married, keep their friendship.

I was enjoying a welcome rest from the travelling that was part of my job when I received a letter from General Sam Cockerham inviting me to visit the US, tour their movements installations and then visit the Pentagon for a few days while staying in Washington as his house guest. Heather was included in the invitation if she could manage it. It was very kind of Sam and Alice and obviously a return match for when we had looked after them during Sam's liaison visit to the UK. I would have liked to see the US Army air and sea movements set-up, but we were then in the period when the union barons were doing their best to bleed the country dry without heed to the consequences. The financial hatches were so firmly battened down in Whitehall during the latter part of the seventies that I doubted if a visit without any concrete return would be sanctioned.

And so it proved. In all conscience I couldn't offer any reason beyond 'liaison and goodwill' for an official visit to the States and the invitation was firmly rejected by our financial overlords. Rather than explain lamely to Sam by letter that official parsimony dictated my rejection of his kind invitation, I explained by phone that 'temporary budgetary restrictions' had caused it to be turned down. "Don't worry. We'll keep at it," he said. I took this to be the end of the matter.

I was not particularly distressed. Globetrotting was a necessary part of my job and by that time, although I had enjoyed my tour as D.Mov, I had become sated with the constant travel. My contemporaries, envious of my travel opportunities, thought I had a 'Bobby's job' as they used to say in the north, and it had been good to get away from Whitehall from time to time. But it wasn't all plain sailing. Movements, by the nature of its operations, and no matter how efficiently the function is carried out, attracts a fair degree of criticism, complaints often being saved up to lay before a visiting director. These had to be dealt with, sometimes on the spot by signal, more often by notes and a report on return.

And except at weekends when travelling there was rarely any time to be spent enjoying the delights of a tourist. Without a wife to return to in the evening or the companionship of a unit mess to enjoy, it could be a lonely existence, usually in anonymous hotels for one or two nights before moving on. It's tough when your washing gets dirty and you haven't time to take advantage of the hotel laundry services. I was coming to the end of my tour of duty and I would be happy to hand over to someone else. But what the hell! In the Service you'd go mad if you didn't play the hand you'd been dealt and anyway the good times had massively eclipsed the bad in the D Mov job despite the constant crises brought on by 'events'.

Assuming that the invitation to the US would remain firmly on the back burner I had reckoned without Sam's tenacity. Shortly after I had had to decline his invitation, the MOD was sent a memo from the Foreign Office stating that the British Embassy in Washington had received a request from the Joint Chiefs of Staff via the State Department for the British Army Director of Movements to visit Washington for 'discussions and research' with his US counterpart. Apparently there was no question of turning it down. I was told that I had to go. Sam Cockerham, like me, sat at high table when the chiefs of staff met, but his contacts were obviously more powerful than mine. During his tour of our installations Sam had visited our military port at Marchwood and had said that he would like me to see the US Army facilities at Oakland on San Francisco Bay, so I suggested that I should combine the trip to the States with a visit to Vancouver to meet our agent there and check on the new supply arrangements for our training area in Canada, then entering the US on the west coast. This gave respectability to the trip and kept the top moneymen reasonably happy, certainly at bay.

Sam readily agreed to map out an itinerary along those lines and I renewed acqaintance with the US immigration service after a second visit to Vancouver. This time there was no problem with my NATO travel order; perhaps the service nationwide had been briefed on its validity. At any rate they were quite content to pass me through without fuss at San Francisco airport where a familiar face greeted me. A few months earlier Heather and I had been the guests of a US Army transportation brigade at Heidelburg in Germany where I had lectured their officers on British Army logistics and we had both enjoyed their hospitality at a formal guest night. The young officer who had acted as a temporary ADC on that occasion was now serving in San Francisco and had been assigned to look after me there.

I hadn't visited the city before and having arrived on a Friday night I was pleased to see 'at leisure' marked on my programme for the whole of the weekend. The brigade commander, a 'one star general', or brigadier to us, had sent his apologies but his weekend had long been tied up and I would see him on Monday. Meanwhile anything I wanted or needed would be provided by my young friend.

"Relax," I said, seeing his anxious expression as I read the brigadier's note. "You can spend the weekend with your family. I'm more than happy to look after myself for a couple of days. It's a rare opportunity on these occasions to see some of the sights. I need a haircut; I want to see Alcatraz, ride a cable car, visit Grant Avenue and Chinatown and of course look at the Golden Gate Bridge."

"Sir," he said. "There are two bridges, but you'll want to see what we call the Harbour Bridge. Golden Gate's an old-fashioned Hollywood expression. You must say Harbour Bridge if you travel by cab or they could take you to the Bay Bridge which is further and a better fare." Lesson one in a weekend of lessons.

I had struck lucky with accommodation. For once I was in an officers' mess rather than a hotel. And what a superb location. I had been allotted the guest room of the bachelor officers' quarters (BOQ) at Fort Mason, a small garrison perched on a high point overlooking the Harbour. From my window Alcatraz stuck out like a forbidding boil on the sweep of that splendid bay. It had long been abandoned as a prison and now gave good service to the City as a tourist attraction. To the left, the Harbour Bridge reared up magnificently to mark the Harbour entrance, familiar to us all from many old Hollywood films. It was actually dressed in dull red. So much for a Golden Gate.

Saturday dawned damp and chilly. There was a sea mist, not unusual in San Francisco I was told, and I was glad of a heavy sports jacket and flannels as I walked to the cable car terminal for a trip into the city to seek a much needed haircut. The ride lived well up to expectations. The car clanked and swayed from side to side, the driver doing wonders with rods and levers up and down the steep hills and the passengers adding to the cheerful atmosphere with noisy, good-natured conversation.

An ambulance pulled up to the kerb beside me as I walked through the commercial centre and two ambulance men with a stretcher rushed into a building. A crowd gathered, arc lights appeared from nowhere and it suddenly dawned on me that the whole episode was being filmed. I asked the man next to me what was going on and he said,

"Right now we're both extras on a TV series called *The Streets of San Francisco*, but don't expect the bastards to give out with any money. It happens all the time here."

I walked on and finally saw what I'd been looking for – a barber's pole above a first floor window. A steep flight of stairs led to a landing with a door either side. I could see nothing to tell me which was the barber so I opened one of the doors and stepped in, to be transfixed by the spectacle before me.

It was a large room, well lit by garish artificial lighting. The centre was rigged as a film set featuring a bed occupied by two naked young women and one young man just about down to his underpants and still disrobing. They became motionless as they realised that a stranger had appeared through the door. There was a shout from a shirtsleeved older man who rushed over to me shouting over his shoulder to a young woman assistant, "How many times do I have to tell you to keep that goddam door locked. What do you want buddy?" all in one breath.

"I'm here," I said inanely, gazing at the weird tableau before me, "for a haircut." Even now I have to laugh at the idiocy of my reply. He took my arm, turned me round and marched me to the other door. "Haircut," he said briefly and vanished. Looking closely at the door I saw that it bore the legend in faded brown paint 'Barber' – almost unreadable in the gloom of the landing.

The barber said that his neighbours made porn video films, mainly for the tired businessman hotel market. He wanted to have his sign repainted but he faced opposition from his regular customers.

"Why," I said "Surely it would save embarrassment all round?"

He rolled his eyes, clearly thinking 'got a right one here.' "Think about it," he said. But it was a good haircut.

True to my accustomed role of an innocent abroad I wandered into a pleasant looking restaurant for lunch, noticing without making anything of it, that the other tables were occupied by pairs of men who were looking at me strangely and clearly discussing my solitary state. It was only when I saw a male pair of new arrivals wander in hand in hand that I realised that I was in an alien environment. I began to feel like a cat in a strange backyard surrounded by small boys debating whether or not to sling me out and I left as soon as I had finished my meal. It was probably a totally unwarranted impression, for I received efficient attention and unwavering courtesy from the restaurant staff, together with an excellent meal. But I don't think it is possible for anyone of my natural inclinations, generation and upbringing to feel as comfortable in a gay environment as our more enlightened children and grandchildren do. From that point of view the world is certainly a better and more tolerant place. I mentioned the incident later to my conducting officer and he told me that San Francisco was bidding to become the 'gay capital' of the United States.

Just opposite the cable car terminal I saw a sign marking Grant Street and pointing in the general direction of Fort Mason. The Flower Drum Song mentioned previously and a great musical show in the late nineteen fifties had been set in San Francisco. 'Grant Avenue' was one of its best numbers and Grant Street was good enough, so I decided to walk that way back to the barracks. As I strolled along the fairly wide city street that sloped gently upwards, I noticed that pedestrians began to look more oriental. I was relaxed about that; the show was set in Chinatown and I was used to Chinese towns and cities.

I walked on, to be confronted by two policemen. They were dressed in black trousers and open necked short sleeved shirts, topped by black peaked caps. They stopped and one said, "Where ya making for, friend?" I looked at them; they were festooned with the tools of their trade. Service handguns at the hip, nightsticks, handcuffs, but as yet no radios, or none visible. The forearm of the hand outraised to stop me looked as thick as my thigh and they were both tall enough to loom over me. I explained as I had done several times before, that I was a visiting British army officer, that I was making my way to Fort Mason at the top of the hill and that I was walking there to get some exercise.

"Well sir," said the second one. "That is not a very good idea. We certainly wouldn't walk by ourselves any further along this road, so we suggest you turn around, go back, take the cable car and make us all happy."

If it is possible to leer in a friendly way, he managed it. I was surprised. I had wandered alone around Singapore, Hong Kong and other cities with a majority Chinese population and not met the slightest trouble. But it would have been foolish to ignore this well meant advice so I retraced my steps. I was told later that Chinatown is one of the sights of San Francisco but it was advisable to see it either by car or in a party.

A visit to Fisherman's Wharf, San Francisco's Blackpool on the Bay, to take the ferry to Alcatraz was on the agenda, but the queue was so immense that I gave it a miss and made do with the view of 'The Rock' from my window.

After a visit to the military port on the east side of the Bay at Oakland, which was in effect a vastly enlarged and much more up to date Marchwood, a visit the US Air Force base at Travis Field was next on the itinerary. This was the home of the mighty C5 transport aircraft, by far the world's biggest at that time.

We travelled by helicopter from the Praesidio, the main Army base in the lea of the Golden Gate Bridge. The trip entailed overflying Alcatraz and I asked the pilot if we could have a look since I had failed to get there by ferry over the weekend.

"Certainly," he said and promptly zoomed down to a hover about three feet above the old exercise yard. We then helicopter – hopped all round the old prison. It was a new experience to examine buildings by helicopter. Short of flying through the corridors I don't think we could have got closer, and if it was the pilot's intention to impress me with his flying ability he certainly succeeded.

We landed at Travis Field to be met by the Commander, a cheery Texan major general, grizzled, tall and rangy as all Texans are to us.

"You spent the weekend on your own in that Hellhole?" he said. "Why didn't someone tell us? We did an exercise to Diego Garcia on Saturday and Sunday. You'd have enjoyed it."

He was wrong. The thought of flying across the Pacific and Indian Oceans and back in a transport aircraft, however famous, in the space of two days, did not attract. But of course I agreed it was a pity.

The visit passed in a flash. We had a light lunch in the Officers' Club, enlivened by the banter of the base seniors but before we were led out to see the C5, my conducting officer and I were treated to a slide presentation of the Base's role and equipment. "We're running a series of experiments," said the general by way of introduction. "So I hope you won't mind if I ask you a few questions at the end."

"Not at all," I replied, mystified. Surely it couldn't be a device for keeping his guests awake?

The slide screen covered almost the width of one wall of the lecture room and there was a smaller slimmer screen on either side of it. Both the slides and the voiceover were of great professional interest to me and there was no question of dozing during the hour long session. I had noticed that the smaller screens were flickering during the presentation but I had paid little attention to that. Both my conducting officer 'shadow' and I were questioned closely at the end of the show and we thought we acquitted ourselves well. The General confirmed this and told us that a number of the questions we had answered correctly bore no relation to what had been shown on the main screen. We had apparently absorbed the material subliminally from the flickering images on the side screens that had flashed before our peripheral vision much too quickly for us to be consciously aware of what we were seeing.

"You've been brainwashed guys," he said. "So remember. If you're captured, name, rank and number only!"

As we walked across the tarmac towards the aircraft dispersal areas, the colonel accompanying us suddenly turned to me and said, quite seriously. "Are you a religious man, sir?"

"No more than the next person," I replied cautiously, wondering what was coming.

"Well," he said. "I asked because we don't want to upset anyone but the fact is, we call this aircraft Jesus Christ."

"Why?"

"Because that's what most everybody says when they see it for the first time!"

And vast it certainly was. Apart from a mind-boggling quantity of stores it could carry, the enormous hold could accommodate guns, heavy trucks and even tanks within limits. Standing on the gallery above the hold it was difficult to believe you were in an aircraft rather than a coastal vessel. A fall over the low rail on to the cargo deck below would certainly mean a broken neck. Sadly, a short flight was out of the question. There were no training flights left in the budget and even the lavish hospitality of the US Army couldn't stretch to a special flight for visitors in this exceptionally expensive flying draught horse.

The short visit to the west coast completed, the next stop was a visit to MAC (Military Airlift Command) in Missouri. Although even Sam couldn't arrange for a brief C5 trip, he had done the next best thing. I flew the 1700 miles to Saint Louis in a USAF executive jet, a journey of great comfort, accompanied by two civilian passengers. They were oldish men; I took them to be high ranking politicians or civil servants and assumed that I was opportunistic supercargo tacked on to some important enterprise that they were embarked upon. But they were surprisingly deferential and it emerged that they were actually retired regular servicemen, 'space available' passengers and that they were the supercargo on an aircraft specifically tasked for my visit.

'Space available' is the US version of the British forces' system of 'indulgence' where serving officers and men may take advantage of otherwise empty space on Service aircraft and ships to travel on duty and very occasionally leave, with their wives. In our case, indulgence passengers pay for their food and accommodation where this is provided. Passage availability, scarce as hen's teeth anyway, is strictly confined to those actually serving and their immediate families. In the US, however, as befits a superpower, passages are available on a worldwide basis to both serving and retired men and women. I didn't discover from my fellow passengers, both retired soldiers, whether or not they paid anything for their food and 1700 mile trip.

We flew a southern route to avoid the San Juan Mountains and their associated turbulence. This took us over a good deal of desert, the Grand Canyon – a great red gash in the earth – being pointed out by the pilot, and we landed for a refuelling stop at a military airstrip 'a million miles from nowhere' as one of my travelling companions said when asked.

Saint Louis, on the mighty Mississippi, is the home of the sternwheeler riverboats of film and musical comedy fame, and they make a pleasant sight lying snugly under the main bridge almost in the shadow of the Gateway to the West, a great gleaming silver archway sited, I was told, on the spot from where the wagon trains started in the nineteenth century to carve out a new life in the untracked wilderness.

MAC had been included in my programme to give me a flavour of the US worldwide military air freight tasking system. I was taken to a viewing gallery overlooking the main tasking room to see a welcome message spelled out on a liquid crystal display…"Military Airlift Command is pleased to welcome the British Army's Director of Movements from London, England." – followed by my name. A nice gesture and by no means debased by the fact that they do it for someone different nearly every day. I then toured the ops centre to be briefed on the array of more state of the art information retrieval and dissemination systems than I had ever seen in one place before.

I would have liked to have seen more of Saint Louis – pronounced locally as Saint Lewis – for it looked an interesting place, but this was a whistle stop tour and Washington DC beckoned. I stayed with Sam and Alice Cockerham in their house in Fairfax County, a leafy suburb just outside the Beltway, as the DC ring road is called. America's capital city, an entity carved out of the State of Virginia, is commonly referred to as just 'DC' to avoid confusion with Washington State and the twenty or so other Washingtons in the US.

After the standard visit to the Pentagon in uniform to talk about professional matters and look at the US systems, Sam sensibly cut me loose.

"There's a lot to see here for first timers," he said. "You've got about a day and a half before you're due to travel down to the east coast military port in North Carolina. "I've booked you in to see the Space Film this afternoon at the Air and Space Museum and you can also see the Smithsonian and the Capitol Building. You can't really wander round in uniform by yourself not knowing where things are so I've arranged for Dolores to escort you. She'll get you back here by about five thirty and we'll go home."

Dolores? She was a civilian on Sam's staff. A pretty and vivacious brunette in her late twenties. Her company was easy to enjoy and she certainly knew her way about Washington. There was a Renoir exhibition at the National Art Gallery that had received wide publicity and I wanted to see it so we varied the tour. On the way I was accosted by a well dressed young man who appeared to know me. He got as far as, "Good afternoon General and nice to see you," when Dolores cut him short with, "We're not interested," and practically dragged me away.

"What was that about?" I said.

"He was a Moonie," she replied. "A way-out religious sect. They're very clever. He knew your rank even though you're wearing a foreign uniform. He would have got you into a conversation, fed you with literature, tried to discover your name and before you know it you're in the paper being quoted as saying something outrageous."

It would never have occurred to me. Obviously Sam was right. First timers in uniform needed a minder.

Dolores was a bewitching young woman and I had an idle and unworthy thought that 'had I been single and twenty years younger…?' But when we returned to Sam's office she said, "I enjoyed our afternoon, general. My husband's just arrived to take me home and I'd like you to meet him."

I turned and had my hand clasped in the massive paw of a beaming uniformed policeman, even bigger than my two friends from San Francisco. 'Maybe not', I thought. Across the room Sam met my eye, and reading my thoughts he grinned, knowingly.

There is a useful and efficient public transport system for visitors to Washington DC. The city is, of course, a Mecca for US citizens, eager to see their capital and tourists throng there from every state in the Union. A bus route has been mapped out with stops at all the sights, the Lincoln Memorial, the Washington Monument with its reflecting pool, the Jefferson Memorial, the Capitol, the museums, Arlington Cemetery and as close to the White House as security will allow. A number of comfortable busses travel the route continuously and for a day ticket costing a few dollars you can see everything worth seeing, jumping on and off a bus at any stop all day and taking as long as you like at each attraction. I passed my 'free day' doing this in plain clothes and it was time well spent. The queue for the White House, however, was so long that I gave it a miss. Perhaps another time?

The following day's visit to the ammunition port at Sunny Point, North Carolina gave me a flavour of small town America. It was a neat and clean little town; it could have been Peyton Place but it was in fact Southport NC, so close to the military port that the Commanding Officer was accepted as one of the town's personalities. I met the CO and was told that we had an appointment for lunch with the Mayor before visiting the port.

The lunch took place in the mayor's favourite restaurant and our host, full of goodwill and bonhomie, told me that he didn't get many English generals visiting his town. He then said he'd recently been visited by the mayor of the English Southport with which his town was twinned. A 'feisty' lady, he said, at which point he was interrupted by a neatly dressed character at another table who seemed to be considerably the worse for wear and released a broadside on the subject of town revenues being spent by the mayor on entertainment for his 'ritzy' friends. The mayor, obviously a consummate politician, went over to the man, clapped him on the shoulder and whispered something in his ear, at which his tormentor got up and walked unsteadily out. Our host then apologised gracefully, dismissed the incident as small town politics and we carried on. The CO later told me that the dissatisfied citizen was the nearest thing they had to a town drunk with frustrated political ambitions.

The port visit, after the customary briefing at the operations centre, also involved a drive round the facilities in an open jeep type vehicle. It was a vast area with a semi-circular quay stretching out to sea and obviously capable of taking several more than the two ocean-going freighters berthed there that afternoon. The inland side of the port was quite well wooded and there were several lakes. As in most relatively undisturbed military installations there was plenty of wildlife and I was delighted to count three families of Ospreys nesting over the lakes. As we drove round, however, I was nagged by an impression that security measures didn't seem to be given much emphasis. There were the great piles of palleted ammunition lying covered with tarpaulins in open spaces with the luxury of being well spaced apart, and there were no security guards on foot that I could see. I mentioned this to the CO who gave me an amused glance.

"Oh, we have regular vehicle patrols," he said. "But we leave what you might call foot security to George and his family."

"George?"

"You'd better meet him. He should be around."

We drove over to one of the ammunition stacks and there, lying in the shade from the afternoon sun, lay an enormous alligator. We stopped and he swivelled an eye at us. "Don't get out," said the CO, a mite unnecessarily. "George has a big family and no one walks around here. We chase them off when we're loading, but all the locals know the score and our scaly friends provide us with low cost security round the clock."

Back in DC it was the last day of my visit and Sam took me to lunch at the United Services Club in downtown Washington. At that time the town, the residential part of DC, as opposed to the centre of administration featuring the Capitol, the White House and the offices of state, had a fearsome reputation for violence and was trying to avoid the title of 'murder capital of the US'. So before we left Sam's parking space the car had to be sealed with all doors locked and windows up with nothing showing on the rear seats that might attract a smash and grab at traffic lights. The geography of the US Club had been selected in better times and it was a comfortably appointed place, but it was a pity that it was unwise to venture outside on foot.

I left Dulles Airport for RAF Brize Norton by the regular VC10 service reflecting that during my first sponsored visit to the US I had absorbed a good deal of useful professional information for what was billed as a 'liaison visit to enhance personal relations' which cynics would probably regard as a euphemism for a 'jolly'.

I returned to a bout of select committeeing. This is a sometimes tricky process that senior directors of the MOD and elsewhere in Whitehall have to undergo at the hands of MPs who are members of parliamentary committees when there are pressing matters of moment to debate – in our case affecting the security of the nation. Our subject was the state of planning for the reinforcement of NATO in the event of the Cold War becoming hot. This would mean that reserve forces would be embodied and could have to be moved to the near continent at short notice. Several MOD staff directors were involved from the three armed services and our supporting civilian directorates.

We formed up as a party and led by a senior civil servant operating as 'question master' we walked to the committee rooms at the House of Commons where we were faced by a cross-party panel of MPs, some of whom were eager to find out if these servicemen could provide them with ammunition to shoot at the Government of the day in the Commons Chamber. The questioning varied in quality from positively banal to very astute and you had to keep your wits about you. MPs become dab hands at extracting answers using the parliamentary device of supplementary questions; it wasn't possible to hide behind security gradings with these, the people's representatives, who were deemed to be screened to a high security classification.

There were several barristers present, leavened by a few 'laymen' with scant knowledge of what went on in the Madhouse. One old chap kept dozing off, attracting the ire of a rear admiral among our number who blew him out of the water in short order. The MP woke up at one stage clearly thinking he ought to contribute. He asked a question to which the admiral replied in his best quarterdeck voice, "I answered that question sir, while you were asleep!"

The Chairman said gently "Yes, well, perhaps we should move on." The admiral was left untouched for the rest of the session.

What is it about admirals? I've met a goodly number and without exception they are affable, likeable and charming folk on the social scene – generally much 'smoother' than their contemporaries in the other two services. But when operating professionally they do tend as a fraternity to have a short fuse. I suppose that unlike their contemporaries in the other services, they spend their working lives at sea coping night and day with the sometimes alarming eccentricities of the Almighty whether there is a war or not; perhaps this causes them to be less tolerant of the pedestrian frailties of their fellow men.

For security reasons the Press was banned from select committee grillings of security classified subjects; thus we had the inestimable advantage of screening the draft minutes – later published as part of a White Paper – to delete anything that we felt for security reasons should not appear in the public domain. We were always conscious, however, that we were operating in a minefield on those occasions.

At one of our Corps evening discussions in Aldershot I found myself talking during the supper afterwards to Freddie Laker, who had given us a talk on the subject of operating an airline. On learning that I was Director of Army Movements he said:

"I used to work for you occasionally – before your time of course. Were you ever in Malaya?"

"Yes."

"Then you'll remember that you had some Fijian soldiers there?"

"Of course."

Freddie grinned. "They caused me a bit of grief," he said. "I got the contract to move them to Malaya from Fiji. We had no idea what they looked like but one of my lads said they were little fellows, like Gurkhas. So I told them to fit some extra seats in the aircraft before they flew out to Fiji, reckoning to make a bob or two extra. The pilots were drinking their orange juice in the tin roofed hut that in those days served as Fiji's terminal building when down the road came marching several bodies of giants in what looked like grass skirts. They were big busty fellows, all over six feet."

"Who are they?" said one of the pilots. "Your passengers," replied the barman.

"Great panic," said Freddie. "We had to rearrange the seating on the spot, turfing out more than the total of the extra seats we had put in. Then there was an extra flight needed. I'd been too clever for my own good and hardly covered my costs on that contract. But you can never win ' em all," he added philosophically.

My job in the Ministry meant reading much civil service generated paper: memos, briefing papers and documents known as 'position papers' circulated between branches for comment by 'principals' as heads of departments were known. The prose was pure but pedantic: in style it veered towards multi-syllable words with Latin or Old French roots; short, expressive Saxon words were rare – quite the opposite of staff college teaching, and both words and phrases appeared and disappeared at the dictates of Whitehall fashion. I recall that 'rehearse' was commonly used for 'repeat' and until it became unfashionable, 'subsume' appeared regularly for 'absorb'. It was easy to have sympathy with the serving officer at MOD who underlined a passage in a report passing across his desk and wrote 'Balls!' in the margin. Then, reflecting that it was perhaps an inappropriate comment for circulation at a Department of State, he erased his pencilled comment and replaced it with 'Round objects!' He was surprised to get it back weeks later with a memo attached, 'Pray who is Mr Round and to what does he object?'

Adjudicating on complaints was a chore that had to be accepted. One of the members of the Army Board found his luggage didn't appear on the carousel after a charter flight to Germany. Not unnaturally he made a fuss and because of the eminence of the complainant, what would normally be a problem for my air movements branch landed on my desk. I rang the managing director of the charter airline who was suitably contrite and although the luggage had been found and arrived a day late, he promised compensation and offered to write a personal letter of apology to the irate senior officer. I said fair enough and told the complainant that the matter was being dealt with and that he'd hear from the airline shortly. The MD sent me a copy of the letter. It read something along the following lines:

'Dear General X,

I have received your complaint about the failure of my organisation to produce your luggage immediately on completion of your recent journey to Dusseldorf. Subsequent investigation has disclosed that it was mistakenly routed to Lourdes. We are normally more efficient than this in our baggage handling department but I well appreciate that with a busy itinerary ahead of you it must have caused you considerable inconvenience. In consequence of this I enclose a cheque with my sincere apologies and hope that it will in some measure compensate you for the delay.

I should perhaps add that while in Lourdes my staff took the opportunity to have your baggage blessed in the hope that it would make you feel better when it was returned to you!'

As the complaining general said to me, still laughing, when he had received the letter, "Game set and match to the MD. How could anyone pursue a complaint after that."

Having the power of decision over the movements budget sometimes paid off for the Service in unusual ways. The Director of Army Training rang me one morning. The RSM at Sandhurst had been invited with his wife to attend a ceremony at the US Military Academy, West Point and while the RSM's application for a passage had been approved, the passage for his wife had been turned down by 'Movements'. How mean can you get, said the DAT. The decision had been contested but our civilian head of Mov (Finance) had again turned it down. It was a pleasure to be able to reverse the decision and to tell the head of the finance branch to get on with it.

The end of the Second World War saw the birth of many old comrades clubs. Most of these faded out as their members spread across the world to get on with their civilian lives. But there were some exceptions that survived the years. One of these is the Movement Control Officers' Club (MCOC).

My job as Director of Movements also made me President of the MCOC. It was a figurehead post – for the tenure of my MOD appointment only, but it was hugely enjoyable. My Corps had inherited the stewardship of this from the Royal Engineers in the nineteen sixties when the Movements function had been transferred to the newly formed RCT. Many, indeed most of its members had remained in the transport and movements field after leaving the Army and it was full of ex-sappers, fiercely loyal to their old Corps but quite happy to embrace the new one. The chairman, himself an ex-sapper colonel and then Deputy Chairman of British Railways, was Bobby Lawrence of BR. He had become a good friend and his death some years later was much mourned. The Club still flourishes as I write nearly sixty years after the Second World War and the monthly 'Beer and Blather' sessions held at the Overseas Club are well attended.

The Army had been directed from on high to relinquish a number of senior appointments at about the time I was due to receive notice of my next and final job after nearly three years in an active and fascinating post. This would mean a sharp reduction in brigadier (one star) and major general (two star) posts and it was on the cards that I wouldn't get another job at all. Five major generals were suddenly 'axed' after only one appointment in the rank and several brigadiers also suffered the chop. It was unlikely that I would get command of my Corps; there was a 'favourite son' lined up for the post, or so I was told. He was a nice fellow, very able and knowledgeable and we all wished him well. Rumours abounded. I heard on the grapevine that I was being 'run' as chief of staff for a large HQ, but then I heard that there was to be a second tranche of redundancies.

The QMG brought the situation back to earth by saying casually one day:

"Have you heard from MS about your next posting yet?"

"No," I replied, "I'm all ears."

"Well you know about the three line whip on the reduction of two star appointments? I'm sorry to say that we've had to give up the two star D Mov job. It's to revert to brigadier and the post of Transport Officer in Chief as head of your Corps is to be retitled Director General of Transport and Movements and responsible for the two functions. Because of your experience of both you are to be the first DGMT. The formal posting order should be on the way to you now."

This was a considerable surprise. I had become reconciled to probable early retirement and had formulated an outline plan for a short career in business, the object being to get together enough money to buy a small place in the country with a bit of land so that we could keep a few animals and have a largely outdoor retirement. The two older girls were married; Kate, our third daughter, was seventeen and about to leave school. Lucy, the youngest, was still at school but into her teens and could board if necessary. This new intelligence, however, forced a quick rethink. I could carry on in the Service for a couple of years and still be young enough on retirement to get a decent job outside. Also the thought of commanding my Corps was mightily attractive. I would be located at the new Logistic Executive near Andover. We could live in our own house near Winchester with Andover only a short drive by staff car to my office. Heather's 'wobbly' as she now called it, was nearly eight years behind her and she had to report for a medical check up only once a year.

I accepted my new appointment without comment. I was to hand over to my old friend Ron Jenkins who, in my opinion, had been robbed of promotion by the climate of reductions. Had the D Mov appointment not been downgraded, he was well qualified to fill it as a major general. It was tough luck.

But with some months before leaving the movements scene and having not taken advantage of the indulgence system during the whole time in my uniquely advantageous appointment, I applied for one way indulgence passages by air to Cyprus for Heather, myself and our two younger girls. Our return a week later was timed to coincide with the return of one of our LSLs from Cyprus. Her Captain, Maurice Salt, was well known to me and was, he said, delighted to agree that he had plenty of spare cabin space for us to return by sea as indulgence passengers. One or two of his officers would have their wives with them during the voyage, which would make it nice for Heather and the girls.

We flew to Cyprus in a RAF VC10 on a 'milk run' trip, hired a car and stayed in a pleasant villa high in the Troodos Mountains. I knew the Island well and so was able to show my family those parts of Cyprus that were still open to us. It was late summer, almost autumn, and the roads were slippery with the purple grape juice dropped from the lorries carrying the harvest to the presses. The weather was glorious; warm, but not oppressively so and charged with that luminous light peculiar to a Mediterranean autumn. We swam in a calm, warm sea at Ladies' Mile close to the RAF station at Akrotiri, the girls became acquainted with the famous Paphos Pelican and most evenings we dined at the lively village of Kakopetria on the slopes of the Troodos.

For the return by sea to UK we were lightered out to LSL Sir Percivale to renew acquaintance with Maurice Salt and meet his officers and his Chinese crew.

The return trip was all I had hoped it would be. The sea behaved itself well; the accommodation was comfortable, the girls proved to be good sailors on the few occasions when the sea became choppy and the journey to the staging stop at Gibraltar passed in a flash. About two days out from Gibraltar the Captain passed me a signal received from the Governor's ADC. I had hoped to avoid official attention; we were on leave after all, but the Governor's staff had obviously picked up our presence from the ship's manifest. The Governor at the time was General Bill Jackson. He sent his apologies through the ADC for being unable to entertain us while passing through Gibraltar but the ADC explained that he was in hospital with 'an injury'. Intriguing. He had been spare and very fit when I had worked for him at the MOD only two years before.

I replied to the effect that I was sorry to hear the news, but that I quite understood and being on leave with my family, I had neither anticipated nor expected to be entertained. But I decided to get in touch with him when we arrived to find out what had happened. I phoned the General when we berthed at Gibraltar. He was obviously using his hospital room as an office, for the ADC answered. Very typical. Bill Jackson would have to be ill indeed to release his grip on affairs. After a whispered conversation the ADC said, "The Governor will speak to you now."

"Your ADC mentioned an injury," I said. "What on earth happened?"

"It's embarrassing," he replied. "I don't much want to talk about it but I'll have to tell you to kill speculation. As a sapper I'm supposed to know about boats. They give me a launch here and somehow I managed to get my leg in between the boat and my jetty at the Convent (the Governor's house in Gibraltar) and it got crushed."

I could do no more than express sympathy and offer hopes for speedy relief. Although lesser mortals might have cursed their luck but enjoyed the enforced leisure, this must have been a severe blow to the pride of a man like Bill Jackson and I resolved to say nothing at home. But of course the jungle drums had been thrumming and when we got back, his misfortune was common knowledge.

There was just time to 'do the Rock' before the ship sailed. We saw the Barbary Apes, the girls bought geegaws in the High Street and I took them to see the small cemetery by the dockyard gates that held the graves of some of the sailors who did not survive Trafalgar. Heather and I were able to entertain Maurice and his First Officer, who was accompanied by his wife, to dinner ashore before we sailed next day.

Three days later, after Cape St Vincent had nobly died away in the other direction, we disembarked at Marchwood Military Port.

26

The Last Lap

A few months later I handed over to Brigadier Ron Jenkins, my appointment having been duly downgraded and added to my new portfolio as DGMT and professional head of The Royal Corps of Transport. I knew, however, that I wouldn't have to worry about the Movements side of the business. It was in good hands.

I took over as Director of my Corps from Peter Benson. It was a short and amicable handover. Heather and I had known Peter and his wife, Betty for many years. We were offered a married quarter a few miles from the Logistic Executive, or LE(A) as it was known with the Army's passion for initials. Although the quarter came with a small staff to run it, we turned it down, preferring to live in our own house. There was a substantial entertainment commitment, with little recompense from the guardians of the Treasury – a situation unheard of in civilian life as I was subsequently to discover. But I asked the authorities to allow me to employ our home help as a civilian batman to replace the three servants we would have had if we had occupied the Army quarter. For the Service it was a magnificent deal – recognised by the guardians of the Army's money and agreed to without delay. In fact our elderly Mrs White carried on as before, helping Heather in the house. Mrs White was a true 'treasure'; she had been in service in her youth and suitably rewarded, she provided willing and expert help when we entertained. As for batman work, aided by my driver I had no difficulty in keeping my belt and shoes up to standard.

I was now on the last lap in the Service. It was technically a command job but in fact it consisted of disseminating Corps policy and keeping the Army's large transport and movements element on an even keel. Policy direction was exercised through a number of brigadiers and colonels, themselves in command appointments and responsible to a series of senior officers commanding field formations in Europe and in such overseas places as we had managed to retain after the almost total loss of Empire. There would be a good deal of travelling but this time I wanted it to be accompanied travel. This should be possible because I would be visiting the units of my Corps and my wife would, as ever, be able to gauge the morale of the families during those visits. In fact the Service tended to recognise this and generally looked favourably on wives accompanying senior officers in command appointments within the UK and Europe, although we would have to rely on the availability of indulgence passages for visits elsewhere overseas.

My HQ at Andover was quite big. I had a brigadier chief of staff assisted by a colonel and a large mixed military and civilian staff to assist them. In addition there was a transport and movements executive staff headed by a brigadier putting into effect the instructions emanating from our movements staff at the MOD. My personal outer office housed my staff captain acting as a watchdog and a civilian lady secretary. It was easily controllable and there was time to think. For the first time as a senior officer I would not be driven by untoward and unexpected 'events', sometimes feeling like the Dutch boy with his finger in the dyke except that in movements it was usually all fingers and now and then thumbs as well.

By the same token it would be easy to become cocooned; easy to let events take over and run their course without interference. Someone once said – a nineteenth century politician I think, 'Very little matters and nothing matters much'- a variation on, 'In the long run we are all dead.' True in the great scheme of things, but hardly an inducement to progress. It was clear that if my professional writ was to run properly through my widely spaced 'command' I would have to devise some method of getting Corps policies through to the ground without spending my whole time travelling and preaching.

After some thought I instituted 'one star' quarterly conferences to discuss Corps matters. All brigadiers employed in specifically RCT appointments would assemble at the Andover HQ at set intervals each year to discuss matters related to their professional activities, working to an agenda prepared over the preceding months. This cast a wide net; we seldom had less than eight brigadiers present and this number was often exceeded by RCT brigadiers employed in staff appointments outside the Corps, who were invited to attend on a voluntary basis and often contributed useful snippets of intelligence. To my great surprise this arrangement was never queried on grounds of expense. It helped, of course, that we controlled the movements budget, but I was told that my successor, Bill Allen, carried on the system as a means of disseminating policy and presumably it became ossified by time.

We all knew each other well and discussions were informal and free. I acted as ringmaster and the only rule was that when a matter was deemed to be thoroughly discussed and a decision had been taken, the issue was closed and not to be discussed again. This worked well and going round units in Europe and elsewhere it was apparent that policies decided at these meetings had certainly reached unit and sub unit level.

For the first year or so the Chief of Staff Logistics, who was located at the LE(A) and co-ordinated its administration, was Paul Travers, now a major general and reporting directly to the Quartermaster General. He went on to become the Vice Quartermaster General, a frequent route to the stars. Could it possibly be that the RCT would bag an Army Board appointment, a first for a professional logistician? Hardly likely, but the air was full of change and sacred cows were being slaughtered with abandon.

It was late 1978 and our country was being described as 'the sick man of Europe'; a shameful situation, the reasons too well known to need much comment, but the ruling Labour government was roundly rejected by the voters the following year. Inflation was raging and civilian 'workers' were just about keeping pace with it financially. Not so the serving public servants, however. Those who were retired and on index-linked pensions were 'riding the pig's back' with aplomb, pensions increasing at up to twenty per cent annually. The Treasury, with the Prime Minister piously intoning his belief that the Services would wish to help the country in its hour of financial need, held back the recommended Service pay increases to six or seven per cent. This had a shattering effect on the morale and living standards of all ranks and the newspapers even hinted at the hitherto unthinkable possibility of some sort of military takeover – a coup no less! Soldiers, with families to keep, were moonlighting in their free hours, serving in pubs and driving taxis, a situation unacceptable to the Manual of Military Law, but who was to blame them?

We were all feeling the pinch, and it was obvious that the British people had had enough of union militancy. A woman Prime Minister, a modern Boadicea, took post in 1979 and set out to put things right without delay although it was obvious that the rot had penetrated deeply and she would have a massive fight on her hands.

It was customary for each new Director of the Corps to do a 'pastoral' tour of his units in the UK and Europe shortly after taking over. This had mutual benefits. The officers, senior NCOs and soldiers wanted to see the new professional head of their Corps and the new man himself needed to get a 'feel' for their concerns while there was time for him to do something about them. Heather and I toured RCT units in Germany within a few months of my arrival in Andover, to find morale considerably higher than it had been at home and things generally in good shape. Our itinerary featured a visit to Berlin, travelling to the city on the British Berlin train, operating on Deutches Bundesbahn metals, starting its journey at Hanover with a break at Marienborn on the East/West German border to pick up Russian guards for the journey through East Germany to the British sector of Berlin.

The train had operated for the whole of the time that Germany had been divided and of course in 1979 the Cold War was still going on. The pause at Marienborn railway station gave one an eerie feeling of a Cold War film in operation. A British army subaltern detailed for the task from any regiment, emerged from the train followed by a RCT warrant officer clutching a briefcase. Both were in uniform, the officer formally attired in service dress and Sam Browne belt and the warrant officer in service dress with leather waistbelt.

They formed up on the platform, and marched in step towards the station office. Before they arrived at the station office, a Russian officer accompanied by a soldier assistant, also dressed formally, emerged on to the platform. The two groups met near to the office and exchanged unsmiling salutes. This little tableau was watched by all the train passengers in silence, the only background noise being a faint hissing sound from the stationary train. Both groups then went into the station office to exchange documentation, emerging to repeat the saluting before retracing their steps. There was then a further short pause while the carriage doors at each end were secured with chains and wooden beams, each door guarded by an armed Russian soldier. This was not designed to prevent the oppressed British or West Germans from leaping into the Soviet dominated paradise of East Germany; it was to prevent the happy citizens of East Germany from leaping on to the train and reaching the sanctuary of West Berlin.

The train was administered by the Berlin Brigade's RCT squadron, our Berlin hosts. I was told that despite the formal and boot faced appearance of both sides during the Marienborn ceremony, in fact they became human once the station office door had closed behind them and bottles of scotch were frequently exchanged for bottles of vodka before they re-emerged.

Despite our years in Germany, neither Heather nor I had visited Berlin before; it was new to us and thus very interesting, although it was still a divided city with the contrast between West Berlin and East Berlin just as striking as we had been led to believe. We were accommodated in Edinburgh House, the British officers' visitors mess and leave hostel, but the General Officer Commanding the British sector and his wife, Bob and Maureen Richardson, had been neighbours at Tidworth during a previous posting and they invited us to join them for an evening on the GOC's launch. An evening literally 'on the Spree' for that is the name of the river that runs through Berlin and is presumably the origin of the phrase.

A pleasant spring evening emerged – just right for a trip on the river. The Spree is navigable for small craft and hazards were well marked. The river ran past the bottom of the GOC's garden and we embarked at his jetty. We were told that there was a huge entertainment commitment tacked on to that appointment; everyone wanted to see the Wall but houses capable of offering good security to public figures were thin on the ground. Bob and Maureen had been hosts to US President Jimmy Carter and his wife Rosalynn only a few months previously.

The launch was long, quite narrow as befits a river craft, but very comfortable. It was a convivial gathering of friends. We chugged along gently with the warrant officer helmsman pointing out interesting riverside features to his GOC's guests. Heather, who had been around boats for the whole of her married life when we were together and was a competent boat handler, was invited to take the wheel under the guidance of the warrant officer while I gazed at the passing scene. The buoys passed by slowly with the river widening and narrowing as we idled along the marked channel. At one stage I noticed an oddly marked buoy go past; there was a notice behind it but it held no significance for me and I didn't draw it to the attention of the helmsman who was deep in conversation with my wife. He looked up suddenly with a start asked me if we'd passed a striped buoy.

"Yes," I said and added helpfully, "there was notice behind it but I didn't notice what its message was."

"Oh, my God! I think we're in East Berlin."

Apparently we had passed the buoy that marked the boundary of the two sectors. Bob masked his disquiet very well. The rules for the divided city allowed occupation forces to travel between sectors, including the Russian sector, but only in uniform and through a recognised checkpoint. Depending on the political climate at the time, much could have been made of two British generals, one a GOC, travelling into the Russian sector in plain clothes and not having passed through a checkpoint. In distance terms though, we were not very much 'offside', only about fifty yards or so. Quietly, and without changing speed, the boat was turned round and driven back into the British sector. We must have got away with it. So far as I know, nothing was made of the incident.

We gawped at the Wall, did the standard tour of East Berlin, a depressing place, reminiscent of a down at heel northern mill town, before returning by air to England. There was, however, an incident in East Berlin that gave us a flavour of the tensions that existed in that divided city.

Our hosts, the RCT squadron commander and his wife, escorted us on the East Berlin visit and took us to lunch at a well known restaurant on the Unter den Linden. We were warned not to expect either Savoy style food or service. We waited in a queue for a table and once seated, a squat, unsmiling and wordless waitress distributed menus. It featured soup and a choice from two main courses. We made our choice that included soup all round and the waitress disappeared. When she had gone my wife asked me what soup we were getting.

"Dumplings," I replied. "I was surprised you didn't refuse it. I know you don't like them much."

"I didn't recognise the German word," she said. "But perhaps they'll have an alternative if you ask her nicely for me."

"Very doubtful," I said. "But I'll try."

The waitress returned with the soup. With a scowl on her face she claimed no knowledge of English, so our hosts and I explained in our imperfect German that my wife had misunderstood the menu and didn't care for dumplings. Could she have another type of soup instead?

The scowl deepened. "You ordered soup. It is here and you will pay for it. If you want something else you would do better to go back to the fat cats on the other side. There is nothing else here."

All this in a rising tone of voice that silenced the talk at the other tables. The male members of our party being in uniform it would have been unwise and unseemly to create the fuss that he situation would have called for in more civilised surroundings, so the rest of the meal was taken in near silence. I don't suppose it bothered our female cold war warrior one bit that she received no tip.

The RCT had a close connection with the Worshipful Company of Carmen, mentioned earlier. The Carmen's Company, while not one of the ten great City livery companies, has a respectable pedigree and ranks well up in the pecking order, being founded in the fifteenth century as the sponsoring guild in the succeeding centuries for the proprietors of haulage concerns. Its membership tends to have close connections with transport in all its forms. The Company presented a sword annually to the young officer entrant to our Corps who was judged to have put up the best performance at Sandhurst. It had become customary for the Director of the Corps to become an honorary liveryman of the Company and to join the Carmen's Court for the tenure of his appointment. I was invited to do so as my predecessors had done and of course I accepted.

Before the induction ceremony it was necessary for a potential liveryman to become a Freeman of the City of London – not as daunting a prospect as it might sound. It's a matter of sponsorship and simple purchase followed by a short ceremony over a silver reproduction of Temple Bar in the office of the City Chamberlain. I was given my Freedom in January 1979, not long after I had assumed my appointment.

There was one other candidate for the Freedom that morning. This was Lord George Brown who told me in conversation that his father had been a RASC driver in the First World War. Afterwards he came to several of our functions as a guest but his secretary warned me on pain of her severe displeasure not to let him break his vow of abstinence. George didn't embarrass us by trying, and he proved to us that he didn't need to be tanked up to be as indiscreet as ever. Knowing that he was among friends he let his hair down.

After the Freedom came the induction to the Livery, a ceremony in a Livery Hall with the Carman's Court present in full regalia. There were solemn promises to be made and hands were bound with silken cords; it was all very impressive. I renewed acquaintance with Denis Baker, now a Court member and once the second in command of the company I'd joined when I transferred from infantry to the RASC many years previously. Denis was now the transport supremo for Tesco. He told me that when he left the army as a major, he had joined Tesco to run its transport fleet.

"Jack," he said, "asked me what I wanted to be called. Well, Lord Cohen, I said, I joined the Army with an ambition to be the Director of Supplies and Transport – the DST. I didn't make it, but if you don't mind I'd like that to be my title in your Company so I can at least claim to have made it somewhere else. Jack laughed and told me to call myself whatever I wanted so long as the goods got to where they were meant to be." So Denis became the DST of Tesco. He crowned an interesting career by becoming Master of his Livery Company before, sadly, he met an untimely end.

My induction to the Freedom and the Livery took place during the mayoralty of Sir Kenneth Cork, Senior Partner in the firm of Cork Gully, chartered accountants in the City, specialising in insolvency. Ken Cork was a strong supporter of my Corps and had wartime connections with its main predecessor, the RASC. He was a great character, almost larger than life, totally without pomp and with a fund of stories told with the verve and fluency of a true raconteur. He had a story about a troop train journey through Italy at the end of the war.

"I was in one of those compartments with a door either end and no corridor. I was bursting for the loo but of course I had to wait for the train to stop at a station. When it did stop it was usually there for a while to let a fast train through so I reckoned I had time for a good recce. Well it stopped at a station somewhere in northern Italy. I got out and looked around – no loo. Then I saw a sign saying 'Uschita'. I didn't speak a word of Italian but I thought, Ah, all these Latin languages are to some extent onomatopoeic – that must be it. I ran along an unending corridor and found myself in the street outside the station! I ran back just as the train was pulling out complete with all my kit."

"What did you do then?" I asked. "I eventually found a loo and then did what everyone did in those days. I blamed Movements for the cock-up!"

He became a regular guest at formal dinner nights in our Headquarters mess and repaid our hospitality royally by inviting me to take fifty of our officers with their wives to an evening at the Mansion House where we were entertained in great style and given a conducted tour of the ancient building.

To mark the centenary of the action at Rorke's Drift that took place in 1879 in Zululand, the film *Zulu* had its premiere in London in the late nineteen seventies. A member of the military Commissariat and Transport Element, Commissary Dalton, had won a VC there, while his assistant, Corporal Attwood of the ASC, won a DCM. The Commissariat was a link in chain of history of our Corps, stretching back to the Royal Waggoners of the eighteenth century and his VC had only recently been acquired from a sale at Spinks to be part of the VC element of our Buller Collection. I was asked to provide two soldiers dressed in period uniform to stand in the aisle at the premiere along with sappers, RAMC and infantry soldiers of the Royal Regiment of Wales whose predecessors, the South Wales Borderers, had formed the main element of the small garrison. The film was a blockbusting success and the soldier volunteers said it was a splendid party afterwards.

Shortly afterwards I received a letter from the War Graves Commission. 'We propose,' they said 'to erect at the site of the Battle of Waterloo, a memorial to the soldiers and officers of The Royal Waggon Train who participated in the action and lost their lives there. As the present day successors to that organisation would you please confirm that the Royal Corps of Transport will arrange an appropriate ceremony and dedication at a date to be mutually decided?' They also indicated, but very politely, that we would have to pay for it all.

I had not realised that the Royal Waggon Train was not commemorated at Waterloo, although they must have been there because my Corps and its predecessors had provided support for all our nation's battles for at least two centuries and as every schoolboy once knew, Waterloo took place in 1815. I was already familiar with the tactical outline of the battle but now more basic research was indicated and I visited the library of the Royal United Services Institute in Whitehall to read it up. Meanwhile my Chief of Staff, Brigadier Bernard Courtis was given the task of organising the arrangements in liaison with our senior man in BAOR, Brigadier

Keith Davis. The omens were good, for Bernard had a French mother; he was completely bilingual and had attended the Belgian Staff College. He was also an excellent and unflappable organiser. This job was right up his street.

The British Ambassador to Belgium readily agreed to do the honours at the ceremony and the Friends of Waterloo, a collection of mainly local dignitaries, were there in force together with the Duke of Wellington, their Patron. The Duke, a gallant soldier in his own right, having fought with the Royal Horse Guards through the Second World War and numbering a Military Cross alongside his many honours, is a retired brigadier. He was good company and appeared to enjoy the ceremony.

After a tour of the battle site we moved to Hougoumont Farm, the Ambassador pulled back the curtain covering the memorial slab, said a few words and together with our wives, we repaired to the village of Waterloo for lunch as guests of The Friends.

My research at the RUSI had uncovered the fact the Royal Waggon Train had produced a genuine hero during the battle. His name was Corporal Brewster and he was an ammunition wagon driver. The Foot Guards had been holding a flank at Hougoumont Farm under intense assault by the French and had almost exhausted their ammunition. Brewster, with his wagon fully loaded, was on the way to another formation fighting close to Hougoumont Farm when he was spotted by a staff officer who was aware of the Guards' plight. Brewster was immediately told to make for the Farm 'with all despatch' and did so, coming under heavy fire on the approach. He delivered his load and the historian relating the incident records a staff officer at the time saying 'I am convinced that the wagon driver's delivery of ammunition at the eleventh hour saved the position at Hougoumont Farm from being overrun'. I related this incident while responding to the toast of my Corps and the Duke told me afterwards that although he had seen the painting by Lady Butler of the wagon being ushered through the Farm gates, he had not heard the story in such detail before I was able to give him its provenance.

Amid all this goodwill and jollity there occurred an incident that we had to gloss over smartly. We had arranged for a presentation to the Friends of Waterloo that consisted of a figurine on a plinth of an officer of the Royal Waggon Train in the full dress of the period together with a framed print of Lady Butler's painting. We had assumed that the Duke would realise that these gifts were specifically for the Waterloo museum, sponsored by the Friends so we had not spelled this out. But he assumed, while thanking us for them, that they were presented to him as personal gifts and he announced that they would look well in his new museum at Stratfield Saye, his house near Basingstoke. Consternation in the ranks of the Friends! The lady secretary had fire in her eyes and it was a blessing to have Bernard Courtis with us. He was able to tell her in rapid French that we would correct the situation and we arranged for Bernard to return shortly afterwards with an identical presentation for the Friends to deposit in the Waterloo museum.

The ceremony attracted the attention of our national press. The Peterborough column in *The Telegraph* made the valid point that anyone visiting the site of the battle for the first time could be forgiven for thinking that Napoleon had won, for effigies of the Emperor are everywhere and his image dominates the items sold in the gift shop. The museum telling the true story is located in the village of Waterloo some distance away from the battlefield.

Another extraneous task that went with my job as DGTM was to be a member of the main organising committee for the Royal Tournament, a tri-service display of traditional military skills and equipment that took place annually at the covered Earl's Court Stadium in west London. It was not an arduous task. The Committee met infrequently under the chairmanship of the major general commanding the Household Brigade and London District. Since Victorian times, I believe, he has been known throughout the Army as 'The Major General', no further explanation being considered necessary; he was, of course, always a guardsman and invariably a pleasant, co-operative and laid back one. The main committee decided policy; there was a sub-committee to do any necessary executive work.

Members of the royal family with military connections appeared regularly to take the salute during the Tournament fortnight and it was usual for any committee member whose regiment or corps had a royal patron to play host to that personage during his or her appearance. For many years the RCT and its predecessor, the RASC, had been connected with the Gloucester family. The Queen's uncle, Prince Henry, Duke of Gloucester, had been the Colonel in Chief of both Corps until his death and his widow, Princess Alice, the Dowager Duchess, had succeeded him by popular request and with the Queen's approval, as Colonel in Chief of the RCT. It therefore fell to me to host Princess Alice at the Tournament on several occasions. This was no hardship. In the late nineteen seventies the Princess was an elderly lady; she had been born in 1901 and such was her charm that we were all devoted to her. She was always happy to attend our parades and social occasions, but the years were passing and it became necessary to apply the brakes to avoid imposing on her willingness to donate her time to us. The Tournament, however, was always enjoyable. Princess Alice usually attended the matinee session and the Royal Box was invariably full of grandchildren making the cream tea vanish at a respectable rate, her two Ladies in Waiting maintaining order as stand in nannies for the occasion. In the second year of my tenure I was asked to look after Major General Hank Small, Director General of the US Army Transportation Corps during his visit to the UK.

He hadn't visited the UK before but we got on well and he seemed to enjoy his trip that had included a short stay at our house near Winchester to give him a flavour of Hampshire's rich history. He was a good friend to Sam Cockerham, still the US Director of Movements in DC, and like Sam on a previous occasion he wanted to play a return match, but this time he particularly asked me to bring Heather so that she could meet his wife and 'socialise' with his family and his headquarters' wives at Fort Eustis, the Transportation Corps HQ.

I was quite keen to do this trip because Hank operated a large training organisation at Fort Eustis and I wanted to see it. Heather had not visited the States before and was also keen to accept the invitation – dependent in her case on the availability of indulgence passages both ways, but there were frequent VC10 runs to Washington DC so the prospects were reasonable. Also Sam came up with an offer of accommodation at his house in DC before we moved south to Fort Eustis, so the omens were favourable. A further plus was that the assistant British Defence Attaché at our embassy in Washington was Colonel Con Carey, a member of my Corps, who maintained close liaison with Fort Eustis and with Sam Cockerham and was bursting to prepare an itinerary for us.

To my surprise the MOD had no objection to the trip. Costs were minimal. No civilian air passages were involved as we would travel RAF both ways and internal travel in the States would be at the expense of the US authorities by road and by helicopter. Indulgence passages were arranged for Heather on the understanding that in the event of a compassionate or sick serviceman or woman needing her return seat, she would be left behind until space became available on another flight. This was a standard caveat and caused no alarm, although we had to aim off for it by fixing emergency accommodation should it become necessary.

We flew from RAF Brize Norton to Dulles Airport near Washington on the morning of a mild spring day, arriving slightly before we had left – because of the five hours gain in time during a flight to North America.

This time my itinerary was different from the programme I had followed on my previous visit to the US as a staff officer. I was to visit training installations and be among working soldiers. But first a weekend stay with Sam and Alice Cockerham at their house in Fairfax County – virtually a suburb of Washington DC. Sam took us to Mount Vernon, the home of George Washington overlooking the Potomac River and perfectly preserved. Should the First President's reincarnation occur, he could go home and find his house more or less as he had left it; furniture and silver in place all clean and highly polished, beds made with new linen, his pictures on the wall and his garden tended. It was a perfect example, to my mind, of the house of an English gentleman from bygone days. Washington had been a British Army officer before he espoused the cause of the American colonists.

I took Heather round the museums and monuments of Washington, a rerun of my visit with the fair Dolores a few years earlier, and next day we visited Annapolis on the Chesapeake Bay – the home of the US Naval College. There was comfortable feeling about all this; it reeked of age and tradition but in fact we were only a few years more than two centuries away from the revolt of the American colonists against the ill judged tax demands of our Hanoverian King. Almost recent history to jaded Europeans.

Sam was keen for us to visit a crab restaurant on the Bay and so we appeared at 'Ernie's Crab House' for supper. It advertised fresh crabs from the Chesapeake and 'lip smackin' beer! At first sight it wasn't at all prepossessing. It looked like an old Nissen hut with its black corrugated tin roof and fading paintwork. But the welcome was cordial and sincere. We sat at a six foot table with benches either side. A functionary appeared with a roll of white paper and rolled it along the table to form a tablecloth. He went away and reappeared with enough hammers, pliers, crab picks and forks to furnish each of us with a set. A gigantic flagon of beer, salad bowls, a monumental salad and two large loaves of bread followed; these were laid at the outer end of the table; we were each provided with a beer mug. Then followed the pièce de résistance – a big basket full of newly cooked crabs. There was no piped music and very little conversation; this was a place for the serious seafood lovers we had professed to be and we all got down to it with a will. It was one of the finest meals I can remember. I can recall Heather leaning towards me and hissing:

"That big lorry driver at the next table has eaten no less than ten crabs."

The deal was that we could eat as many crabs as we could for a set fee. I imagine that taken across the board Ernie didn't lose by it. Learning that we were from England he took us out to his cookhouse and store to show us baskets of crabs caught that day, waving their claws and waiting patiently to be cooked. Sam drove back with his passengers deep in gluttonous slumber.

I had been looking forward to our visit to Fort Eustis, Virginia. It was not only a very large transport and movements training organisation with a great deal to offer an interested professional in the way of specialist techniques, the area was also steeped in early American history. Located on the banks of the James River that rises in the Appalachian Mountains and drains into the southern edge of the Chesapeake Bay, it is the site of one of the earliest landing places for the first colonists from England to the New World early in the seventeenth century. History tells us that having landed they were assailed by disease and the unpleasant attentions of the native tribes; the survivors were on the brink of returning home when they saw the second shipload of colonists arriving. Some of the earlier settlers stayed and joined the new arrivals; the result was a number of successful settlements surviving to this day as the cities and townships on and around the river named for James I, England's king when the colonists arrived.

Con Carey, friend and defence attaché, drove us down to Fort Eustis in an Embassy car to be met on arrival by General Hank Small, our host, who had indicated that Con and I should arrive in uniform – working dress would be fine, he had said. He told me that there was an 'Honors Ceremony' laid on and that I was to be the inspecting officer.

"That's very kind," I replied, but, I thought privately, unnecessarily lavish for a brief fraternal visit. I could have had no idea how lavish it was to be.

We reached the parade ground to be confronted by a vast array of soldiers drawn up for inspection. They were dressed in disruptive pattern combat clothing with weapons and I noticed that there were many fresh-faced young women among them.

At our host's signal a band struck up, the parade commander reported to me that his troops were ready for inspection. The inspecting party, Con and I with the parade commander, walked along the ranks – so far nothing out of the ordinary – but not realising that it is not the done thing on American parades to talk to individuals in the ranks, I made the mistake of asking a young woman soldier how long she had been in the army – to face blank incomprehension.

It was a bit embarrassing; I repeated my question and she managed a strangled "Que?" – just like Manuel from Fawlty Towers. A sergeant at the end of the front rank a few paces away said out of the corner of his mouth, "She don't speak English too good, General." Wordlessly I finished the inspection and returned to the saluting place, assuming that there would be a march past. There was, but not yet. Standing to attention I heard the command 'Fire One' and the boom of a field artillery piece. Open mouthed I listened, I think, to nine more as the whole parade ground was wreathed in gunsmoke. This was totally unexpected. In Britain we do our best to look after visiting heads of equivalent corps and regiments, but our efforts fall considerably short of artillery salutes.

The parade marched past to the strains of what I had known in Korea as the US Field Artillery song, but Hank told me later that it had been adopted as the US Army song. It's a rousing march – popularly known as "Those caissons go rolling along" and having taken the salute I was presented with a shell case bearing a brass plate with my name, the date and the legend 'Honors Ceremony. Fort Eustis, Virginia. First

Round Fired'. A useful and practical memento and still holding fire irons in my fireplace.

Training facilities at Fort Eustis were superb. The US Army was and probably still is much more aware of the importance of logistics than our Army used to be, although I get an impression that our views are changing for the better as time passes and the mastery of supply, transport and distribution becomes more important in wars and campaigns.

Heather operated to a separate itinerary, mainly touring the many locations along the James River where the first settlements are reproduced for the tourists with the inhabitants wearing seventeenth century dress and doing their best to speak in the accents of the period. We shared experiences at the end of each day. She met all the wives of Hank's officers and reflected to me that army wives across the globe must share similar concerns for she got on famously with them and was sorry to leave. Wise old Kipling, with his 'sisters under the skin'.

The hospitality of the US Army Transportation Corps could not be faulted and rather late in my career I added to my store of knowledge of transport and movement training methods and techniques.

We stayed with Con Carey and his wife in their house on the outskirts of DC for the weekend before leaving for home and on the Saturday we decided to visit the shopping mall a mile or so away for some last minute present buying.

"I'll drive you," said Con.

"Don't worry. We could both do with a walk and it's a nice day."

But he did look worried.

"Well, do be careful. Nobody walks around here and there are no pavements on the way, so keep to the grass verge. They don't all keep to the speed limit."

There was quite a wide grass verge and we set off happily; shopping malls were an unfamiliar concept to us then and we were looking forward to seeing this one. It was new and supposed to be pretty plush.

About halfway along the road with the shopping mall in view and no habitation on either side of the road, a patrolling police car passed us then drew in to the side of the road as we approached. A policeman got out and said politely, "Can I help you? Have you broken down? Where's your car?"

"No," I replied, equally politely. "We're going for a walk to the shopping mall over there. We don't have a car." I was curious to see his reaction. Casual walkers were probably either outside his experience or were up to no good. On the other hand we were outwardly respectable.

He surveyed us for a good minute. A hard stare.

"Well if you don't have a car you won't have a driving licence. Any other means of identification?"

I pulled out my military identity card and offered it to him; it bore my uniformed photograph. "This lady is my wife," I said, paraphrasing the old music hall joke. "We're visitors. Staying with friends."

He read it, grinned at me and turning his head he spoke to his companion, still in the car but watching the exchange closely.

"It's OK Joe. They're English. Going for a walk – it's what they do sometimes." He saluted. "Enjoy your walk sir. But watch the traffic." They sped off.

Arriving home I found that in my absence I had been appointed a Colonel Commandant of the Corps. This is an honorary post usually offered to recently retired senior officers of a regiment or corps. The Royal Corps of Transport had a ration of six colonels commandant, other establishments boasted a smaller or larger number, depending on their size. Their function is to look after dress and ceremonial aspects of their organisation, represent the Colonel in Chief – who is usually but not always a royal personage – when he or she is not able to be present. We met three or four times a year at the Corps Headquarters Mess in Aldershot. As the serving Director I found it useful to have the experience of several of my predecessors to call on and their wise words were absorbed and often, but not always, acted on.

Shortly after our return from the States, Heather began to suffer back pain. This was very unusual. She had always been tall and slim; except when bearing our children she had varied no more than a pound or so in thirty years of marriage. She made light of it and although the discovery of her cancer was now ten years behind us and she had a check up only once each year, I felt a vague disquiet and without telling her had a private chat with our village GP. He knew her history and agreed with me that expert investigation was indicated. I was content to be berated for 'making a fuss' but finally she agreed to see the oncologist at the Millbank Hospital. I knew that she was far more worried than she ever admitted and to our horror the medics decided that the cancer had reappeared.

This was the start of a truly ghastly time. I had about a year left before retirement and Heather began to spend time in and out of hospital having radiation treatment, chemical therapy and other indignities that were truly shattering to a quiet, sensitive and lovely woman. She had always had great courage, however, and insisted that I got on with my job as though she was still in good health. The Millbank Military Hospital was then dispossessed to make room for an extension to the Tate Gallery and the hospital was re-established at Woolwich, a tortuous journey across South London.

My contemporaries at Andover knew nothing of all this as Heather had insisted that her problems should remain confidential, but eventually I had tell the Chief of Staff Logistics because we had to turn down so many invitations. Robert Staveley had replaced Paul Travers in the post and he and his wife, Airlie, were friends from our teaching stint at the Staff College.

Shortly after I had replaced the telephone after a discussion with the doctor at Woolwich one morning, I received an unexpected visit from the Quarter Master General, now Dick Worsley, or more formally, General Sir Richard. A few moments earlier I had been told that Heather's condition was terminal and he must have found me in a very strange mood. I loved my wife deeply. It was a strong and fulfilling relationship. I am not outwardly an emotional person but that morning I could feel myself on the brink of tears. A man of quick perceptions, the QMG sensed something was wrong and jumped to the conclusion that it was to do with the handling of my Corps. He was sympathetic and said he hoped that the problem could be mastered.

Anxious only to get him to leave as quickly as possible, I let him think that his analysis was correct. In fact nothing could have been further from the truth. The Corps was running like clockwork. The directing team had coalesced to the degree that one word in the right place brought results.

But this was my Rubicon; by the end of the morning I had firmly decided to leave the Army before my retirement was due and look after Heather until the inevitable overtook us. The doctors had given her until October – the month when I was due to reach the age of fifty-five and so retire. It was now November, eleven months to go. There was no question of any further trips outside the UK. A farewell visit to units in BAOR had to be cancelled as well as a journey to the Far East for which Air Commodore Alf Biell, the RAF's Director of Movements, had arranged for Heather to accompany me on an indulgence basis. It was a dolorous time, made more so by an inability to make known the real reason.

Conscious that I was sparking on only four of my six cylinders, I decided to leave in the spring of 1981 and not take on a civilian job until late in that year. I 'put my papers in' as we say in the Service, in February of that year. Early retirement was accepted instantly, to take effect in April. I even received a letter from General Roly Guy, then the Military Secretary, thanking me for leaving early and so easing his efforts to place too many able people into too few senior appointments.

Of course I had let it be known among civilian contacts that I was leaving the army and would be looking for a suitable job later in the year. I wanted to enter the commercial world, hopefully in the transport industry, and preferably in an organisation standing on its own feet and working for profit. I had no interest in returning to the Service as a retired officer or heading up a charity. Fortunately, it seemed that my experience as a logistician had some value. I had several approaches. It was interesting to see how it was done.

For instance I had not seen or spoken to Sir Kenneth Cork for some time but he rang me in my office one morning. He had finished his year as Lord Mayor and was now back at work as senior partner of Cork Gully, long regarded as the City liquidators. "I hear you're leaving. Is that so?"

"Yes. I put my papers in a couple of weeks ago."

"Interesting," he said. "Anything lined up?"

"Not really. For domestic reasons I won't be available until the autumn and I haven't started looking yet."

"That's OK. Might fit nicely."

I was intrigued. "Well, come on. What's this all about?"

"You'll know that the Foden Company had been put into administration?"

"Yes," I said. I had been saddened to hear that this famous old English truck manufacturer had gone bust. I had met the Foden brothers and had regularly attended their annual dinner at the Cavalry Club.

"Well, I've sold the assets and goodwill to an American multinational." He went on. "It's a public company but it's still mainly family owned and run. It's called Paccar – stands for Pacific Car Company – they build those massive Peterbilt and Kenworth trucks in the States and they plan to resurrect Fodens. They're putting a board together and they've asked me to recommend someone who knows the military transport scene. I thought of you as a possibility. Would you be interested?"

"Of course," I said. "I've got to find a job. Good of you to think of me. But two questions. First, what would it entail? Secondly, if it comes off, when would I start?"

"Hold your horses. It isn't a full time post. There'll be an American MD. You'd be a non-executive director attending board meetings three or four times a year. Nothing much will happen for a bit and then probably in late summer the Chairman, Charles – likes to be known as Chuck – Piggott will invite you to lunch at Claridges, where they plan to hold their UK board meetings. He'll look you over and if he thinks you'll do, you're in. I don't know what they'd pay you but it wouldn't be peanuts for what you'd have to do."

This was promising. But it can't all be that easy, I thought. I still need a full-time job. I began to scan the appointments section of *The Times*. There didn't seem to be much in my line on offer and I consoled myself with the thought that there was plenty of down time. Then one evening at a Livery function, the Chairman of the Road Haulage Association (RHA) and his predecessor, both proprietors of large haulage companies, fell in alongside me; I had met them, having attended several RHA annual dinners. It was, and is, a very large employers' association organised on a nationwide basis and with over eleven thousand companies in membership. Most of its board members were liverymen of the Carmen's Company. The usual gambit emerged.

"When are you leaving?"

"In about two months time," I said. "Why do you ask?" They looked around. No one was in earshot.

"George Newman is retiring this year. We shall be looking for a replacement. Would you be interested?"

George Newman, a barrister who had left the Bar to take on the job of Director General of the RHA, had been in post for about twenty years and his job would be a splendid challenge. I would certainly be interested and said so, making the point that I wouldn't be available for at least six months.

"That's all right. George will be more than happy to stay on until his successor arrives. But we have to advertise the post and draw up a short list. Perhaps you would write to us with your CV?" I promised to do so.

There were two more surprises. Bobby Lawrence, now Chairman of the National Freight Company and incidentally, an RHA member, also rang me and said that the British Oxygen Company (BOC) were looking for a new transport supremo and would like to talk to me. Then Harry Edmondson, a retired RASC brigadier and head of logistics at Geests, the banana and general fruit distributors based in Spalding, got in touch and offered a lunch with his managing director with a view to sizing me up for Harry's job when he was due to retire at the end of the year. This was mightily tempting; Harry was also MD of the Geest shipping line and part of his job was to negotiate the banana contract each year in the Windward Islands, entailing an annual visit to the Caribbean.

It was all very heady stuff and I had not yet left the Service, although the die was cast.

I realised that it would be bad tactics to try to keep all the possibilities alive and that I should pursue only one full-time job prospect. Naturally I discussed it with Heather. She had already ruled out Spalding. We had visited it at what was admittedly its worst time of year and she had decided that she didn't want to go there. I wrote to Mr Vivian, the MD, who had kindly asked me to lunch and to Harry Edmonton, leaving BOC and the RHA in the frame. Both organisations were based in London, the RHA in Woburn Place, close to Euston Station, and BOC further out at Brentford. BOC had been kind enough to send me off on a whistle stop tour of their installations in mainland Britain. It was clear that it was an alive and hard working organisation and that full-time and hands on management would be called for. The salary being tentatively mentioned was tempting.

"Look at it this way," said Heather. "At BOC you'd be a medium sized fish in a large pool and you know nothing about oxygen, their primary concern, so there'd be little chance of advancement. On the other hand, at the RHA you'd be a big fish in a sizeable pool; you could call the tune with the Board's agreement. You could adjust and reorganise to your heart's content. We could live in London during

St Kilda. RCT logistic landing craft beaching at Village Bay ready to offload vehicles and stores.

Hugoumont Farm. Brigadier Keith Davis and Mrs Davis with The Duke of Wellington, Patron of The Friends of Waterloo.

the week and Hampshire at weekends. It would be convenient for my trips to Woolwich."

She was right, as usual, and I never regretted my decision to pursue the RHA appointment.

I left the Army in April 1981 and became Director General and Chief Executive of the Road Haulage Association later that year. Counting my service in the Fleet Air Arm and the infantry before demob and my return to the Amy in 1950, I had completed over thirty-five years in the Service. I was a civilian again.

Heather outlived the medical assessment by some months; she died in March the following year at the Woolwich Military Hospital. As she had predicted, we were living in our London flat during the week and at home in Hampshire at weekends. There are no plus points to bring to book in the progress of that dire and insidious disease but it is some consolation to know that with two of our daughters also living in London, she was surrounded by her family at the end.

Chuck Pigott, Chairman of Paccar, the new proprietors of Foden Trucks, did get in touch and I became a non executive director of the reborn Fodens for fifteen subsequent years. In due course I picked up by invitation several other non executive jobs in the transport world including the chairmanship of the British Railways London Midland Region Board. This ensured that bearing in mind my circumstances at that time, there was a great deal to do. The RHA, my main job, was not only a major employers' association and political pressure group, it was also a substantial commercial enterprise with seventeen fully staffed regional branches around Britain and a strong international haulage connection. Although cash poor it was property rich and ripe for a sweeping reorganisation. This was to take two difficult years, leaving me no time to brood.

During the ensuing years I was often asked if I missed the Service. I replied that it was best to take whatever further years were granted and not to look back too closely, but that given the chance I'd do it all again. Why? Because it is a life like no other. I joined the Royal Navy at the age of seventeen years and some months. We were boys, revelling in the freedom of what we saw as release from the unwanted disciplines of family life and like most boys we gave no thought to the possibility that we might encounter dangers. There was a war on, to be sure, but we, of course, were near as makes no matter, immortal. It was

Hugoumont Farm Ceremony. Second from left: HM Ambassador to Belgium.

not until I witnessed the bloody realities of man's inhumanity to man in Calcutta two years later that I grew up and even then, at nineteen I was two years short of official maturity. The ensuing years, packed with travel and incident and buttressed by a strong family life, both personal and professional, passed in a procession of highlights and lowlights; but even the low points were part of a sometimes exciting and always interesting pattern.

If I were to be asked by a young person today if I could recommend the Service as a career, my answer would be a resounding 'Yes', for the one quality that shines out above the rest is the strength of the comradeship. One inevitably makes lifelong friends – the Service does not go in for fair weather friends. There is a freemasonry that comes to the fore when times are bleak – your comrades are 'there for you'. "Good company and good discourse are the very sinews of virtue" wrote Izaak Walton in *The Compleat Angler*, his seventeenth century classic. I would add laughter, the love of family and the fellowship of friends. For the better part of four decades the Service provided me with a good measure of all these, together with abiding memories. For this I am truly and deeply grateful.

@ fAt & Freddie's 5/22/06 I weighed

13 stones 12 pounds (14# to a stone)